**Waiting for Spring** **14**

Anashin

Waiting
for Spring
vol.14

Presented by
Anashin

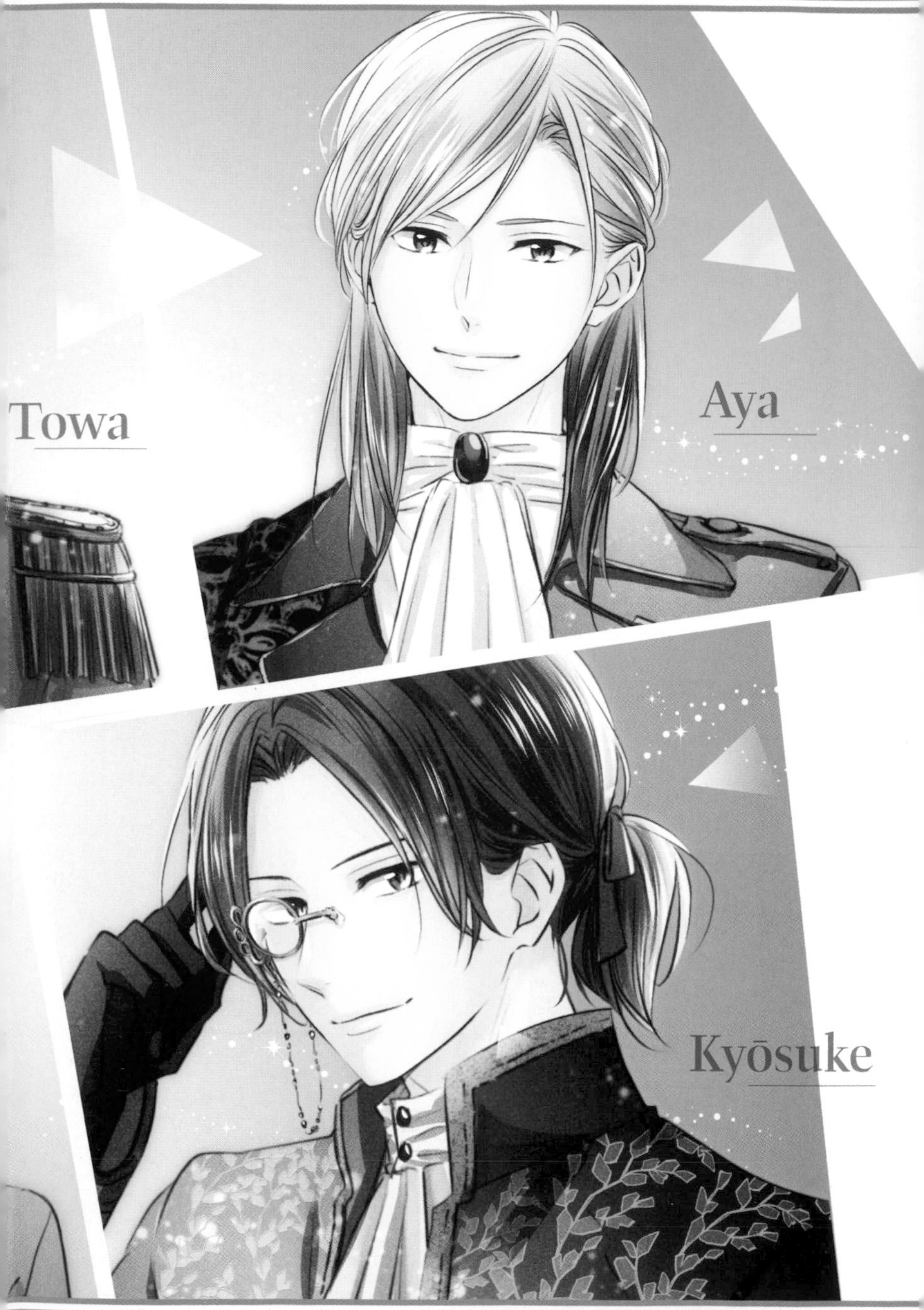
Aya
Towa
Kyōsuke

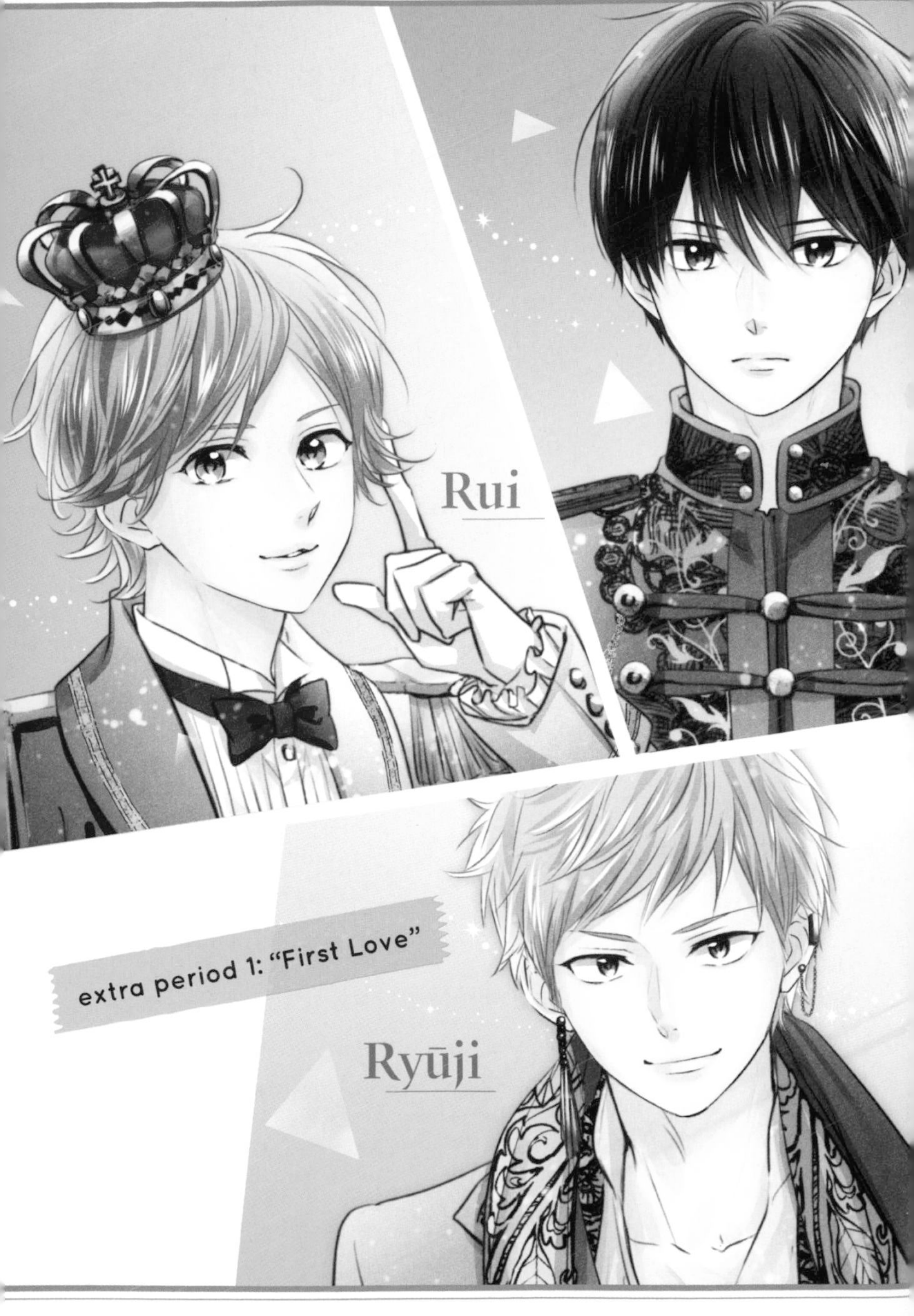
Rui
extra period 1: "First Love"
Ryūji

# CONTENTS

**WAITING FOR SPRING**
Harumatsu Bokura

extra period 1
"First Love"

2

half time 1
Bonus Collection 1 – 5

49

extra period 2
"Summer Vacation"

69

half time 2
Bonus Collection 6 – 9

113

extra period 3
"Thank You"
130

////////////////////////////////////////////////////////////////

······ Hello! Anashin here. (ᵔ◡ᵔ) ······

Thank you so much for buying volume 14! The last volume!!

Note: Volume 14 contains 3 one-shot extra chapters
that I wrote after I finished the main story, and
9 bonus mini-chapters that take place between
each volume of the main story.

······ I really hope you enjoy them! ⋄ᵇ ······

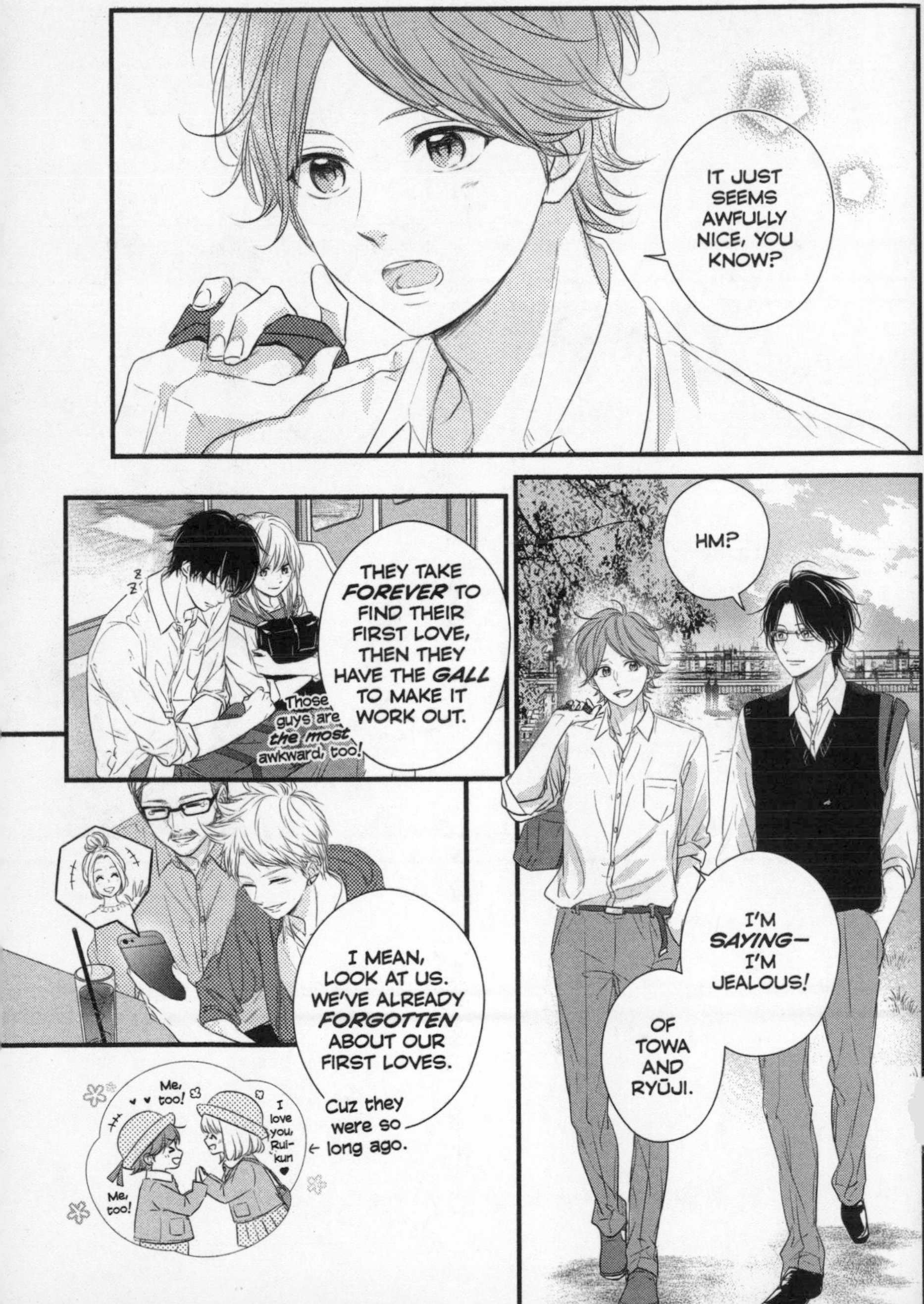
IT JUST SEEMS AWFULLY NICE, YOU KNOW?
HM?
I'M SAYING— I'M JEALOUS!
OF TOWA AND RYŪJI.
THEY TAKE FOREVER TO FIND THEIR FIRST LOVE, THEN THEY HAVE THE GALL TO MAKE IT WORK OUT.
Those guys are the most awkward, too!
I MEAN, LOOK AT US. WE'VE ALREADY FORGOTTEN ABOUT OUR FIRST LOVES.
Cuz they were so long ago.
I love you, Rui-kun
Me, too!
Me, too!

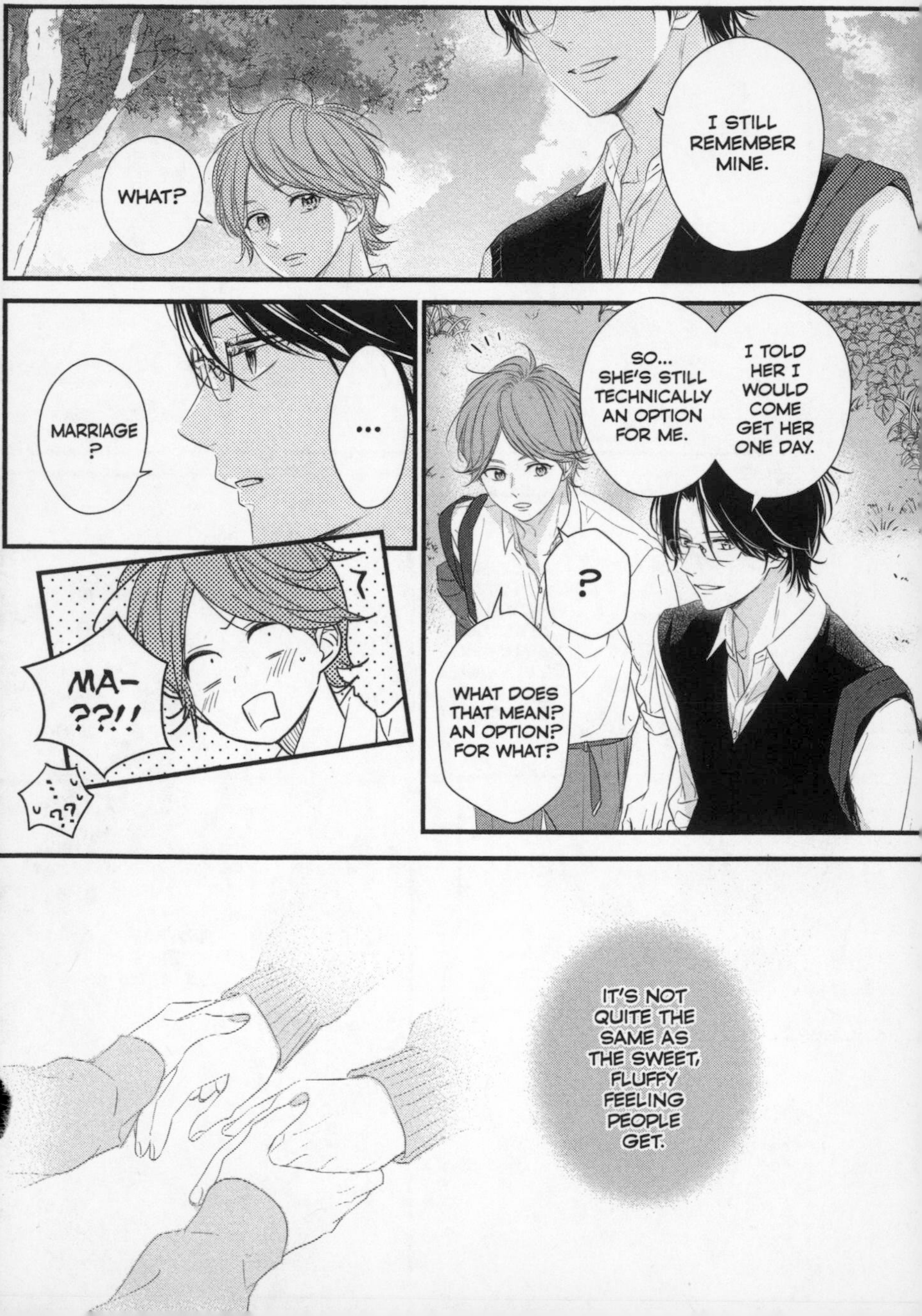
I STILL REMEMBER MINE.
WHAT?
I TOLD HER I WOULD COME GET HER ONE DAY.
SO... SHE'S STILL TECHNICALLY AN OPTION FOR ME.
?
WHAT DOES THAT MEAN? AN OPTION? FOR WHAT?
...
MARRIAGE ?
MA- ??!!
IT'S NOT QUITE THE SAME AS THE SWEET, FLUFFY FEELING PEOPLE GET.

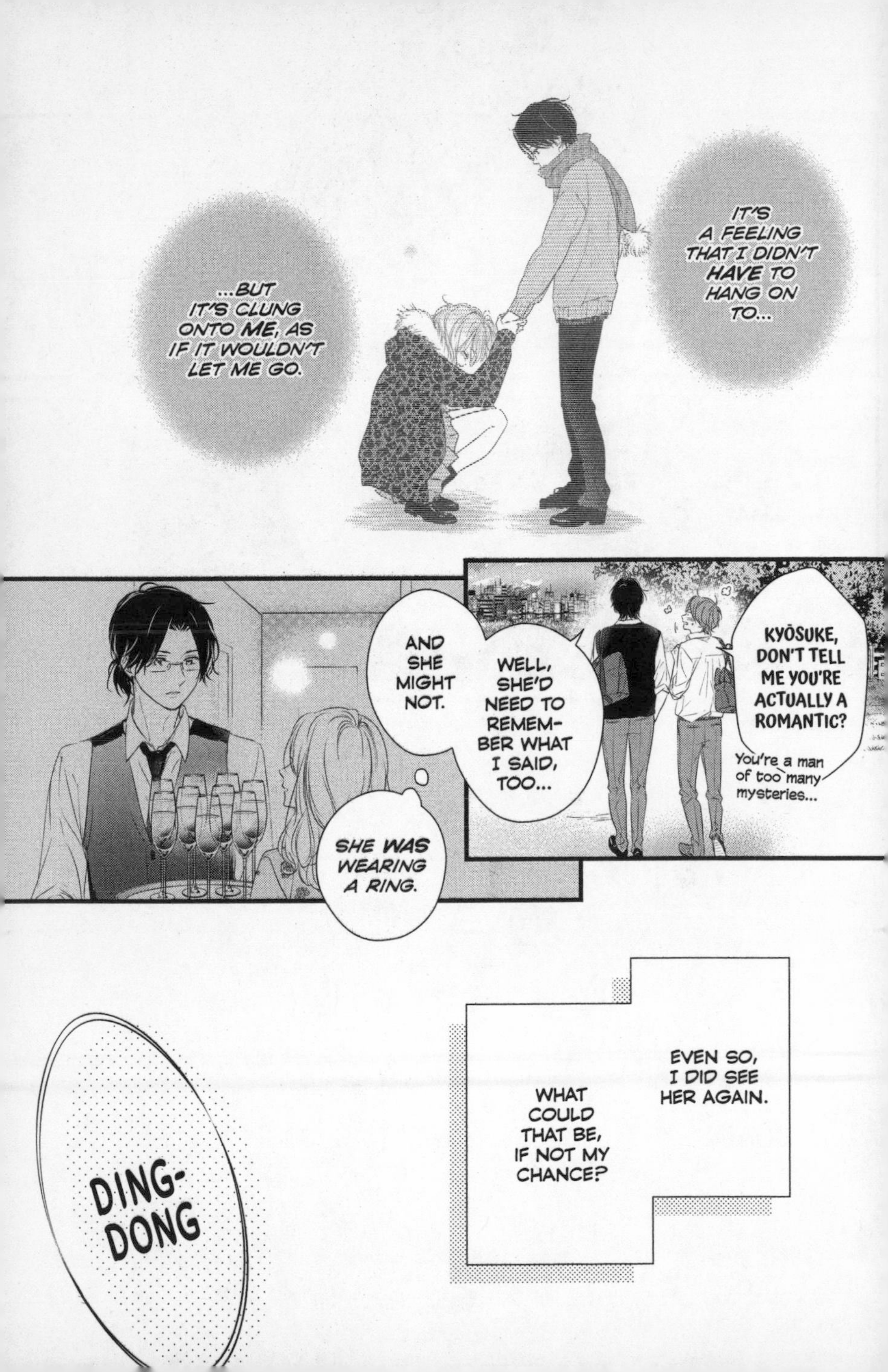
IT'S A FEELING THAT I DIDN'T HAVE TO HANG ON TO...
...BUT IT'S CLUNG ONTO ME, AS IF IT WOULDN'T LET ME GO.
KYŌSUKE, DON'T TELL ME YOU'RE ACTUALLY A ROMANTIC?
You're a man of too many mysteries...
WELL, SHE'D NEED TO REMEMBER WHAT I SAID, TOO...
AND SHE MIGHT NOT.
SHE WAS WEARING A RING.
EVEN SO, I DID SEE HER AGAIN.
WHAT COULD THAT BE, IF NOT MY CHANCE?
DING-DONG

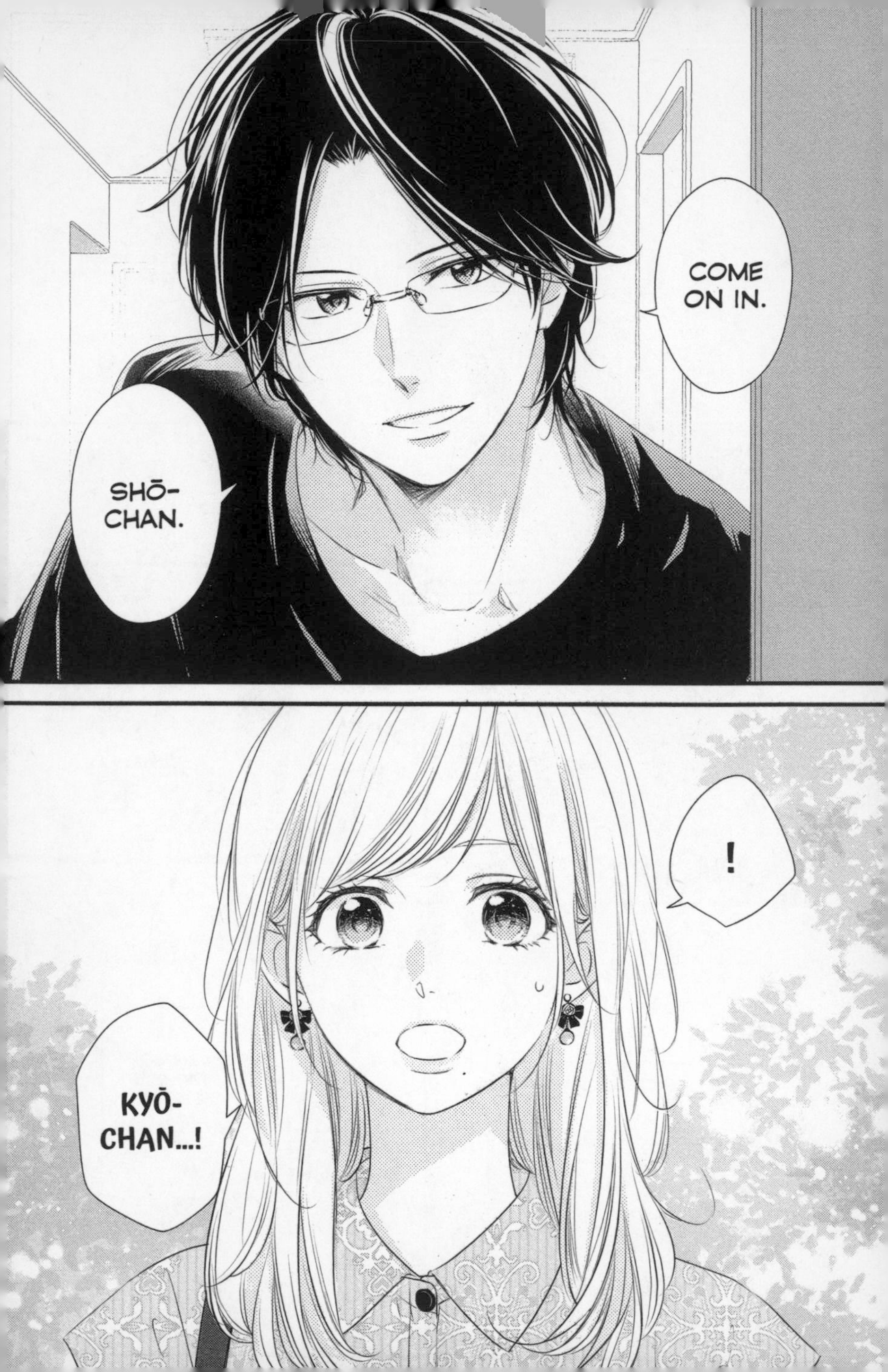
COME ON IN.
SHŌ-CHAN.
!
KYŌ-CHAN...!

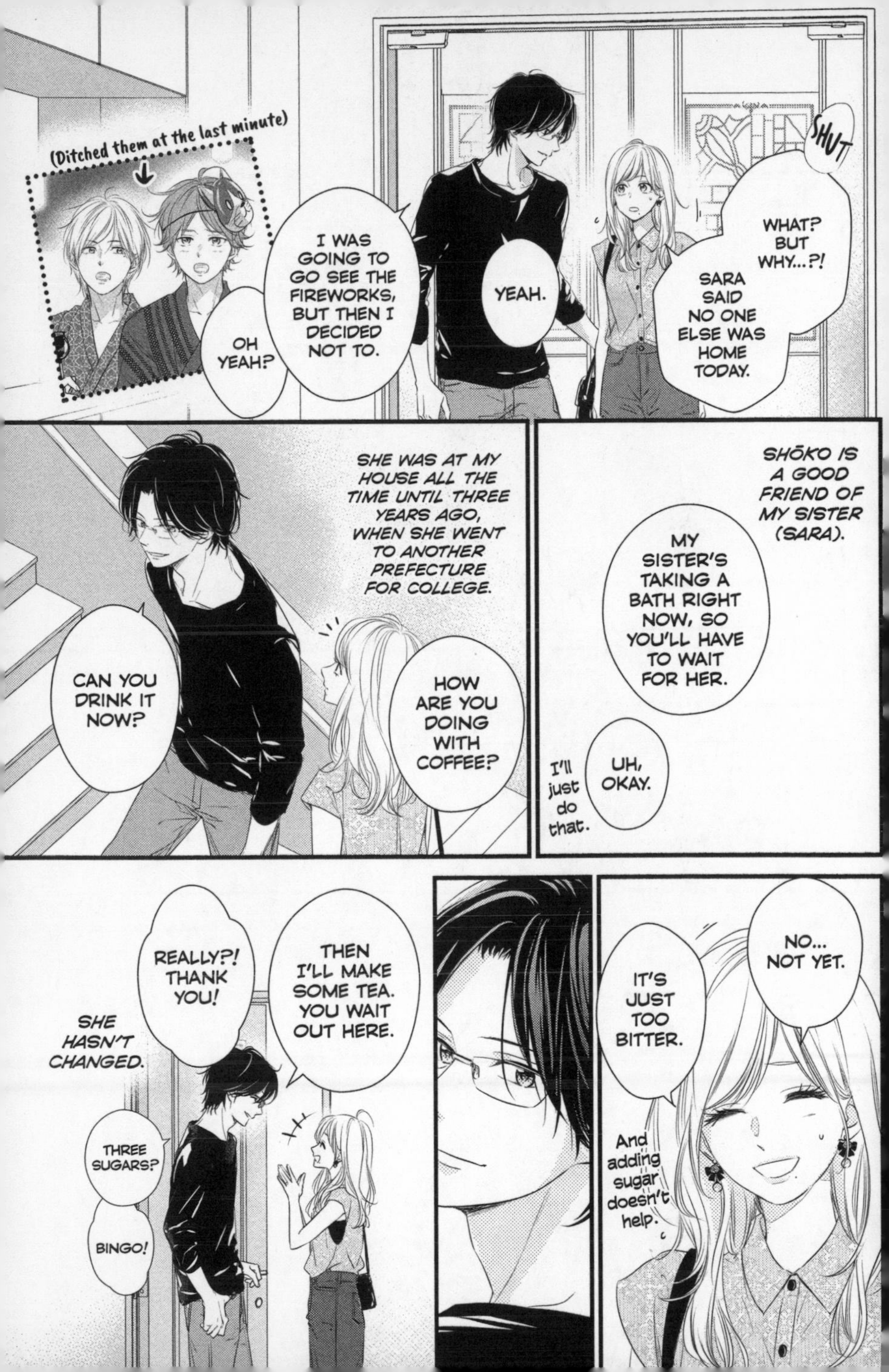
SHUT
WHAT? BUT WHY...?!
SARA SAID NO ONE ELSE WAS HOME TODAY.
YEAH.
I WAS GOING TO GO SEE THE FIREWORKS, BUT THEN I DECIDED NOT TO.
OH YEAH?
(Ditched them at the last minute)
SHŌKO IS A GOOD FRIEND OF MY SISTER (SARA).
MY SISTER'S TAKING A BATH RIGHT NOW, SO YOU'LL HAVE TO WAIT FOR HER.
UH, OKAY.
I'll just do that.
SHE WAS AT MY HOUSE ALL THE TIME UNTIL THREE YEARS AGO, WHEN SHE WENT TO ANOTHER PREFECTURE FOR COLLEGE.
HOW ARE YOU DOING WITH COFFEE?
CAN YOU DRINK IT NOW?
NO... NOT YET.
IT'S JUST TOO BITTER.
And adding sugar doesn't help.
THEN I'LL MAKE SOME TEA. YOU WAIT OUT HERE.
REALLY?! THANK YOU!
SHE HASN'T CHANGED.
THREE SUGARS?
BINGO!

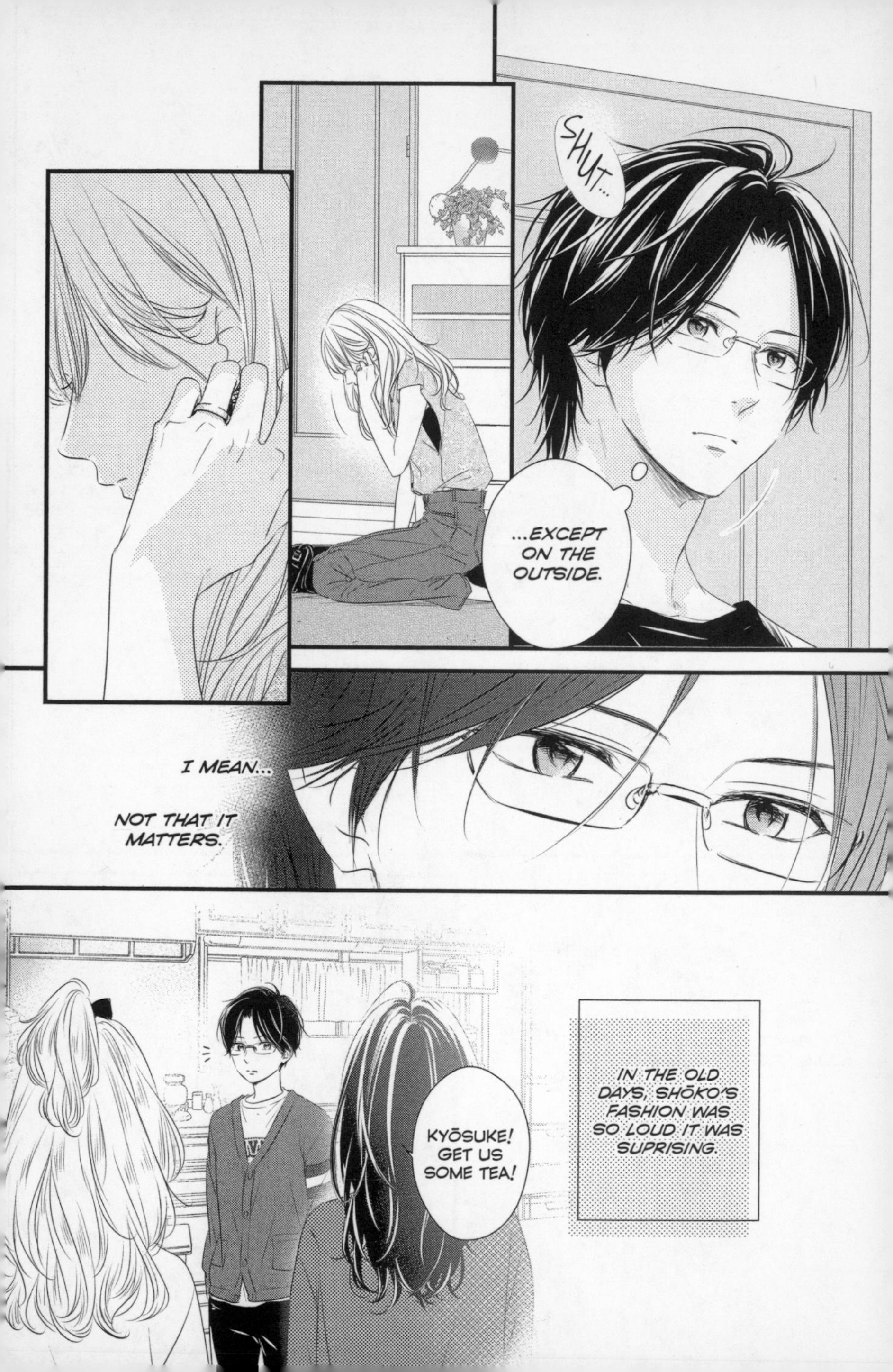
SHUT...
...EXCEPT ON THE OUTSIDE.
I MEAN...
NOT THAT IT MATTERS.
IN THE OLD DAYS, SHŌKO'S FASHION WAS SO LOUD IT WAS SUPRISING.
KYŌSUKE! GET US SOME TEA!

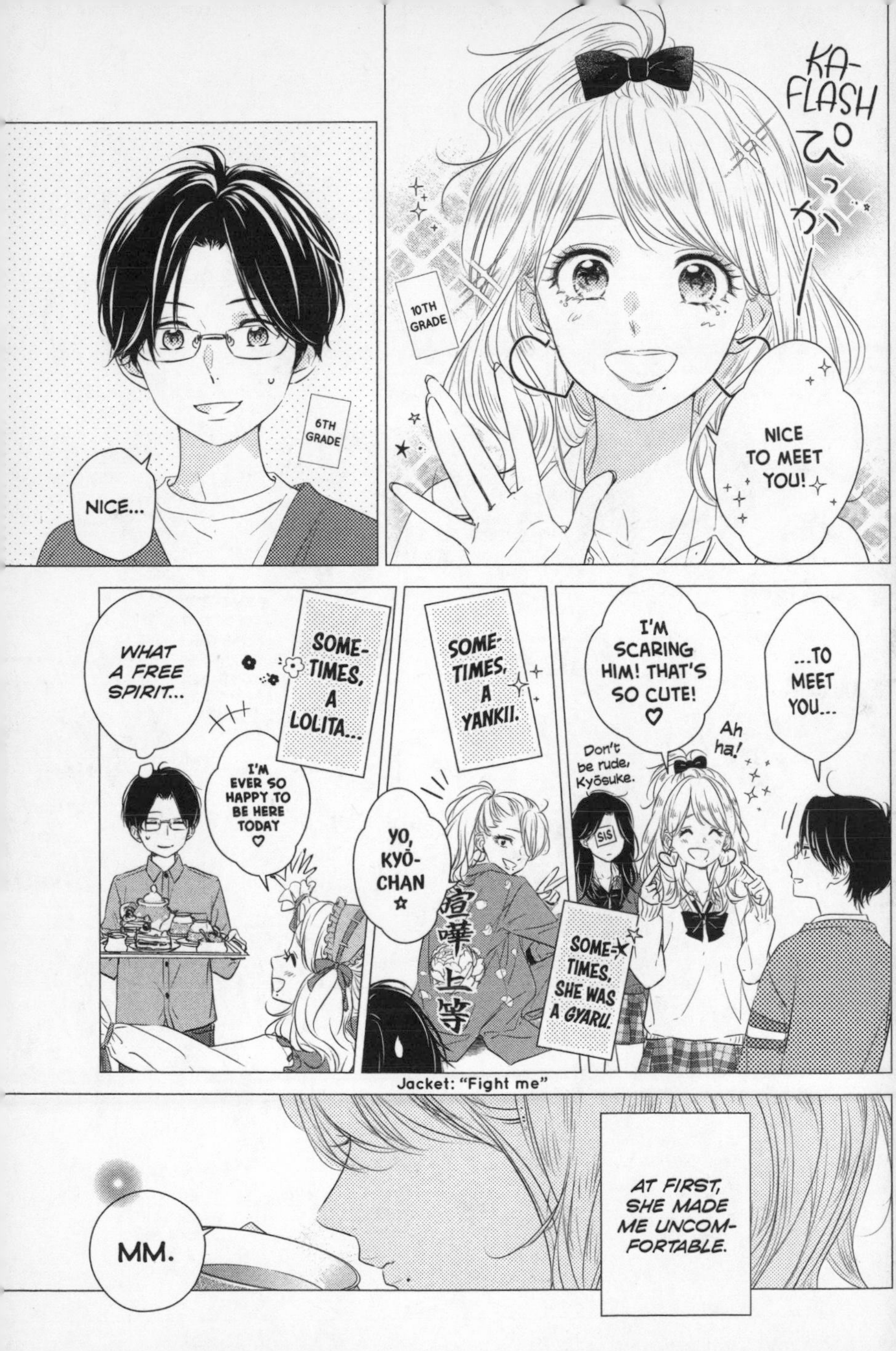
KA-FLASH
ぴっかー
10TH GRADE
NICE TO MEET YOU!
6TH GRADE
NICE...
...TO MEET YOU...
I'M SCARING HIM! THAT'S SO CUTE! ♡
Ah ha!
Don't be rude, Kyōsuke.
SIS
SOME-TIMES, SHE WAS A GYARU.
SOME-TIMES, A YANKII.
YO, KYŌ-CHAN ☆
喧嘩上等
SOME-TIMES, A LOLITA...
WHAT A FREE SPIRIT...
I'M EVER SO HAPPY TO BE HERE TODAY ♡
Jacket: "Fight me"
AT FIRST, SHE MADE ME UNCOM-FORTABLE.
MM.

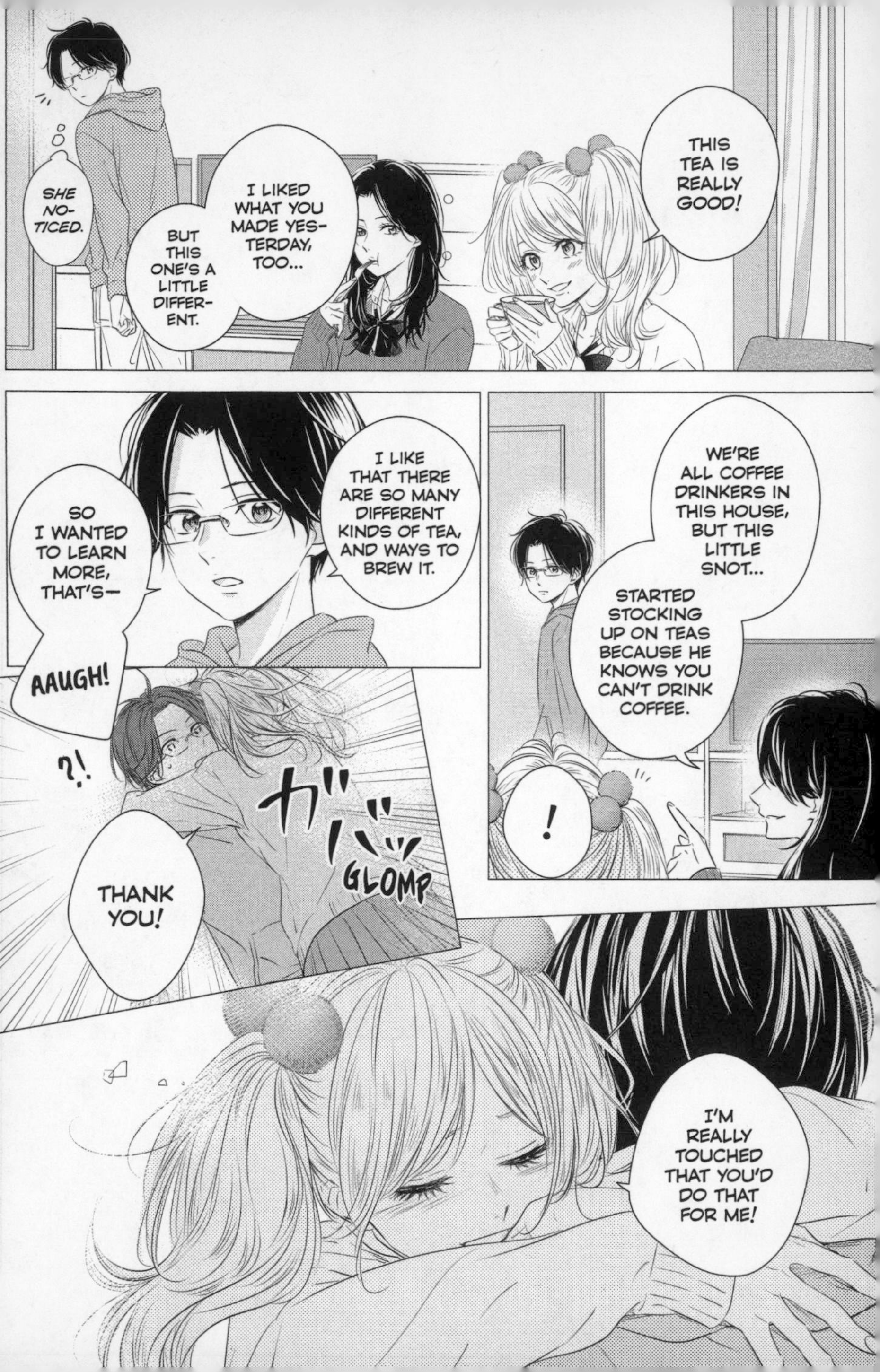
THIS TEA IS REALLY GOOD!
I LIKED WHAT YOU MADE YESTERDAY, TOO...
BUT THIS ONE'S A LITTLE DIFFERENT.
SHE NOTICED.
WE'RE ALL COFFEE DRINKERS IN THIS HOUSE, BUT THIS LITTLE SNOT...
STARTED STOCKING UP ON TEAS BECAUSE HE KNOWS YOU CAN'T DRINK COFFEE.
!
I LIKE THAT THERE ARE SO MANY DIFFERENT KINDS OF TEA, AND WAYS TO BREW IT.
SO I WANTED TO LEARN MORE, THAT'S—
GLOMP
AAUGH!
?!
THANK YOU!
I'M REALLY TOUCHED THAT YOU'D DO THAT FOR ME!

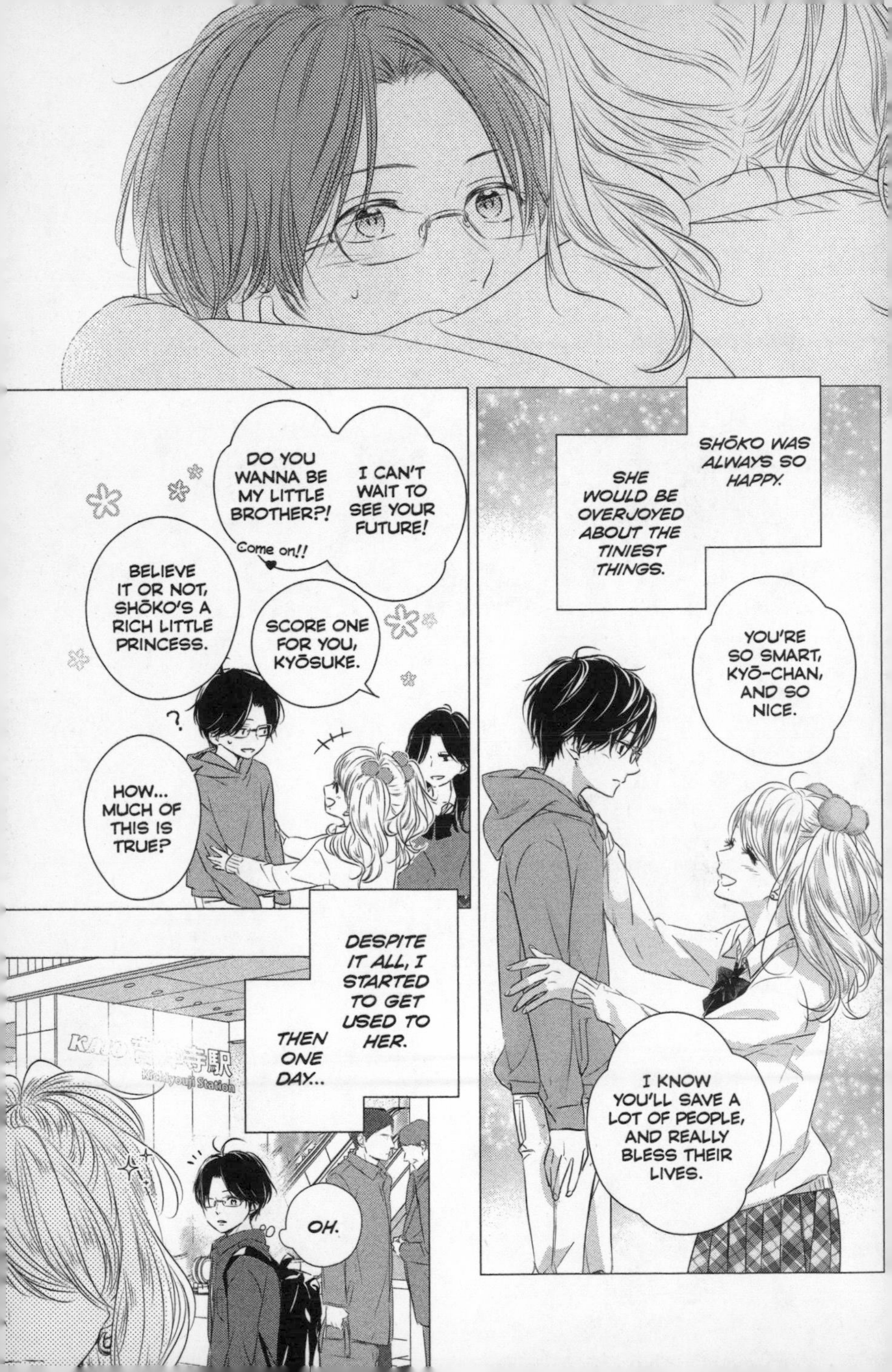
SHŌKO WAS ALWAYS SO HAPPY.
SHE WOULD BE OVERJOYED ABOUT THE TINIEST THINGS.
YOU'RE SO SMART, KYŌ-CHAN, AND SO NICE.
I KNOW YOU'LL SAVE A LOT OF PEOPLE, AND REALLY BLESS THEIR LIVES.
I CAN'T WAIT TO SEE YOUR FUTURE!
DO YOU WANNA BE MY LITTLE BROTHER?!
Come on!!
SCORE ONE FOR YOU, KYŌSUKE.
BELIEVE IT OR NOT, SHŌKO'S A RICH LITTLE PRINCESS.
?
HOW... MUCH OF THIS IS TRUE?
DESPITE IT ALL, I STARTED TO GET USED TO HER.
THEN ONE DAY...
OH.

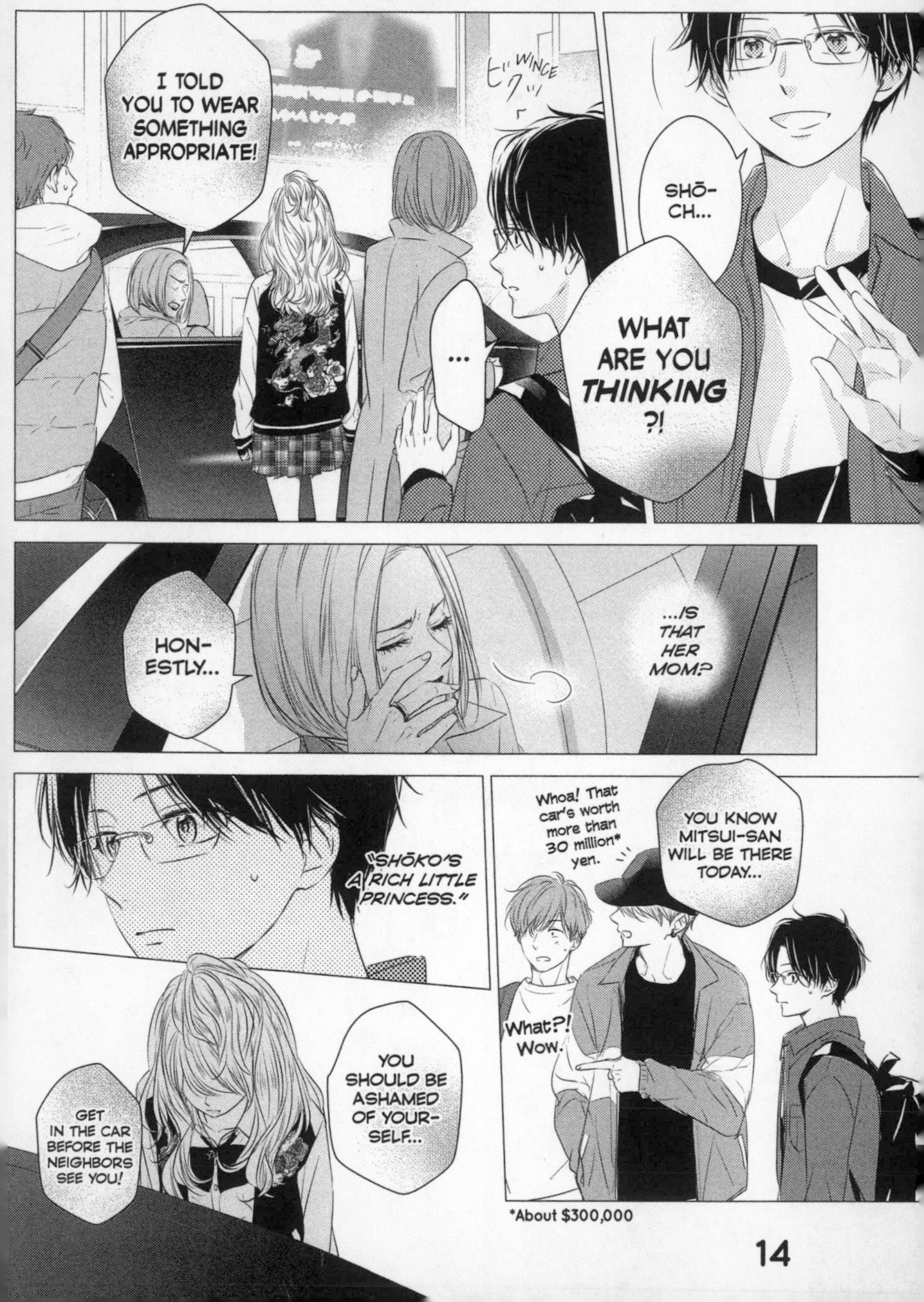
SHŌ-
CH...
WHAT ARE YOU THINKING ?!
WINCE
I TOLD YOU TO WEAR SOMETHING APPROPRIATE!
...
...IS THAT HER MOM?
HON-ESTLY...
YOU KNOW MITSUI-SAN WILL BE THERE TODAY...
Whoa! That car's worth more than 30 million* yen.
What?! Wow.
"SHŌKO'S A RICH LITTLE PRINCESS."
YOU SHOULD BE ASHAMED OF YOUR-SELF...
GET IN THE CAR BEFORE THE NEIGHBORS SEE YOU!

*About $300,000

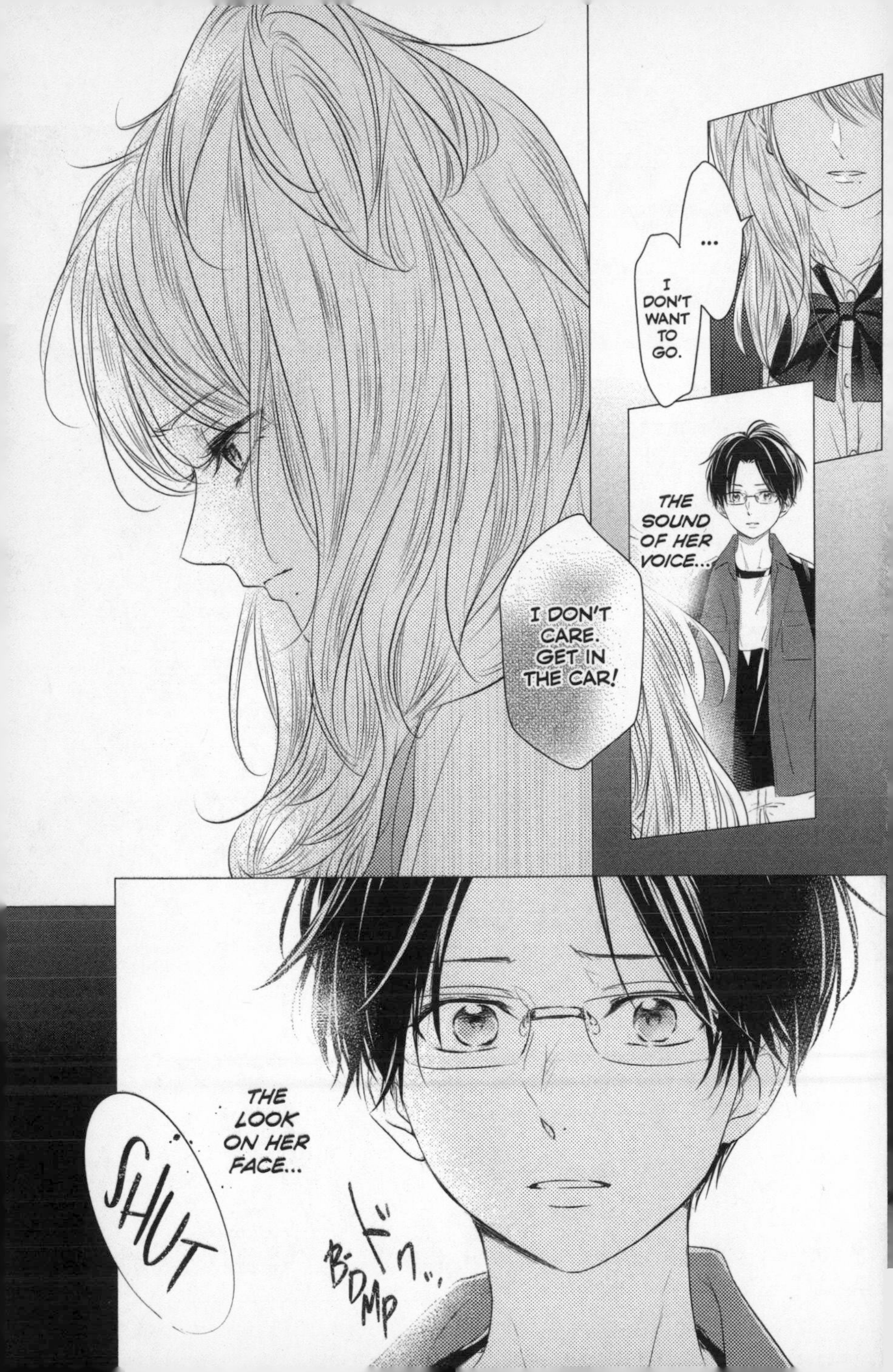
...
I DON'T WANT TO GO.
THE SOUND OF HER VOICE...
I DON'T CARE. GET IN THE CAR!
THE LOOK ON HER FACE...
SHUT
B-DMP

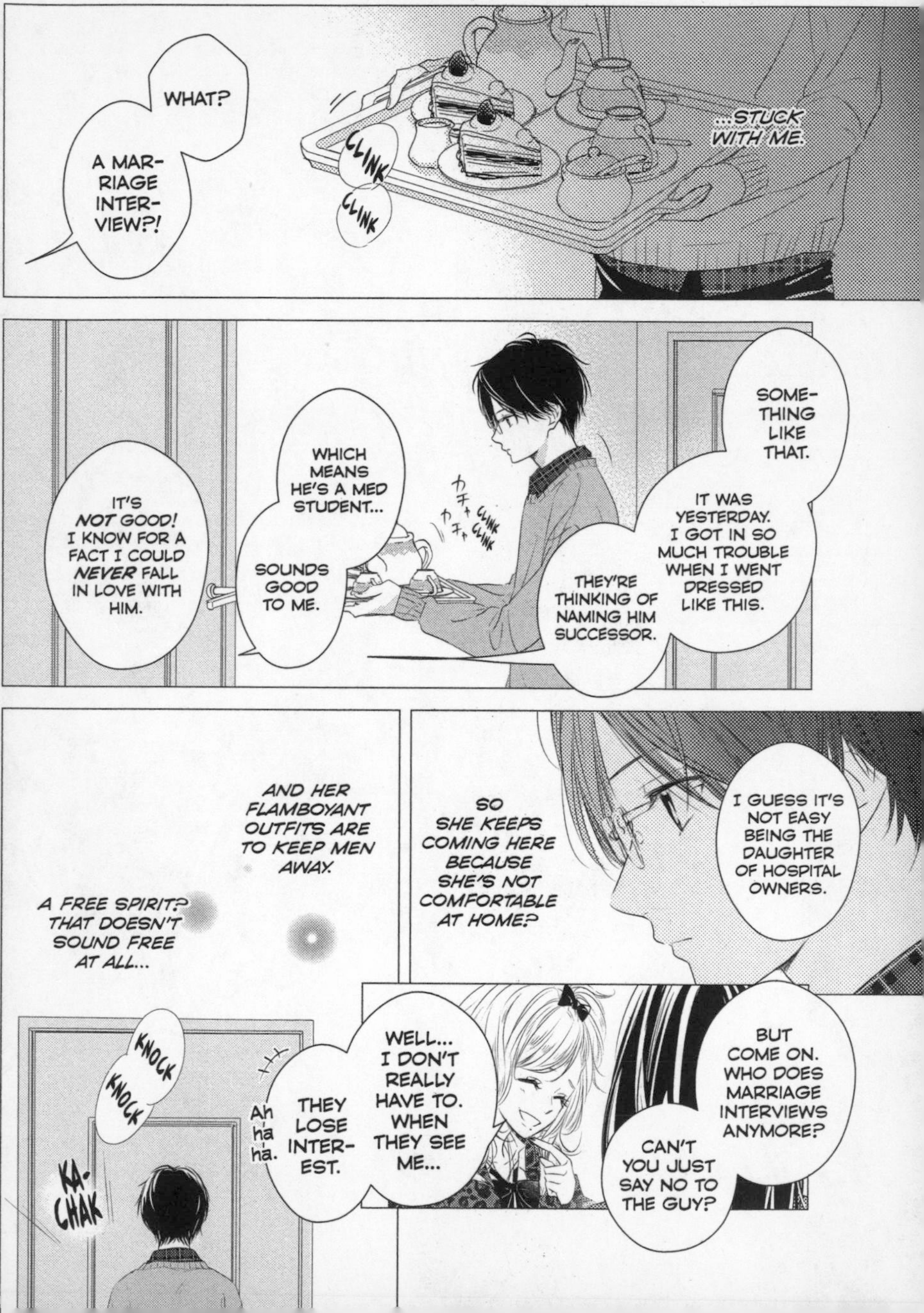
...STUCK WITH ME.
CLINK
CLINK
WHAT?
A MAR-RIAGE INTER-VIEW?!
SOME-THING LIKE THAT.
IT WAS YESTERDAY. I GOT IN SO MUCH TROUBLE WHEN I WENT DRESSED LIKE THIS.
THEY'RE THINKING OF NAMING HIM SUCCESSOR.
カチャ CLINK
カチャ CLINK
WHICH MEANS HE'S A MED STUDENT...
SOUNDS GOOD TO ME.
IT'S *NOT* GOOD! I KNOW FOR A FACT I COULD *NEVER* FALL IN LOVE WITH HIM.
I GUESS IT'S NOT EASY BEING THE DAUGHTER OF HOSPITAL OWNERS.
SO SHE KEEPS COMING HERE BECAUSE SHE'S NOT COMFORTABLE AT HOME?
AND HER FLAMBOYANT OUTFITS ARE TO KEEP MEN AWAY.
A FREE SPIRIT? THAT DOESN'T SOUND FREE AT ALL...
BUT COME ON. WHO DOES MARRIAGE INTERVIEWS ANYMORE?
CAN'T YOU JUST SAY NO TO THE GUY?
WELL... I DON'T REALLY HAVE TO. WHEN THEY SEE ME...
THEY LOSE INTER-EST.
Ah ha ha.
KNOCK
KNOCK
KA-CHAK

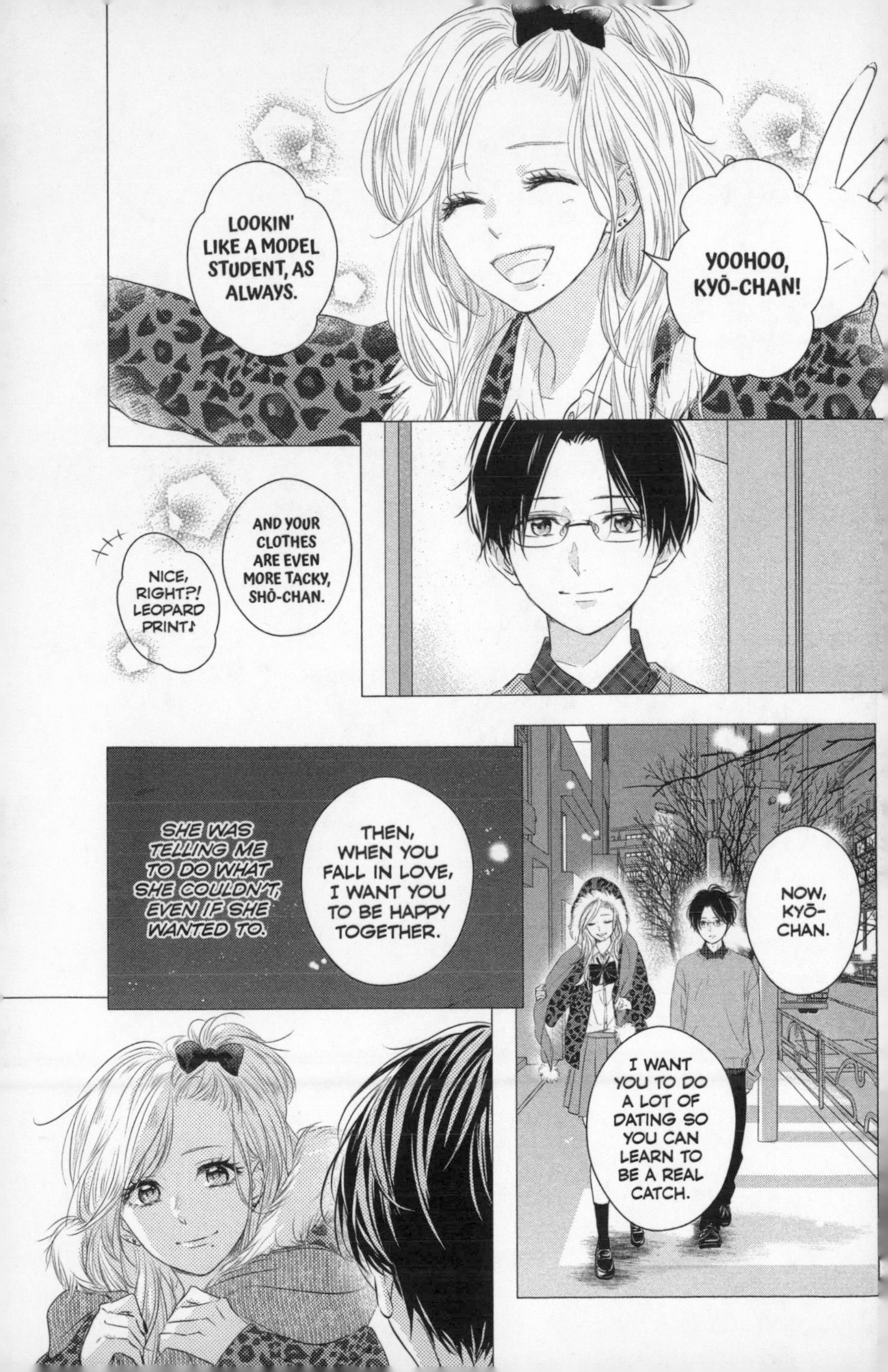
YOOHOO, KYŌ-CHAN!
LOOKIN' LIKE A MODEL STUDENT, AS ALWAYS.
AND YOUR CLOTHES ARE EVEN MORE TACKY, SHŌ-CHAN.
NICE, RIGHT?! LEOPARD PRINT♪
NOW, KYŌ-CHAN.
I WANT YOU TO DO A LOT OF DATING SO YOU CAN LEARN TO BE A REAL CATCH.
THEN, WHEN YOU FALL IN LOVE, I WANT YOU TO BE HAPPY TOGETHER.
SHE WAS TELLING ME TO DO WHAT SHE COULDN'T, EVEN IF SHE WANTED TO.

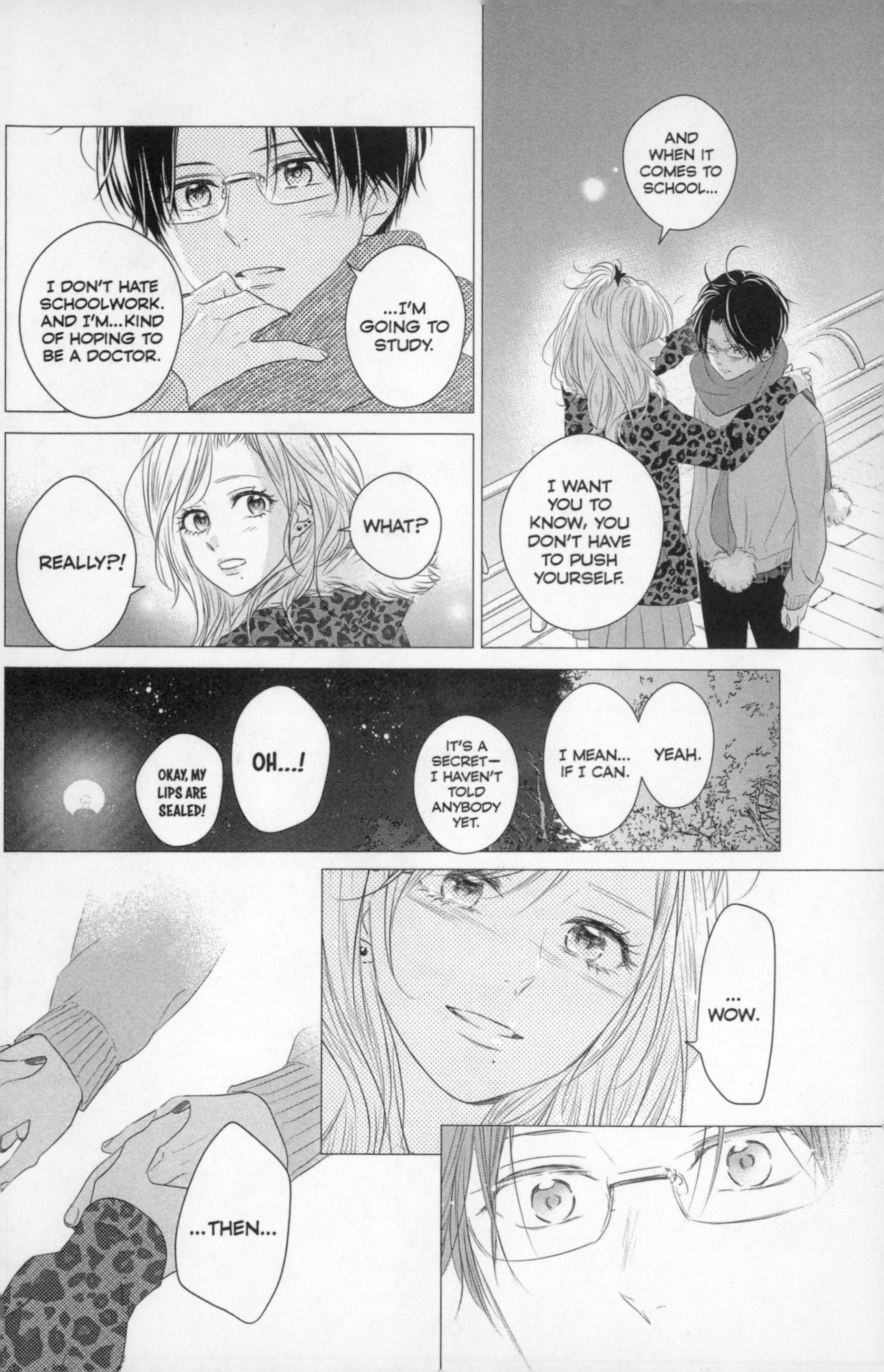
AND WHEN IT COMES TO SCHOOL...
I WANT YOU TO KNOW, YOU DON'T HAVE TO PUSH YOURSELF.
...I'M GOING TO STUDY.
I DON'T HATE SCHOOLWORK. AND I'M...KIND OF HOPING TO BE A DOCTOR.
WHAT?
REALLY?!
YEAH.
I MEAN... IF I CAN.
IT'S A SECRET— I HAVEN'T TOLD ANYBODY YET.
OH...!
OKAY, MY LIPS ARE SEALED!
... WOW.
...THEN...

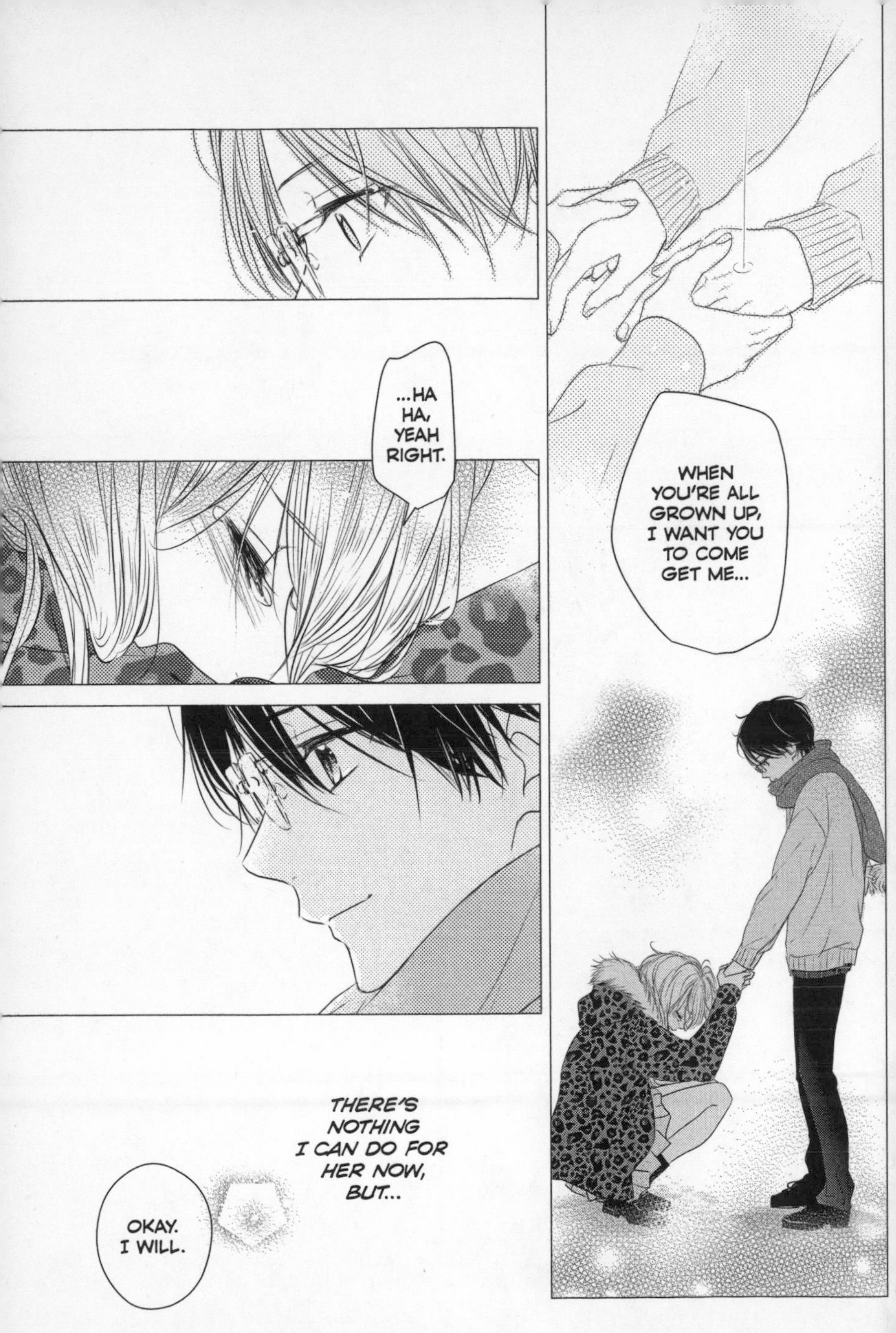
WHEN YOU'RE ALL GROWN UP, I WANT YOU TO COME GET ME...
...HA HA, YEAH RIGHT.
THERE'S NOTHING I CAN DO FOR HER NOW, BUT...
OKAY. I WILL.

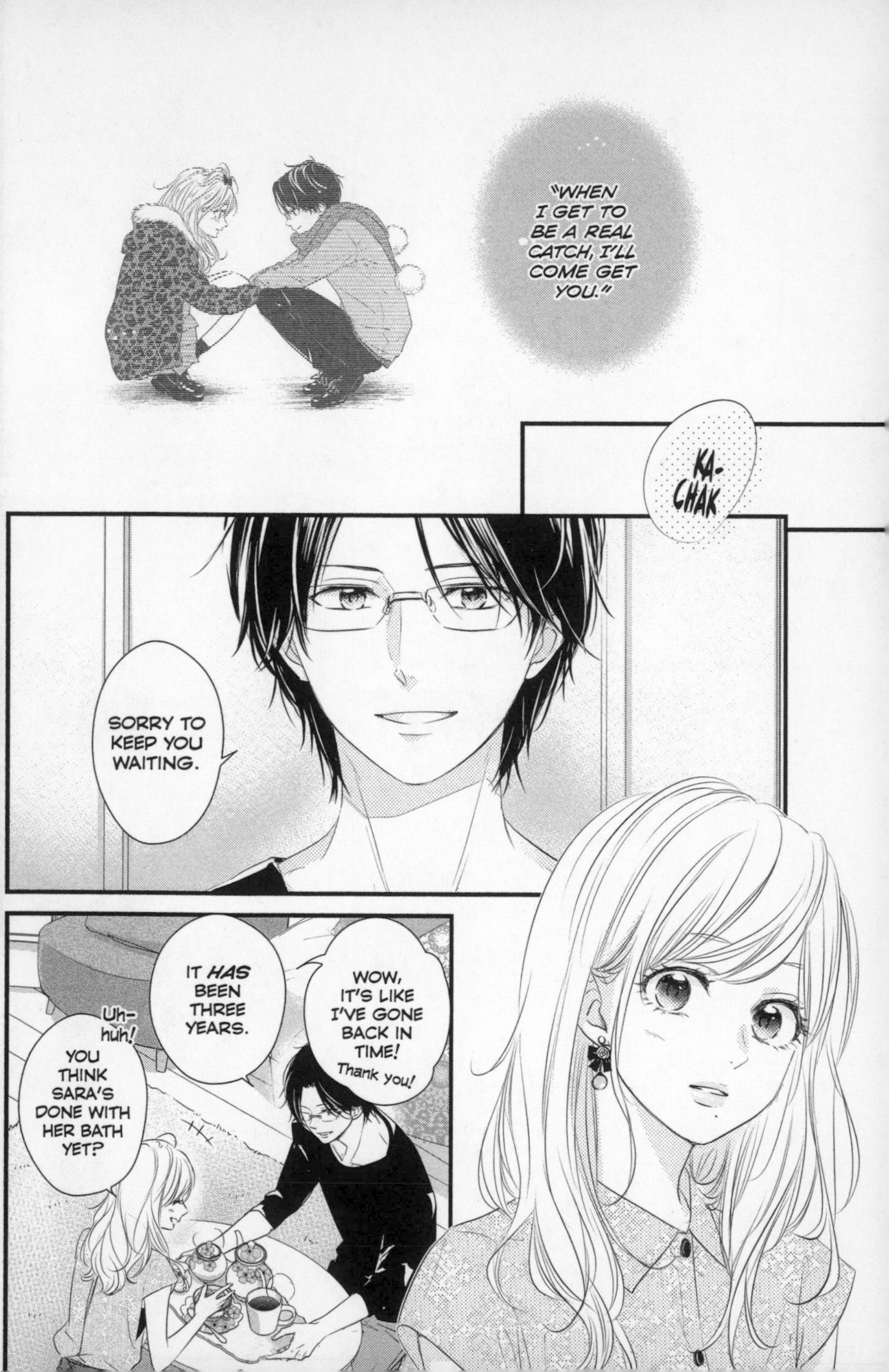
"WHEN I GET TO BE A REAL CATCH, I'LL COME GET YOU."
KA-CHAK
SORRY TO KEEP YOU WAITING.
WOW, IT'S LIKE I'VE GONE BACK IN TIME!
Thank you!
IT *HAS* BEEN THREE YEARS.
Uh-huh!
YOU THINK SARA'S DONE WITH HER BATH YET?

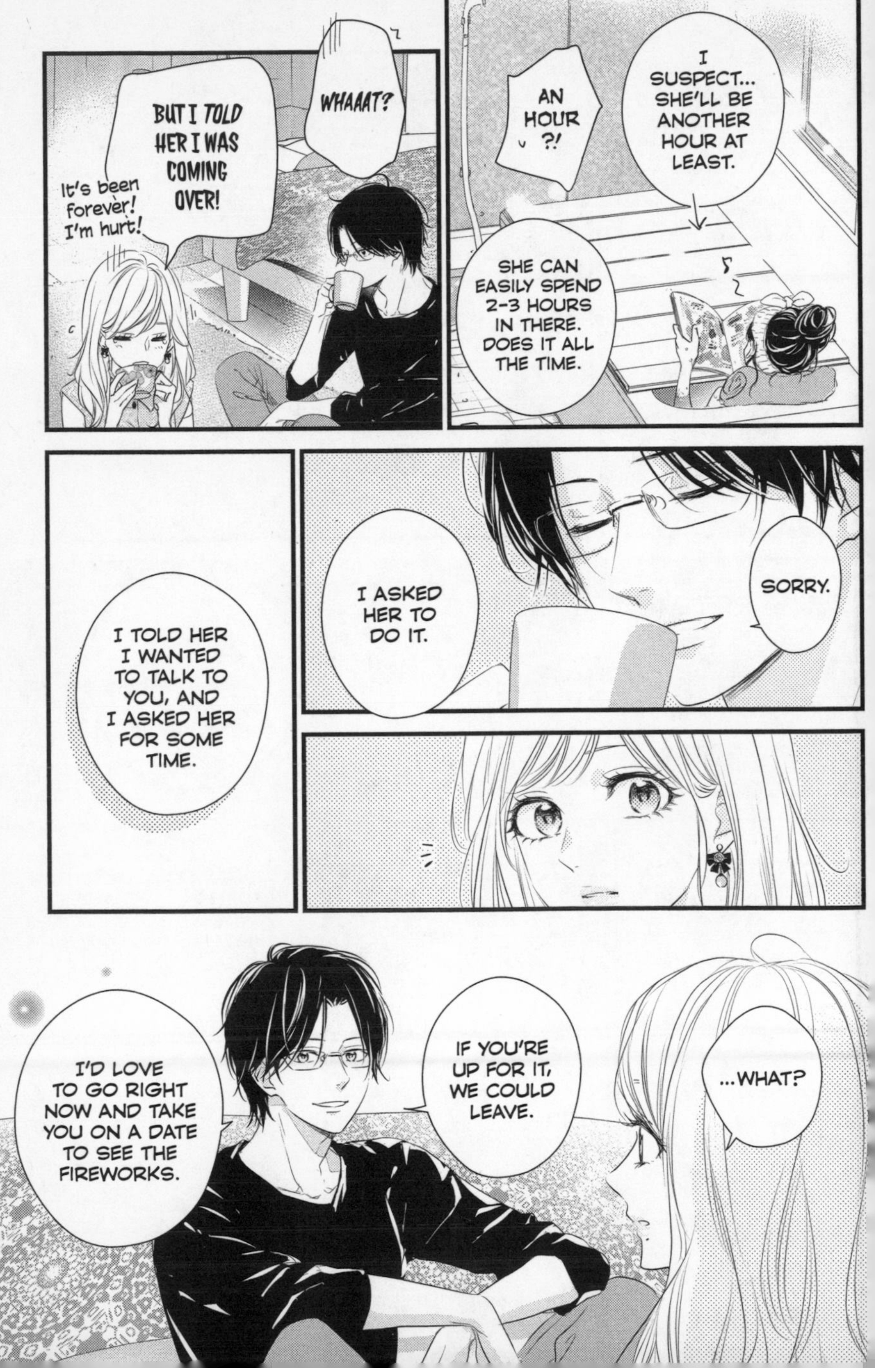
I SUSPECT... SHE'LL BE ANOTHER HOUR AT LEAST.
AN HOUR ?!
SHE CAN EASILY SPEND 2-3 HOURS IN THERE. DOES IT ALL THE TIME.
WHAAAT?
BUT I TOLD HER I WAS COMING OVER!
It's been forever! I'm hurt!
SORRY.
I ASKED HER TO DO IT.
I TOLD HER I WANTED TO TALK TO YOU, AND I ASKED HER FOR SOME TIME.
...WHAT?
IF YOU'RE UP FOR IT, WE COULD LEAVE.
I'D LOVE TO GO RIGHT NOW AND TAKE YOU ON A DATE TO SEE THE FIREWORKS.

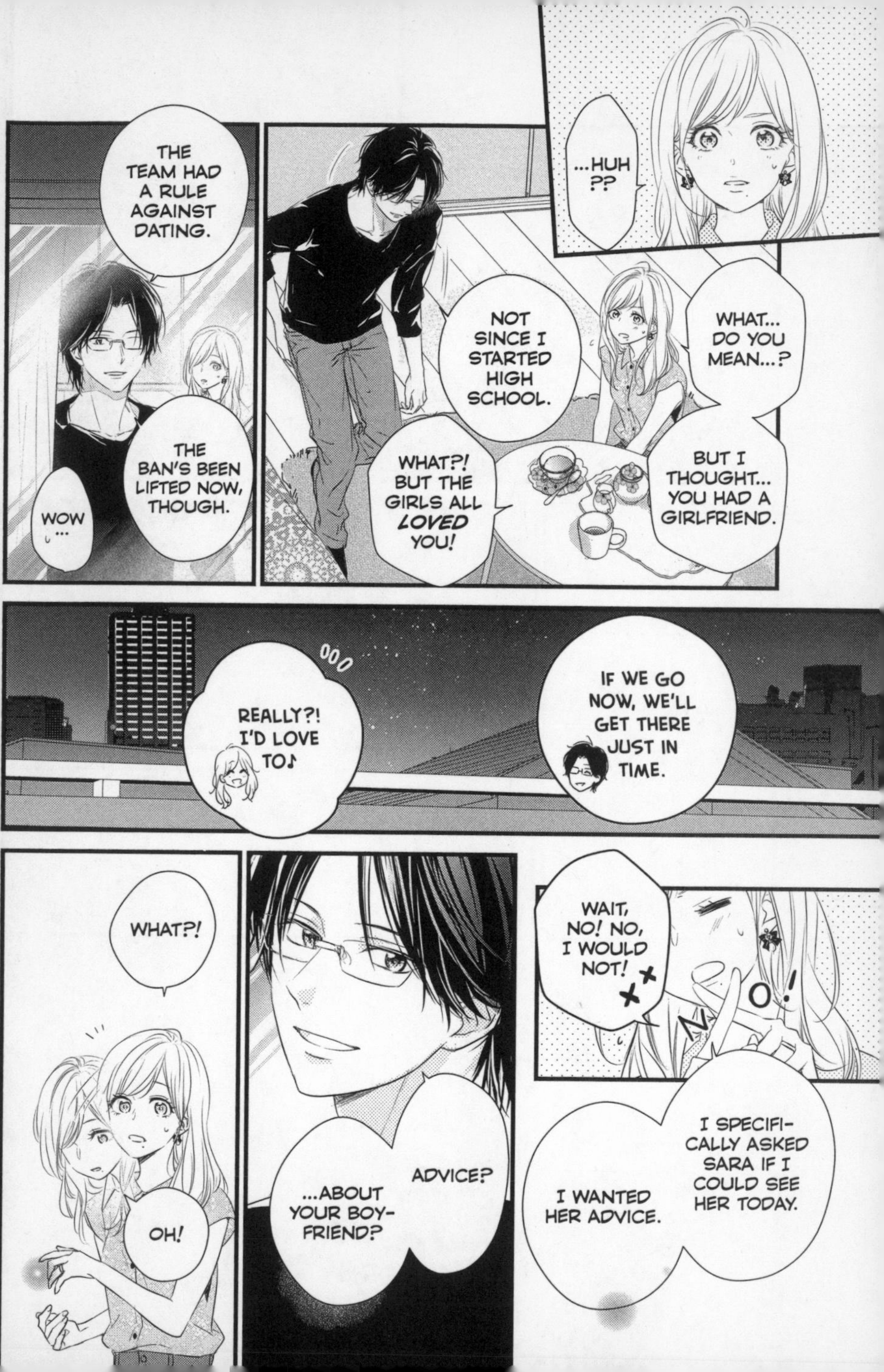
...HUH??
WHAT... DO YOU MEAN...?
NOT SINCE I STARTED HIGH SCHOOL.
BUT I THOUGHT... YOU HAD A GIRLFRIEND.
WHAT?! BUT THE GIRLS ALL *LOVED* YOU!
THE TEAM HAD A RULE AGAINST DATING.
THE BAN'S BEEN LIFTED NOW, THOUGH.
WOW...
IF WE GO NOW, WE'LL GET THERE JUST IN TIME.
OOO
REALLY?! I'D LOVE TO♪
WAIT, NO! NO, I WOULD NOT!
NO!
I SPECIFI-CALLY ASKED SARA IF I COULD SEE HER TODAY.
I WANTED HER ADVICE.
ADVICE?
...ABOUT YOUR BOY-FRIEND?
WHAT?!
OH!

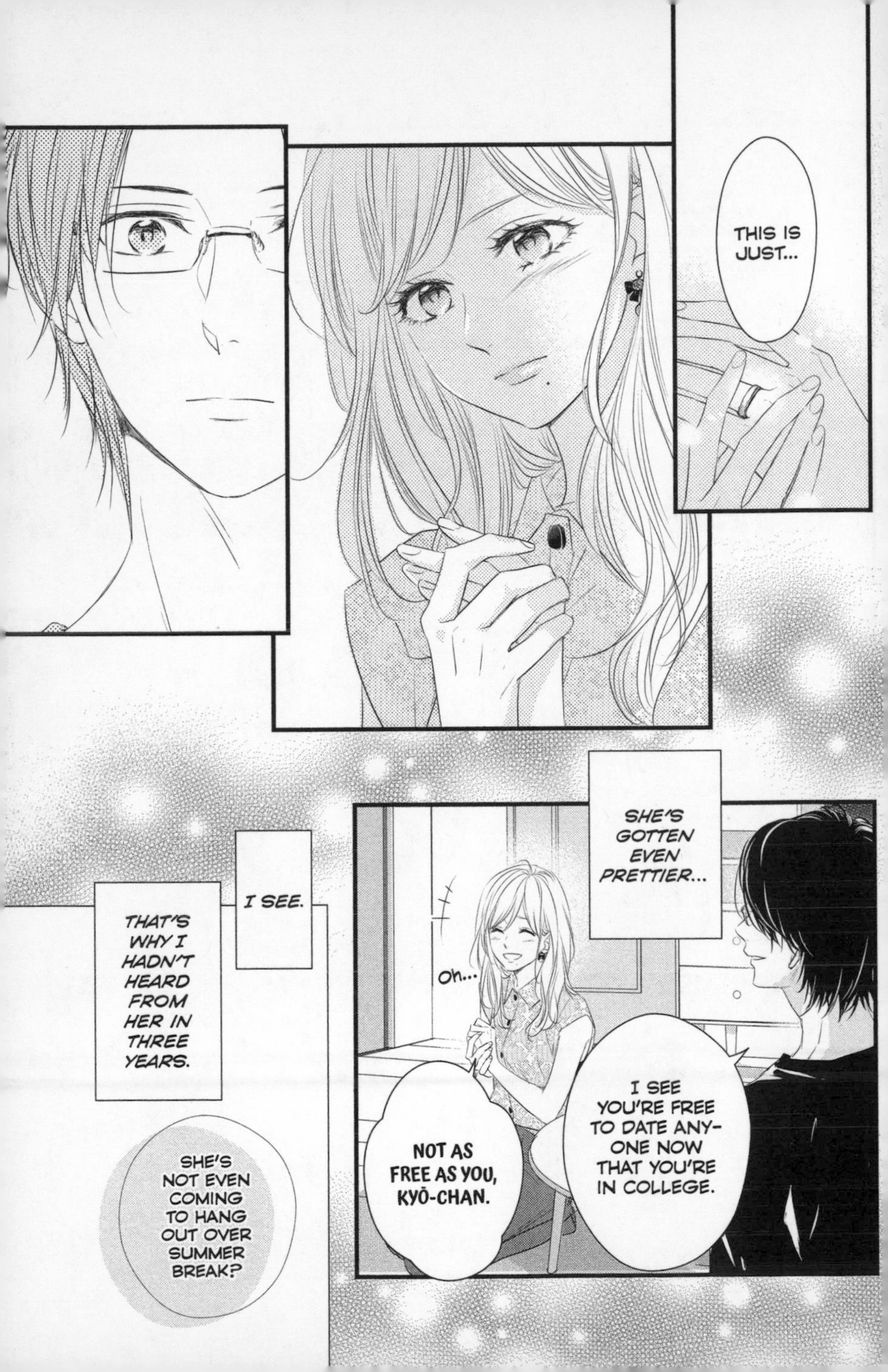

THIS IS JUST...
SHE'S GOTTEN EVEN PRETTIER...
I SEE YOU'RE FREE TO DATE ANY-ONE NOW THAT YOU'RE IN COLLEGE.
Oh...
NOT AS FREE AS YOU, KYŌ-CHAN.
I SEE.
THAT'S WHY I HADN'T HEARD FROM HER IN THREE YEARS.
SHE'S NOT EVEN COMING TO HANG OUT OVER SUMMER BREAK?

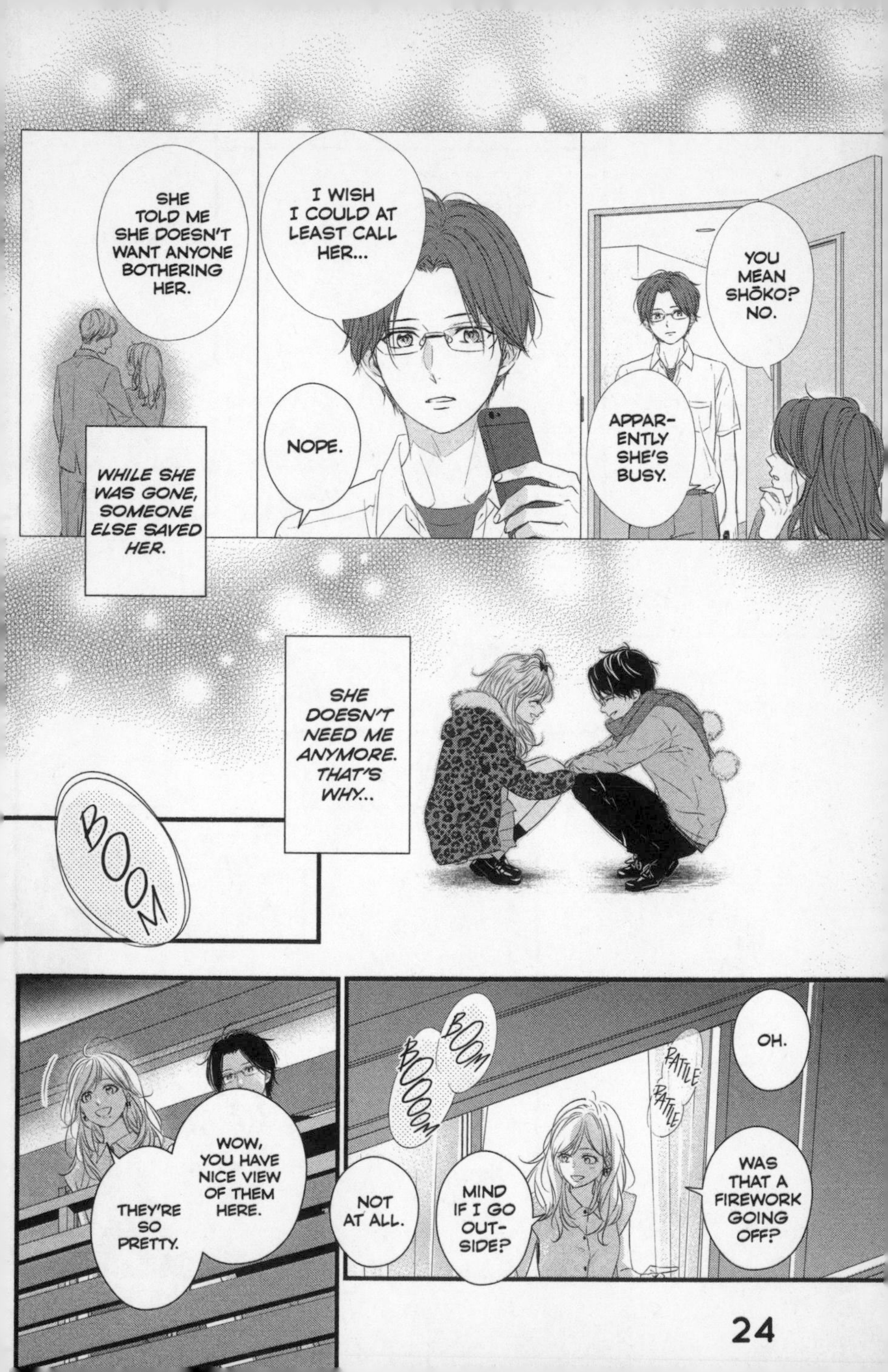
YOU MEAN SHŌKO? NO.
APPAR-ENTLY SHE'S BUSY.
I WISH I COULD AT LEAST CALL HER...
NOPE.
SHE TOLD ME SHE DOESN'T WANT ANYONE BOTHERING HER.
WHILE SHE WAS GONE, SOMEONE ELSE SAVED HER.
SHE DOESN'T NEED ME ANYMORE. THAT'S WHY...
BOOM
OH.
RATTLE RATTLE
BOOM
BOOOOM
WAS THAT A FIREWORK GOING OFF?
MIND IF I GO OUT-SIDE?
NOT AT ALL.
WOW, YOU HAVE NICE VIEW OF THEM HERE.
THEY'RE SO PRETTY.

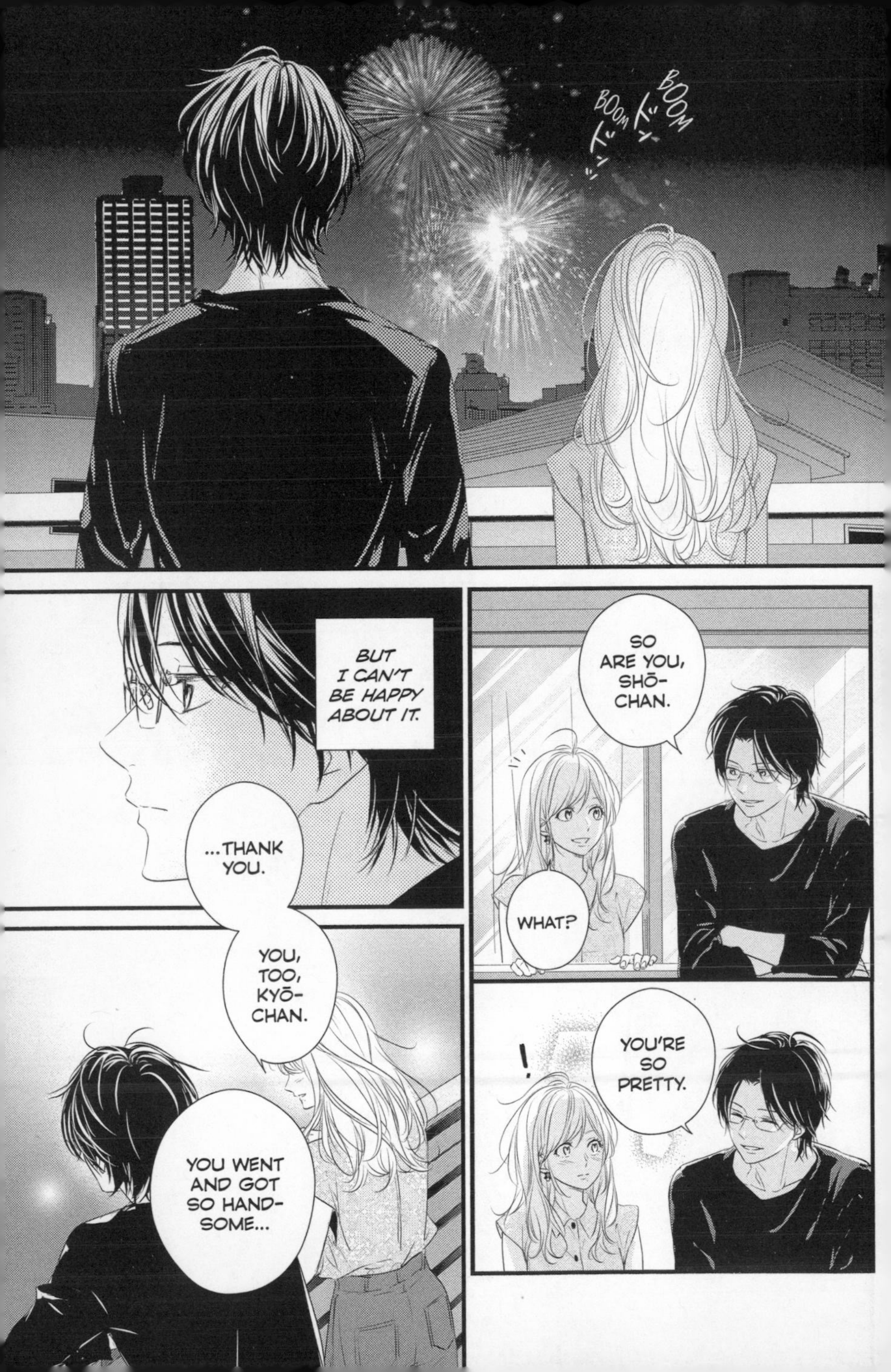
BOOM
BOOM
SO ARE YOU, SHŌ-CHAN.
WHAT?
YOU'RE SO PRETTY.
!
BUT I CAN'T BE HAPPY ABOUT IT.
...THANK YOU.
YOU, TOO, KYŌ-CHAN.
YOU WENT AND GOT SO HAND-SOME...

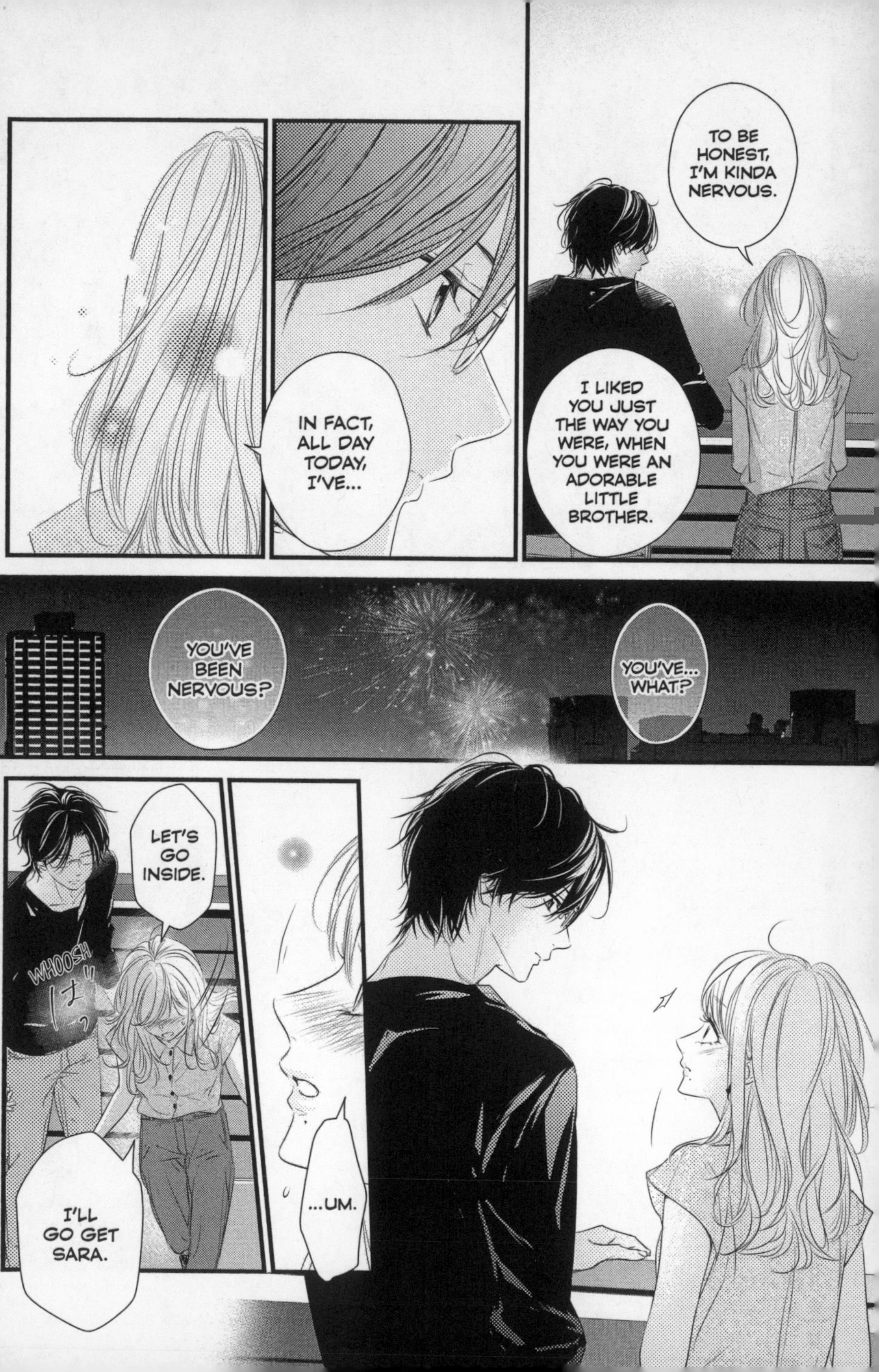
TO BE HONEST, I'M KINDA NERVOUS.
I LIKED YOU JUST THE WAY YOU WERE, WHEN YOU WERE AN ADORABLE LITTLE BROTHER.
IN FACT, ALL DAY TODAY, I'VE...
YOU'VE... WHAT?
YOU'VE BEEN NERVOUS?
...UM.
LET'S GO INSIDE.
WHOOSH
はっ
I'LL GO GET SARA.

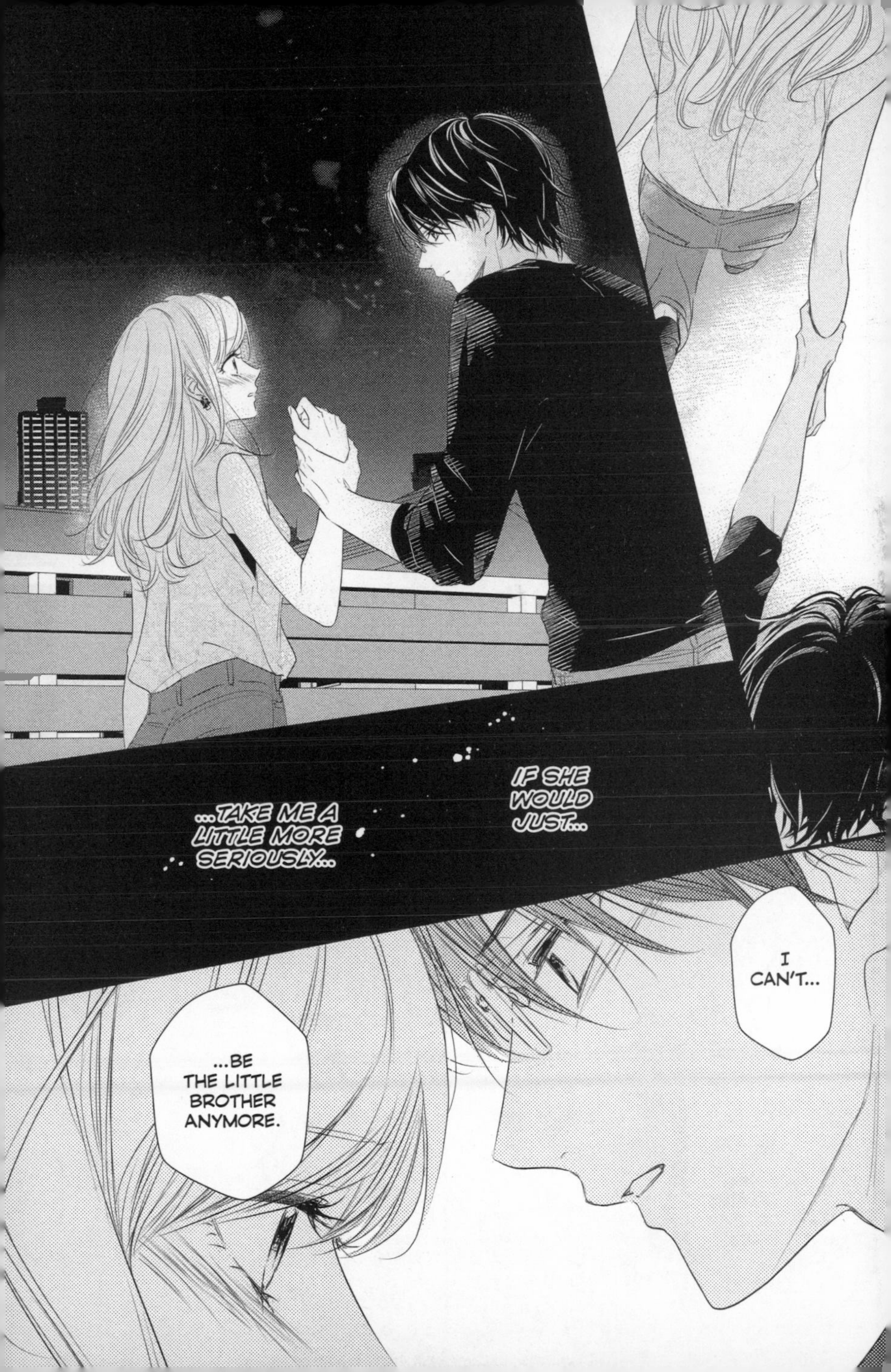
IF SHE WOULD JUST...
...TAKE ME A LITTLE MORE SERIOUSLY...
I CAN'T...
...BE THE LITTLE BROTHER ANYMORE.

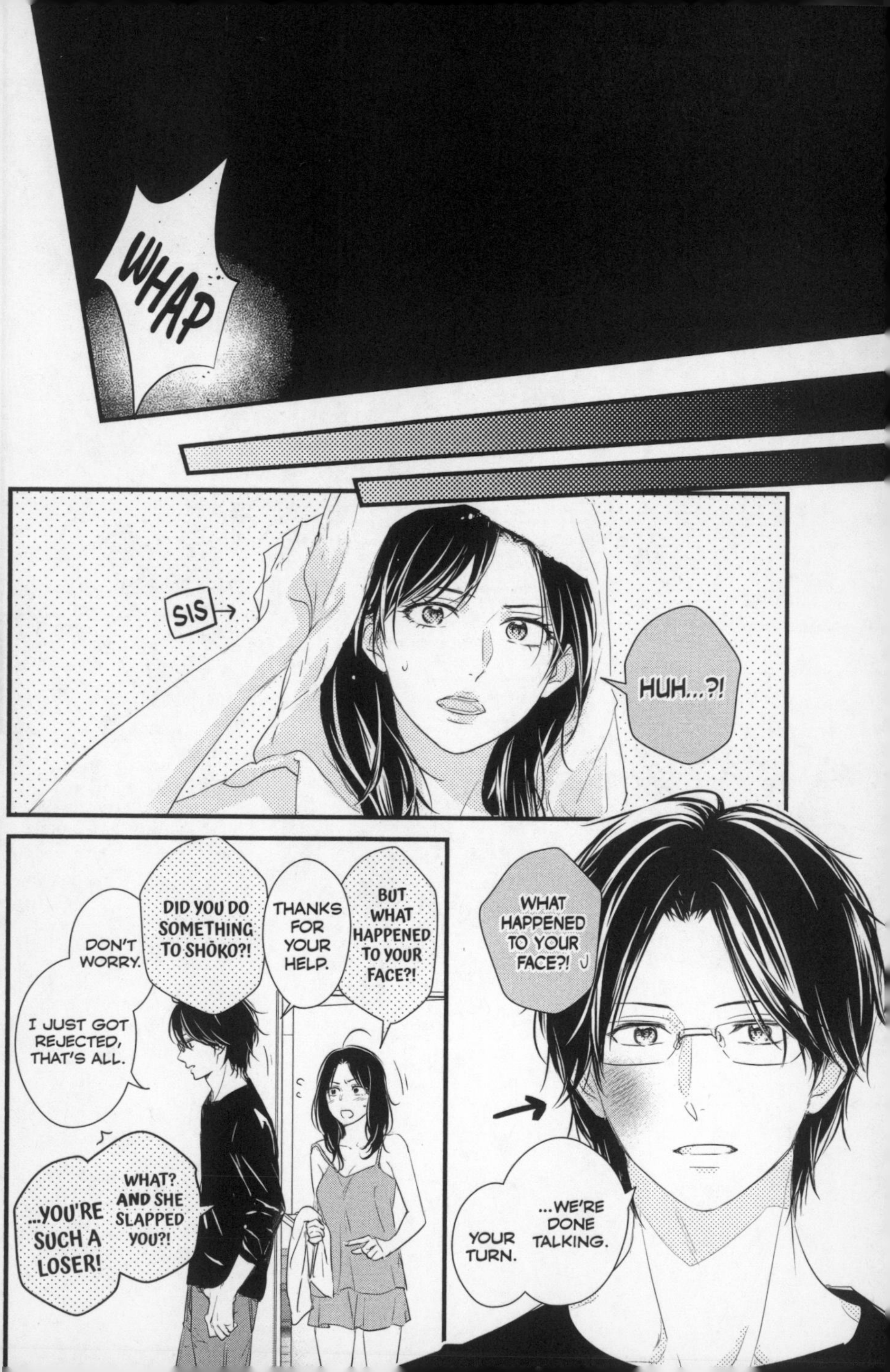
WHAP
SIS →
HUH...?!
WHAT HAPPENED TO YOUR FACE?!
...WE'RE DONE TALKING.
YOUR TURN.
THANKS FOR YOUR HELP.
BUT WHAT HAPPENED TO YOUR FACE?!
DID YOU DO SOMETHING TO SHŌKO?!
DON'T WORRY.
I JUST GOT REJECTED, THAT'S ALL.
WHAT? AND SHE SLAPPED YOU?!
...YOU'RE SUCH A LOSER!

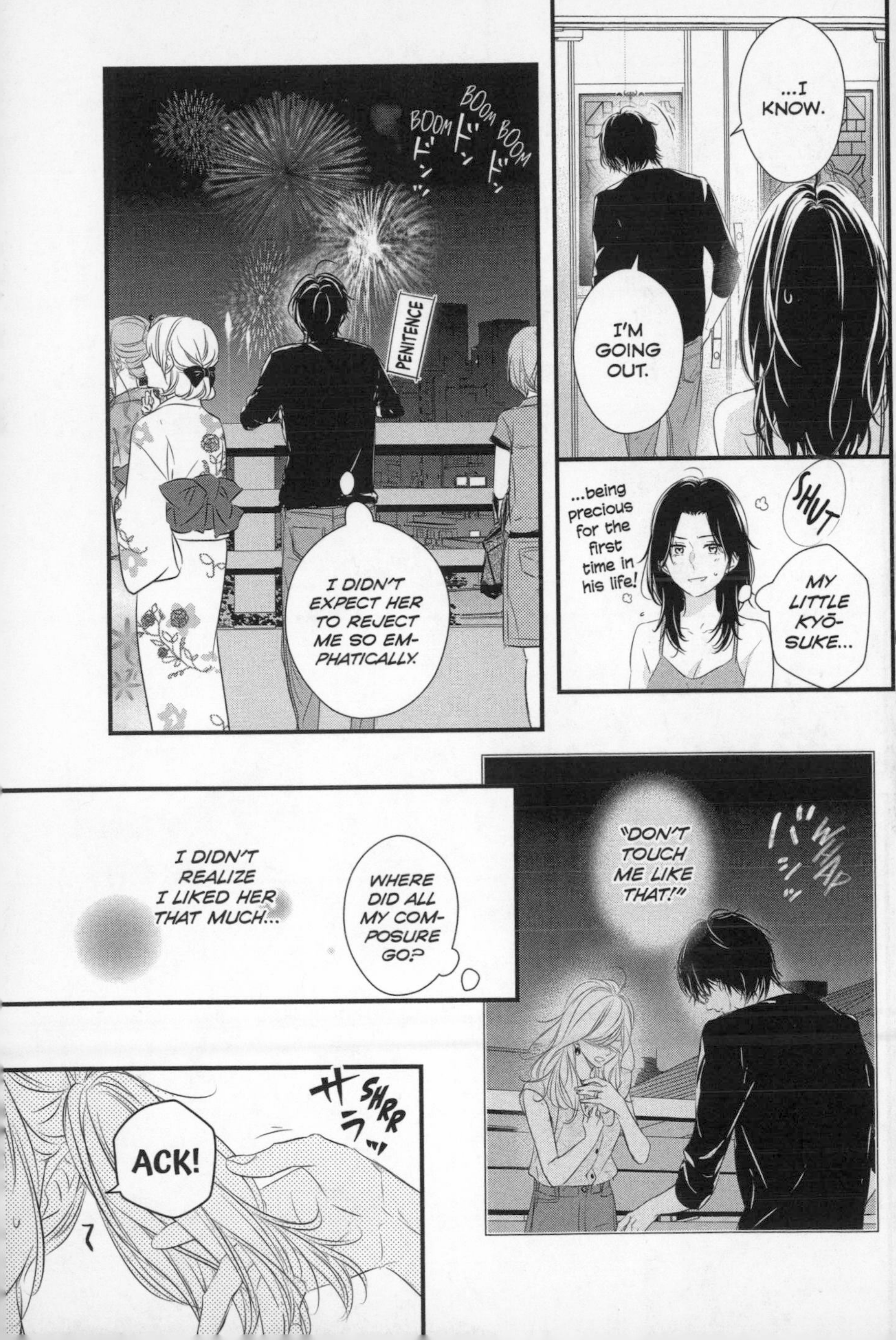

...I KNOW.
I'M GOING OUT.
SHUT
MY LITTLE KYŌ-SUKE...
...being precious for the first time in his life!
BOOM BOOM BOOM BOOM
ドンドンドン
PENITENCE
I DIDN'T EXPECT HER TO REJECT ME SO EMPHATICALLY.
WHAP
バシッ
"DON'T TOUCH ME LIKE THAT!"
WHERE DID ALL MY COMPOSURE GO?
I DIDN'T REALIZE I LIKED HER THAT MUCH...
SHRR
サラッ
ACK!

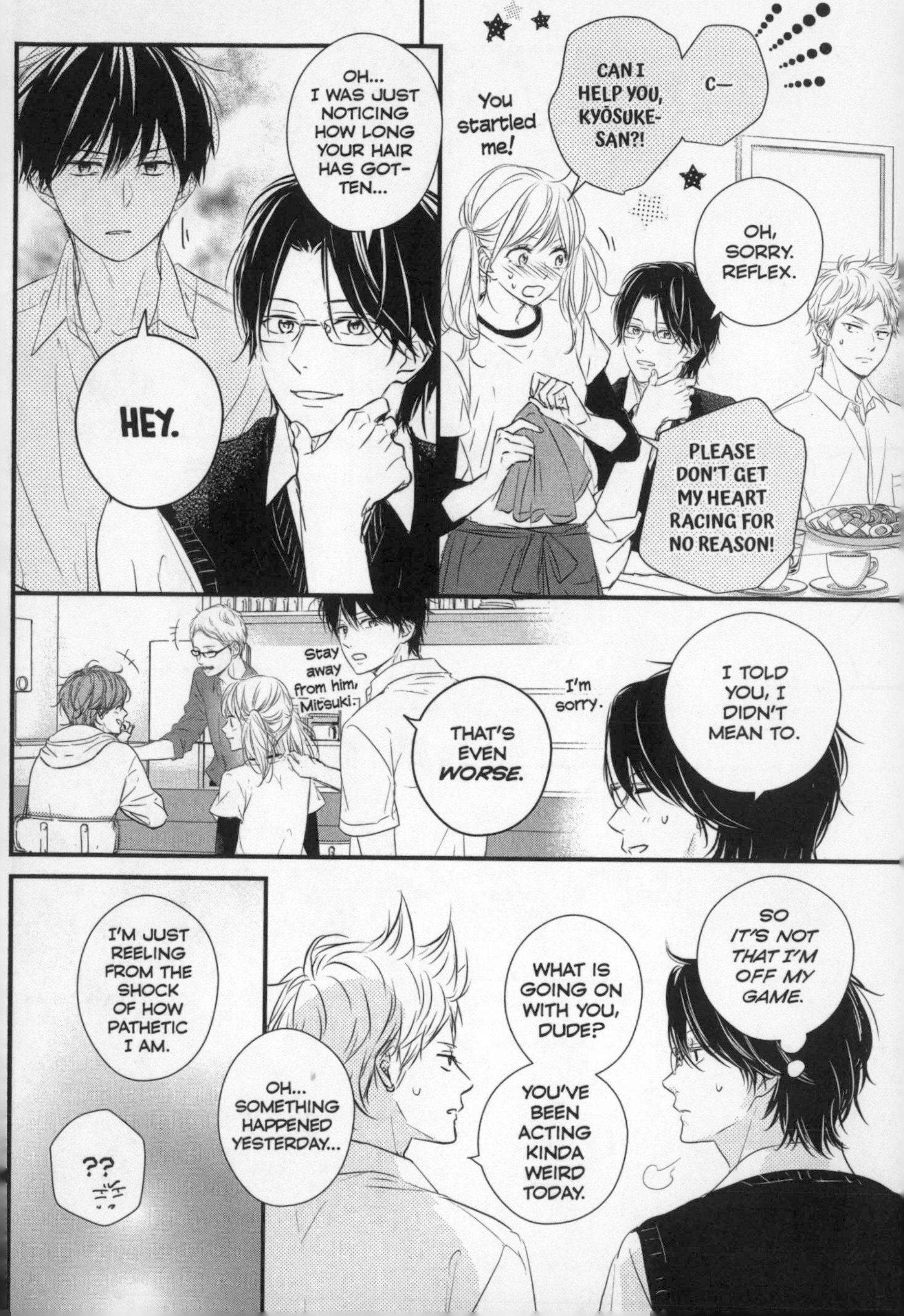
C—
CAN I HELP YOU, KYŌSUKE-SAN?!
You startled me!
OH, SORRY. REFLEX.
PLEASE DON'T GET MY HEART RACING FOR NO REASON!
OH... I WAS JUST NOTICING HOW LONG YOUR HAIR HAS GOTTEN...
HEY.
I TOLD YOU, I DIDN'T MEAN TO.
I'm sorry.
THAT'S EVEN WORSE.
Stay away from him, Mitsuki.
SO IT'S NOT THAT I'M OFF MY GAME.
WHAT IS GOING ON WITH YOU, DUDE?
YOU'VE BEEN ACTING KINDA WEIRD TODAY.
OH... SOMETHING HAPPENED YESTERDAY...
I'M JUST REELING FROM THE SHOCK OF HOW PATHETIC I AM.
??

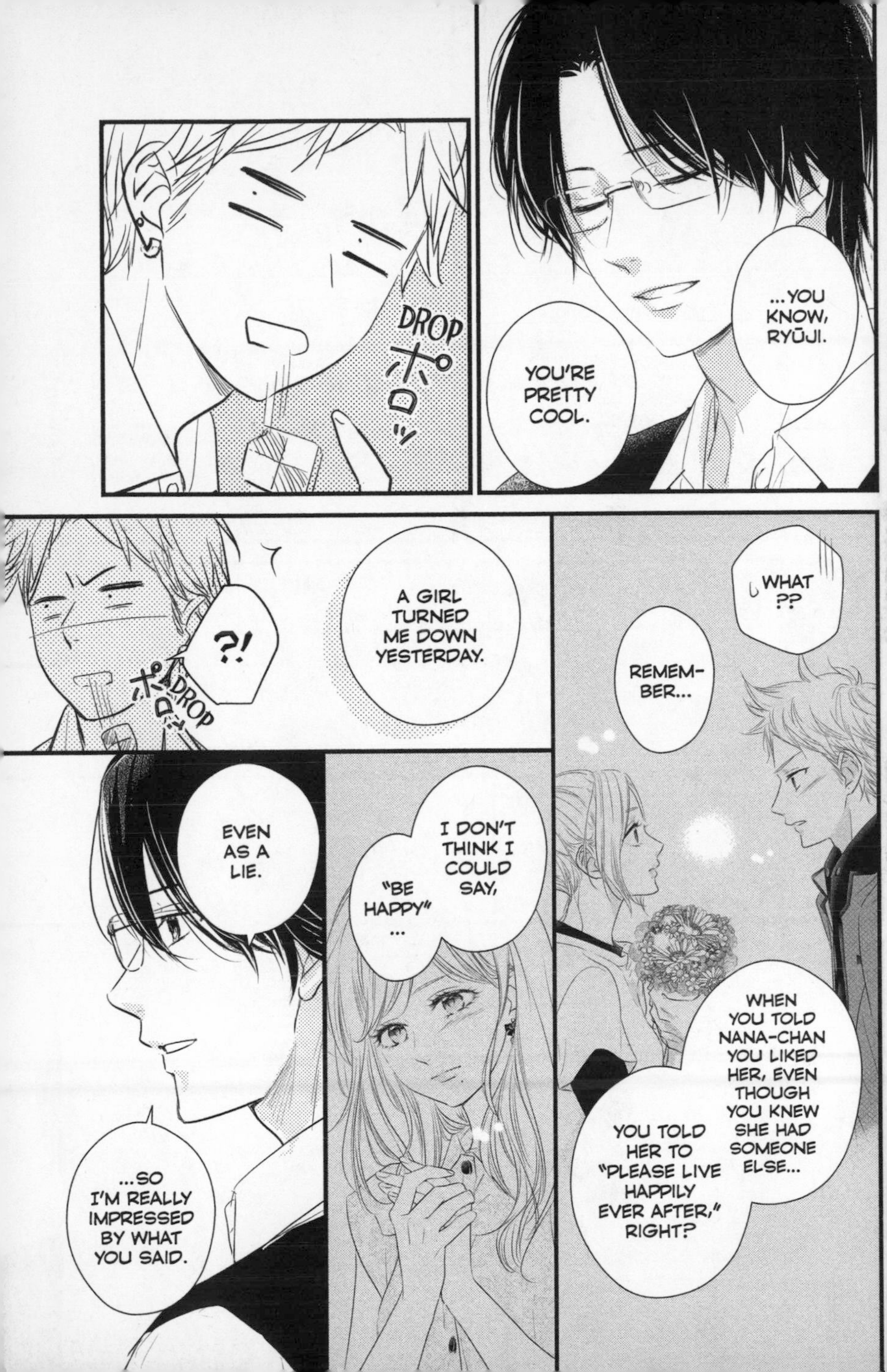
...YOU KNOW, RYŪJI.
YOU'RE PRETTY COOL.
DROP
WHAT ??
REMEMBER...
WHEN YOU TOLD NANA-CHAN YOU LIKED HER, EVEN THOUGH YOU KNEW SHE HAD SOMEONE ELSE...
YOU TOLD HER TO "PLEASE LIVE HAPPILY EVER AFTER," RIGHT?
A GIRL TURNED ME DOWN YESTERDAY.
?!
DROP
I DON'T THINK I COULD SAY,
"BE HAPPY" ...
EVEN AS A LIE.
...SO I'M REALLY IMPRESSED BY WHAT YOU SAID.

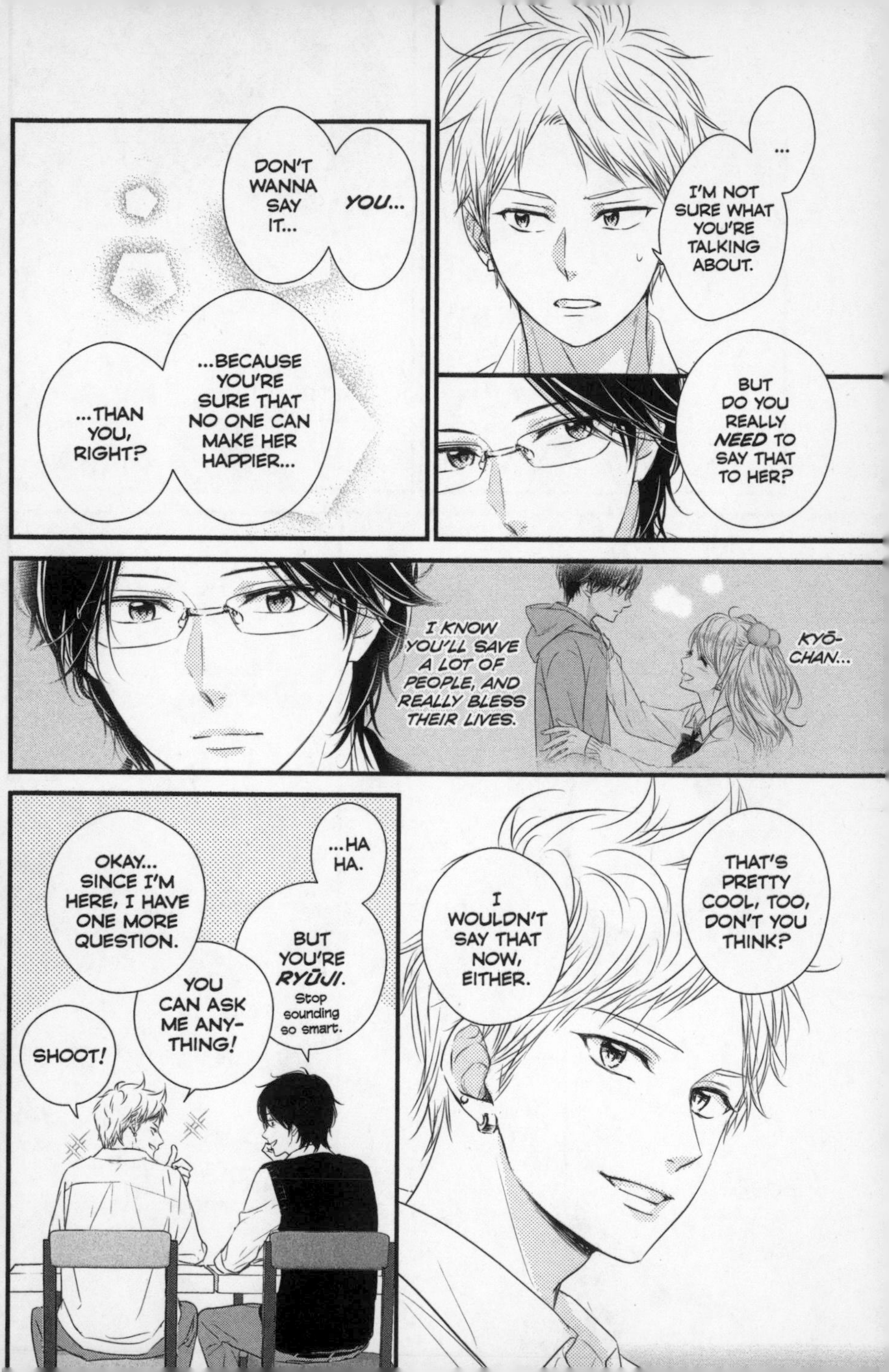
...
I'M NOT SURE WHAT YOU'RE TALKING ABOUT.
BUT DO YOU REALLY *NEED* TO SAY THAT TO HER?
*YOU...*
DON'T WANNA SAY IT...
...BECAUSE YOU'RE SURE THAT NO ONE CAN MAKE HER HAPPIER...
...THAN YOU, RIGHT?
KYŌ-CHAN...
I KNOW YOU'LL SAVE A LOT OF PEOPLE, AND REALLY BLESS THEIR LIVES.
THAT'S PRETTY COOL, TOO, DON'T YOU THINK?
I WOULDN'T SAY THAT NOW, EITHER.
...HA HA.
BUT YOU'RE *RYŪJI*. Stop sounding so smart.
OKAY... SINCE I'M HERE, I HAVE ONE MORE QUESTION.
YOU CAN ASK ME ANY-THING!
SHOOT!

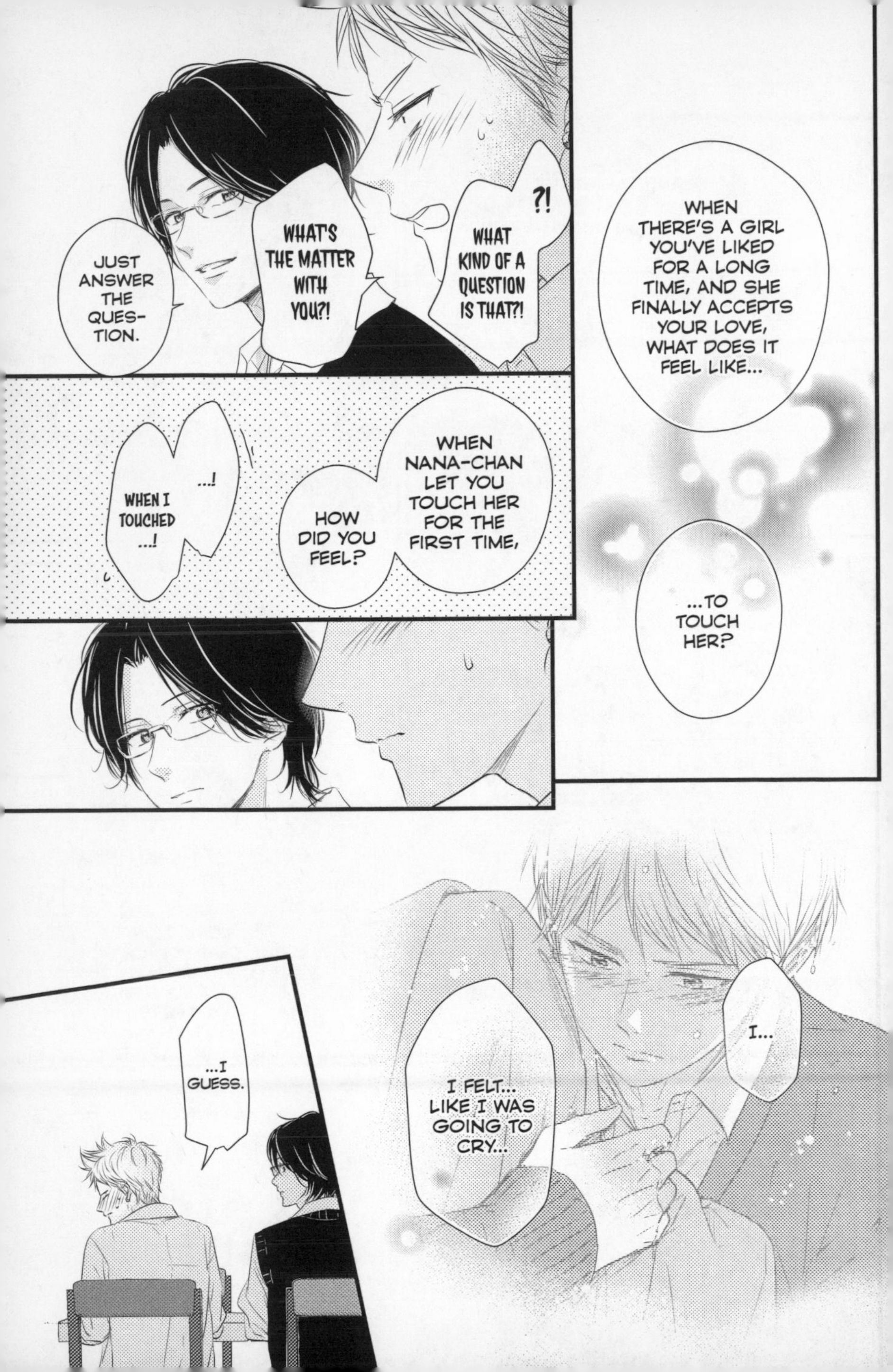
WHEN THERE'S A GIRL YOU'VE LIKED FOR A LONG TIME, AND SHE FINALLY ACCEPTS YOUR LOVE, WHAT DOES IT FEEL LIKE...
...TO TOUCH HER?
?!
WHAT KIND OF A QUESTION IS THAT?!
WHAT'S THE MATTER WITH YOU?!
JUST ANSWER THE QUES- TION.
WHEN NANA-CHAN LET YOU TOUCH HER FOR THE FIRST TIME,
HOW DID YOU FEEL?
...!
WHEN I TOUCHED ...!
I...
I FELT... LIKE I WAS GOING TO CRY...
...I GUESS.

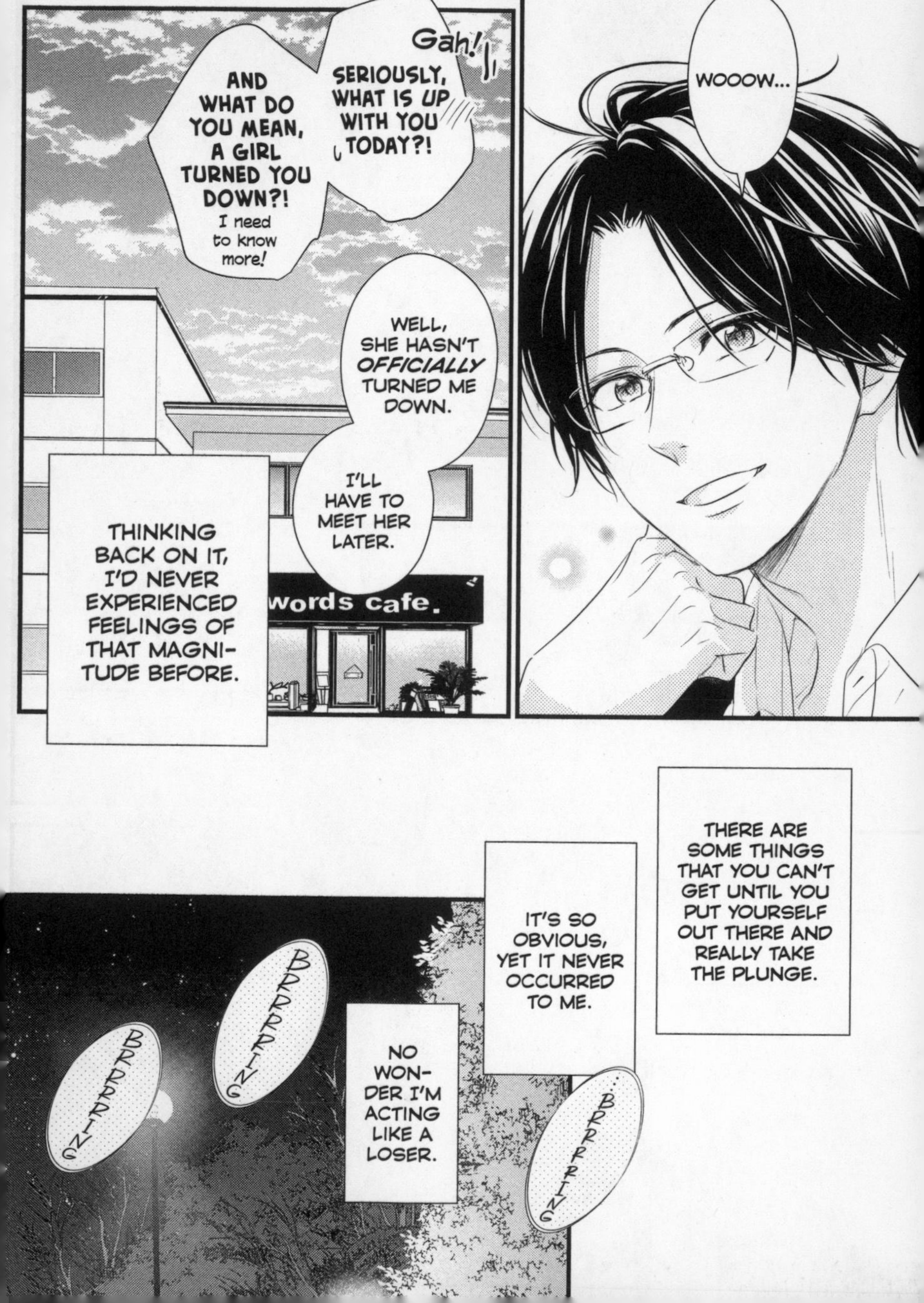
WOOOW...
Gah!
SERIOUSLY, WHAT IS UP WITH YOU TODAY?!
AND WHAT DO YOU MEAN, A GIRL TURNED YOU DOWN?! I need to know more!
WELL, SHE HASN'T OFFICIALLY TURNED ME DOWN.
I'LL HAVE TO MEET HER LATER.
words cafe.
THINKING BACK ON IT, I'D NEVER EXPERIENCED FEELINGS OF THAT MAGNITUDE BEFORE.
THERE ARE SOME THINGS THAT YOU CAN'T GET UNTIL YOU PUT YOURSELF OUT THERE AND REALLY TAKE THE PLUNGE.
IT'S SO OBVIOUS, YET IT NEVER OCCURRED TO ME.
...BRRRRING
NO WONDER I'M ACTING LIKE A LOSER.
BRRRRING
BRRRRING

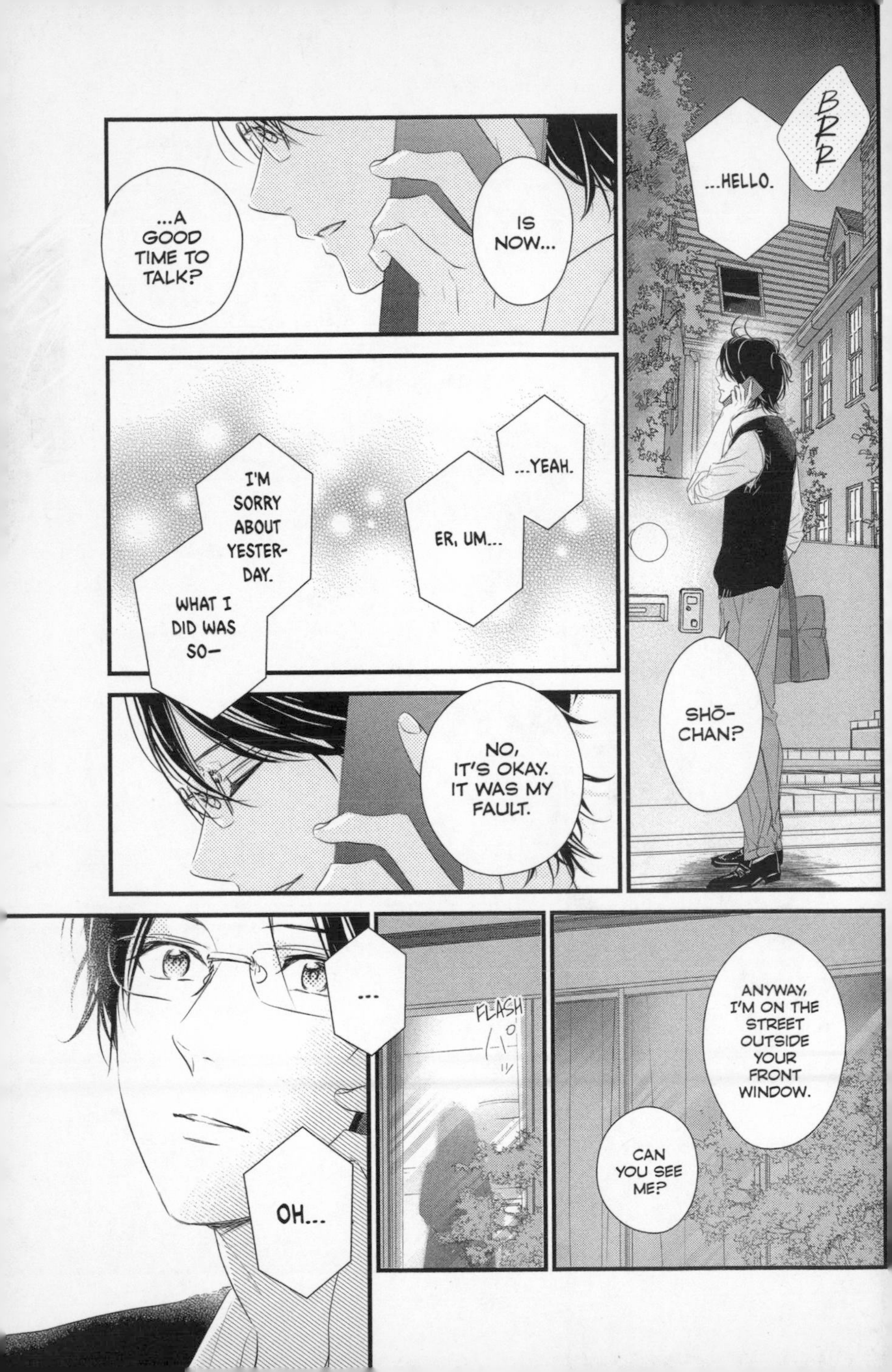
BRR
...HELLO.
SHŌ-CHAN?
IS NOW...
...A GOOD TIME TO TALK?
...YEAH.
ER, UM...
I'M SORRY ABOUT YESTER-DAY.
WHAT I DID WAS SO—
NO, IT'S OKAY. IT WAS MY FAULT.
ANYWAY, I'M ON THE STREET OUTSIDE YOUR FRONT WINDOW.
CAN YOU SEE ME?
FLASH
...
OH...

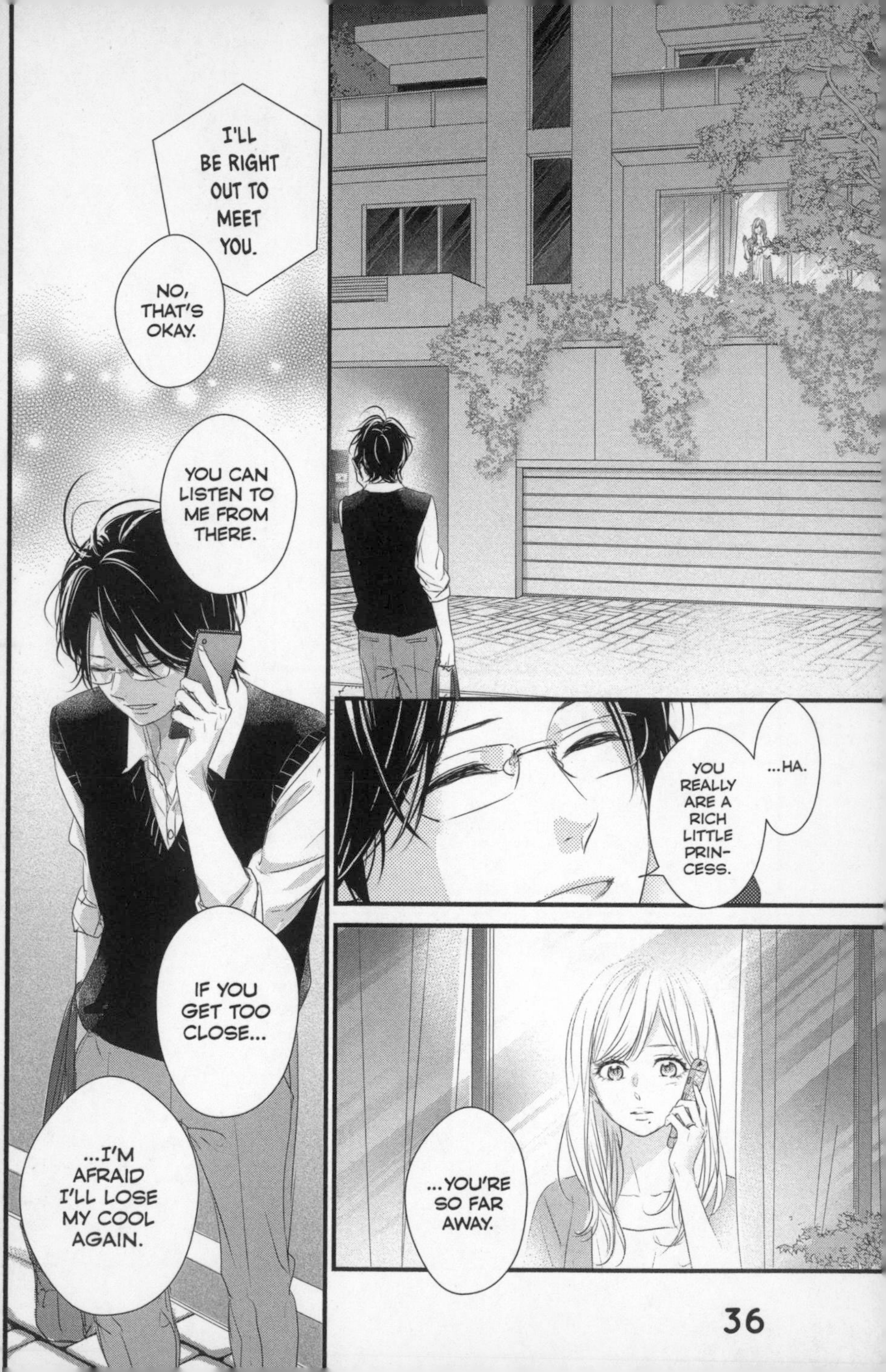
...HA.
YOU REALLY ARE A RICH LITTLE PRINCESS.
...YOU'RE SO FAR AWAY.
I'LL BE RIGHT OUT TO MEET YOU.
NO, THAT'S OKAY.
YOU CAN LISTEN TO ME FROM THERE.
IF YOU GET TOO CLOSE...
...I'M AFRAID I'LL LOSE MY COOL AGAIN.

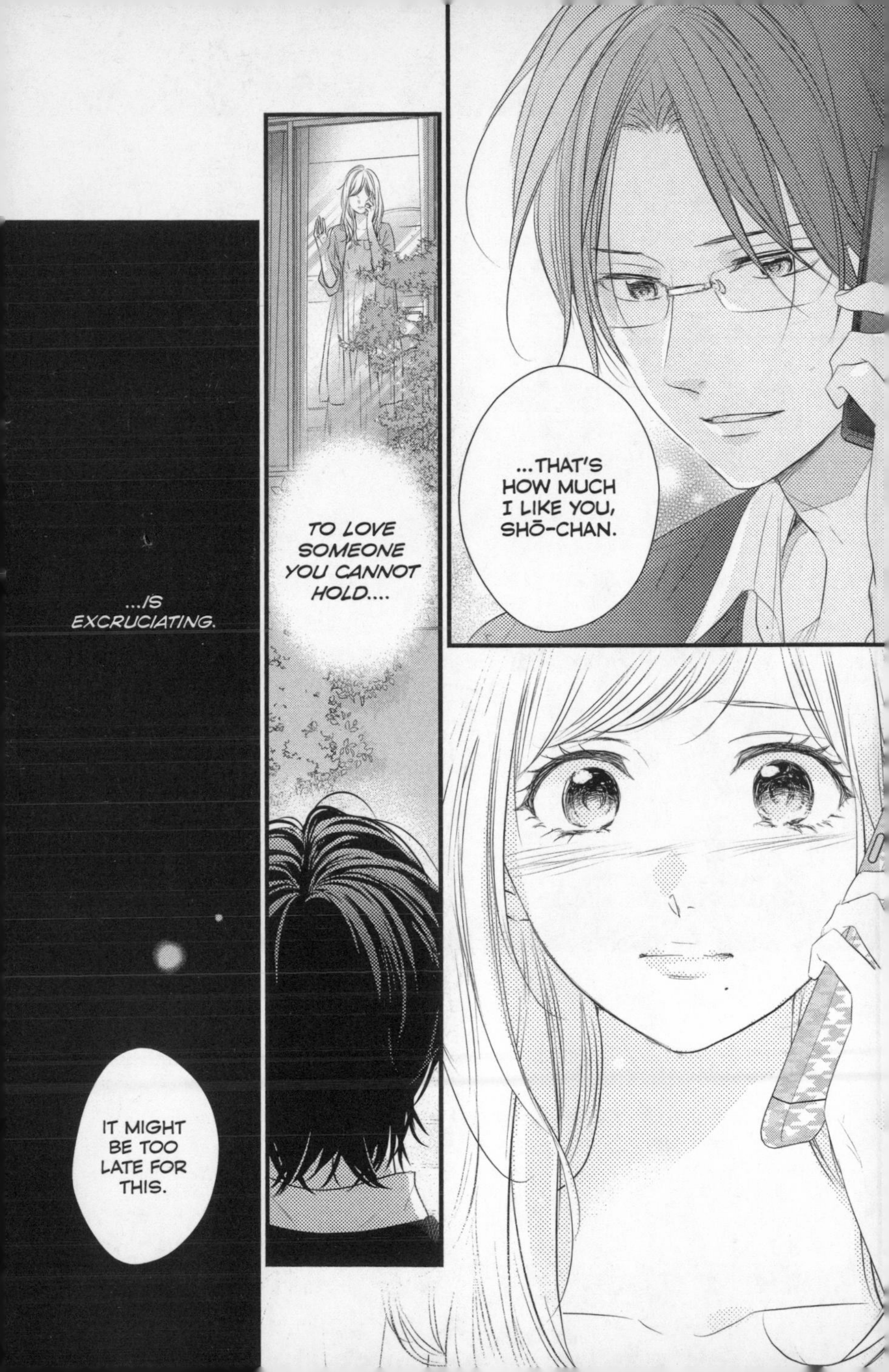
...THAT'S HOW MUCH I LIKE YOU, SHŌ-CHAN.
TO LOVE SOMEONE YOU CANNOT HOLD....
...IS EXCRUCIATING.
IT MIGHT BE TOO LATE FOR THIS.

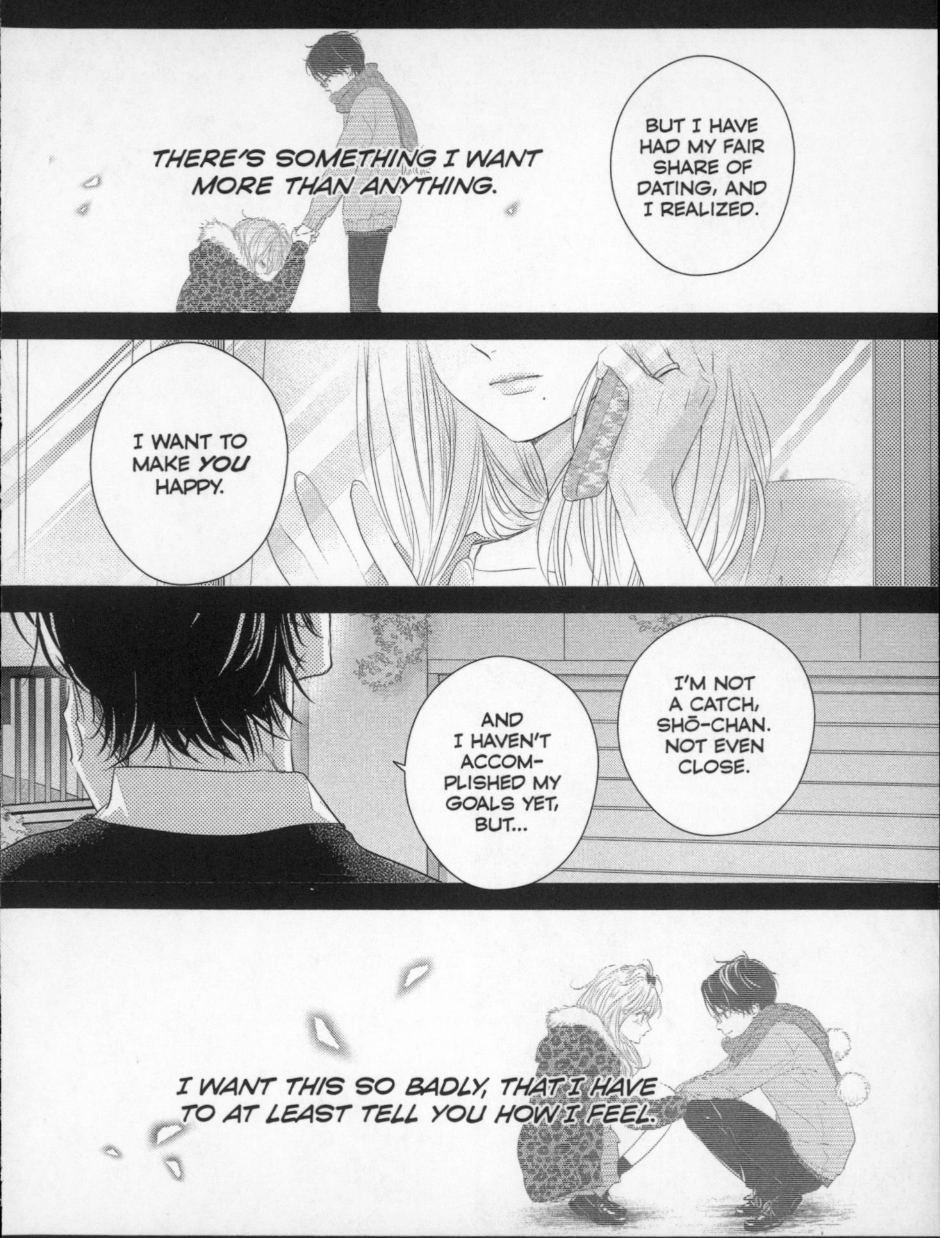
BUT I HAVE HAD MY FAIR SHARE OF DATING, AND I REALIZED.
THERE'S SOMETHING I WANT MORE THAN ANYTHING.
I WANT TO MAKE *YOU* HAPPY.
I'M NOT A CATCH, SHŌ-CHAN. NOT EVEN CLOSE.
AND I HAVEN'T ACCOMPLISHED MY GOALS YET, BUT...
I WANT THIS SO BADLY, THAT I HAVE TO AT LEAST TELL YOU HOW I FEEL.

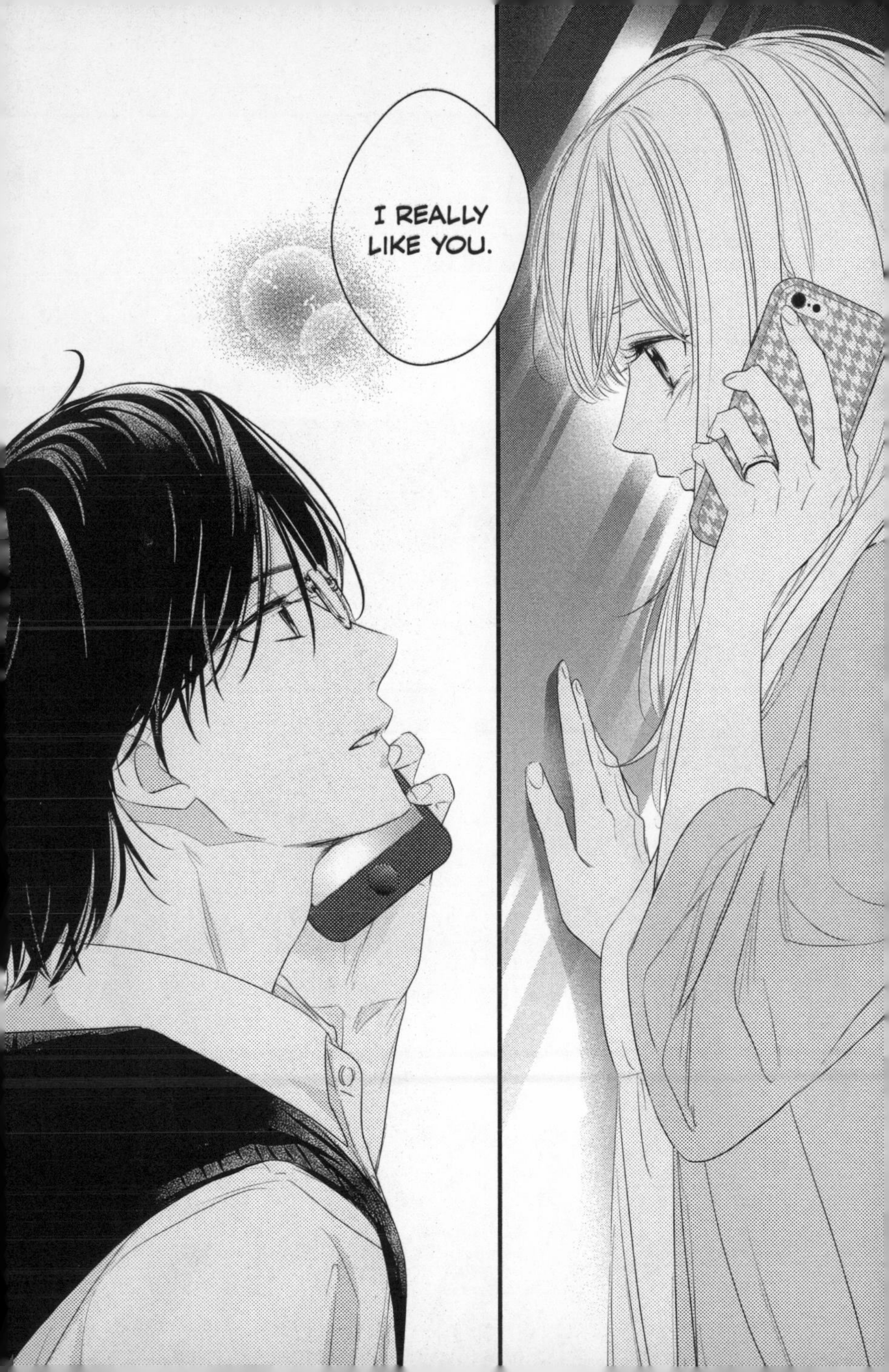
I REALLY LIKE YOU.

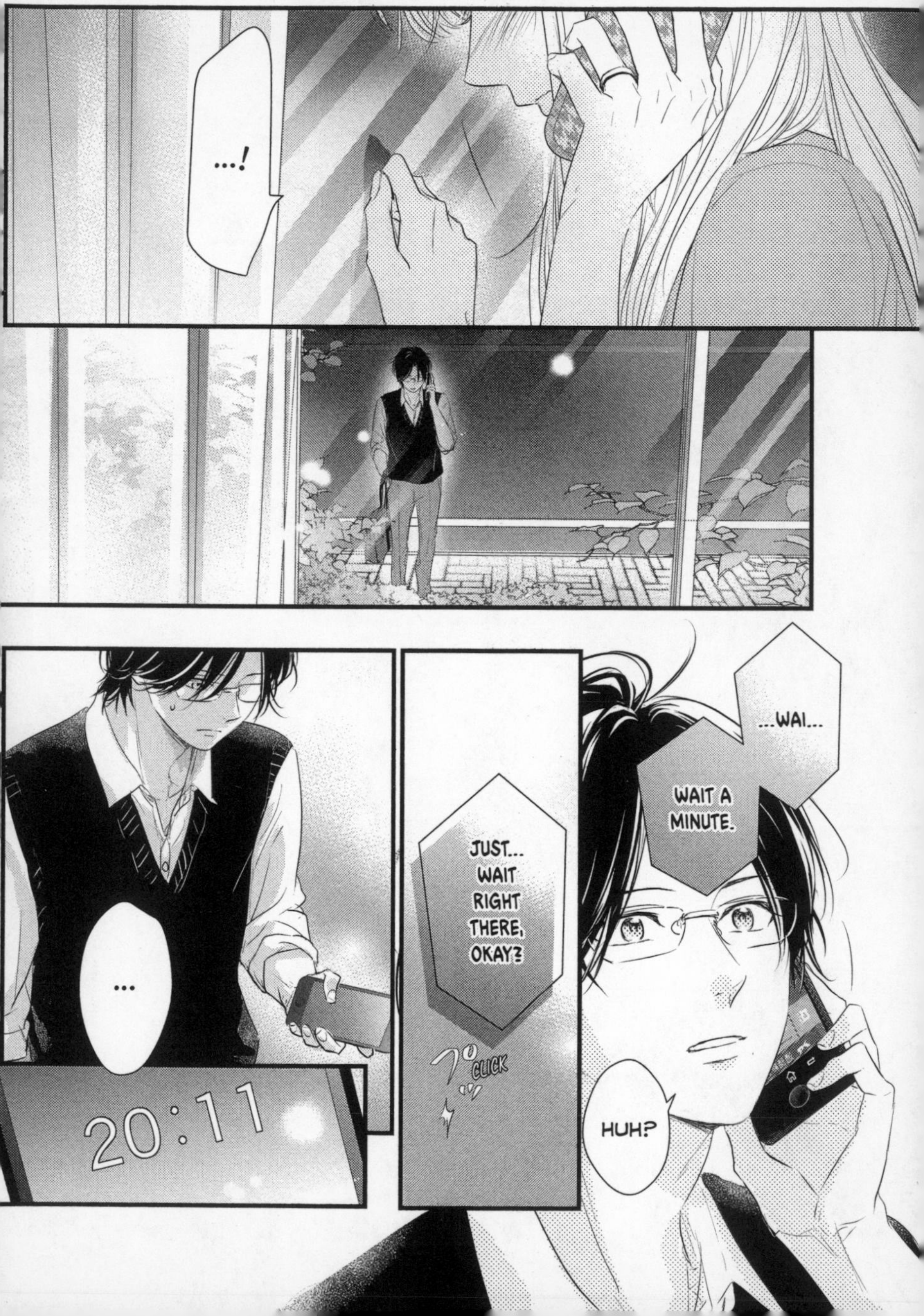
...!
...WAI...
WAIT A MINUTE.
HUH?
JUST... WAIT RIGHT THERE, OKAY?!
CLICK
...
20:11

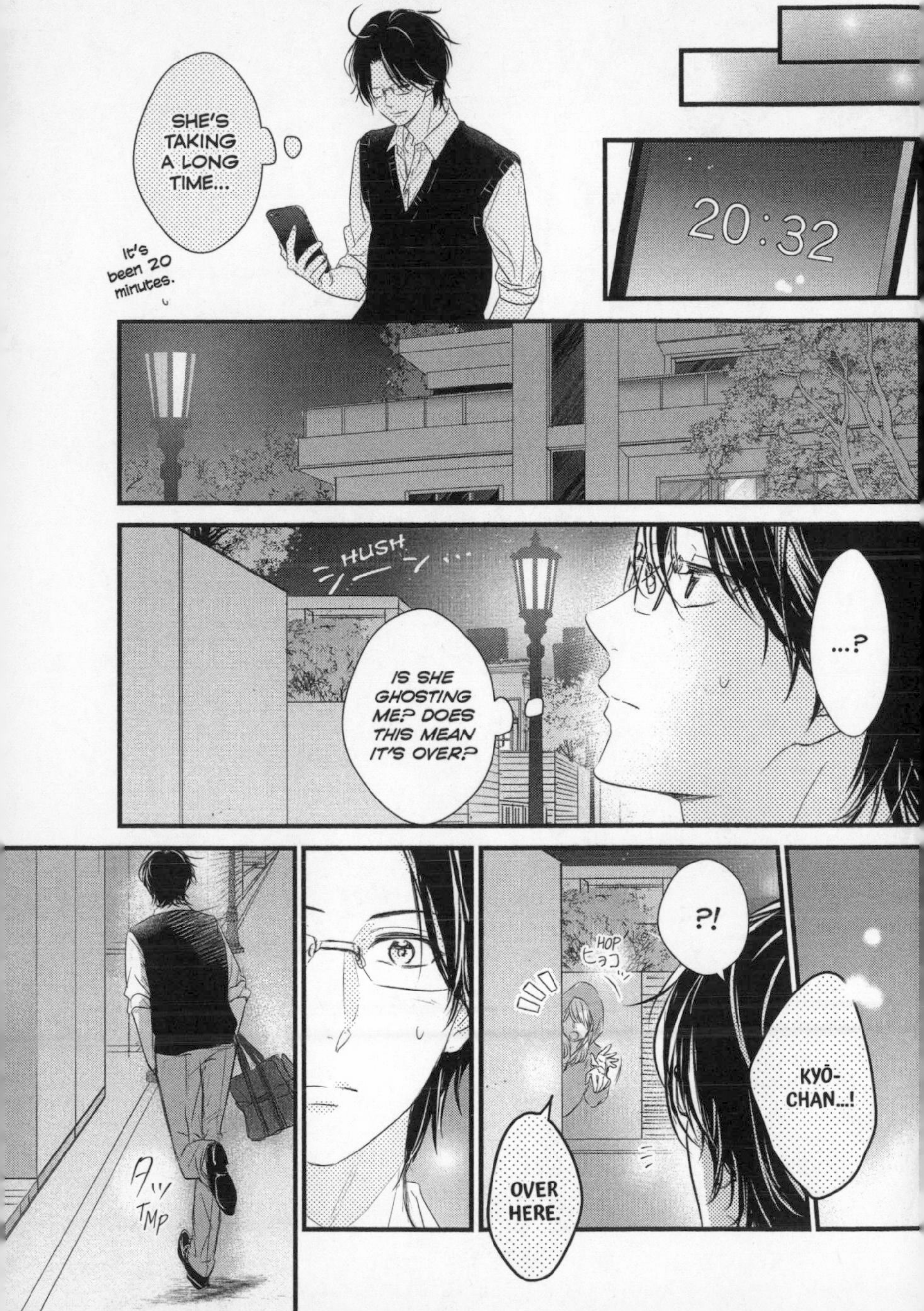
20:32
SHE'S TAKING A LONG TIME...
It's been 20 minutes.
...?
HUSH
IS SHE GHOSTING ME? DOES THIS MEAN IT'S OVER?
?!
HOP
ヒョコ
KYŌ-CHAN...!
OVER HERE.
タッ
TMP

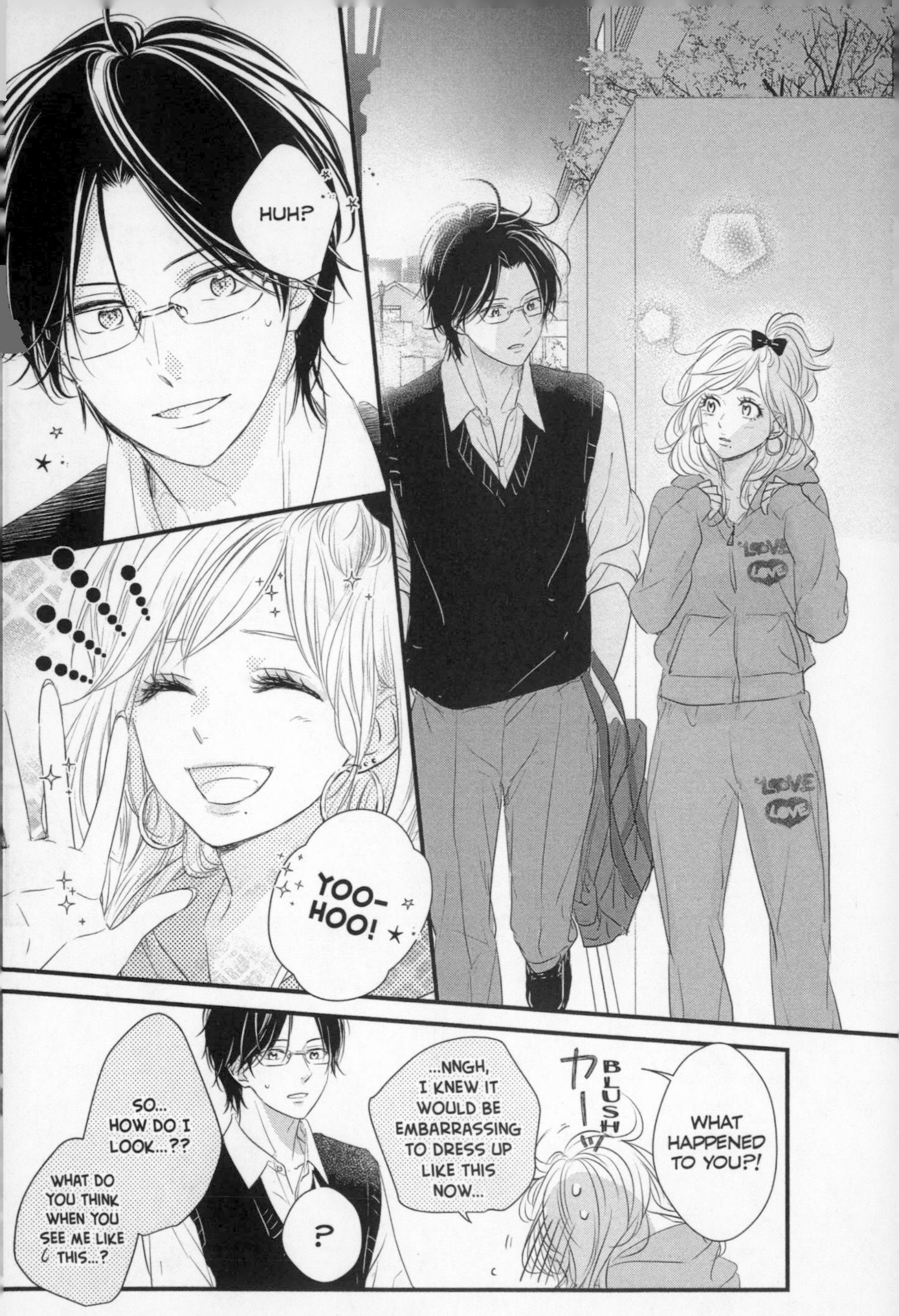
HUH?
YOO-HOO!
WHAT HAPPENED TO YOU?!
BLUSH
...NNGH, I KNEW IT WOULD BE EMBARRASSING TO DRESS UP LIKE THIS NOW...
?
SO... HOW DO I LOOK...??
WHAT DO YOU THINK WHEN YOU SEE ME LIKE THIS...?

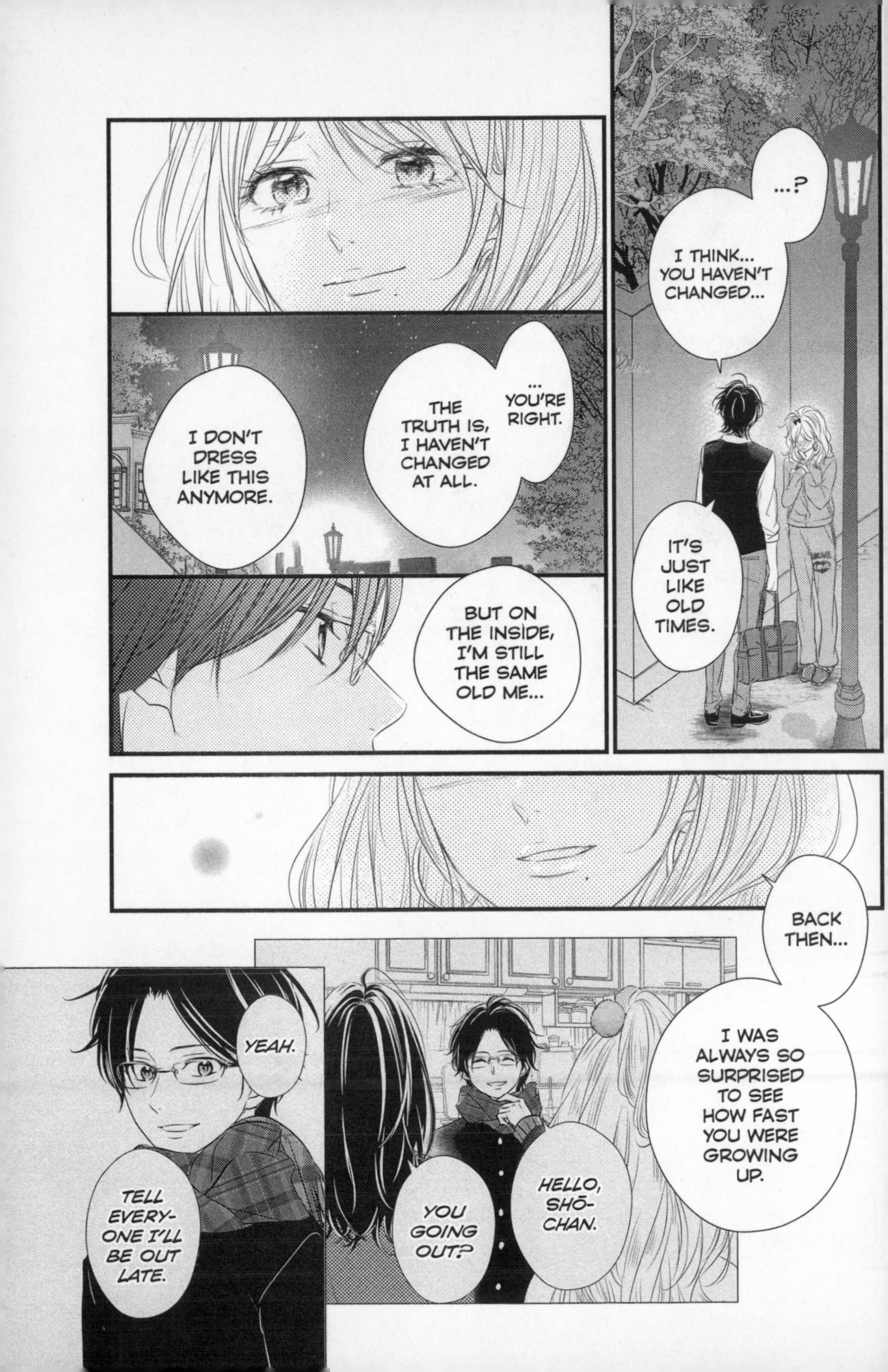
...?
I THINK... YOU HAVEN'T CHANGED...
IT'S JUST LIKE OLD TIMES.
... YOU'RE RIGHT.
THE TRUTH IS, I HAVEN'T CHANGED AT ALL.
I DON'T DRESS LIKE THIS ANYMORE.
BUT ON THE INSIDE, I'M STILL THE SAME OLD ME...
BACK THEN...
I WAS ALWAYS SO SURPRISED TO SEE HOW FAST YOU WERE GROWING UP.
HELLO, SHŌ-CHAN.
YOU GOING OUT?
YEAH.
TELL EVERY-ONE I'LL BE OUT LATE.

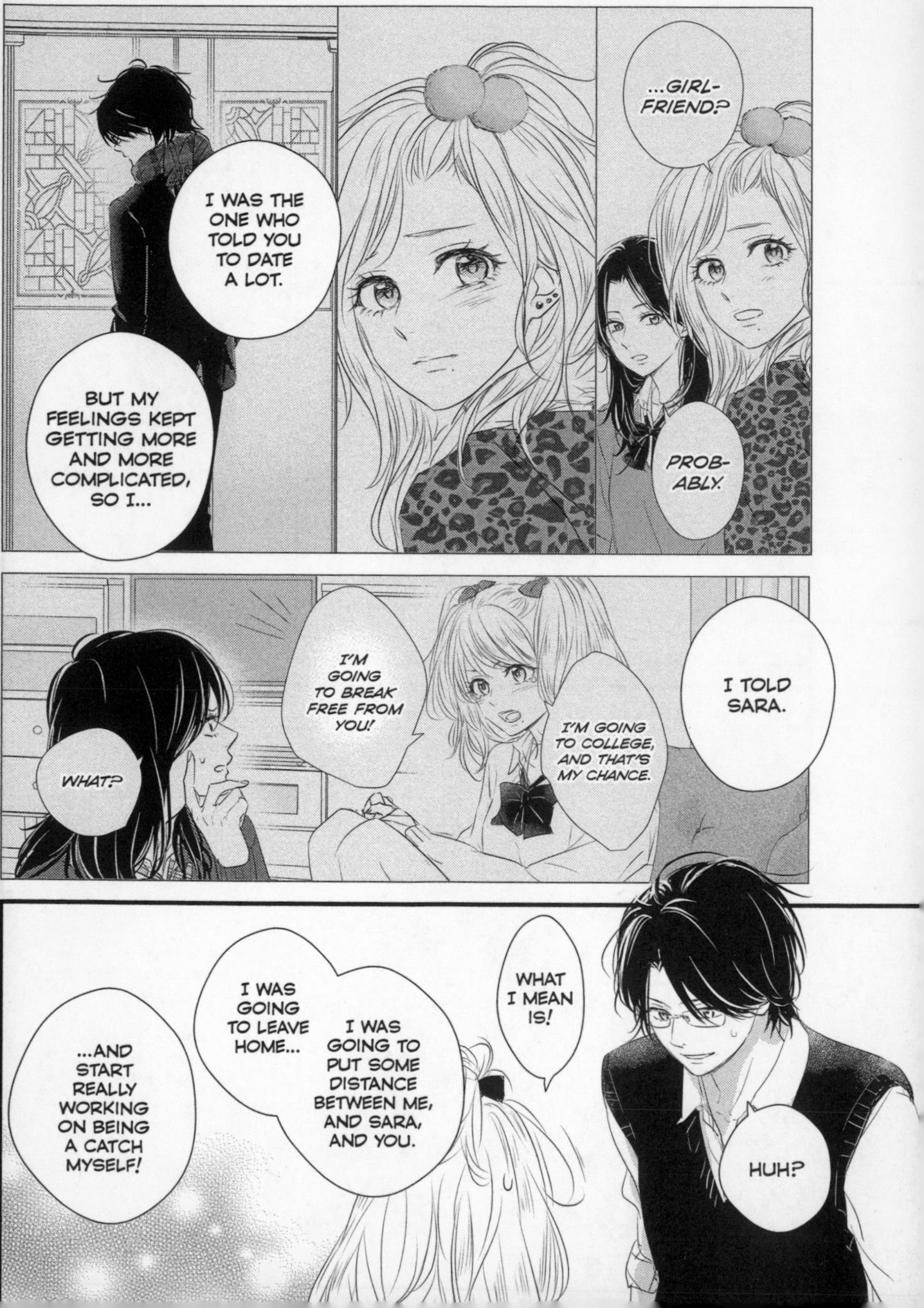
...GIRL-FRIEND?
PROB-ABLY.
I WAS THE ONE WHO TOLD YOU TO DATE A LOT.
BUT MY FEELINGS KEPT GETTING MORE AND MORE COMPLICATED, SO I...
I TOLD SARA.
I'M GOING TO COLLEGE, AND THAT'S MY CHANCE.
I'M GOING TO BREAK FREE FROM YOU!
WHAT?
WHAT I MEAN IS!
HUH?
I WAS GOING TO LEAVE HOME...
I WAS GOING TO PUT SOME DISTANCE BETWEEN ME, AND SARA, AND YOU.
...AND START REALLY WORKING ON BEING A CATCH MYSELF!

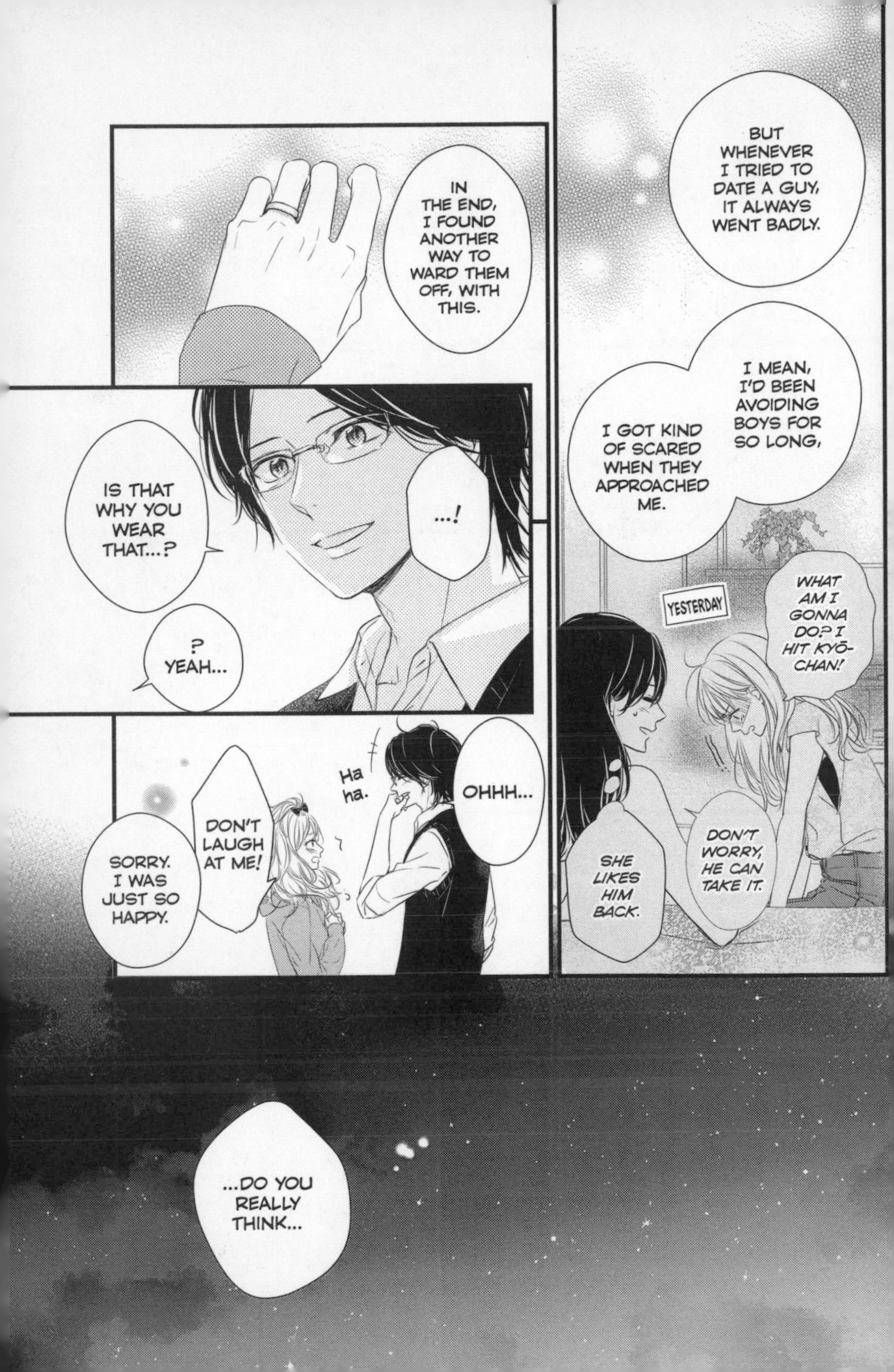
BUT WHENEVER I TRIED TO DATE A GUY, IT ALWAYS WENT BADLY.
I MEAN, I'D BEEN AVOIDING BOYS FOR SO LONG,
I GOT KIND OF SCARED WHEN THEY APPROACHED ME.
YESTERDAY
WHAT AM I GONNA DO?! I HIT KYŌ-CHAN!
DON'T WORRY, HE CAN TAKE IT.
SHE LIKES HIM BACK.
IN THE END, I FOUND ANOTHER WAY TO WARD THEM OFF, WITH THIS.
...!
IS THAT WHY YOU WEAR THAT...?
? YEAH...
OHHH...
Ha ha.
DON'T LAUGH AT ME!
SORRY. I WAS JUST SO HAPPY.
...DO YOU REALLY THINK...

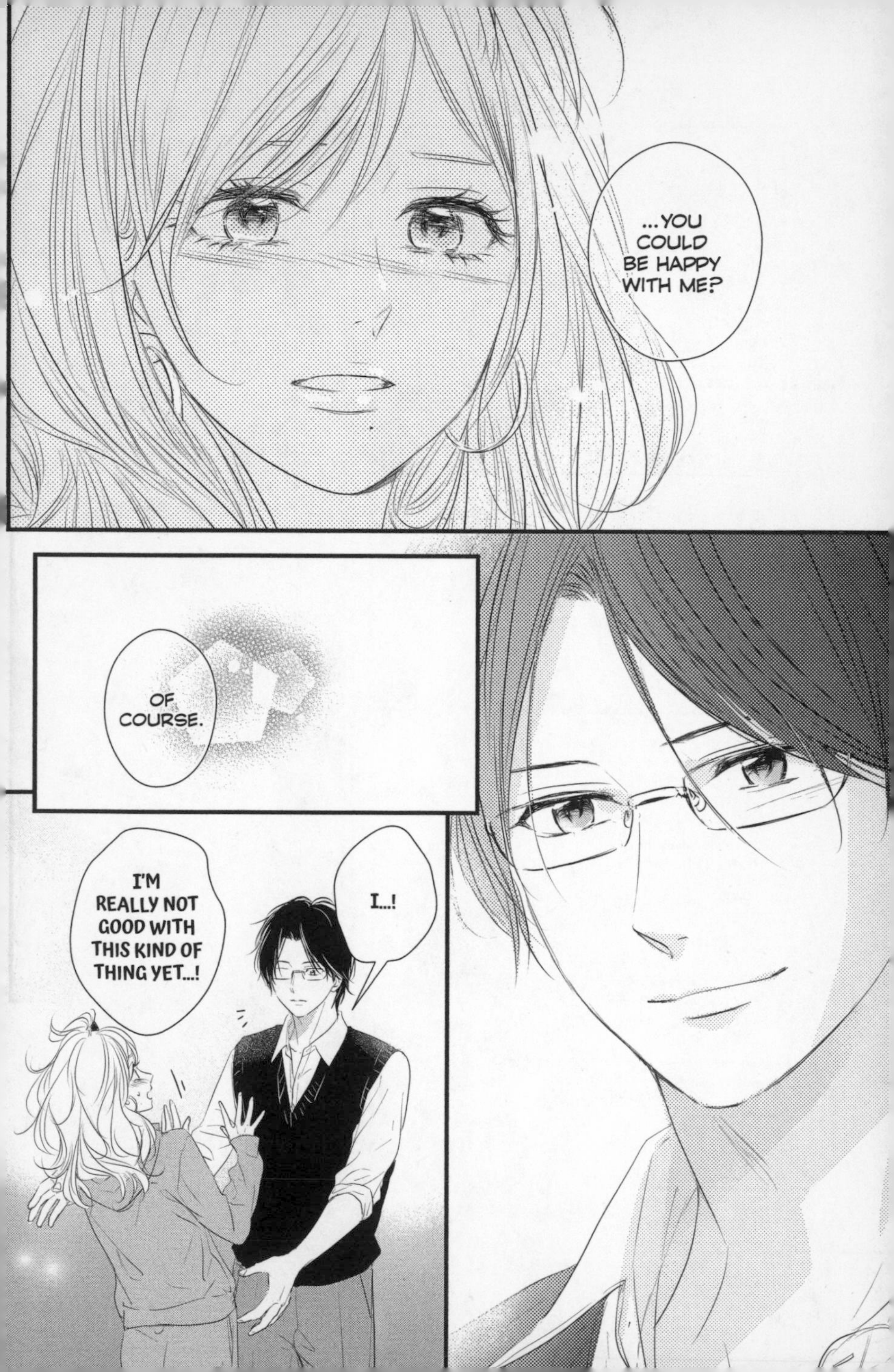
...YOU COULD BE HAPPY WITH ME?
OF COURSE.
I...!
I'M REALLY NOT GOOD WITH THIS KIND OF THING YET...!

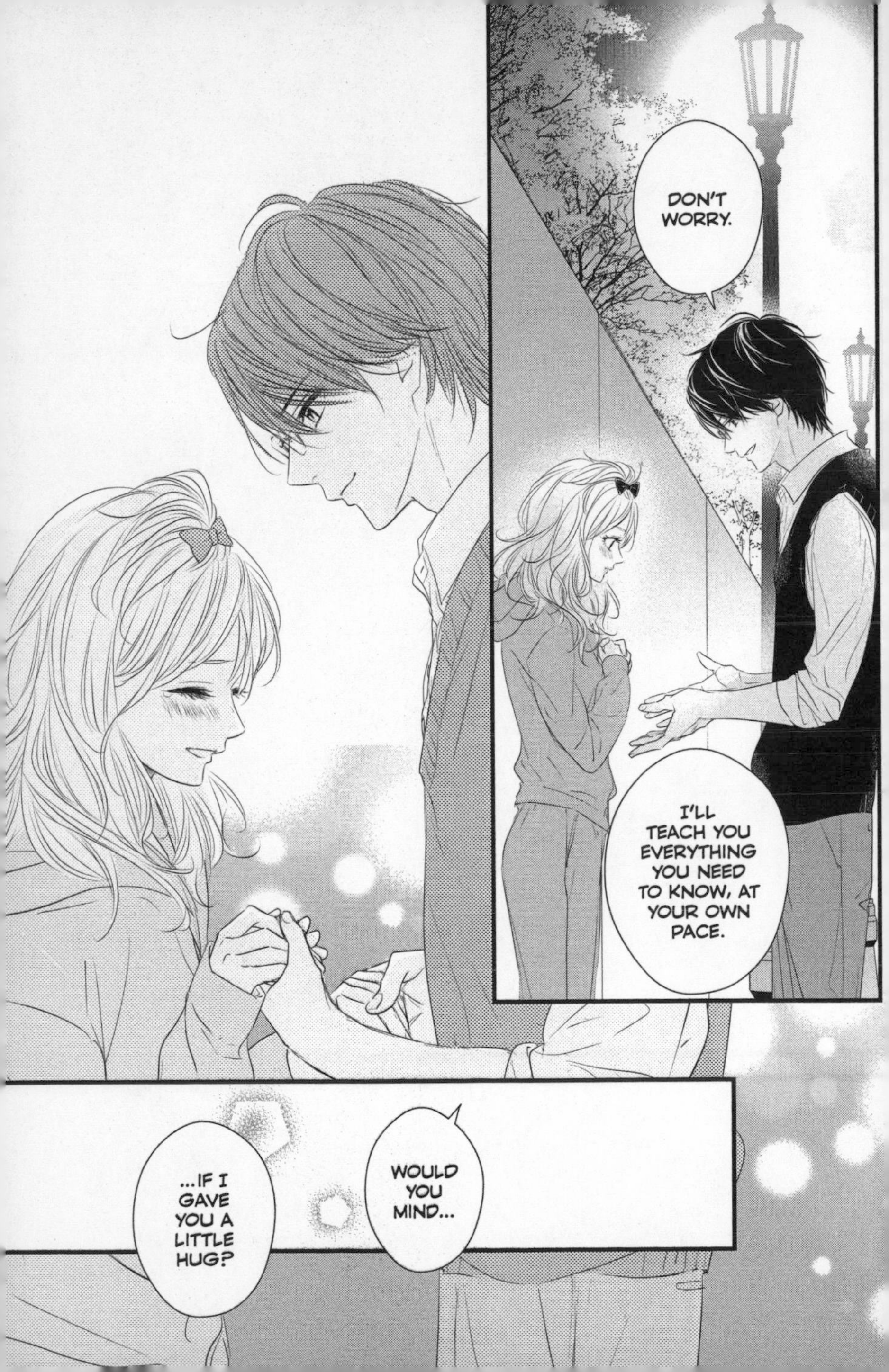
DON'T WORRY.
I'LL TEACH YOU EVERYTHING YOU NEED TO KNOW, AT YOUR OWN PACE.
WOULD YOU MIND...
...IF I GAVE YOU A LITTLE HUG?

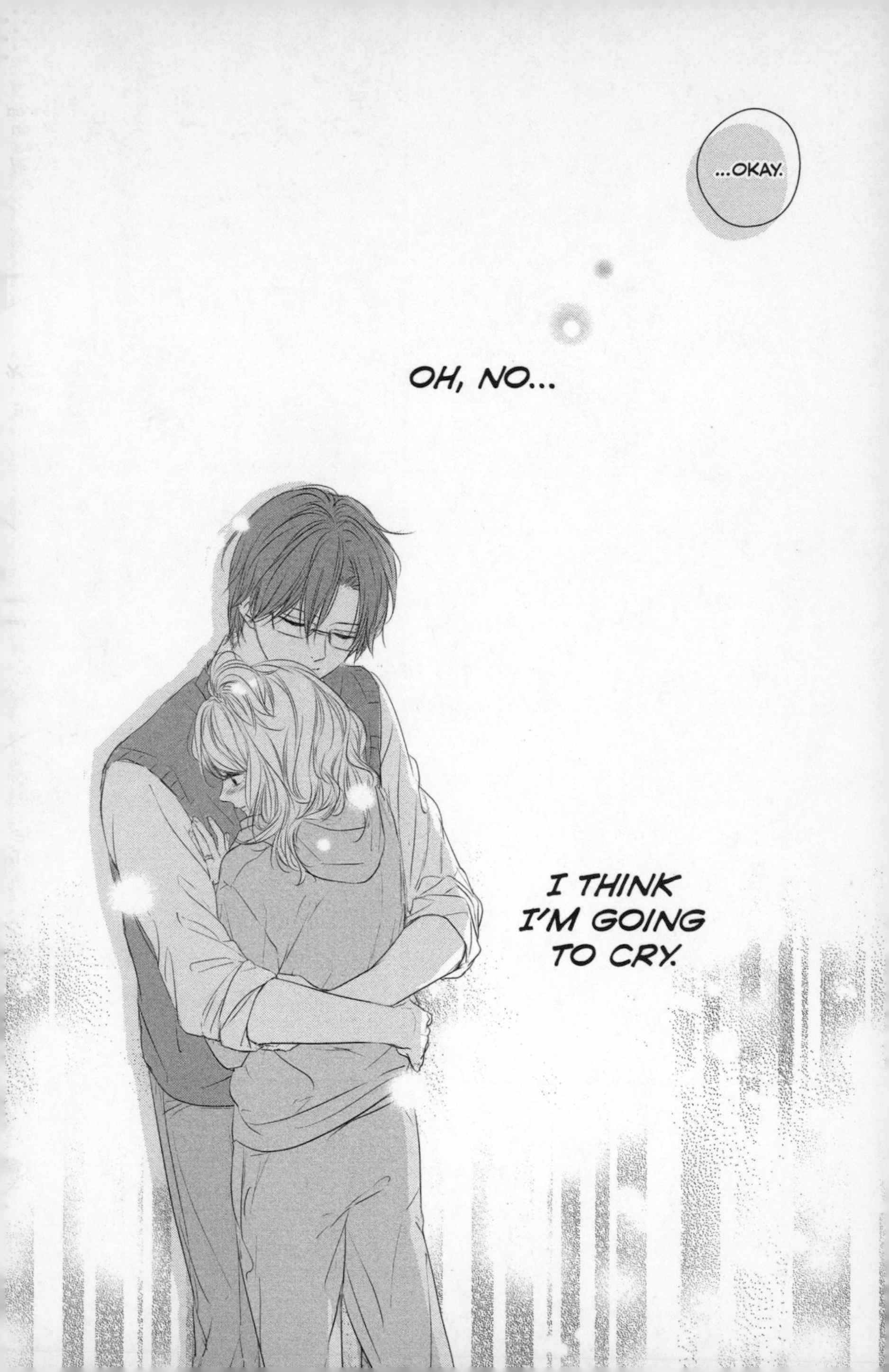
...OKAY.
OH, NO...
I THINK I'M GOING TO CRY.

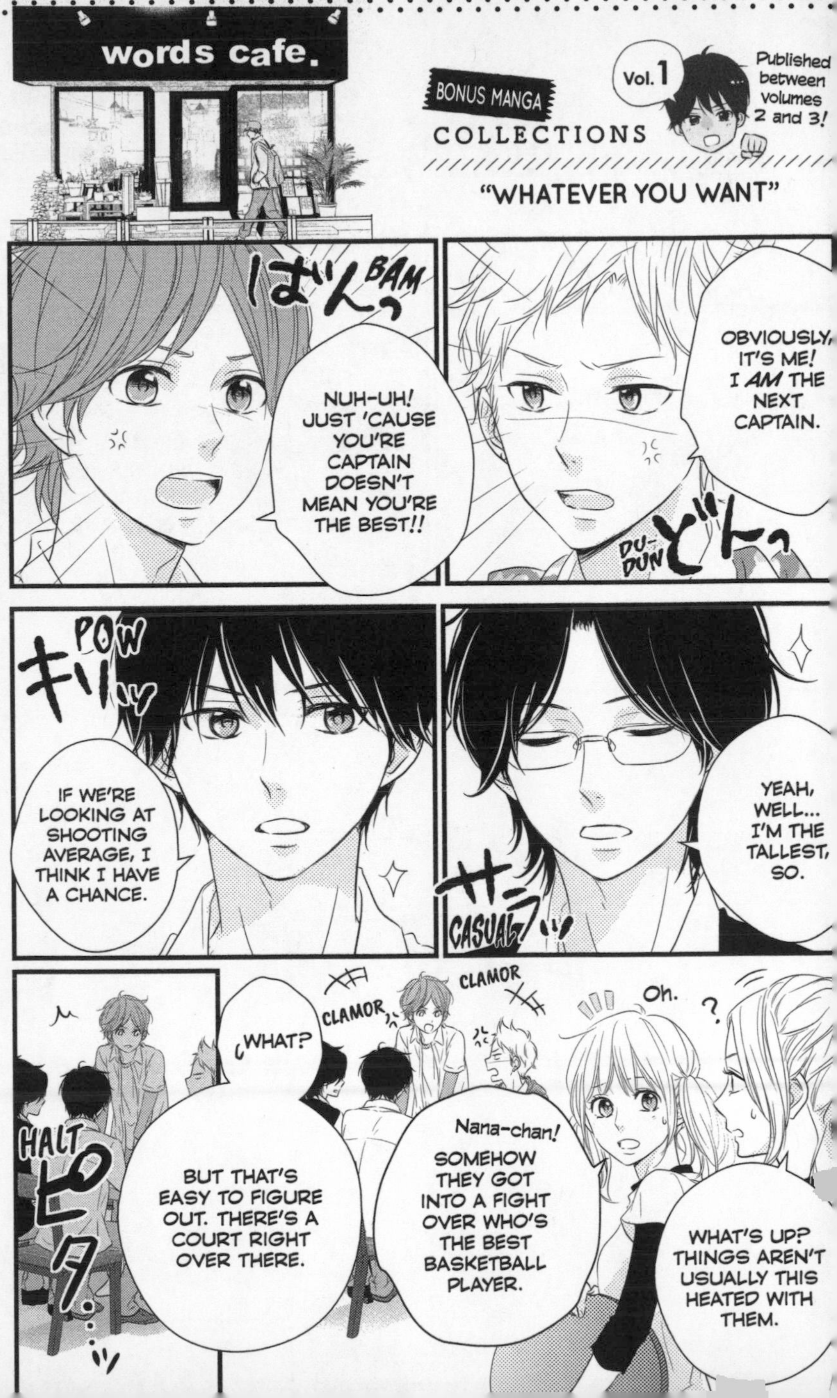
BONUS MANGA
COLLECTIONS
Vol. 1
Published between volumes 2 and 3!
"WHATEVER YOU WANT"
words cafe.
OBVIOUSLY, IT'S ME! I AM THE NEXT CAPTAIN.
DU-DUN
BAM
NUH-UH! JUST 'CAUSE YOU'RE CAPTAIN DOESN'T MEAN YOU'RE THE BEST!!
YEAH, WELL... I'M THE TALLEST, SO.
CASUAL
POW
IF WE'RE LOOKING AT SHOOTING AVERAGE, I THINK I HAVE A CHANCE.
Oh.
?
WHAT'S UP? THINGS AREN'T USUALLY THIS HEATED WITH THEM.
Nana-chan!
SOMEHOW THEY GOT INTO A FIGHT OVER WHO'S THE BEST BASKETBALL PLAYER.
CLAMOR
CLAMOR
WHAT?
BUT THAT'S EASY TO FIGURE OUT. THERE'S A COURT RIGHT OVER THERE.
HALT

★BONUS MINI-COMICS THAT WERE ONCE MAGAZINE-EXCLUSIVE ARE NOW HERE IN ONE COLLECTION!

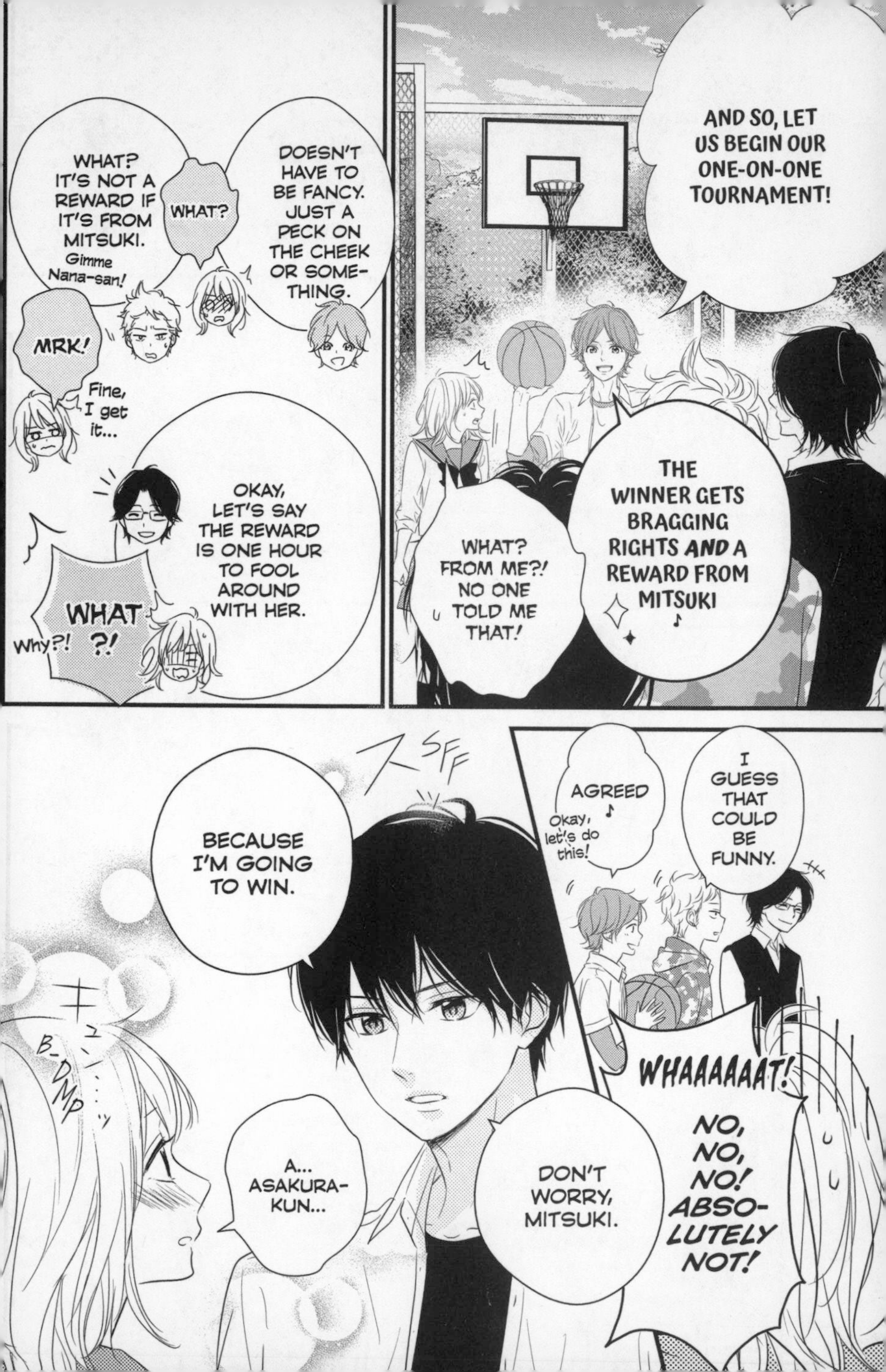
AND SO, LET US BEGIN OUR ONE-ON-ONE TOURNAMENT!
THE WINNER GETS BRAGGING RIGHTS AND A REWARD FROM MITSUKI ♪
WHAT? FROM ME?! NO ONE TOLD ME THAT!
DOESN'T HAVE TO BE FANCY. JUST A PECK ON THE CHEEK OR SOME-THING.
WHAT?
WHAT? IT'S NOT A REWARD IF IT'S FROM MITSUKI.
Gimme Nana-san!
MRK!
Fine, I get it...
OKAY, LET'S SAY THE REWARD IS ONE HOUR TO FOOL AROUND WITH HER.
WHAT ?!
Why?!
I GUESS THAT COULD BE FUNNY.
AGREED ♪
Okay, let's do this!
WHAAAAAAT!
NO, NO, NO! ABSO-LUTELY NOT!
SFF
DON'T WORRY, MITSUKI.
BECAUSE I'M GOING TO WIN.
B-DMP
A... ASAKURA-KUN...

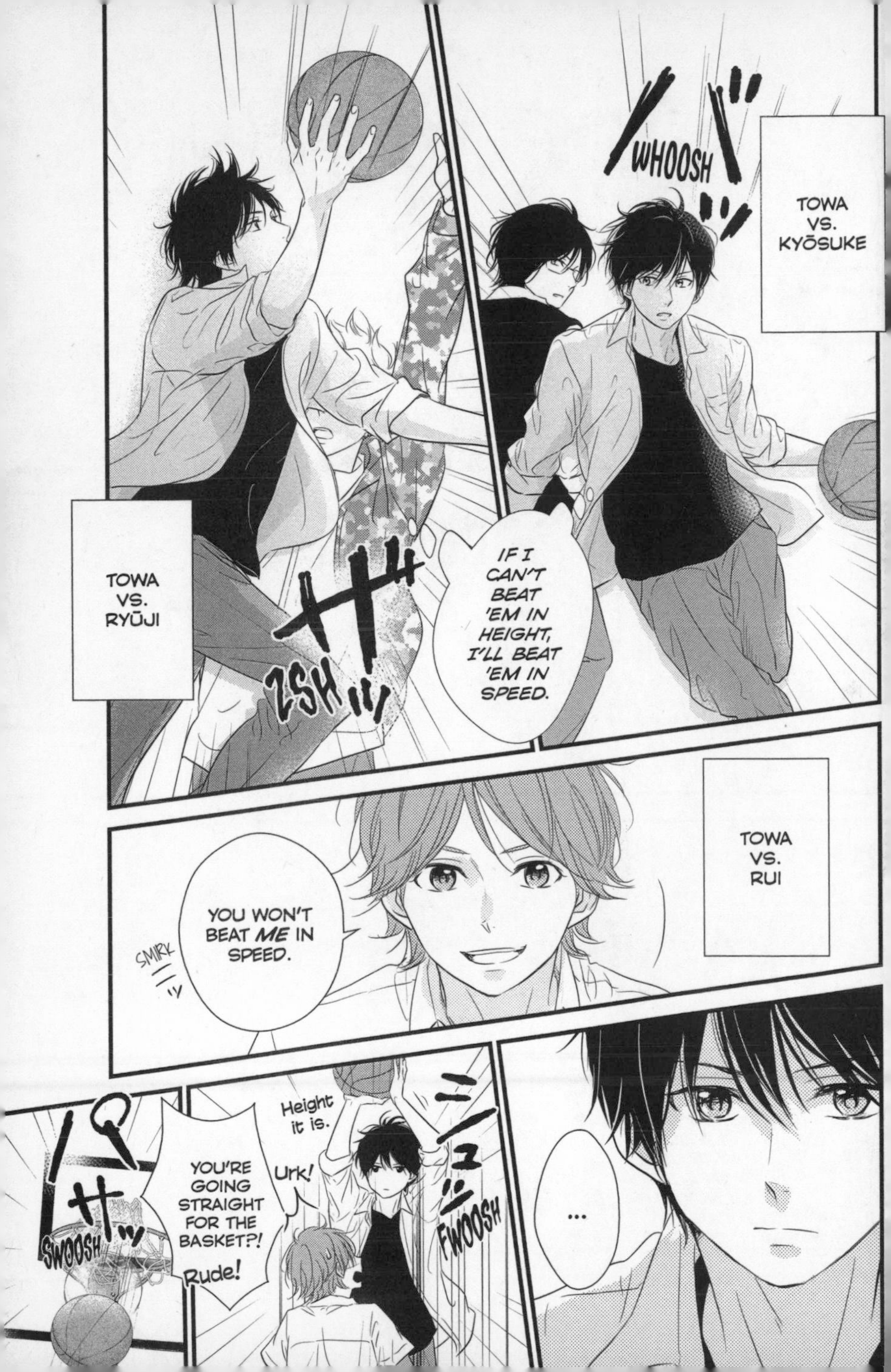

WHOOSH
TOWA VS. KYŌSUKE
IF I CAN'T BEAT 'EM IN HEIGHT, I'LL BEAT 'EM IN SPEED.
TOWA VS. RYŪJI
ZSH
TOWA VS. RUI
YOU WON'T BEAT *ME* IN SPEED.
SMIRK
...
Height it is.
FWOOSH
YOU'RE GOING STRAIGHT FOR THE BASKET?!
Urk!
Rude!
SWOOSH

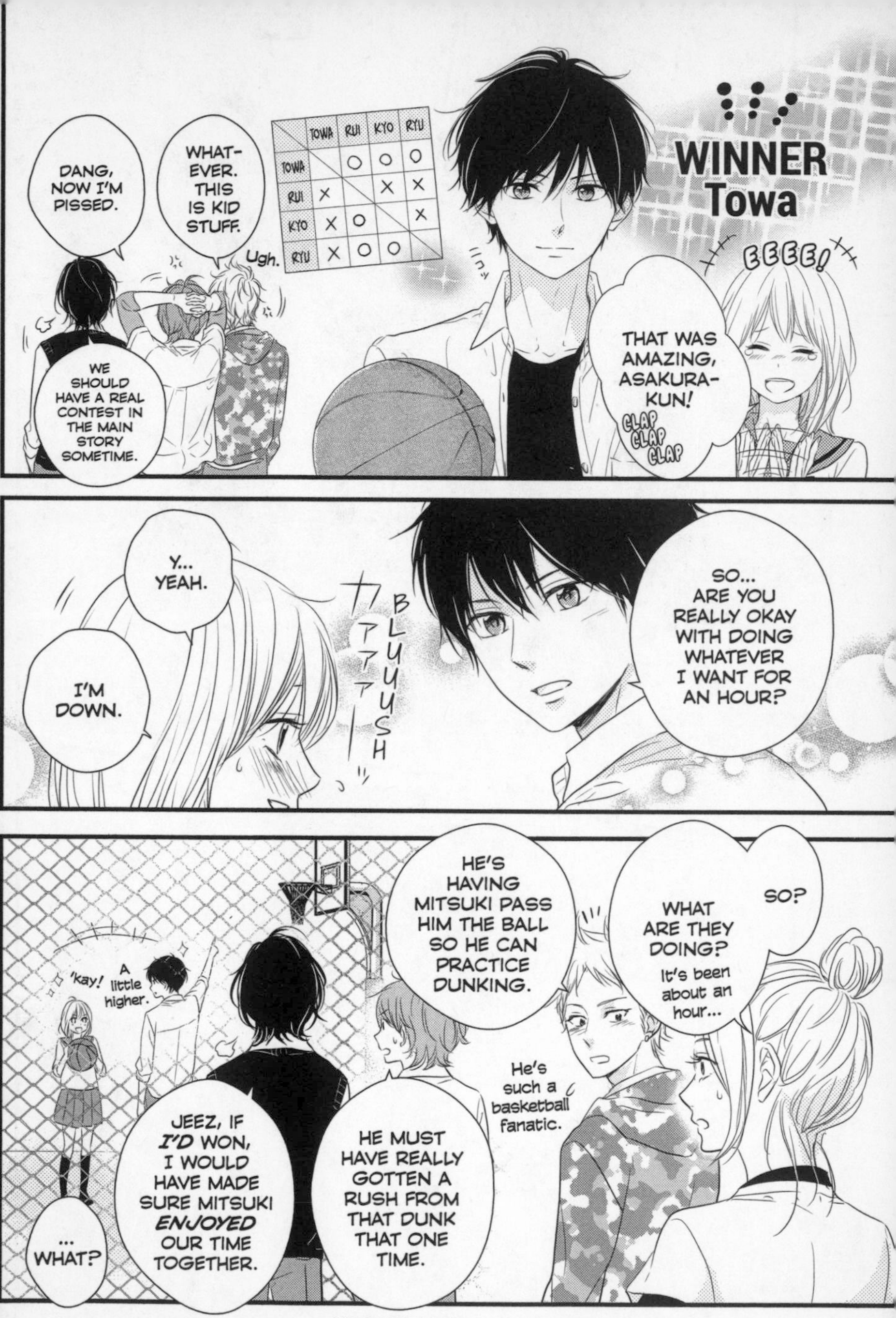
WINNER Towa
EEEE!
THAT WAS AMAZING, ASAKURA-KUN!
CLAP CLAP CLAP
TOWA RUI KYO RYU
WHAT-EVER. THIS IS KID STUFF.
Ugh.
DANG, NOW I'M PISSED.
WE SHOULD HAVE A REAL CONTEST IN THE MAIN STORY SOMETIME.
SO... ARE YOU REALLY OKAY WITH DOING WHATEVER I WANT FOR AN HOUR?
BLUUUSH
Y... YEAH.
I'M DOWN.
SO?
WHAT ARE THEY DOING?
It's been about an hour...
HE'S HAVING MITSUKI PASS HIM THE BALL SO HE CAN PRACTICE DUNKING.
He's such a basketball fanatic.
HE MUST HAVE REALLY GOTTEN A RUSH FROM THAT DUNK THAT ONE TIME.
JEEZ, IF *I'D* WON, I WOULD HAVE MADE SURE MITSUKI *ENJOYED* OUR TIME TOGETHER.
A little higher.
'kay!
... WHAT?

※ SEE VOL.2 CH.7

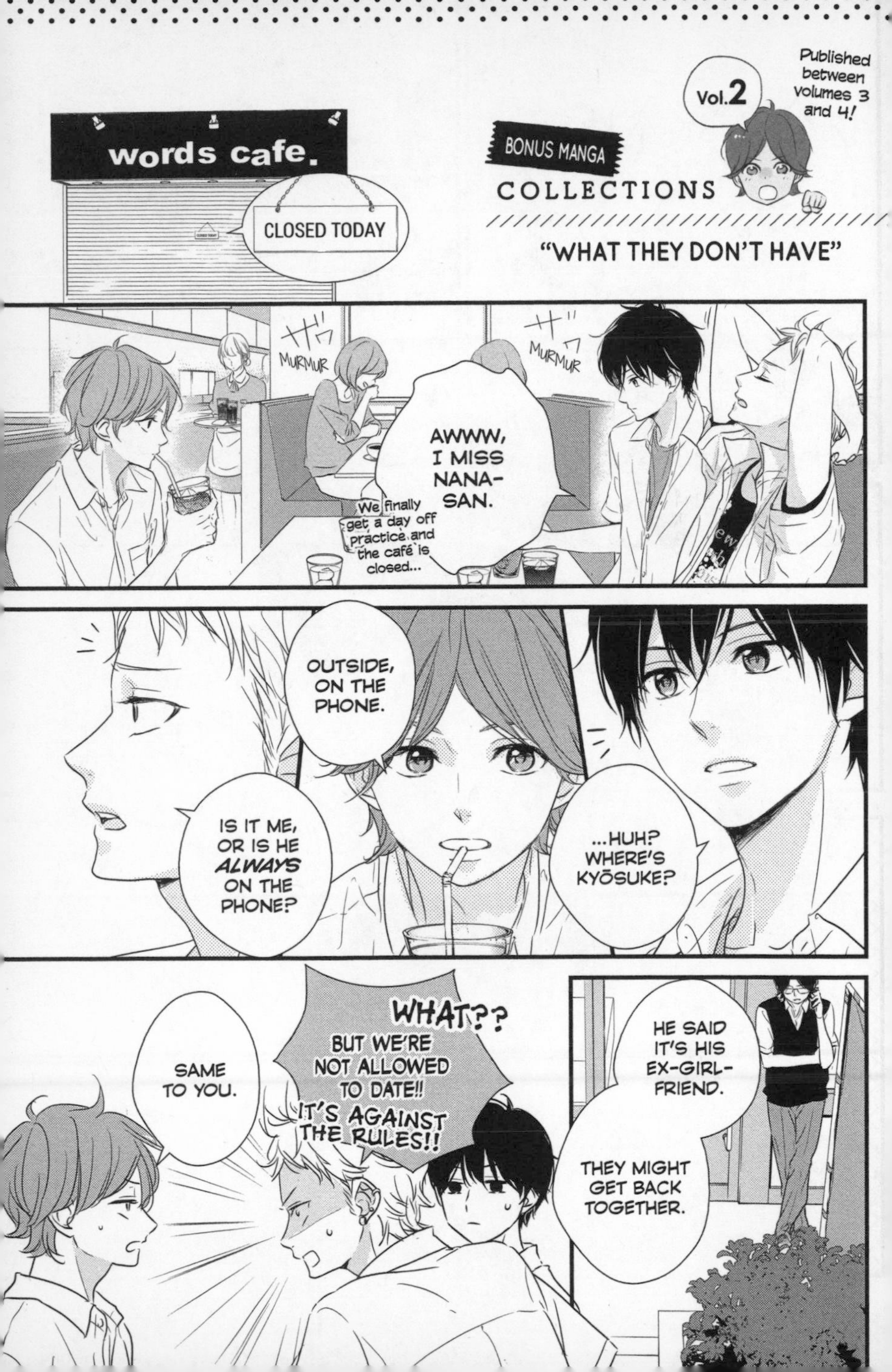
Vol.2
Published between volumes 3 and 4!
BONUS MANGA
COLLECTIONS
"WHAT THEY DON'T HAVE"
words cafe.
CLOSED TODAY
ザワ MURMUR
ザワ MURMUR
AWWW, I MISS NANA-SAN.
We finally get a day off practice and the café is closed...
...HUH? WHERE'S KYŌSUKE?
OUTSIDE, ON THE PHONE.
IS IT ME, OR IS HE ALWAYS ON THE PHONE?
HE SAID IT'S HIS EX-GIRLFRIEND.
THEY MIGHT GET BACK TOGETHER.
WHAT??
BUT WE'RE NOT ALLOWED TO DATE!! IT'S AGAINST THE RULES!!
SAME TO YOU.

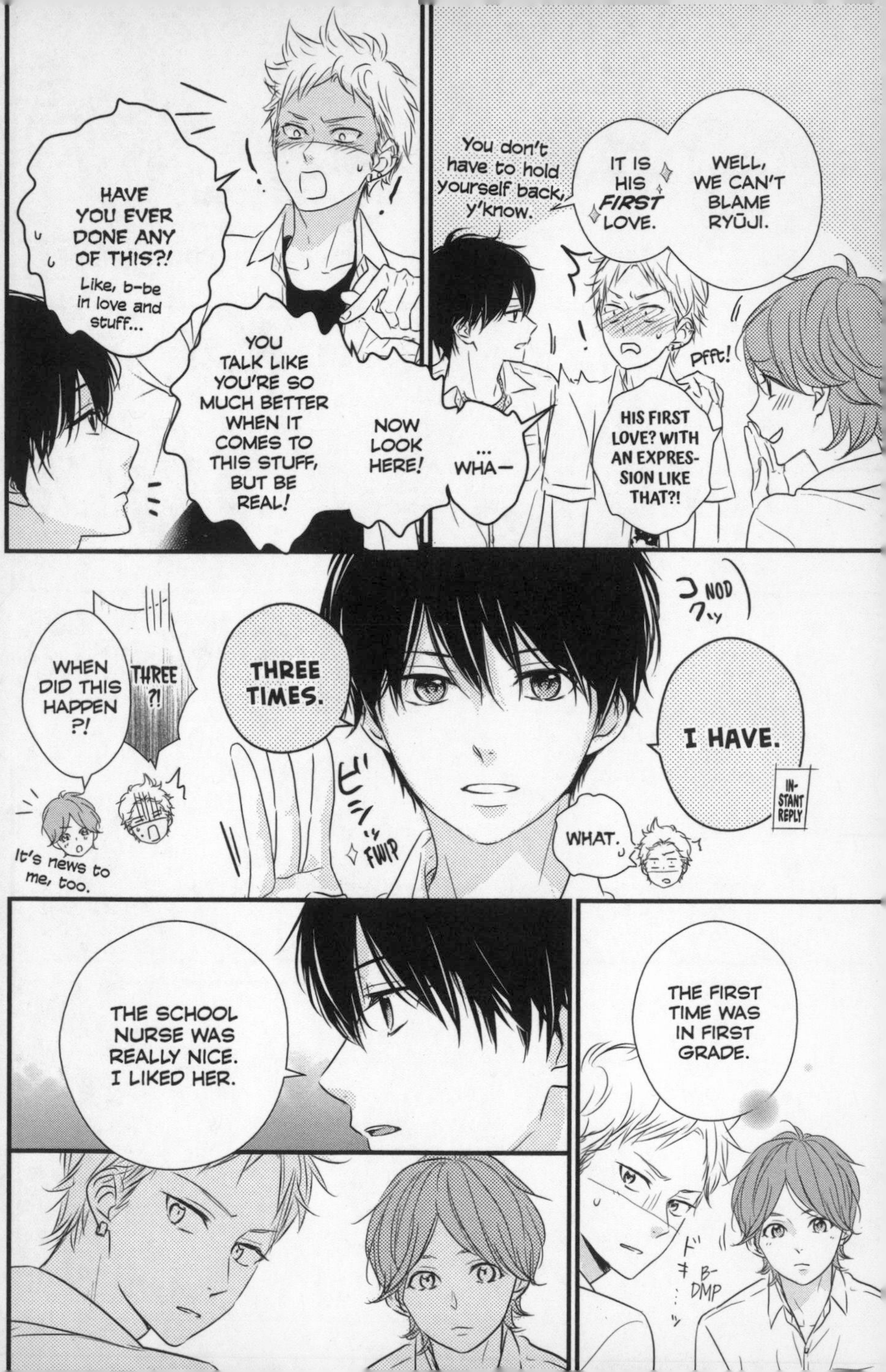
WELL, WE CAN'T BLAME RYŪJI.
IT IS HIS FIRST LOVE.
You don't have to hold yourself back, y'know.
Pfft!
HIS FIRST LOVE? WITH AN EXPRESSION LIKE THAT?!
... WHA—
NOW LOOK HERE!
YOU TALK LIKE YOU'RE SO MUCH BETTER WHEN IT COMES TO THIS STUFF, BUT BE REAL!
HAVE YOU EVER DONE ANY OF THIS?!
Like, b-be in love and stuff...
NOD
I HAVE.
INSTANT REPLY
WHAT.
THREE TIMES.
FWIP
THREE ?!
WHEN DID THIS HAPPEN ?!
It's news to me, too.
THE FIRST TIME WAS IN FIRST GRADE.
B-DMP
THE SCHOOL NURSE WAS REALLY NICE. I LIKED HER.

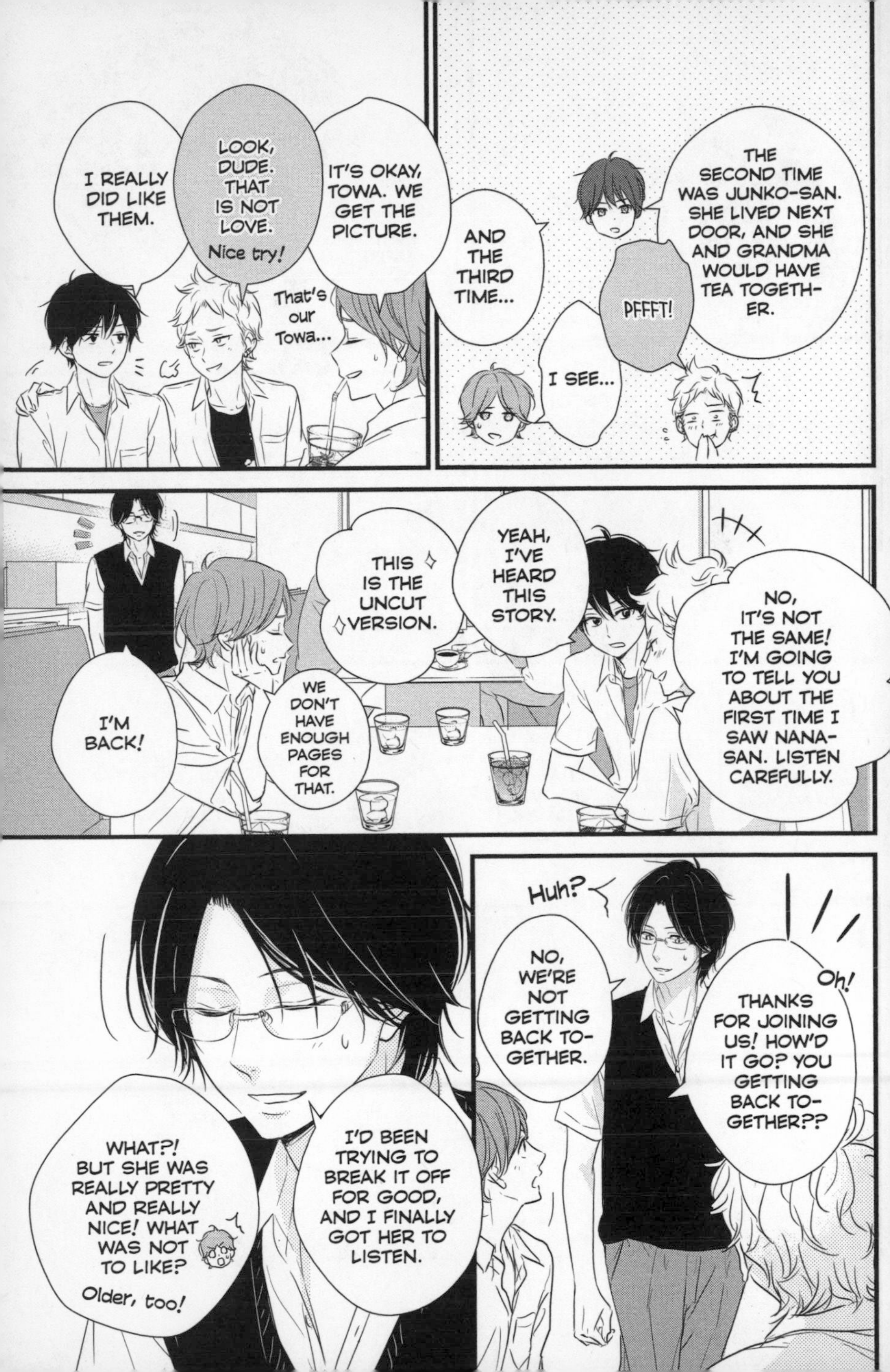
THE SECOND TIME WAS JUNKO-SAN. SHE LIVED NEXT DOOR, AND SHE AND GRANDMA WOULD HAVE TEA TOGETH-ER.
PFFFT!
AND THE THIRD TIME...
I SEE...
IT'S OKAY, TOWA. WE GET THE PICTURE.
That's our Towa...
LOOK, DUDE. THAT IS NOT LOVE.
Nice try!
I REALLY DID LIKE THEM.
NO, IT'S NOT THE SAME! I'M GOING TO TELL YOU ABOUT THE FIRST TIME I SAW NANA-SAN. LISTEN CAREFULLY.
YEAH, I'VE HEARD THIS STORY.
THIS IS THE UNCUT VERSION.
WE DON'T HAVE ENOUGH PAGES FOR THAT.
I'M BACK!
Oh!
THANKS FOR JOINING US! HOW'D IT GO? YOU GETTING BACK TO-GETHER??
Huh?
NO, WE'RE NOT GETTING BACK TO-GETHER.
I'D BEEN TRYING TO BREAK IT OFF FOR GOOD, AND I FINALLY GOT HER TO LISTEN.
WHAT?! BUT SHE WAS REALLY PRETTY AND REALLY NICE! WHAT WAS NOT TO LIKE?
Older, too!

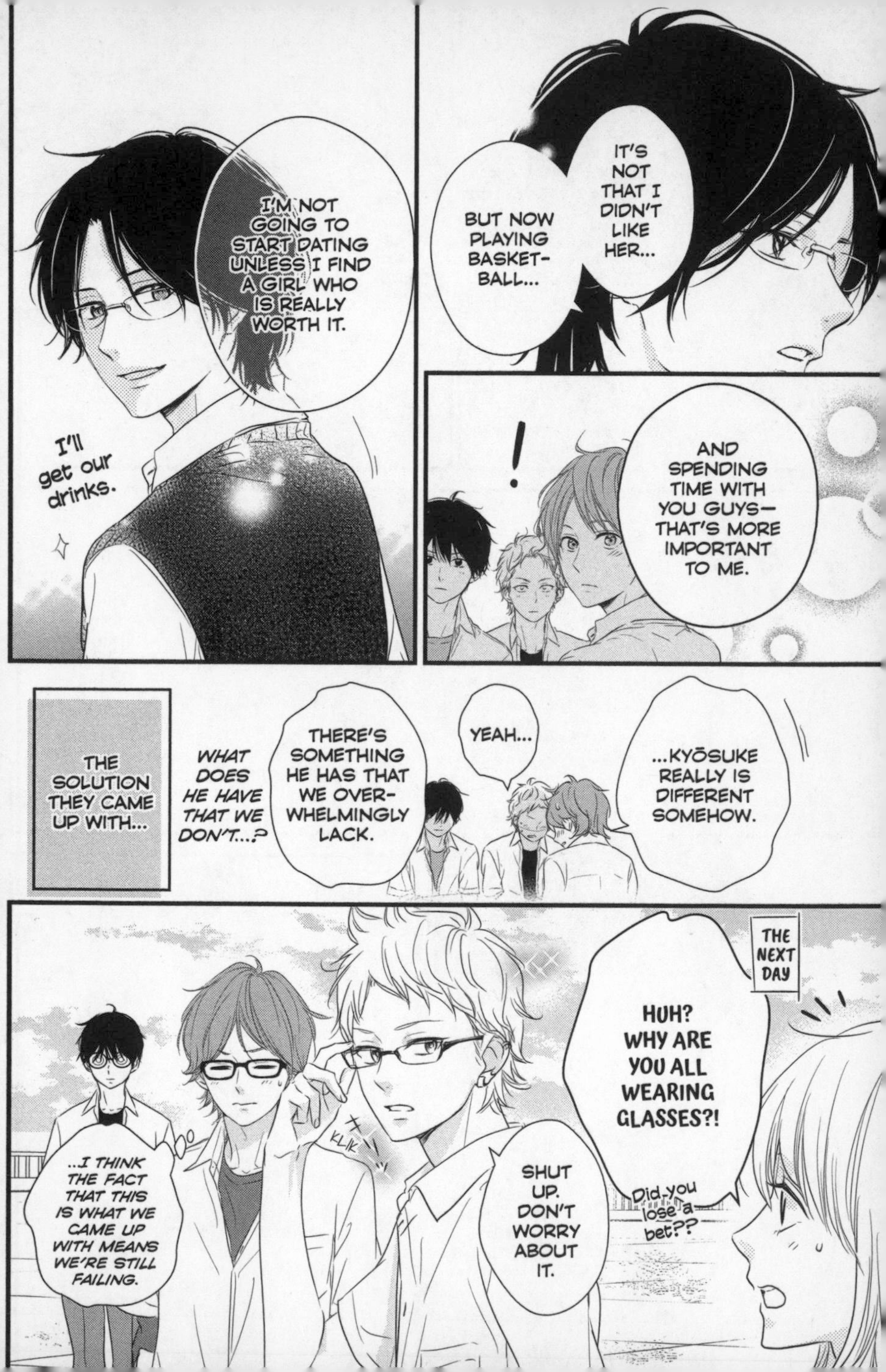
IT'S NOT THAT I DIDN'T LIKE HER...
BUT NOW PLAYING BASKET-BALL...
AND SPENDING TIME WITH YOU GUYS— THAT'S MORE IMPORTANT TO ME.
!
I'M NOT GOING TO START DATING UNLESS I FIND A GIRL WHO IS REALLY WORTH IT.
I'll get our drinks.
...KYŌSUKE REALLY IS DIFFERENT SOMEHOW.
YEAH...
THERE'S SOMETHING HE HAS THAT WE OVER-WHELMINGLY LACK.
WHAT DOES HE HAVE THAT WE DON'T...?
THE SOLUTION THEY CAME UP WITH...
THE NEXT DAY
HUH? WHY ARE YOU ALL WEARING GLASSES?!
Did you lose a bet??
SHUT UP. DON'T WORRY ABOUT IT.
KLIK
...I THINK THE FACT THAT THIS IS WHAT WE CAME UP WITH MEANS WE'RE STILL FAILING.

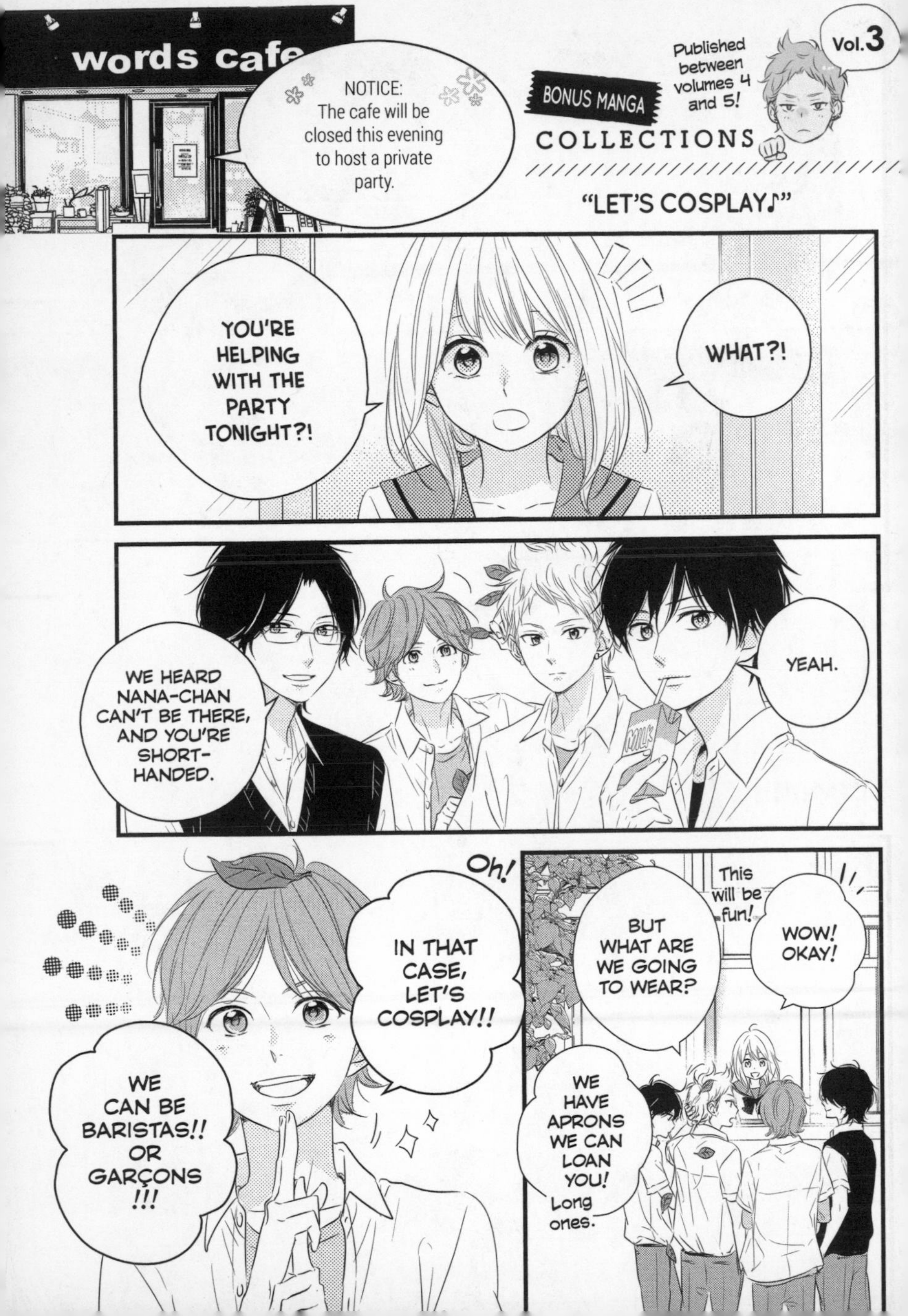
Vol.3
Published between volumes 4 and 5!
BONUS MANGA
COLLECTIONS
"LET'S COSPLAY♪"
words cafe
NOTICE: The cafe will be closed this evening to host a private party.
WHAT?!
YOU'RE HELPING WITH THE PARTY TONIGHT?!
YEAH.
WE HEARD NANA-CHAN CAN'T BE THERE, AND YOU'RE SHORT-HANDED.
WOW! OKAY!
This will be fun!
BUT WHAT ARE WE GOING TO WEAR?
WE HAVE APRONS WE CAN LOAN YOU!
Long ones.
Oh!
IN THAT CASE, LET'S COSPLAY!!
WE CAN BE BARISTAS!! OR GARÇONS!!!

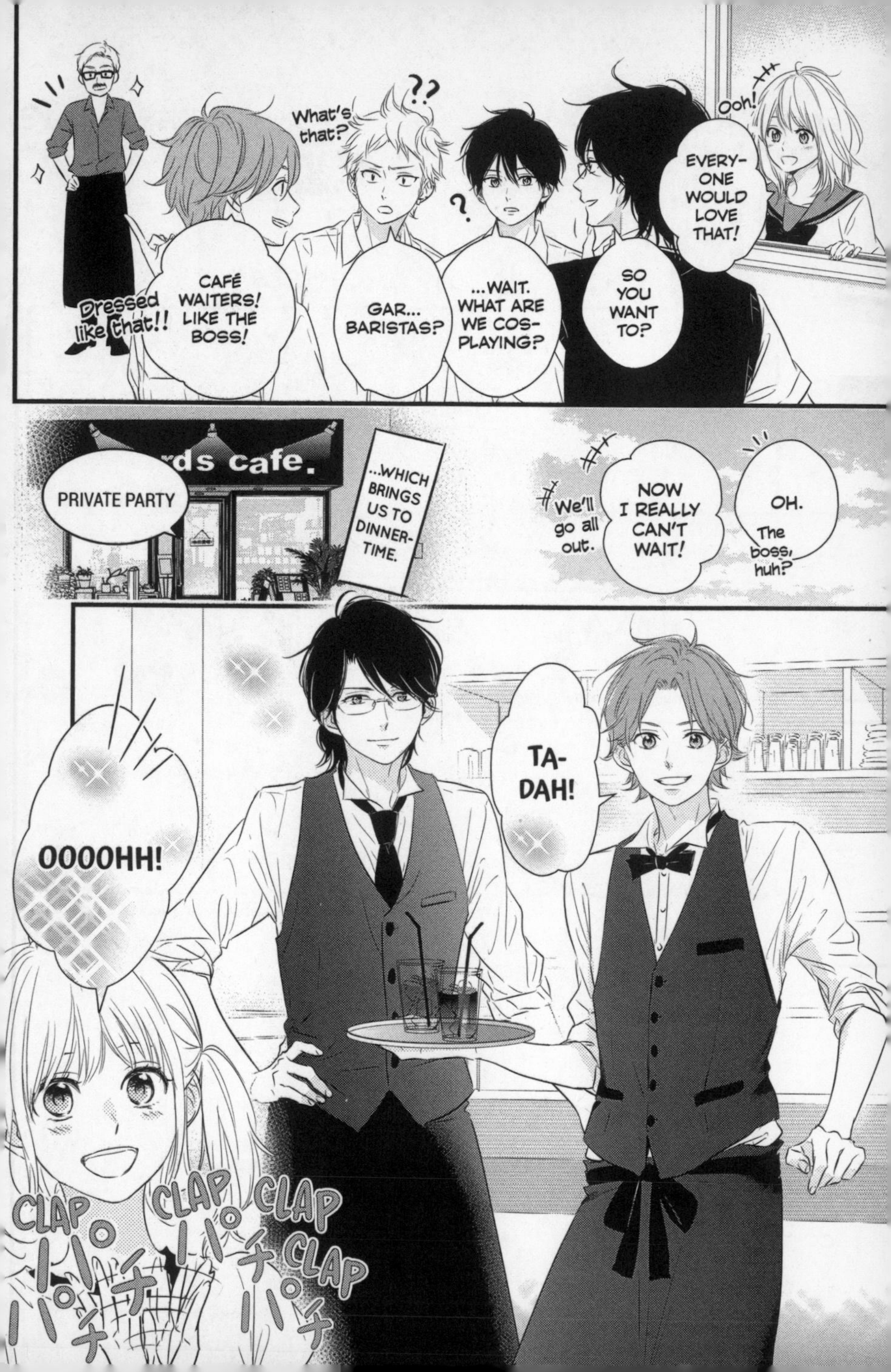
Ooh!
EVERY-ONE WOULD LOVE THAT!
SO YOU WANT TO?
...WAIT. WHAT ARE WE COS-PLAYING?
What's that?
GAR... BARISTAS?
CAFÉ WAITERS! LIKE THE BOSS!
Dressed like that!!
OH.
The boss, huh?
NOW I REALLY CAN'T WAIT!
We'll go all out.
...WHICH BRINGS US TO DINNER-TIME.
rds cafe.
PRIVATE PARTY
TA-DAH!
OOOOHH!
CLAP CLAP CLAP CLAP
パチパチ パチパチ パチ

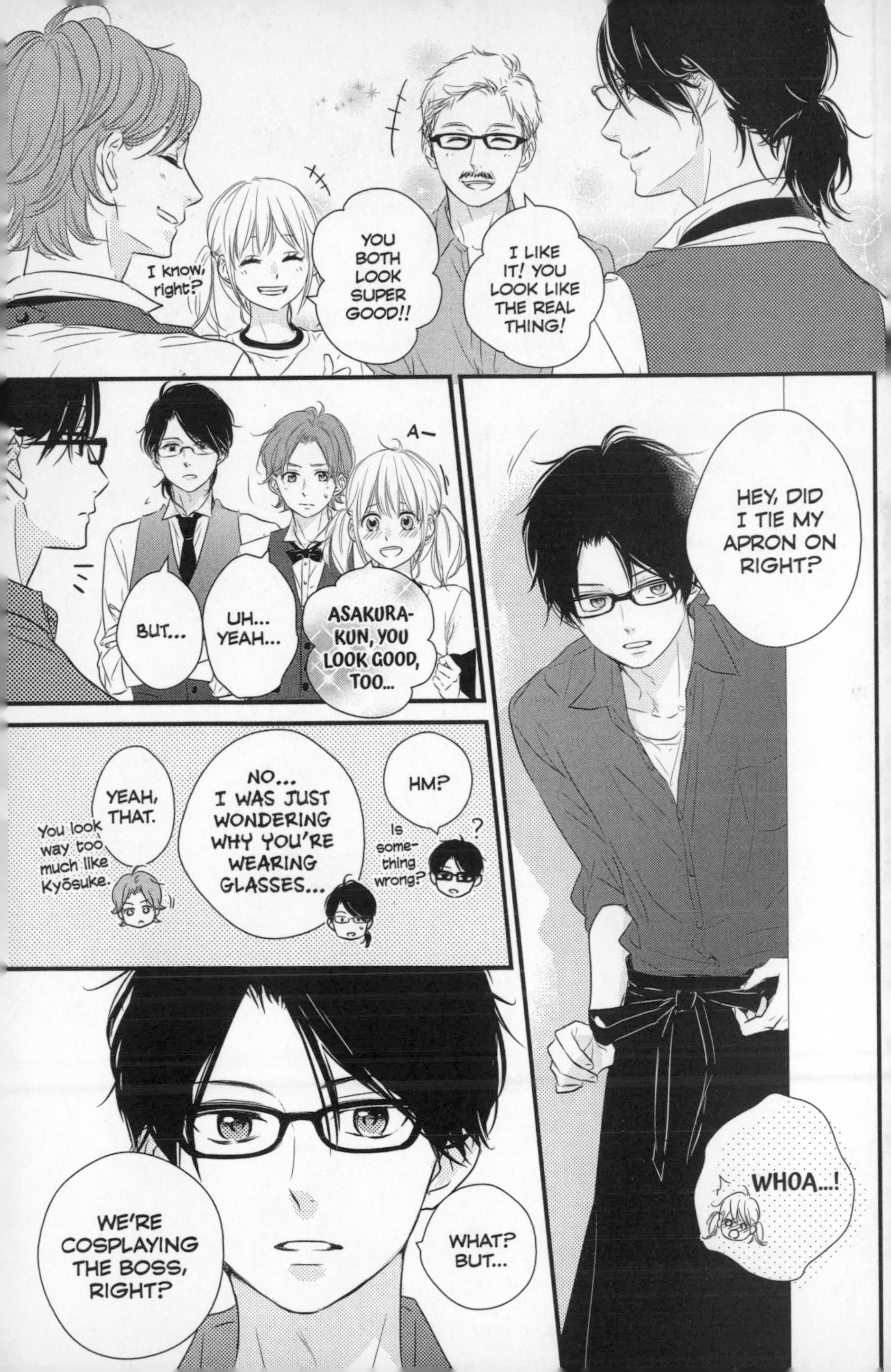
I LIKE IT! YOU LOOK LIKE THE REAL THING!
YOU BOTH LOOK SUPER GOOD!!
I know, right?
HEY, DID I TIE MY APRON ON RIGHT?
WHOA...!
A—
ASAKURA-KUN, YOU LOOK GOOD, TOO...
UH... YEAH...
BUT...
HM?
Is something wrong?
NO... I WAS JUST WONDERING WHY YOU'RE WEARING GLASSES...
YEAH, THAT.
You look way too much like Kyōsuke.
WHAT? BUT...
WE'RE COSPLAYING THE BOSS, RIGHT?

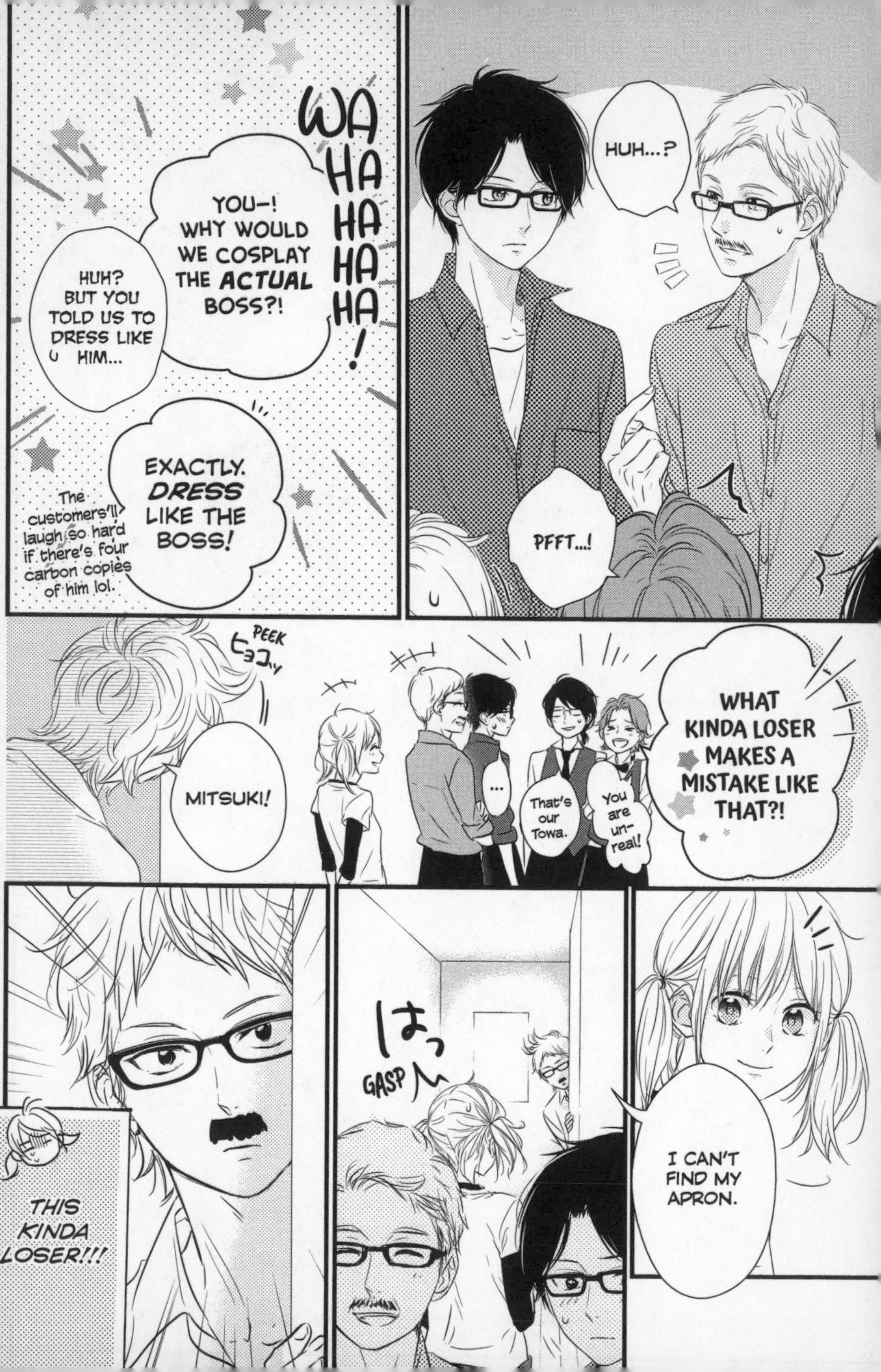
HUH...?
PFFT...!
WAHAHAHAHAHA!
YOU-! WHY WOULD WE COSPLAY THE ACTUAL BOSS?!
HUH? BUT YOU TOLD US TO DRESS LIKE HIM...
EXACTLY. DRESS LIKE THE BOSS!
The customers'll laugh so hard if there's four carbon copies of him lol.
WHAT KINDA LOSER MAKES A MISTAKE LIKE THAT?!
You are unreal!
That's our Towa.
...
MITSUKI!
PEEK ヒョコッ
I CAN'T FIND MY APRON.
はっ GASP
THIS KINDA LOSER!!!

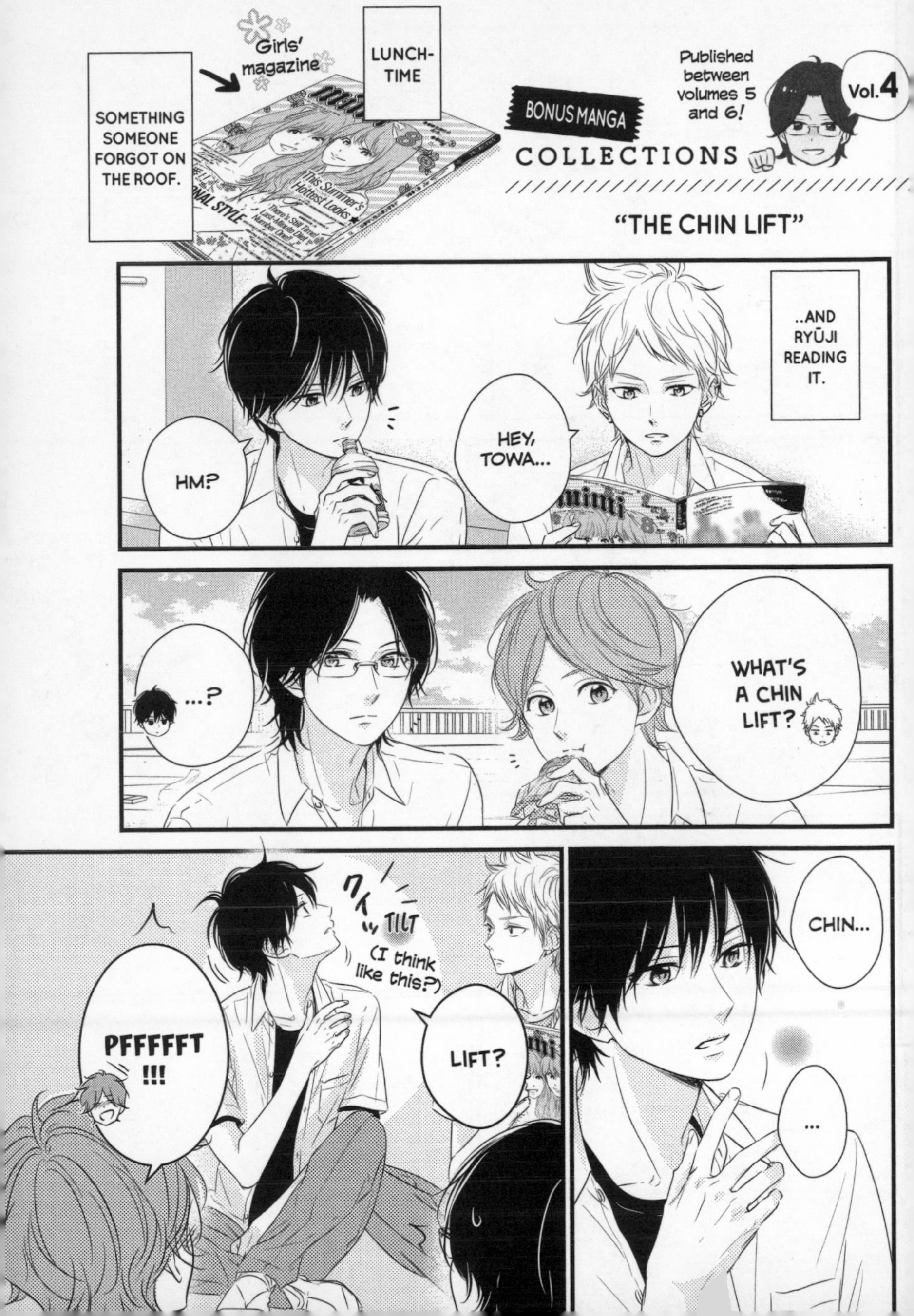
Vol.4
Published between volumes 5 and 6!
BONUS MANGA
COLLECTIONS
"THE CHIN LIFT"
LUNCH-TIME
Girls' magazine
SOMETHING SOMEONE FORGOT ON THE ROOF.
This Summer's Hottest Looks★
..AND RYŪJI READING IT.
HEY, TOWA...
HM?
WHAT'S A CHIN LIFT?
...?
CHIN...
...
TILT
(I think like this?)
LIFT?
PFFFFFT !!!

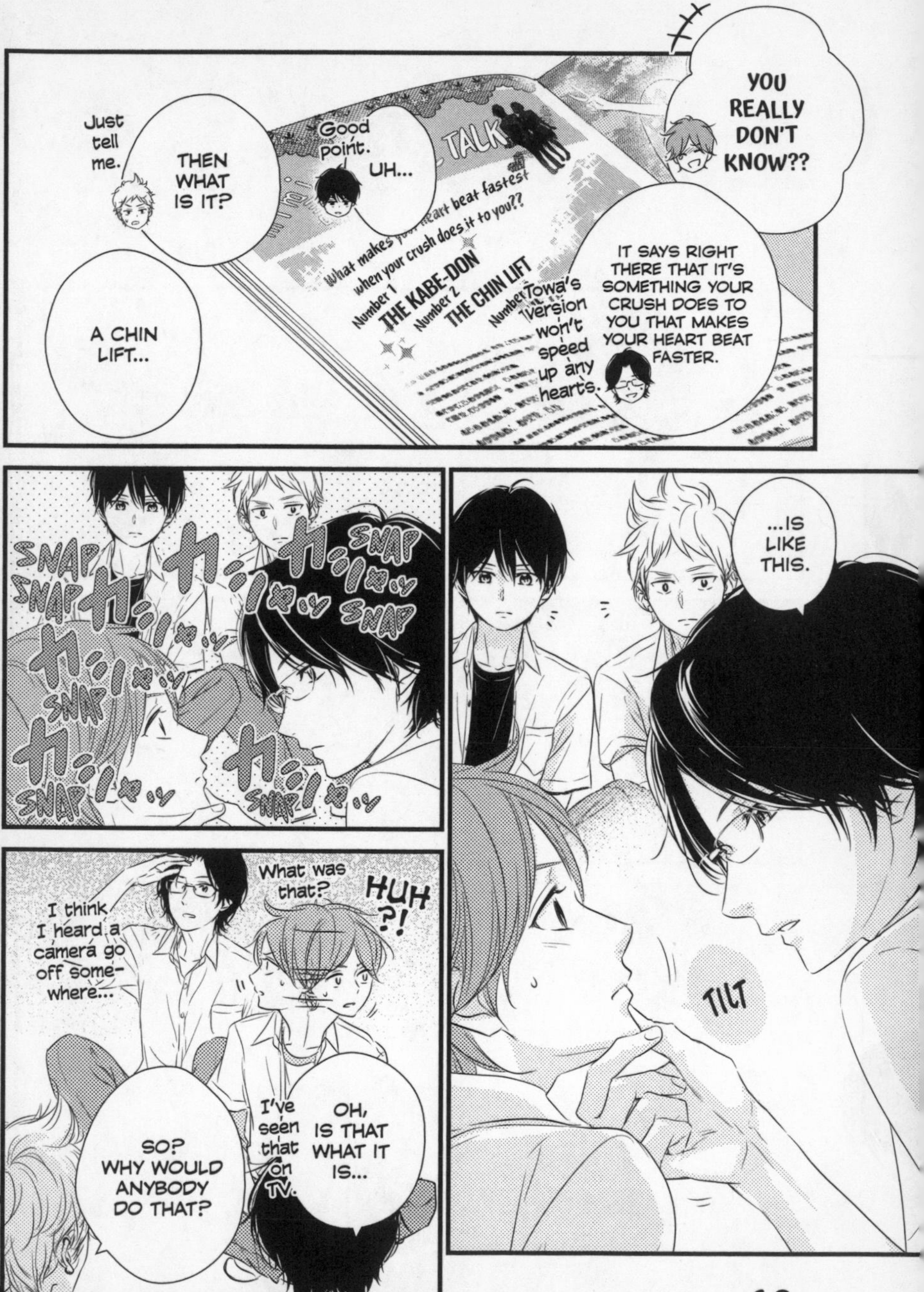
YOU REALLY DON'T KNOW??
TALK
when your crush does it to you??
Number 1 THE KABE-DON
Number 2 THE CHIN LIFT
Number
IT SAYS RIGHT THERE THAT IT'S SOMETHING YOUR CRUSH DOES TO YOU THAT MAKES YOUR HEART BEAT FASTER.
Towa's version won't speed up any hearts.
Good point.
UH...
THEN WHAT IS IT?
Just tell me.
A CHIN LIFT...
...IS LIKE THIS.
TILT
SNAP SNAP SNAP SNAP SNAP SNAP SNAP
HUH ?!
What was that?
I think I heard a camera go off somewhere...
OH, IS THAT WHAT IT IS...
I've seen that on TV.
SO? WHY WOULD ANYBODY DO THAT?

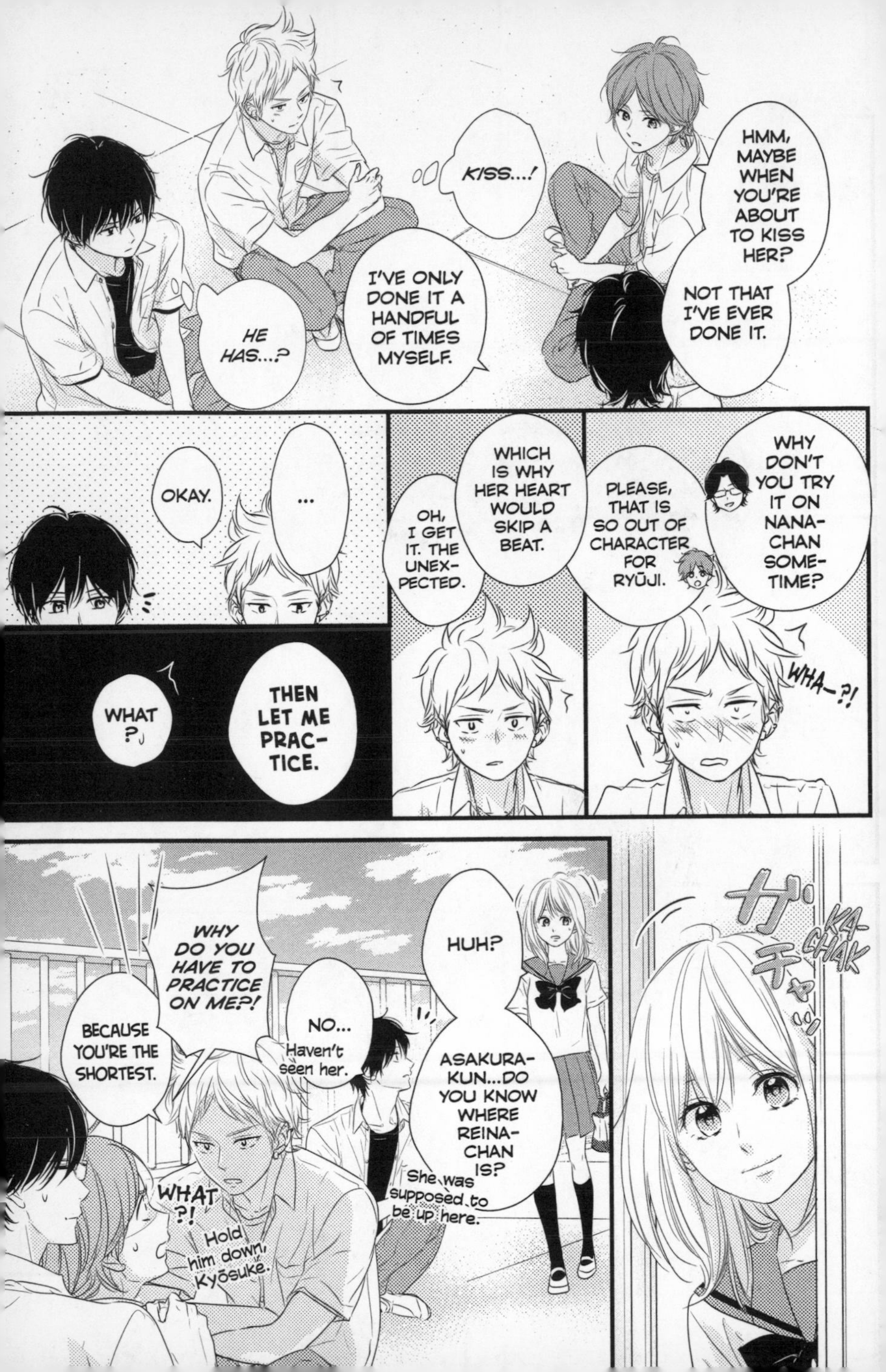
HMM, MAYBE WHEN YOU'RE ABOUT TO KISS HER?
NOT THAT I'VE EVER DONE IT.
KISS...!
I'VE ONLY DONE IT A HANDFUL OF TIMES MYSELF.
HE HAS...?
WHY DON'T YOU TRY IT ON NANA-CHAN SOME-TIME?
PLEASE, THAT IS SO OUT OF CHARACTER FOR RYŪJI.
WHA-?!
WHICH IS WHY HER HEART WOULD SKIP A BEAT.
OH, I GET IT. THE UNEX-PECTED.
...
OKAY.
THEN LET ME PRAC-TICE.
WHAT?
KA-CHAK
HUH?
ASAKURA-KUN...DO YOU KNOW WHERE REINA-CHAN IS?
She was supposed to be up here.
NO... Haven't seen her.
WHY DO YOU HAVE TO PRACTICE ON ME?!
BECAUSE YOU'RE THE SHORTEST.
WHAT?!
Hold him down, Kyōsuke.

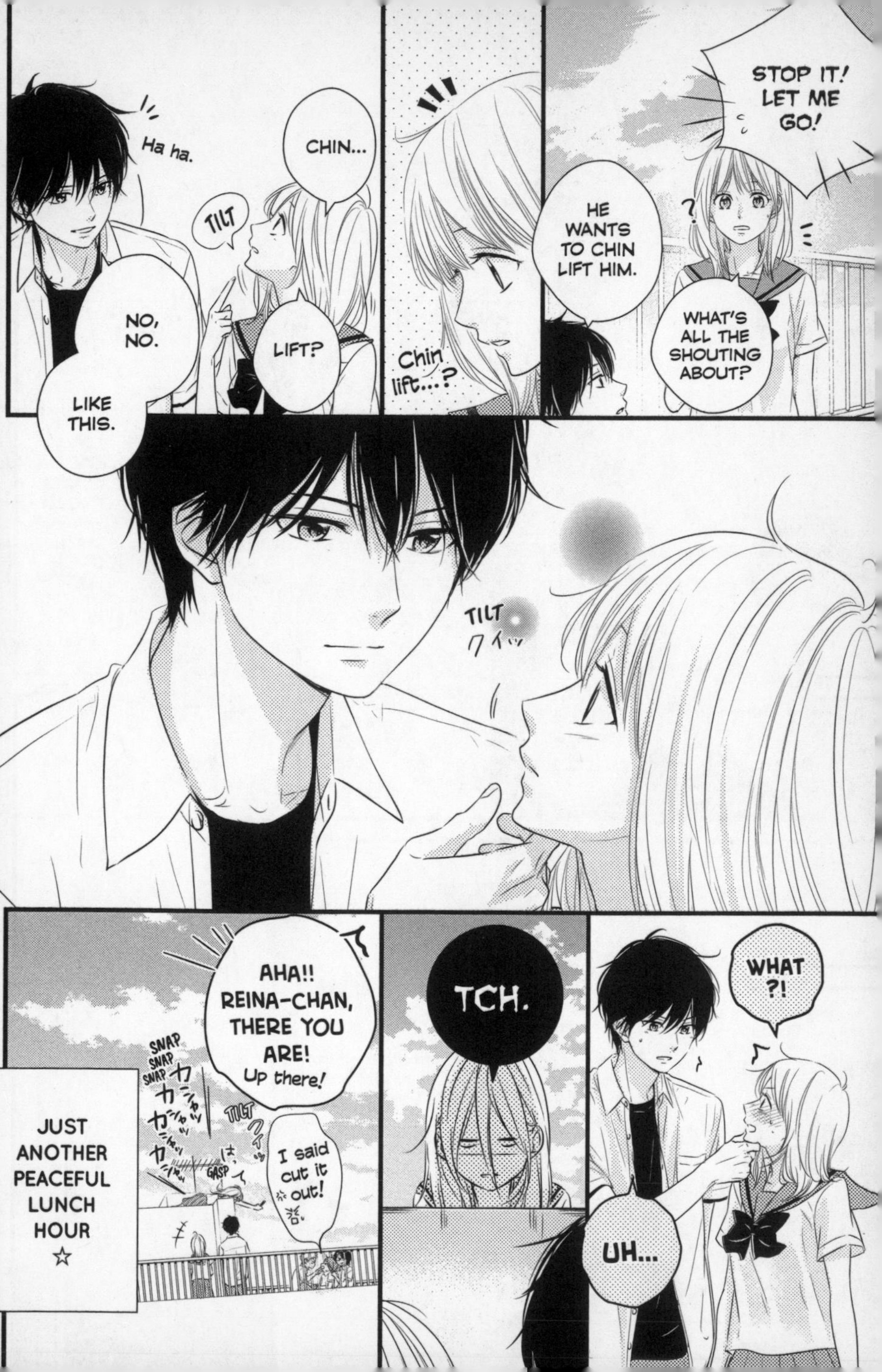
STOP IT! LET ME GO!
WHAT'S ALL THE SHOUTING ABOUT?
HE WANTS TO CHIN LIFT HIM.
Chin lift...?
CHIN...
TILT
Ha ha.
LIFT?
NO, NO.
LIKE THIS.
TILT
クイッ
WHAT?!
UH...
TCH.
AHA!! REINA-CHAN, THERE YOU ARE! Up there!
I said cut it out!
TILT
SNAP SNAP SNAP
GASP
JUST ANOTHER PEACEFUL LUNCH HOUR ☆

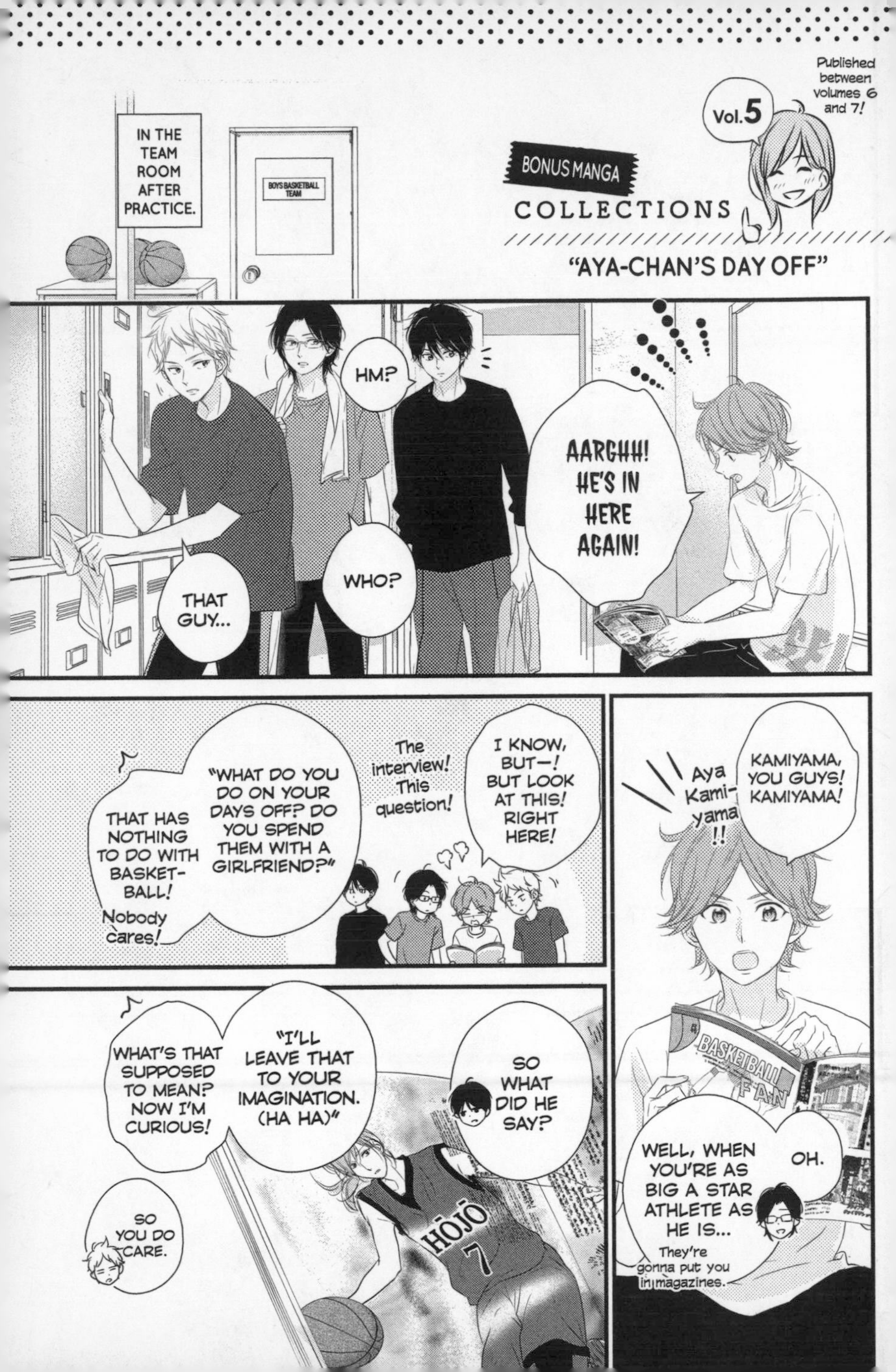
Published between volumes 6 and 7!
Vol.5
BONUS MANGA
COLLECTIONS
"AYA-CHAN'S DAY OFF"
IN THE TEAM ROOM AFTER PRACTICE.
BOYS BASKETBALL TEAM
AARGHH! HE'S IN HERE AGAIN!
HM?
WHO?
THAT GUY...
KAMIYAMA, YOU GUYS! KAMIYAMA!
Aya Kami-yama!!
BASKETBALL FAN
OH.
WELL, WHEN YOU'RE AS BIG A STAR ATHLETE AS HE IS...
They're gonna put you in magazines.
I KNOW, BUT—! BUT LOOK AT THIS! RIGHT HERE!
The interview! This question!
"WHAT DO YOU DO ON YOUR DAYS OFF? DO YOU SPEND THEM WITH A GIRLFRIEND?"
THAT HAS NOTHING TO DO WITH BASKET-BALL!
Nobody cares!
SO WHAT DID HE SAY?
"I'LL LEAVE THAT TO YOUR IMAGINATION. (HA HA)"
WHAT'S THAT SUPPOSED TO MEAN? NOW I'M CURIOUS!
HŌJŌ 7
SO YOU DO CARE.

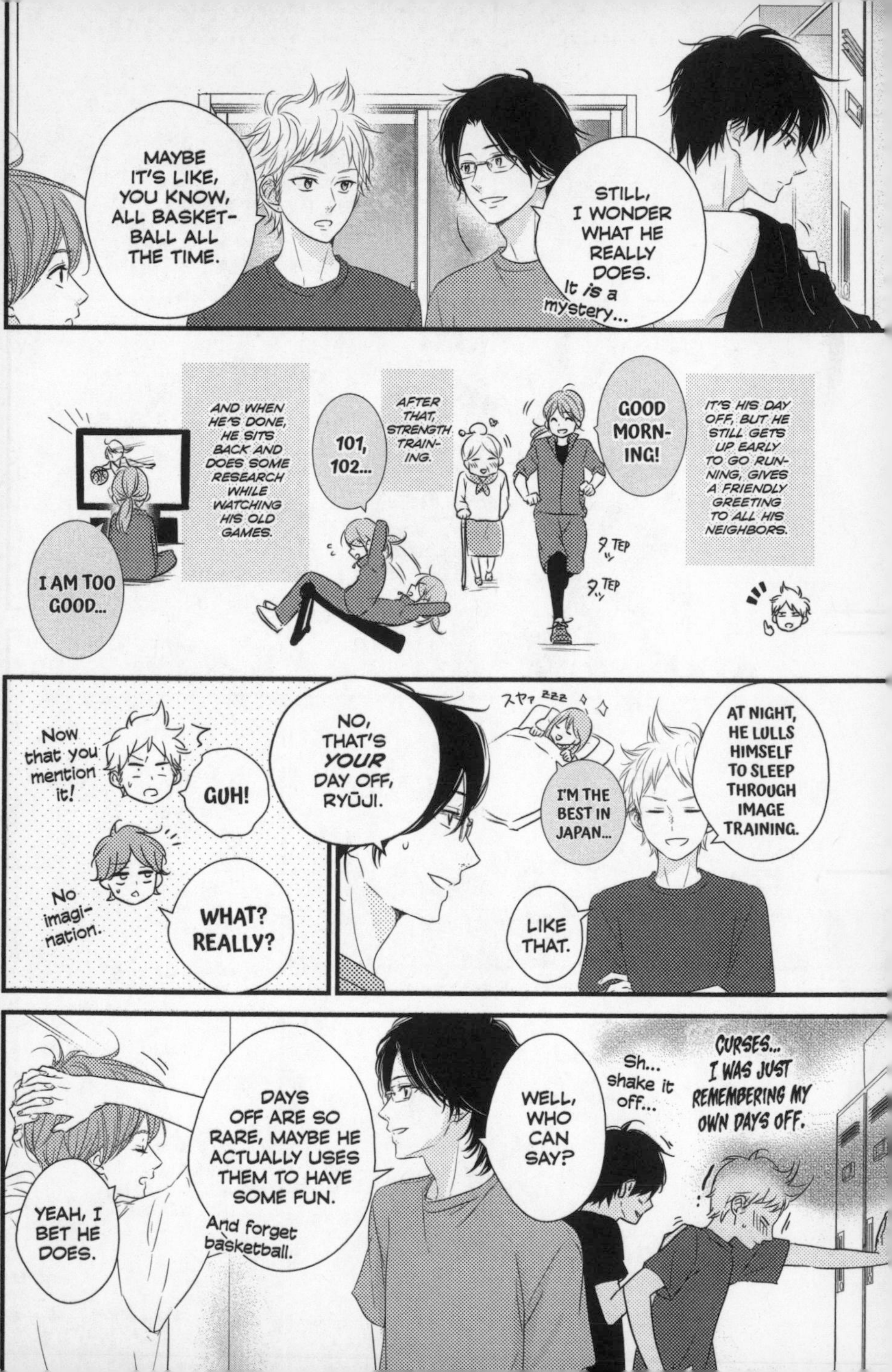
STILL, I WONDER WHAT HE REALLY DOES.
It is a mystery...
MAYBE IT'S LIKE, YOU KNOW, ALL BASKETBALL ALL THE TIME.
IT'S HIS DAY OFF, BUT HE STILL GETS UP EARLY TO GO RUNNING, GIVES A FRIENDLY GREETING TO ALL HIS NEIGHBORS.
GOOD MORNING!
TEP
TEP
AFTER THAT, STRENGTH TRAINING.
101, 102...
AND WHEN HE'S DONE, HE SITS BACK AND DOES SOME RESEARCH WHILE WATCHING HIS OLD GAMES.
I AM TOO GOOD...
AT NIGHT, HE LULLS HIMSELF TO SLEEP THROUGH IMAGE TRAINING.
zzz
I'M THE BEST IN JAPAN...
LIKE THAT.
NO, THAT'S *YOUR* DAY OFF, RYŪJI.
GUH!
Now that you mention it!
WHAT? REALLY?
No imagination.
CURSES... I WAS JUST REMEMBERING MY OWN DAYS OFF.
Sh... shake it off...
WELL, WHO CAN SAY?
DAYS OFF ARE SO RARE, MAYBE HE ACTUALLY USES THEM TO HAVE SOME FUN.
And forget basketball.
YEAH, I BET HE DOES.

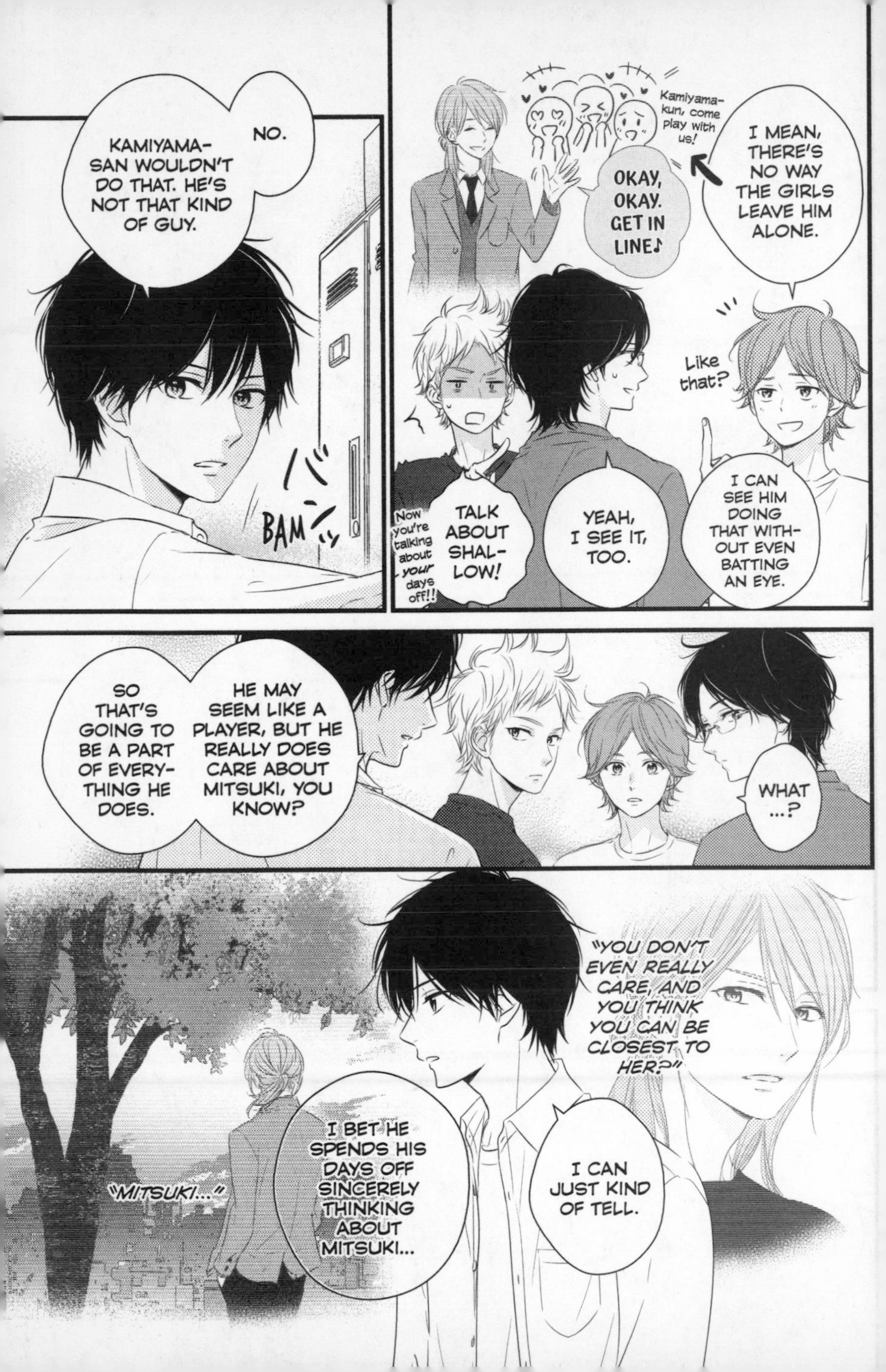
I MEAN, THERE'S NO WAY THE GIRLS LEAVE HIM ALONE.
Kamiyama-kun, come play with us!
OKAY, OKAY. GET IN LINE♪
Like that?
I CAN SEE HIM DOING THAT WITH-OUT EVEN BATTING AN EYE.
YEAH, I SEE IT, TOO.
TALK ABOUT SHAL-LOW!
Now you're talking about *your* days off!!
NO.
KAMIYAMA-SAN WOULDN'T DO THAT. HE'S NOT THAT KIND OF GUY.
バ
BAM
WHAT ...?
HE MAY SEEM LIKE A PLAYER, BUT HE REALLY DOES CARE ABOUT MITSUKI, YOU KNOW?
SO THAT'S GOING TO BE A PART OF EVERY-THING HE DOES.
"YOU DON'T EVEN REALLY CARE, AND YOU THINK YOU CAN BE CLOSEST TO HER?"
I CAN JUST KIND OF TELL.
I BET HE SPENDS HIS DAYS OFF SINCERELY THINKING ABOUT MITSUKI...
"MITSUKI..."

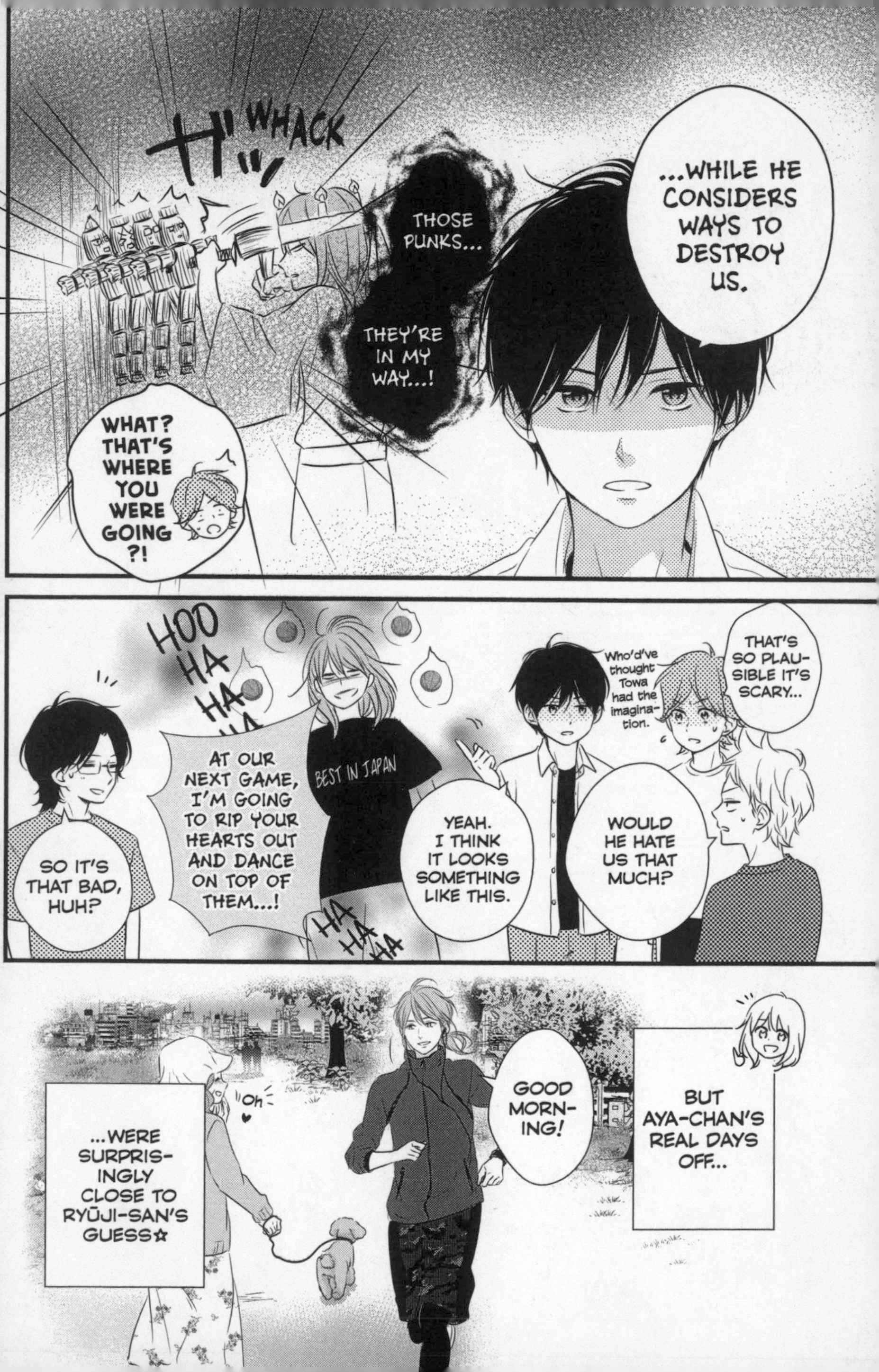
...WHILE HE CONSIDERS WAYS TO DESTROY US.
WHACK
THOSE PUNKS...
THEY'RE IN MY WAY...!
WHAT? THAT'S WHERE YOU WERE GOING?!
THAT'S SO PLAUSIBLE IT'S SCARY...
Who'd've thought Towa had the imagination.
WOULD HE HATE US THAT MUCH?
YEAH. I THINK IT LOOKS SOMETHING LIKE THIS.
HOO HA HA
BEST IN JAPAN
AT OUR NEXT GAME, I'M GOING TO RIP YOUR HEARTS OUT AND DANCE ON TOP OF THEM...!
HA HA HA
SO IT'S THAT BAD, HUH?
BUT AYA-CHAN'S REAL DAYS OFF...
GOOD MORNING!
Oh
...WERE SURPRISINGLY CLOSE TO RYŪJI-SAN'S GUESS☆

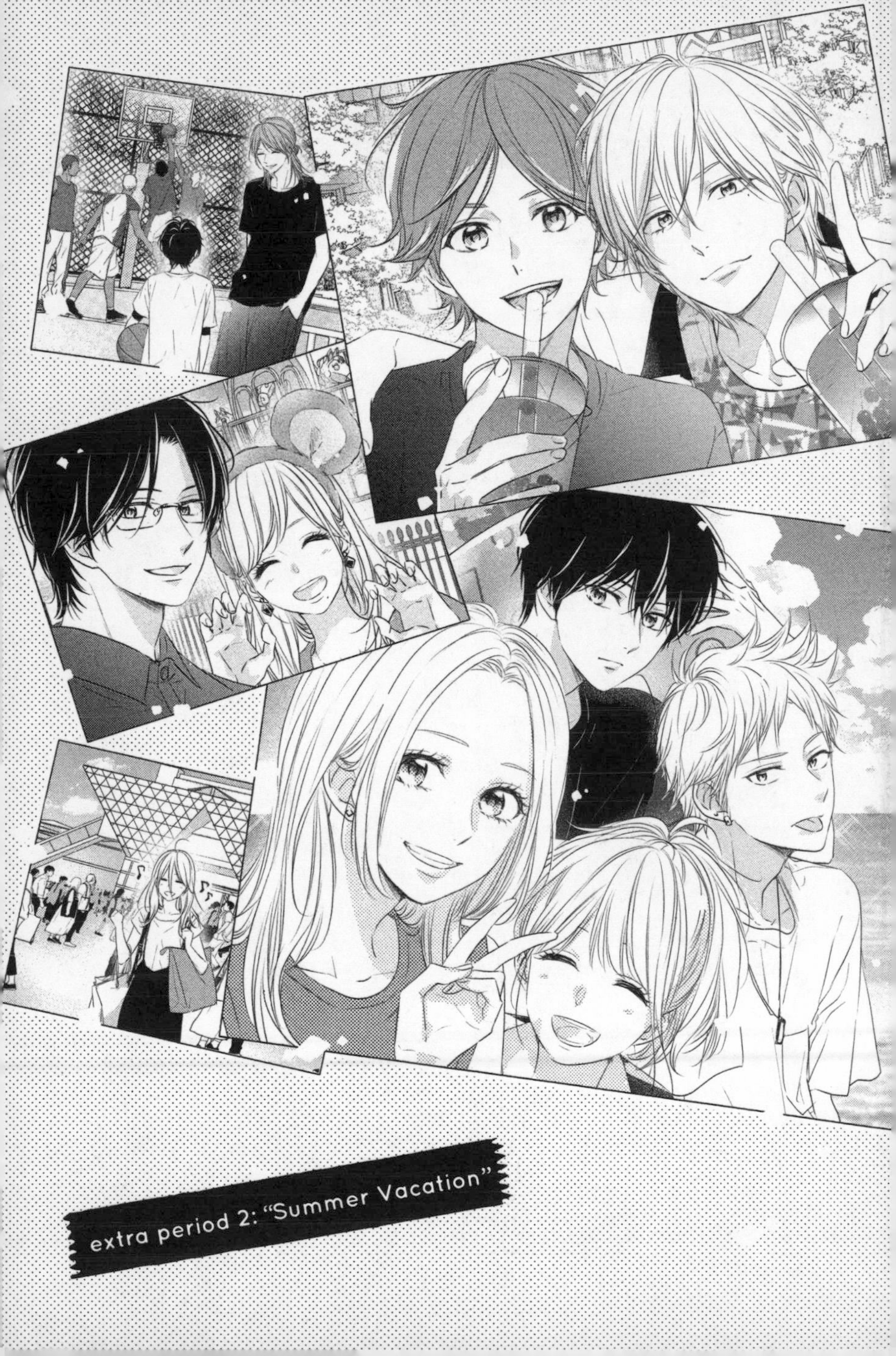

# extra period 2: "Summer Vacation"

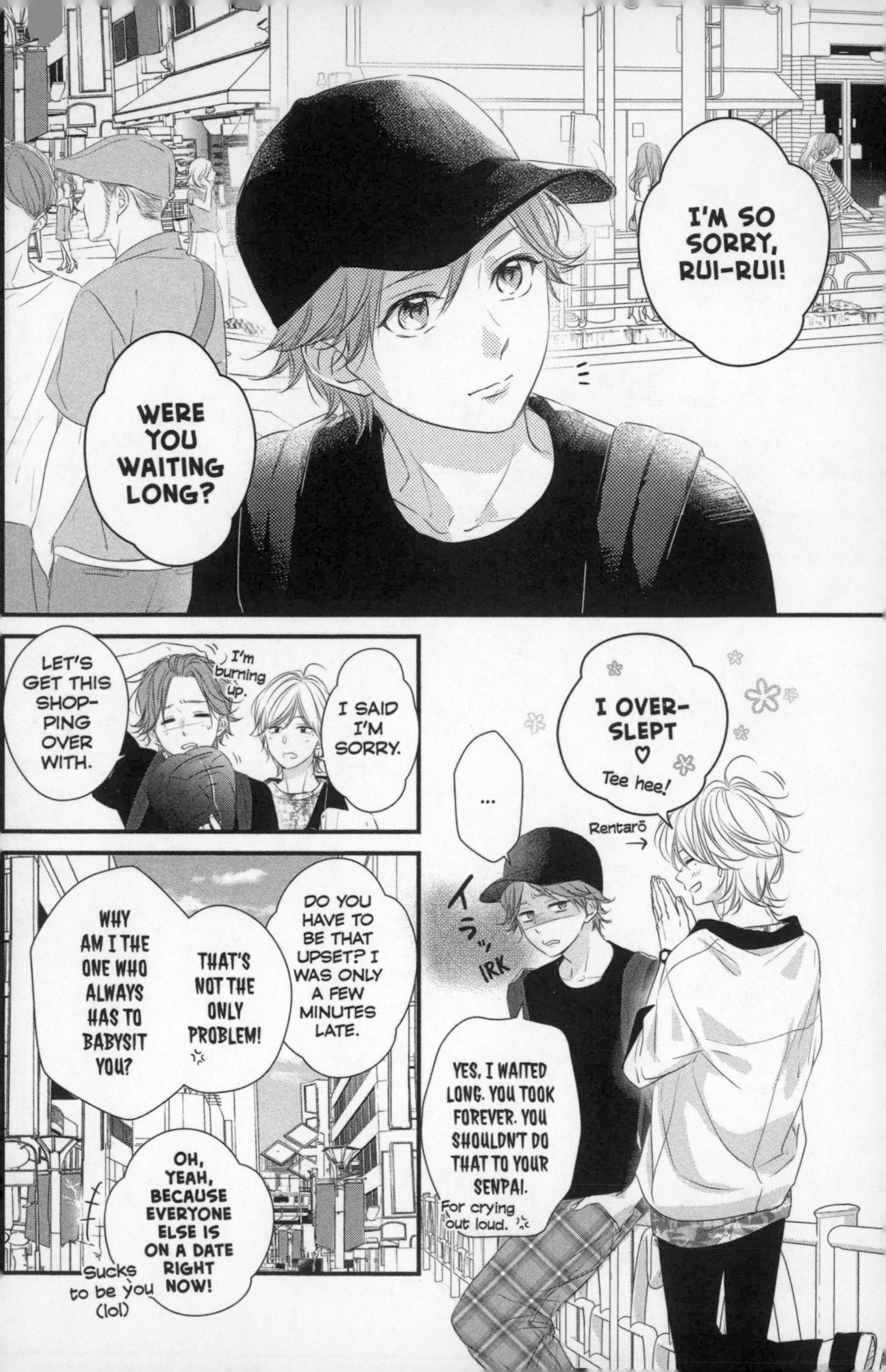
I'M SO SORRY, RUI-RUI!
WERE YOU WAITING LONG?
I OVER-SLEPT ♡
Tee hee!
Rentarō →
...
IRK
YES, I WAITED LONG. YOU TOOK FOREVER. YOU SHOULDN'T DO THAT TO YOUR SENPAI.
For crying out loud.
I SAID I'M SORRY.
I'm burning up.
LET'S GET THIS SHOP-PING OVER WITH.
DO YOU HAVE TO BE THAT UPSET? I WAS ONLY A FEW MINUTES LATE.
THAT'S NOT THE ONLY PROBLEM!
WHY AM I THE ONE WHO ALWAYS HAS TO BABYSIT YOU?
OH, YEAH, BECAUSE EVERYONE ELSE IS ON A DATE RIGHT NOW!
Sucks to be you (lol)

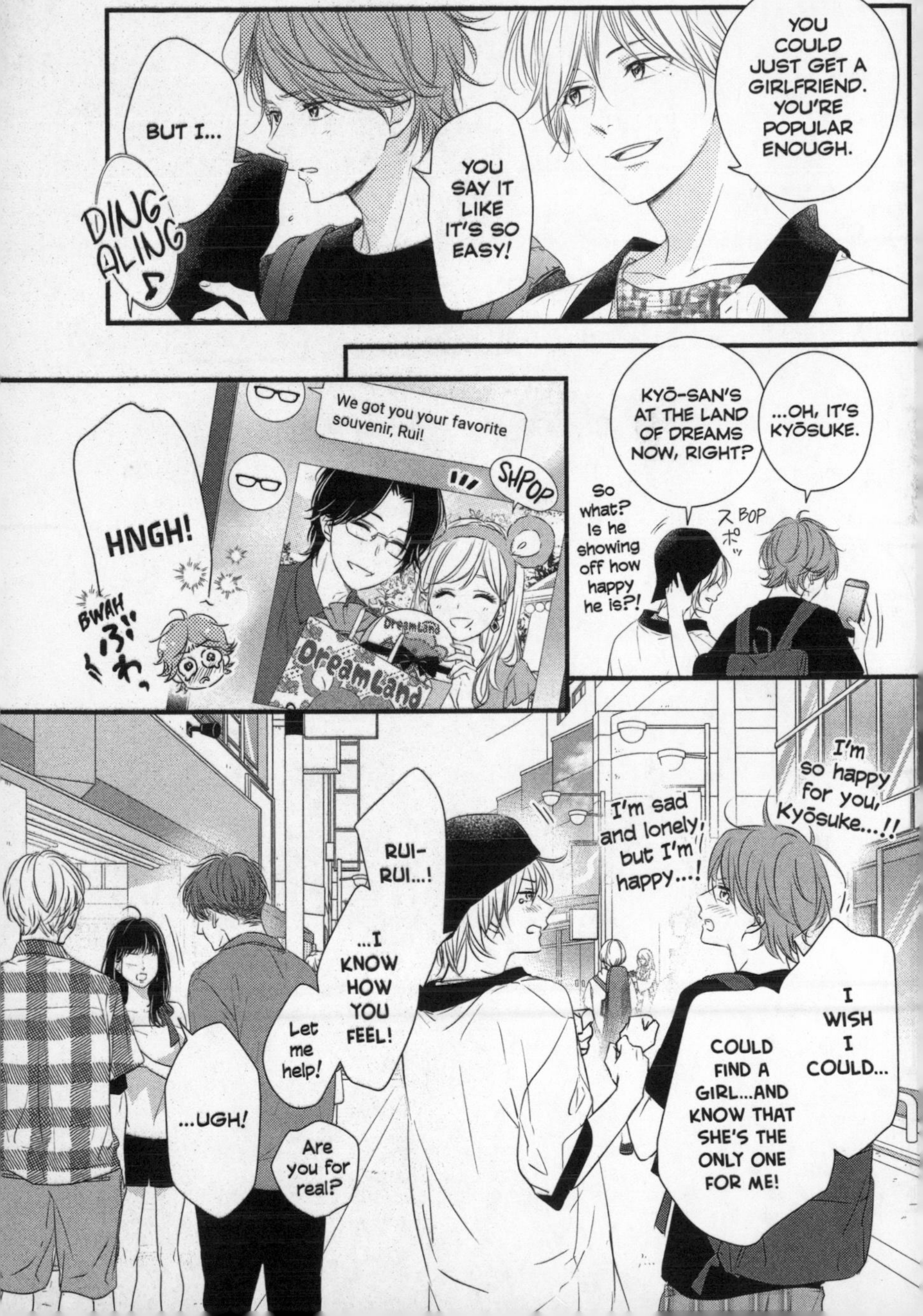

YOU COULD JUST GET A GIRLFRIEND. YOU'RE POPULAR ENOUGH.
YOU SAY IT LIKE IT'S SO EASY!
BUT I...
DING-ALING
...OH, IT'S KYŌSUKE.
KYŌ-SAN'S AT THE LAND OF DREAMS NOW, RIGHT?
BOP
スポッ
So what? Is he showing off how happy he is?!
SHPOP
We got you your favorite souvenir, Rui!
DreamLand
HNGH!
BWAH
ぶわっ
I'm so happy for you, Kyōsuke...!!
I'm sad and lonely, but I'm happy...!
I WISH I COULD...
COULD FIND A GIRL...AND KNOW THAT SHE'S THE ONLY ONE FOR ME!
RUI-RUI...!
...I KNOW HOW YOU FEEL!
Let me help!
...UGH!
Are you for real?

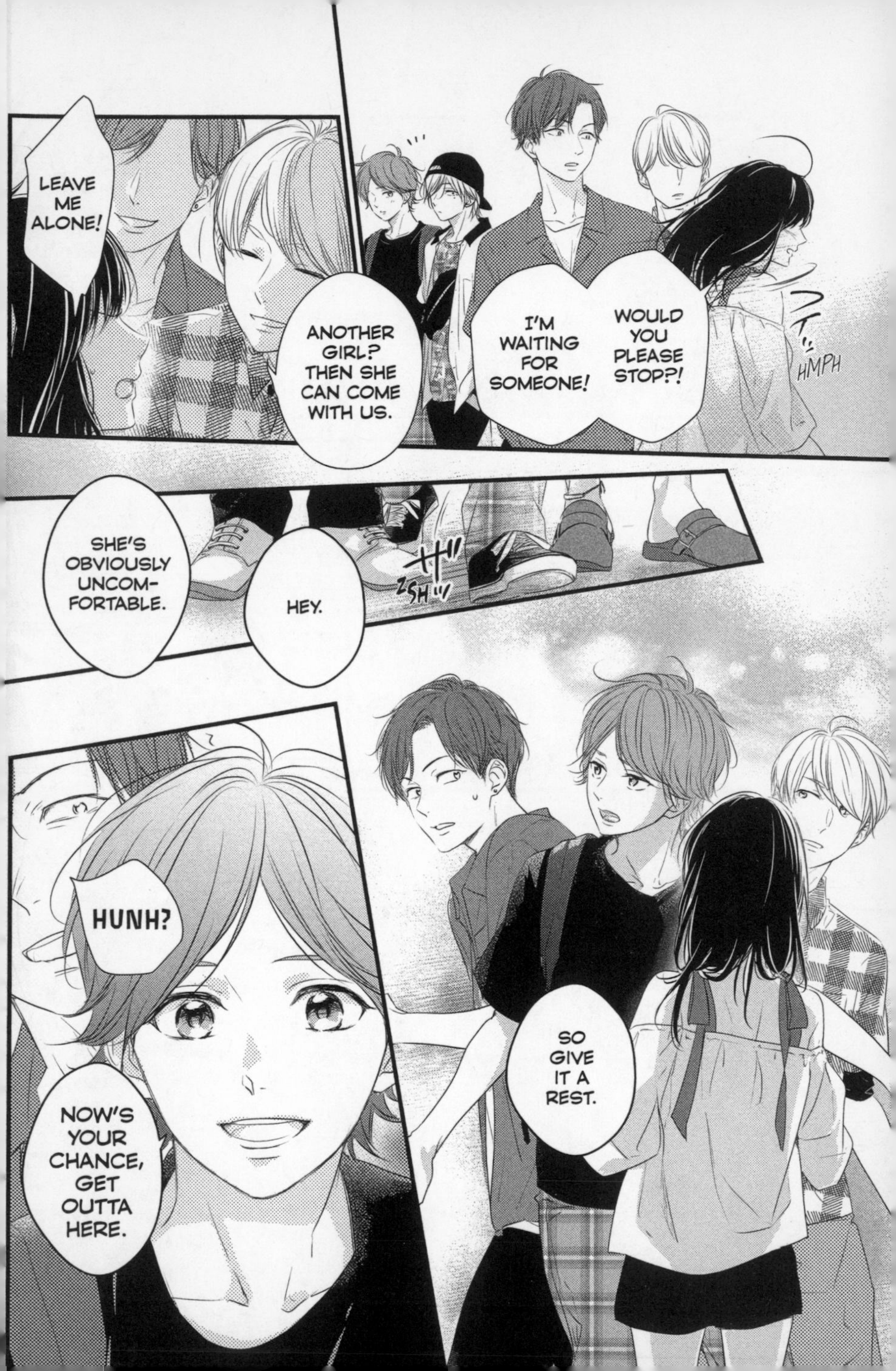
WOULD YOU PLEASE STOP?!
I'M WAITING FOR SOMEONE!
HMPH
ANOTHER GIRL? THEN SHE CAN COME WITH US.
LEAVE ME ALONE!
ZSH
HEY.
SHE'S OBVIOUSLY UNCOM-FORTABLE.
SO GIVE IT A REST.
HUNH?
NOW'S YOUR CHANCE, GET OUTTA HERE.

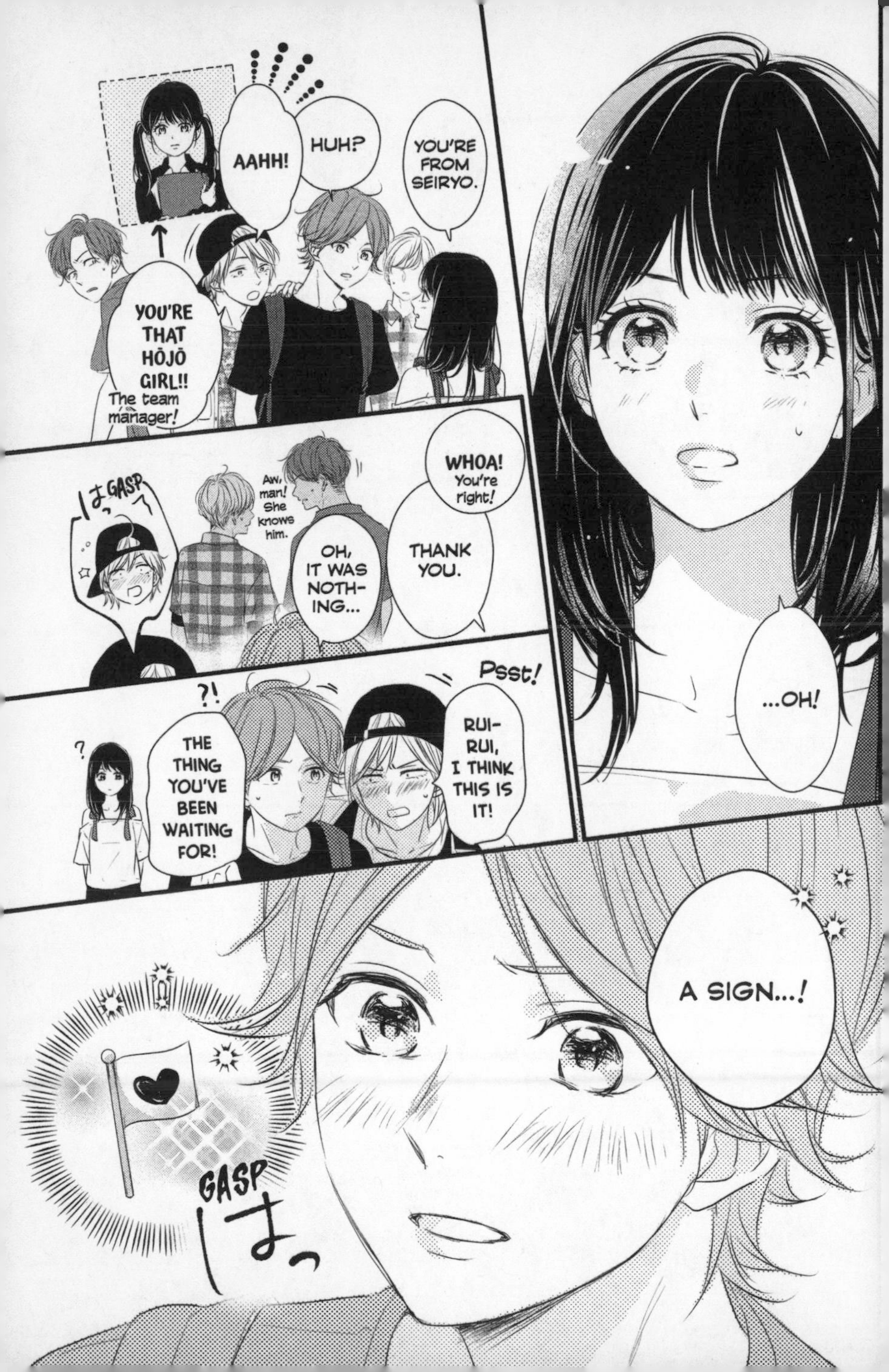
...OH!
YOU'RE FROM SEIRYO.
HUH?
AAHH!
YOU'RE THAT HŌJŌ GIRL!!
The team manager!
WHOA! You're right!
THANK YOU.
OH, IT WAS NOTHING...
Aw, man! She knows him.
は GASP
Psst!
RUI-RUI, I THINK THIS IS IT!
THE THING YOU'VE BEEN WAITING FOR!
?!
?
A SIGN...!
GASP はっ

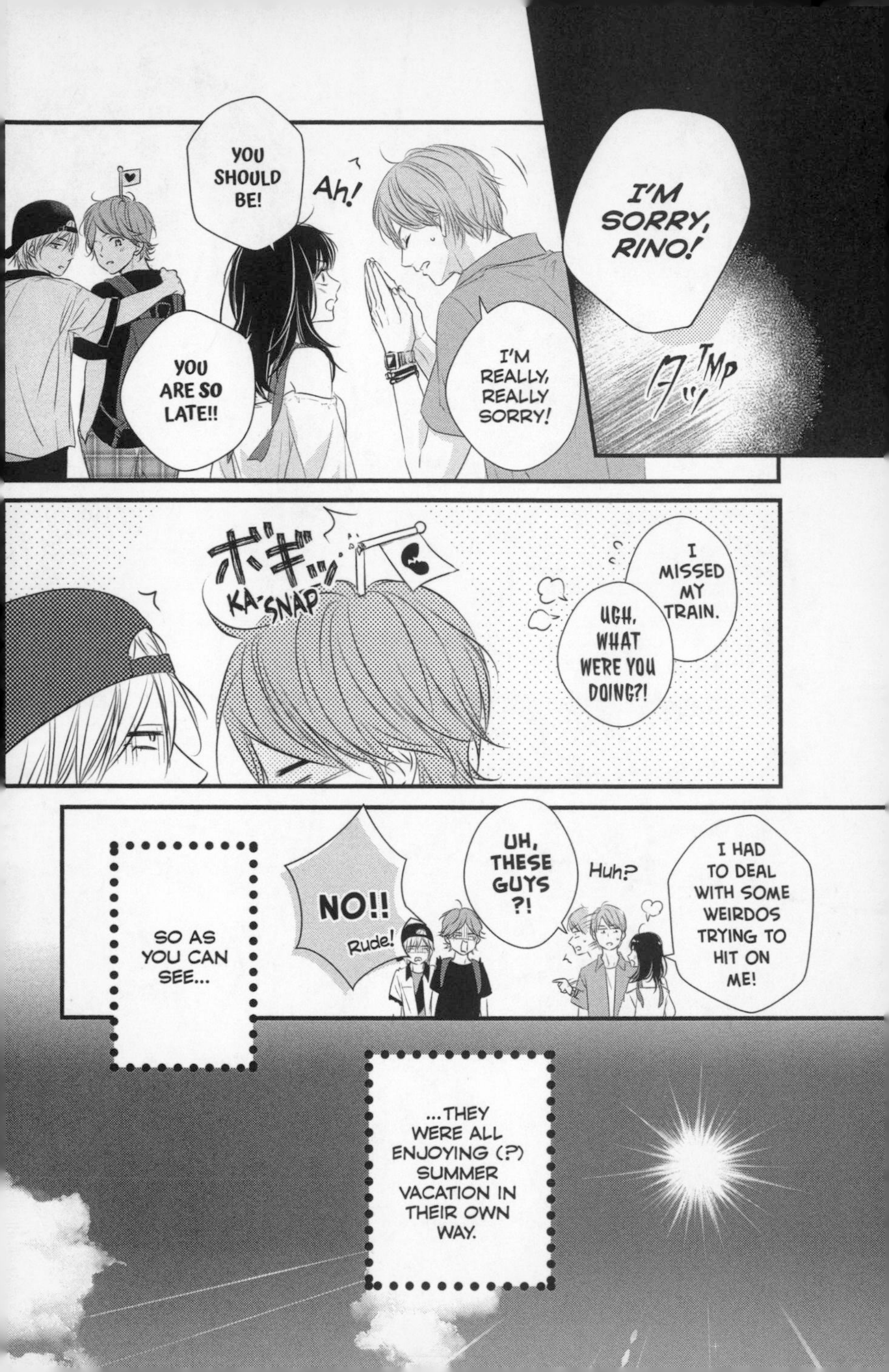
I'M SORRY, RINO!
TMP
Ah!
I'M REALLY, REALLY SORRY!
YOU ARE SO LATE!!
YOU SHOULD BE!
I MISSED MY TRAIN.
UGH, WHAT WERE YOU DOING?!
KA-SNAP
I HAD TO DEAL WITH SOME WEIRDOS TRYING TO HIT ON ME!
Huh?
UH, THESE GUYS?!
NO!!
Rude!
SO AS YOU CAN SEE...
...THEY WERE ALL ENJOYING (?) SUMMER VACATION IN THEIR OWN WAY.

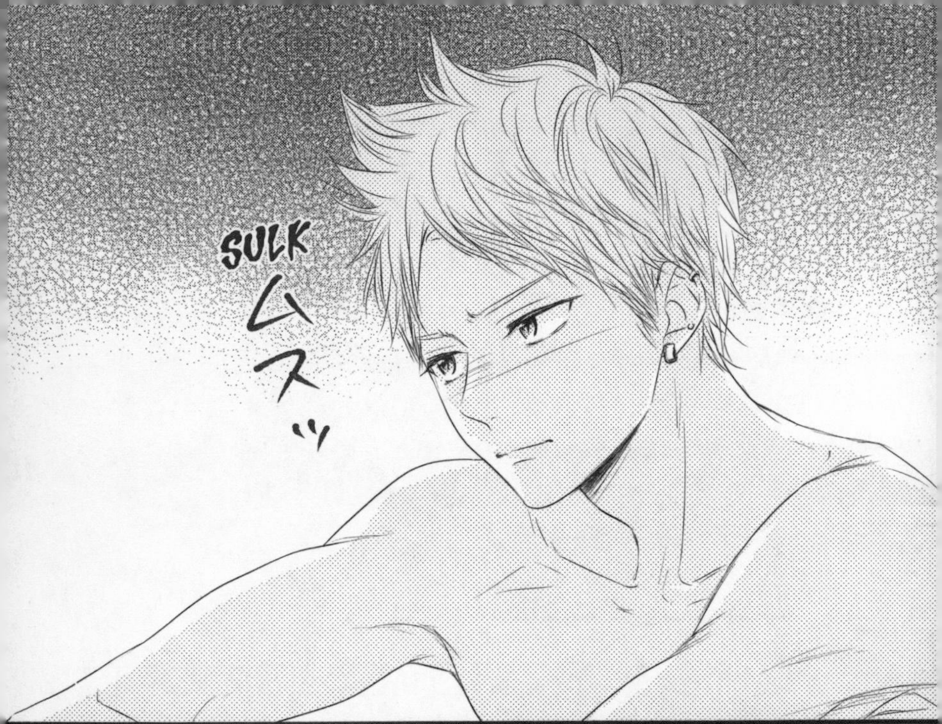
SULK
ムスッ

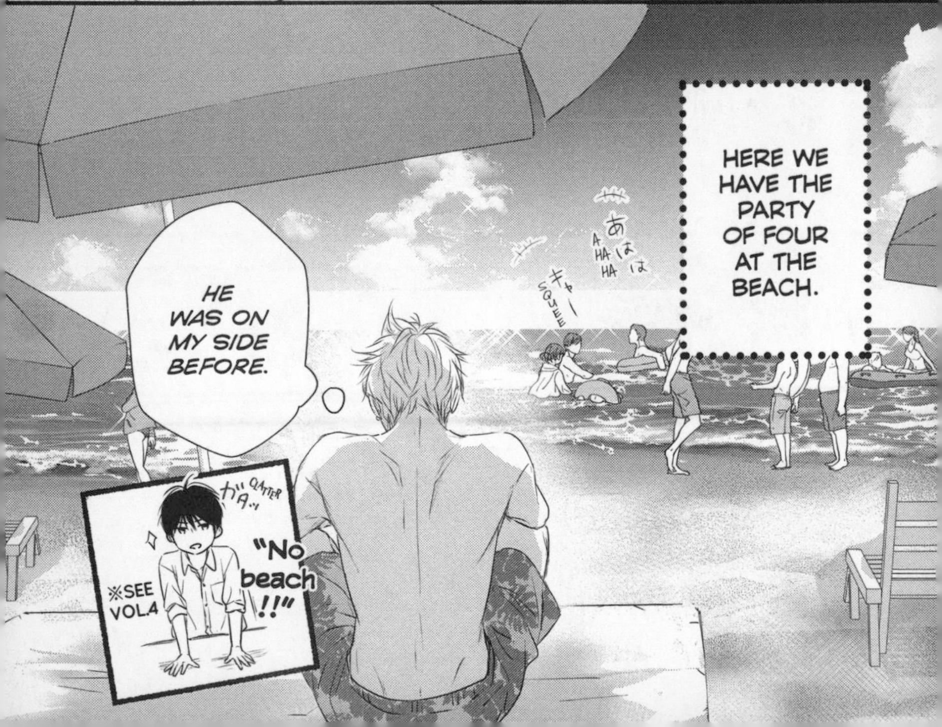
HERE WE HAVE THE PARTY OF FOUR AT THE BEACH.
あはは
A HA HA
キャー
SQUEE
HE WAS ON MY SIDE BEFORE.
ガタッ
CLATTER
"No beach!!"
※SEE VOL.4

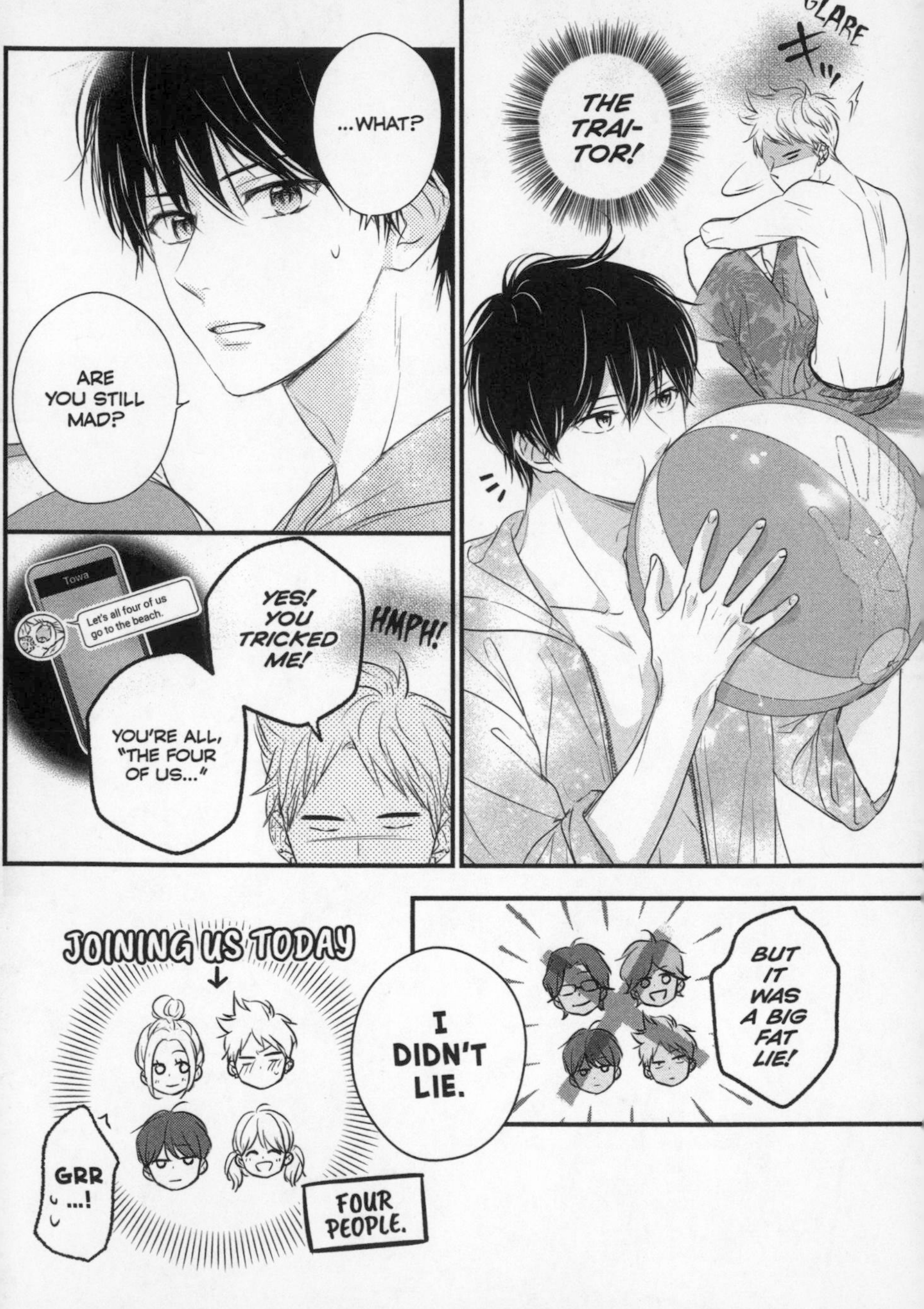
GLARE
THE TRAI-TOR!
...WHAT?
ARE YOU STILL MAD?
Towa
Let's all four of us go to the beach.
HMPH!
YES! YOU TRICKED ME!
YOU'RE ALL, "THE FOUR OF US..."
BUT IT WAS A BIG FAT LIE!
I DIDN'T LIE.
JOINING US TODAY
FOUR PEOPLE.
GRR...!

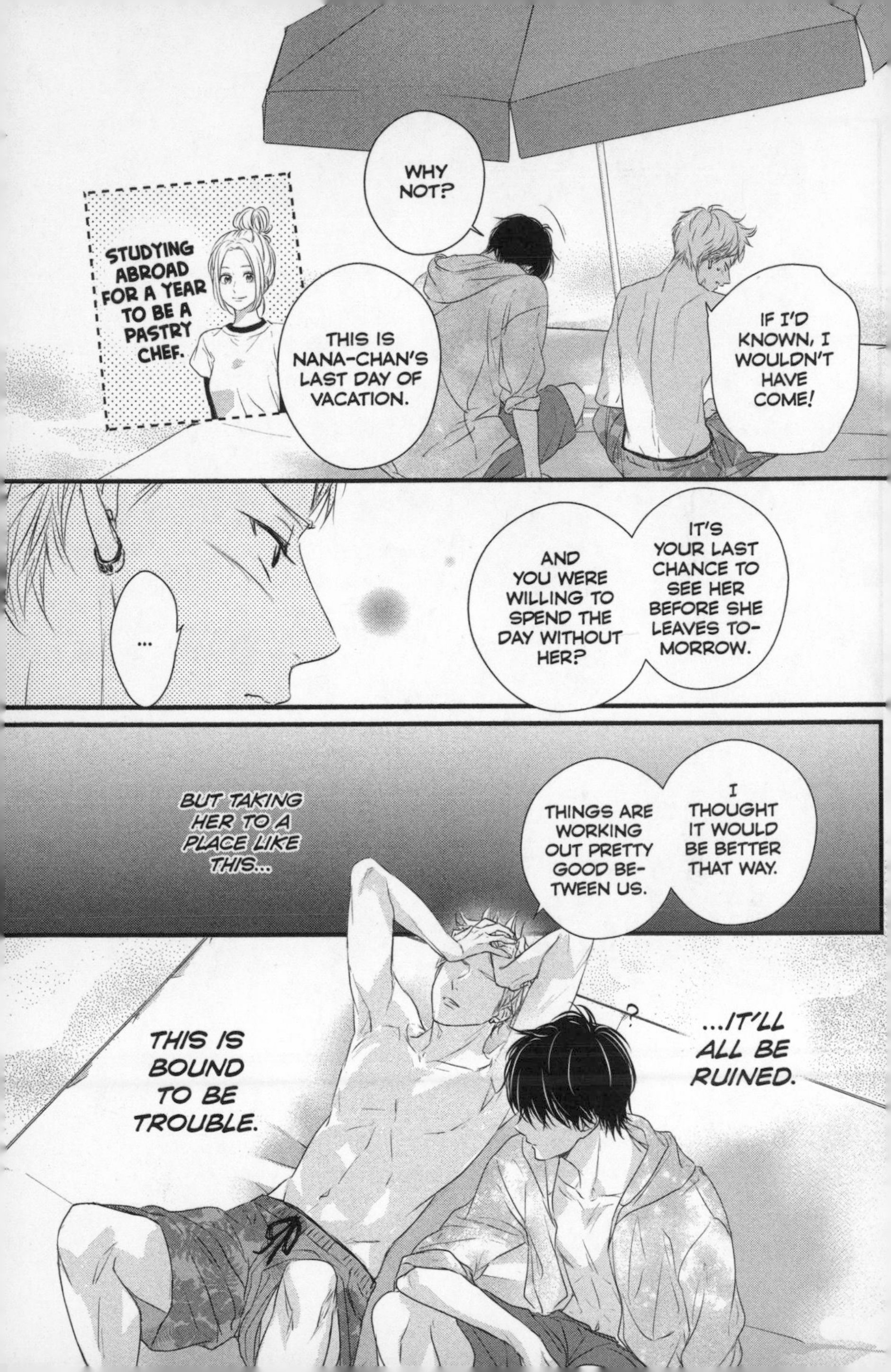
IF I'D KNOWN, I WOULDN'T HAVE COME!
WHY NOT?
THIS IS NANA-CHAN'S LAST DAY OF VACATION.
STUDYING ABROAD FOR A YEAR TO BE A PASTRY CHEF.
IT'S YOUR LAST CHANCE TO SEE HER BEFORE SHE LEAVES TO-MORROW.
AND YOU WERE WILLING TO SPEND THE DAY WITHOUT HER?
...
I THOUGHT IT WOULD BE BETTER THAT WAY.
THINGS ARE WORKING OUT PRETTY GOOD BE-TWEEN US.
BUT TAKING HER TO A PLACE LIKE THIS...
...IT'LL ALL BE RUINED.
THIS IS BOUND TO BE TROUBLE.

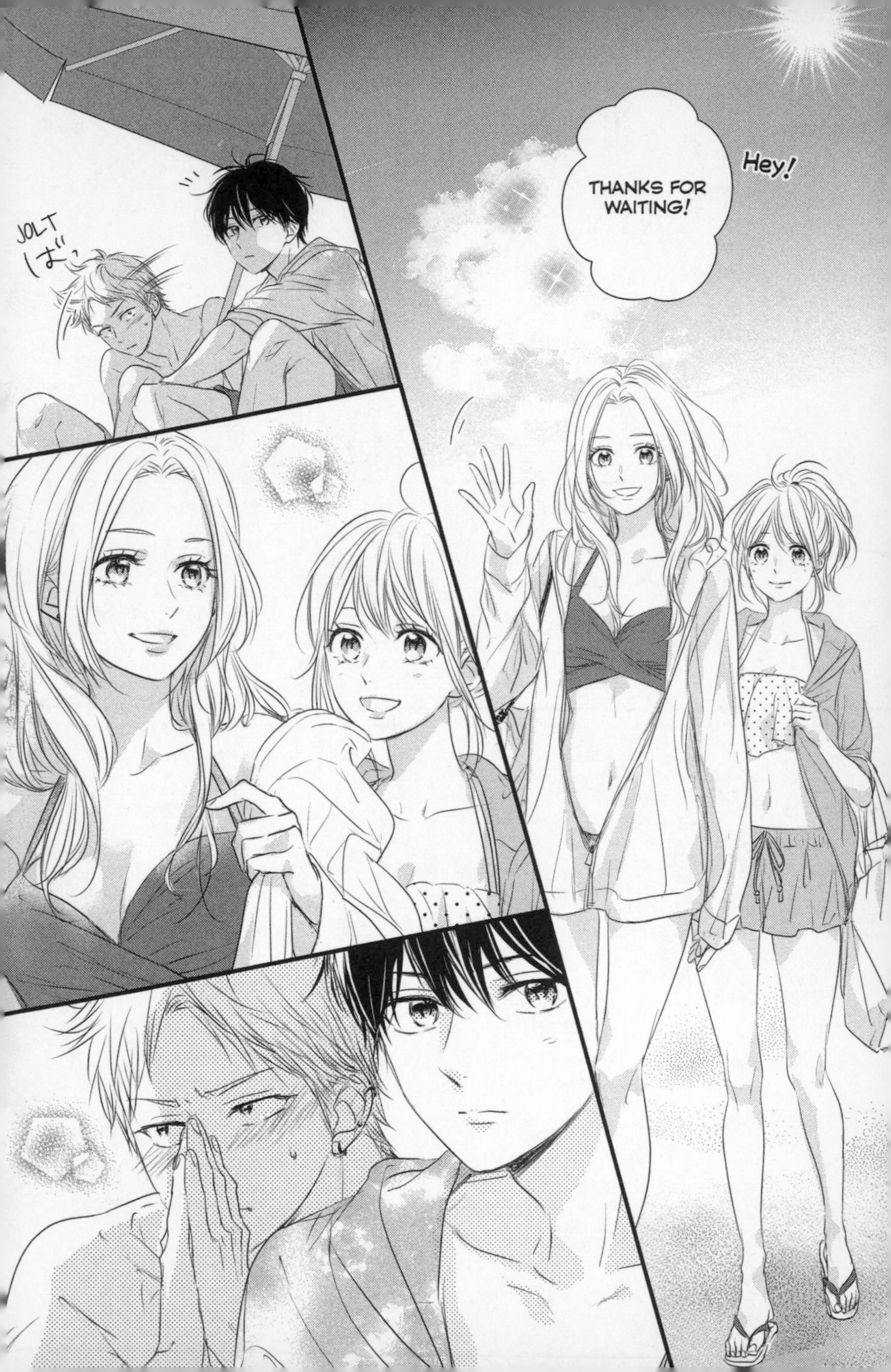
Hey!
THANKS FOR WAITING!
JOLT
ばっ

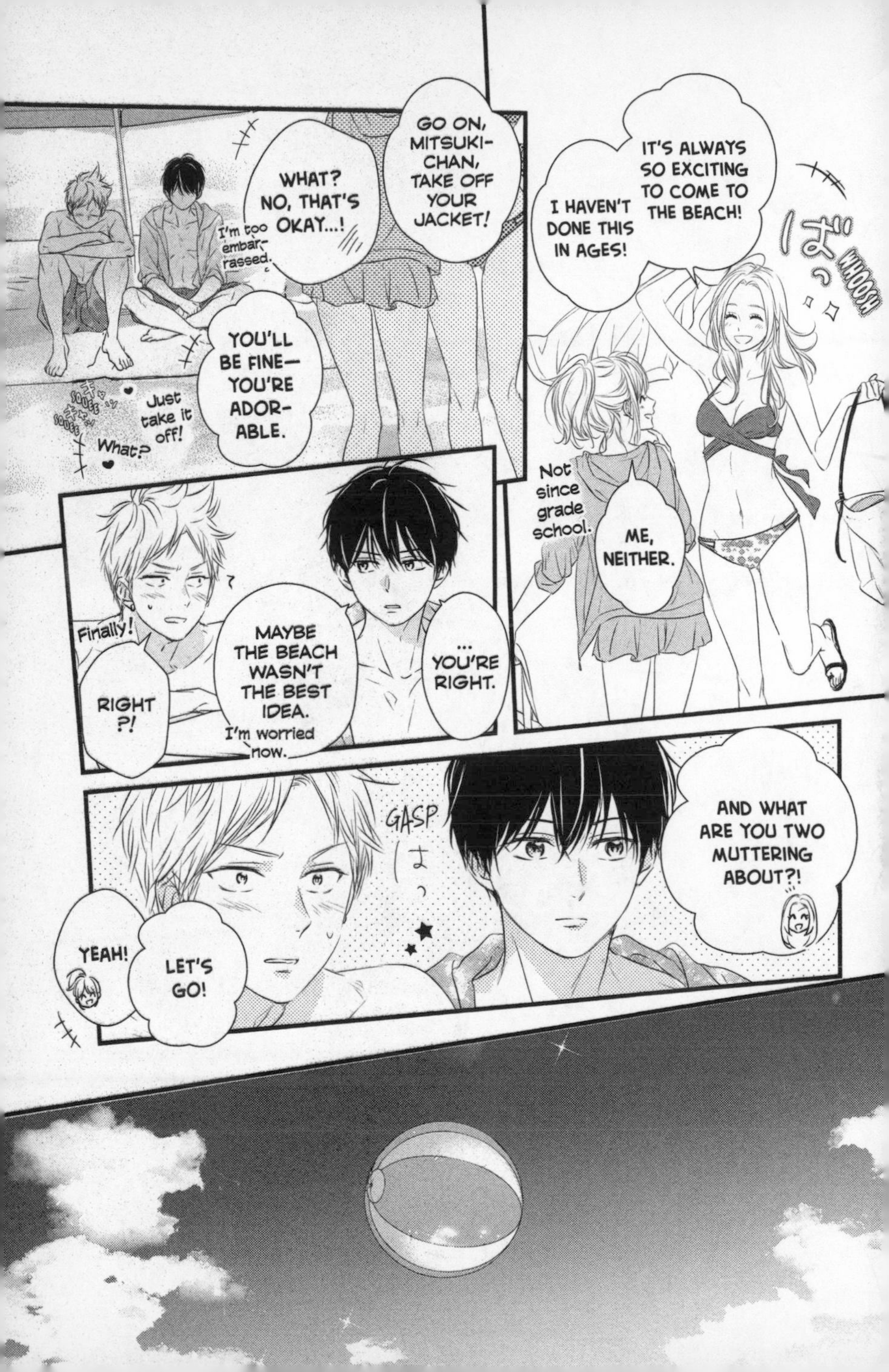
IT'S ALWAYS SO EXCITING TO COME TO THE BEACH!
I HAVEN'T DONE THIS IN AGES!
WHOOSH
ME, NEITHER.
Not since grade school.
GO ON, MITSUKI-CHAN, TAKE OFF YOUR JACKET!
WHAT? NO, THAT'S OKAY...!
I'm too embarrassed.
YOU'LL BE FINE—YOU'RE ADORABLE.
Just take it off!
SQUEE
SQUEE
What?
... YOU'RE RIGHT.
MAYBE THE BEACH WASN'T THE BEST IDEA.
I'm worried now.
Finally!
RIGHT?!
AND WHAT ARE YOU TWO MUTTERING ABOUT?!
GASP
LET'S GO!
YEAH!

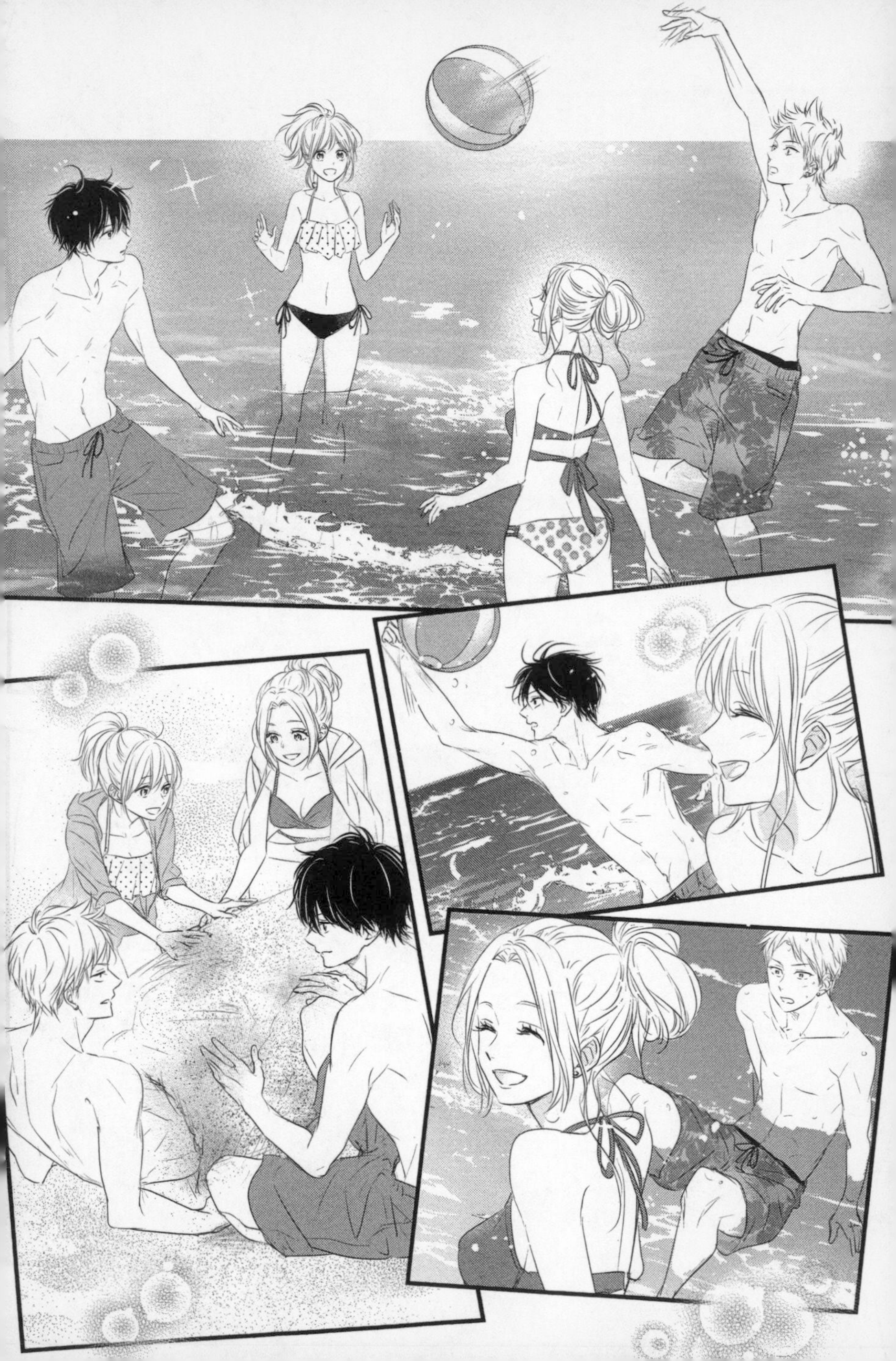

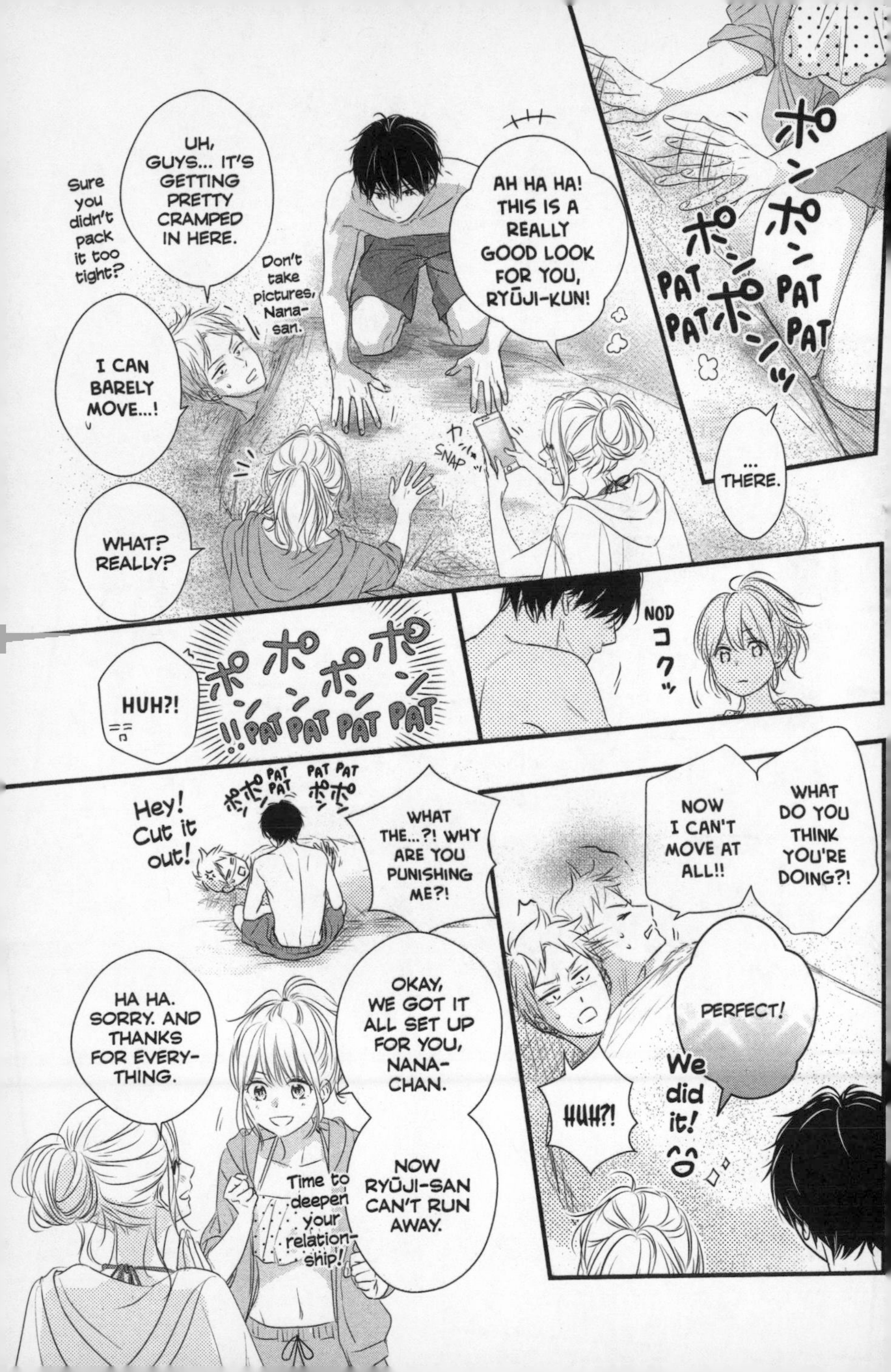
PAT PAT PAT PAT PAT
... THERE.
AH HA HA! THIS IS A REALLY GOOD LOOK FOR YOU, RYŪJI-KUN!
Don't take pictures, Nana-san.
UH, GUYS... IT'S GETTING PRETTY CRAMPED IN HERE.
Sure you didn't pack it too tight?
I CAN BARELY MOVE...!
SNAP
WHAT? REALLY?
NOD
HUH?!
!! PAT PAT PAT PAT
WHAT DO YOU THINK YOU'RE DOING?!
NOW I CAN'T MOVE AT ALL!!
PERFECT!
We did it!
HUH?!
PAT PAT
PAT PAT
WHAT THE...?! WHY ARE YOU PUNISHING ME?!
Hey! Cut it out!
OKAY, WE GOT IT ALL SET UP FOR YOU, NANA-CHAN.
NOW RYŪJI-SAN CAN'T RUN AWAY.
Time to deepen your relationship!
HA HA. SORRY. AND THANKS FOR EVERYTHING.

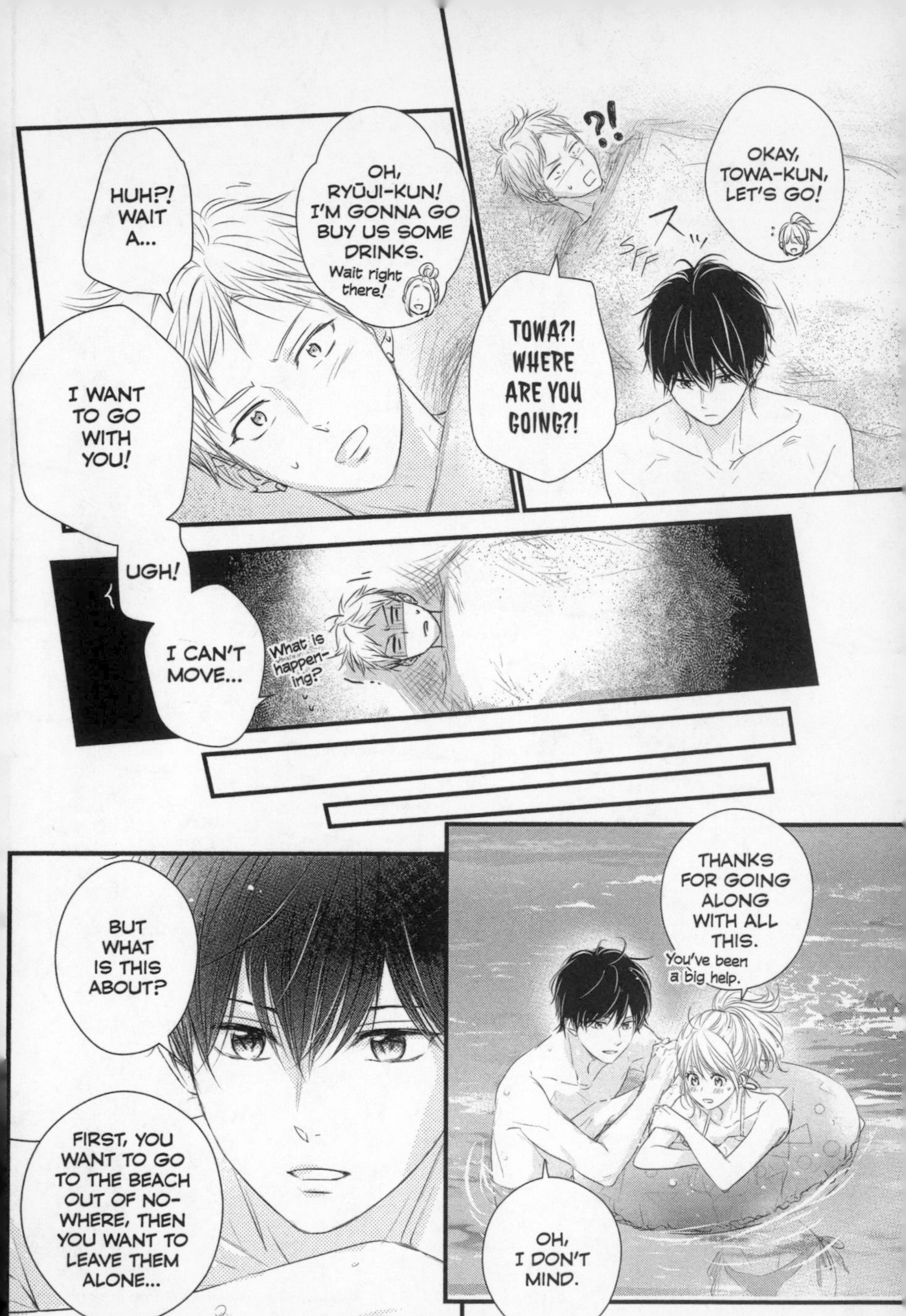

OKAY, TOWA-KUN, LET'S GO!
?!
SFF
TOWA?! WHERE ARE YOU GOING?!
OH, RYŪJI-KUN! I'M GONNA GO BUY US SOME DRINKS.
Wait right there!
HUH?! WAIT A...
I WANT TO GO WITH YOU!
UGH!
I CAN'T MOVE...
What is happen-ing?
THANKS FOR GOING ALONG WITH ALL THIS.
You've been a big help.
OH, I DON'T MIND.
BUT WHAT IS THIS ABOUT?
FIRST, YOU WANT TO GO TO THE BEACH OUT OF NO-WHERE, THEN YOU WANT TO LEAVE THEM ALONE...

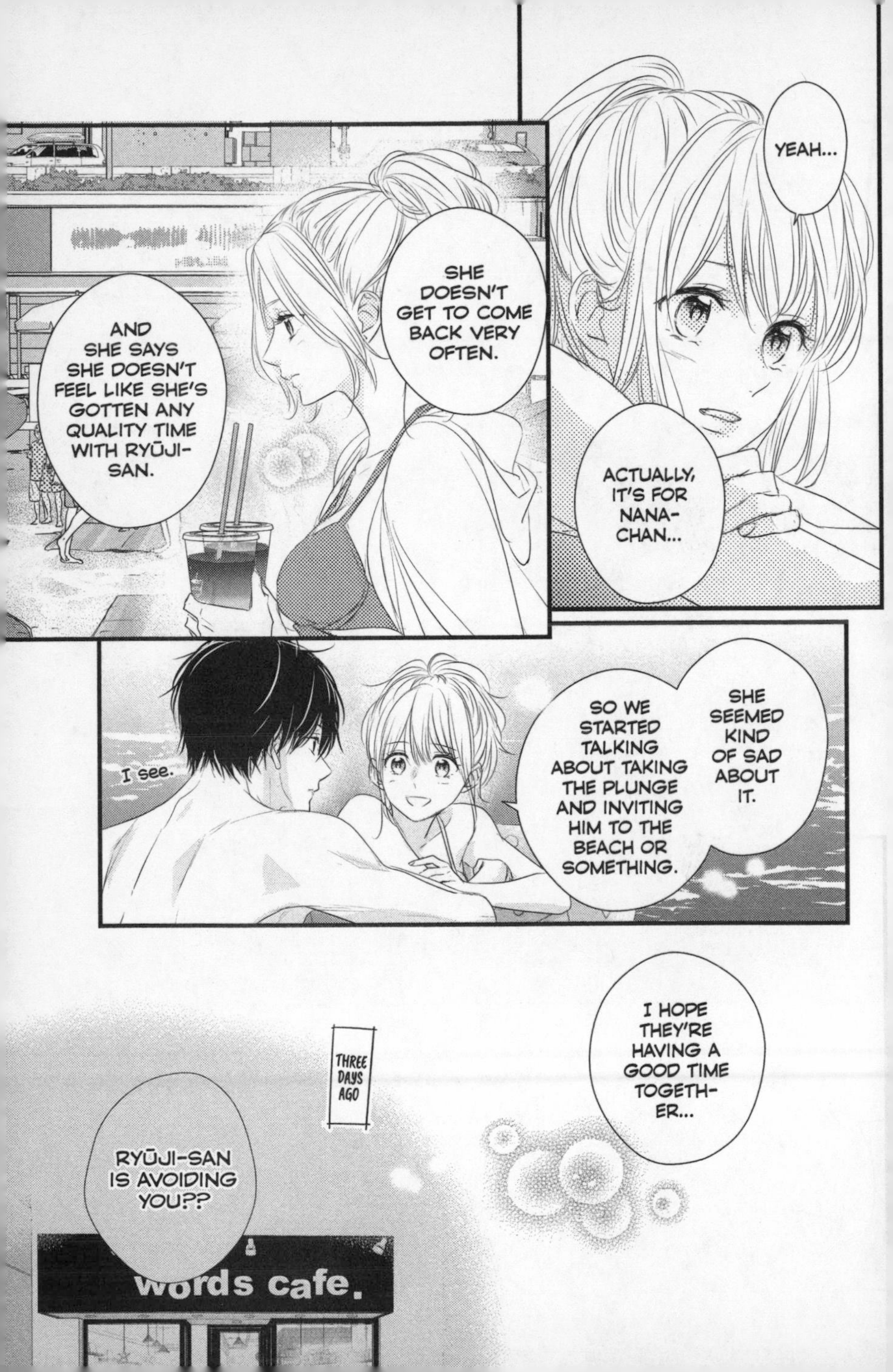
YEAH...
ACTUALLY, IT'S FOR NANA-CHAN...
SHE DOESN'T GET TO COME BACK VERY OFTEN.
AND SHE SAYS SHE DOESN'T FEEL LIKE SHE'S GOTTEN ANY QUALITY TIME WITH RYŪJI-SAN.
SHE SEEMED KIND OF SAD ABOUT IT.
SO WE STARTED TALKING ABOUT TAKING THE PLUNGE AND INVITING HIM TO THE BEACH OR SOMETHING.
I see.
I HOPE THEY'RE HAVING A GOOD TIME TOGETH-ER...
THREE DAYS AGO
RYŪJI-SAN IS AVOIDING YOU??
words cafe.

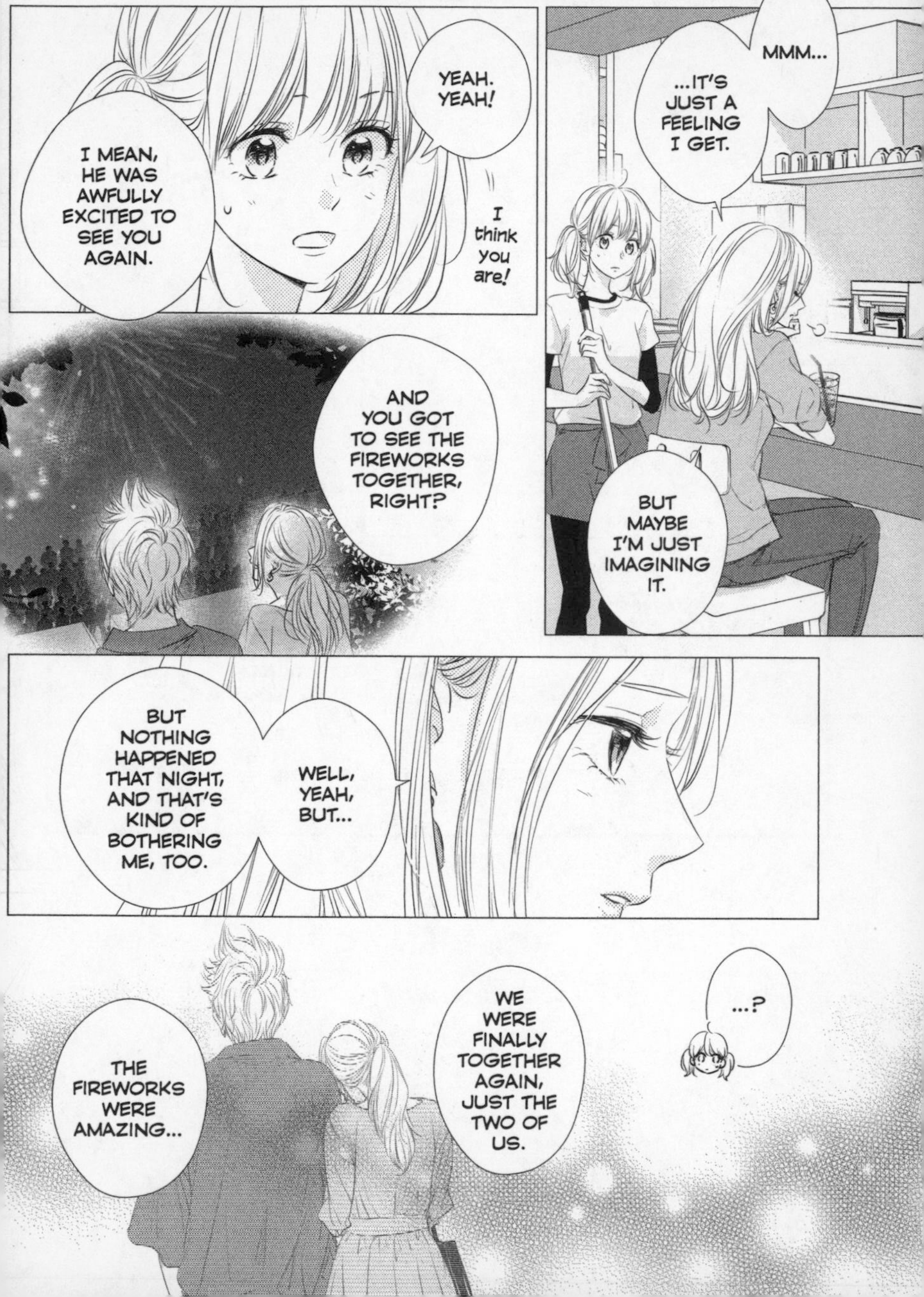
MMM...
...IT'S JUST A FEELING I GET.
BUT MAYBE I'M JUST IMAGINING IT.
YEAH. YEAH!
I think you are!
I MEAN, HE WAS AWFULLY EXCITED TO SEE YOU AGAIN.
AND YOU GOT TO SEE THE FIREWORKS TOGETHER, RIGHT?
WELL, YEAH, BUT...
BUT NOTHING HAPPENED THAT NIGHT, AND THAT'S KIND OF BOTHERING ME, TOO.
...?
WE WERE FINALLY TOGETHER AGAIN, JUST THE TWO OF US.
THE FIREWORKS WERE AMAZING...

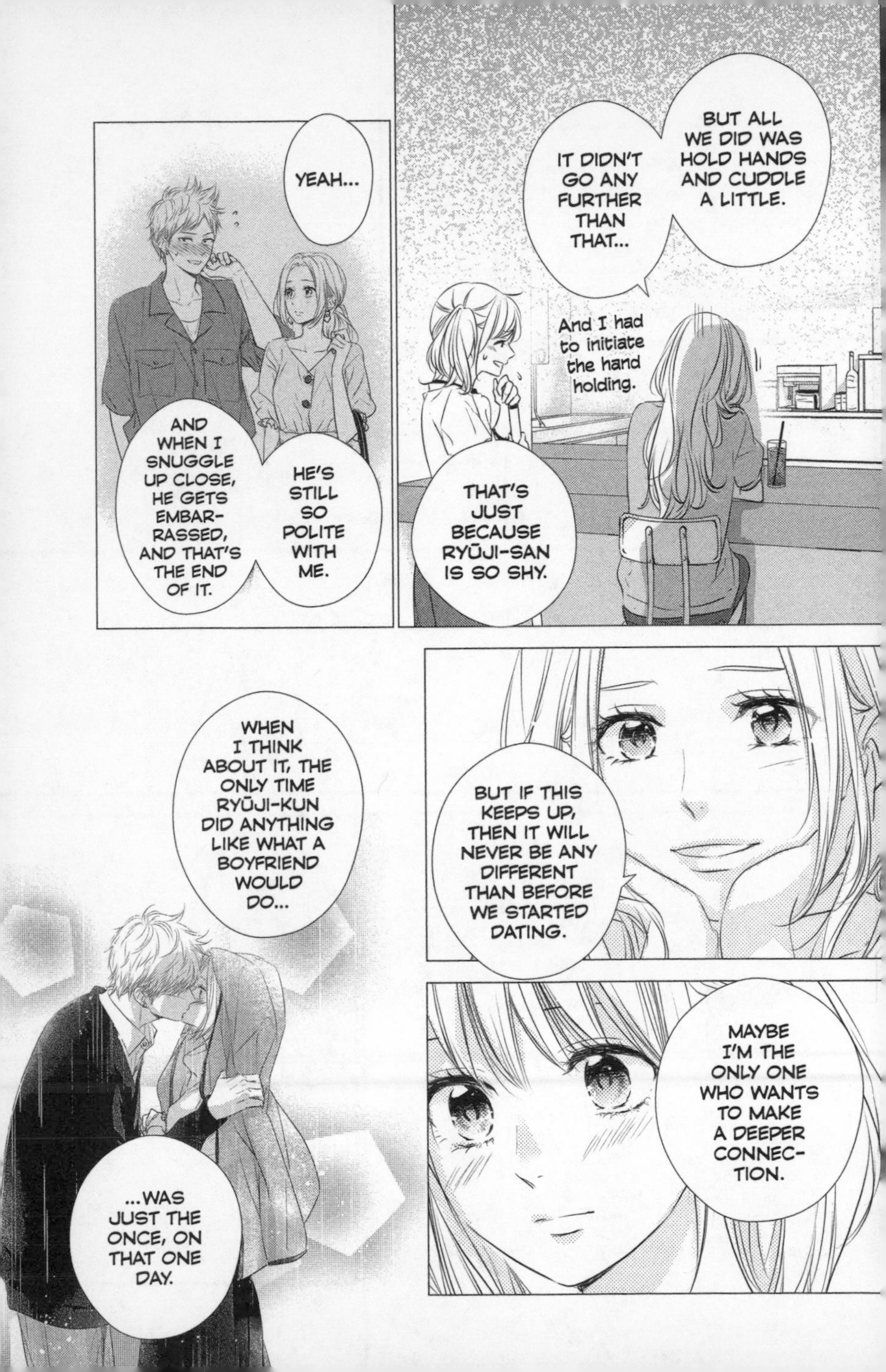
BUT ALL WE DID WAS HOLD HANDS AND CUDDLE A LITTLE.
IT DIDN'T GO ANY FURTHER THAN THAT...
And I had to initiate the hand holding.
THAT'S JUST BECAUSE RYŪJI-SAN IS SO SHY.
YEAH...
HE'S STILL SO POLITE WITH ME.
AND WHEN I SNUGGLE UP CLOSE, HE GETS EMBAR-RASSED, AND THAT'S THE END OF IT.
BUT IF THIS KEEPS UP, THEN IT WILL NEVER BE ANY DIFFERENT THAN BEFORE WE STARTED DATING.
MAYBE I'M THE ONLY ONE WHO WANTS TO MAKE A DEEPER CONNEC-TION.
WHEN I THINK ABOUT IT, THE ONLY TIME RYŪJI-KUN DID ANYTHING LIKE WHAT A BOYFRIEND WOULD DO...
...WAS JUST THE ONCE, ON THAT ONE DAY.

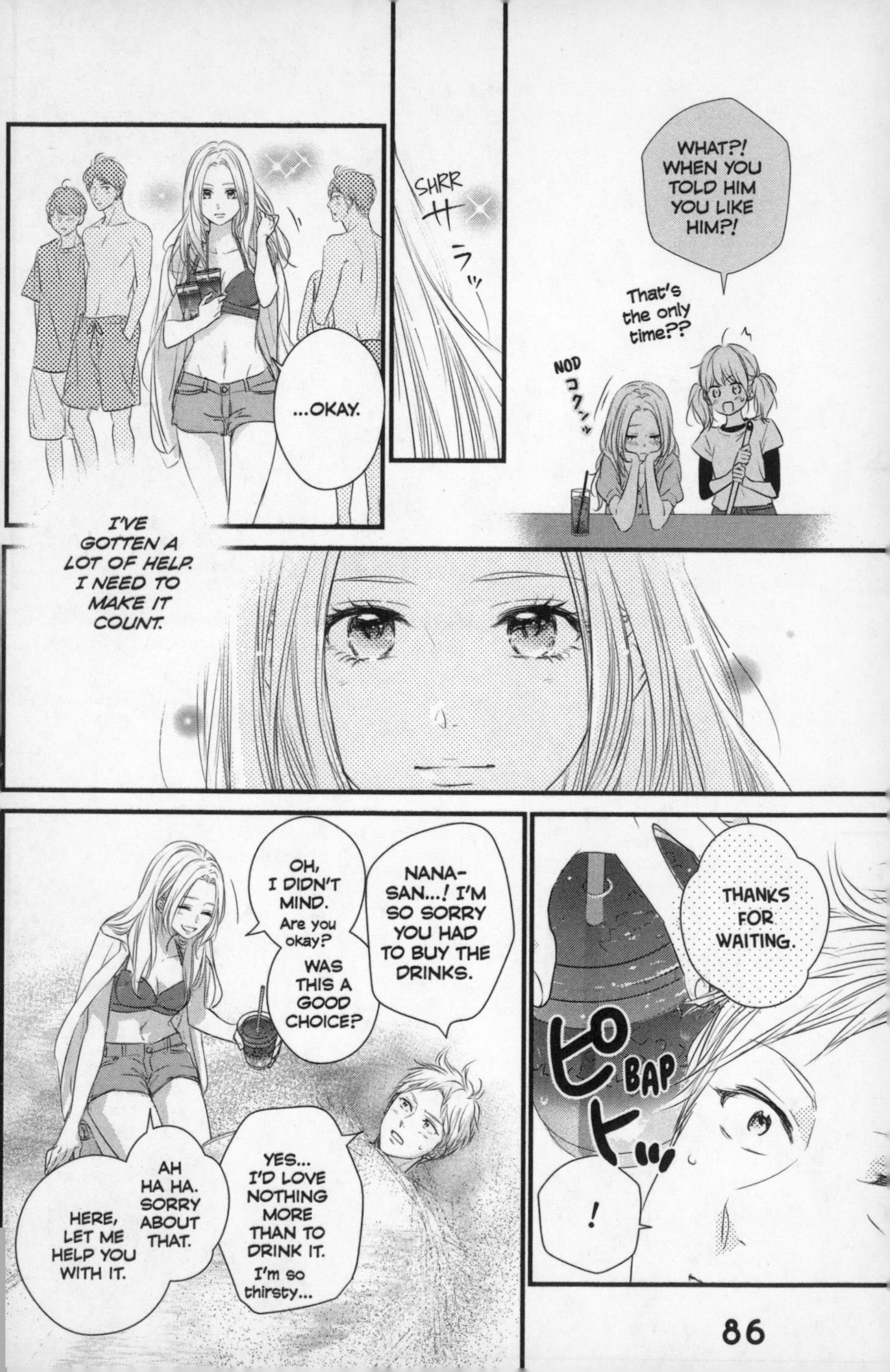
WHAT?! WHEN YOU TOLD HIM YOU LIKE HIM?!
That's the only time??
NOD
コクンッ
SHRR
ラッ
...OKAY.
I'VE GOTTEN A LOT OF HELP. I NEED TO MAKE IT COUNT.
THANKS FOR WAITING.
BAP
ピトッ
!
NANA-SAN...! I'M SO SORRY YOU HAD TO BUY THE DRINKS.
OH, I DIDN'T MIND. Are you okay?
WAS THIS A GOOD CHOICE?
YES... I'D LOVE NOTHING MORE THAN TO DRINK IT. I'm so thirsty...
AH HA HA. SORRY ABOUT THAT.
HERE, LET ME HELP YOU WITH IT.

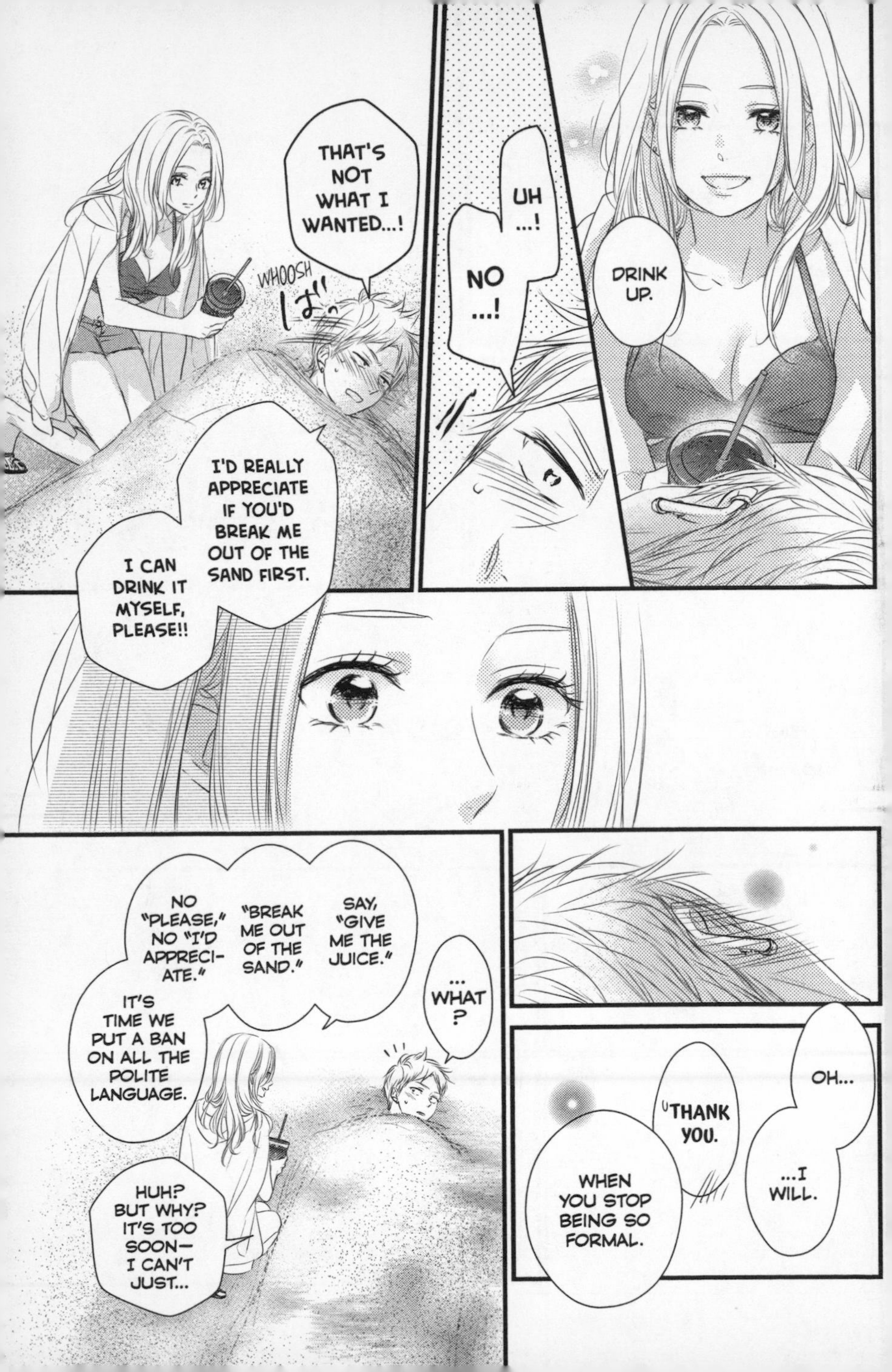
DRINK UP.
UH ...!
NO ...!
THAT'S NOT WHAT I WANTED...!
WHOOSH
I'D REALLY APPRECIATE IF YOU'D BREAK ME OUT OF THE SAND FIRST.
I CAN DRINK IT MYSELF, PLEASE!!
OH...
THANK YOU.
...I WILL.
WHEN YOU STOP BEING SO FORMAL.
SAY, "GIVE ME THE JUICE." "BREAK ME OUT OF THE SAND." NO "PLEASE," NO "I'D APPRECIATE."
... WHAT?
IT'S TIME WE PUT A BAN ON ALL THE POLITE LANGUAGE.
HUH? BUT WHY? IT'S TOO SOON— I CAN'T JUST...

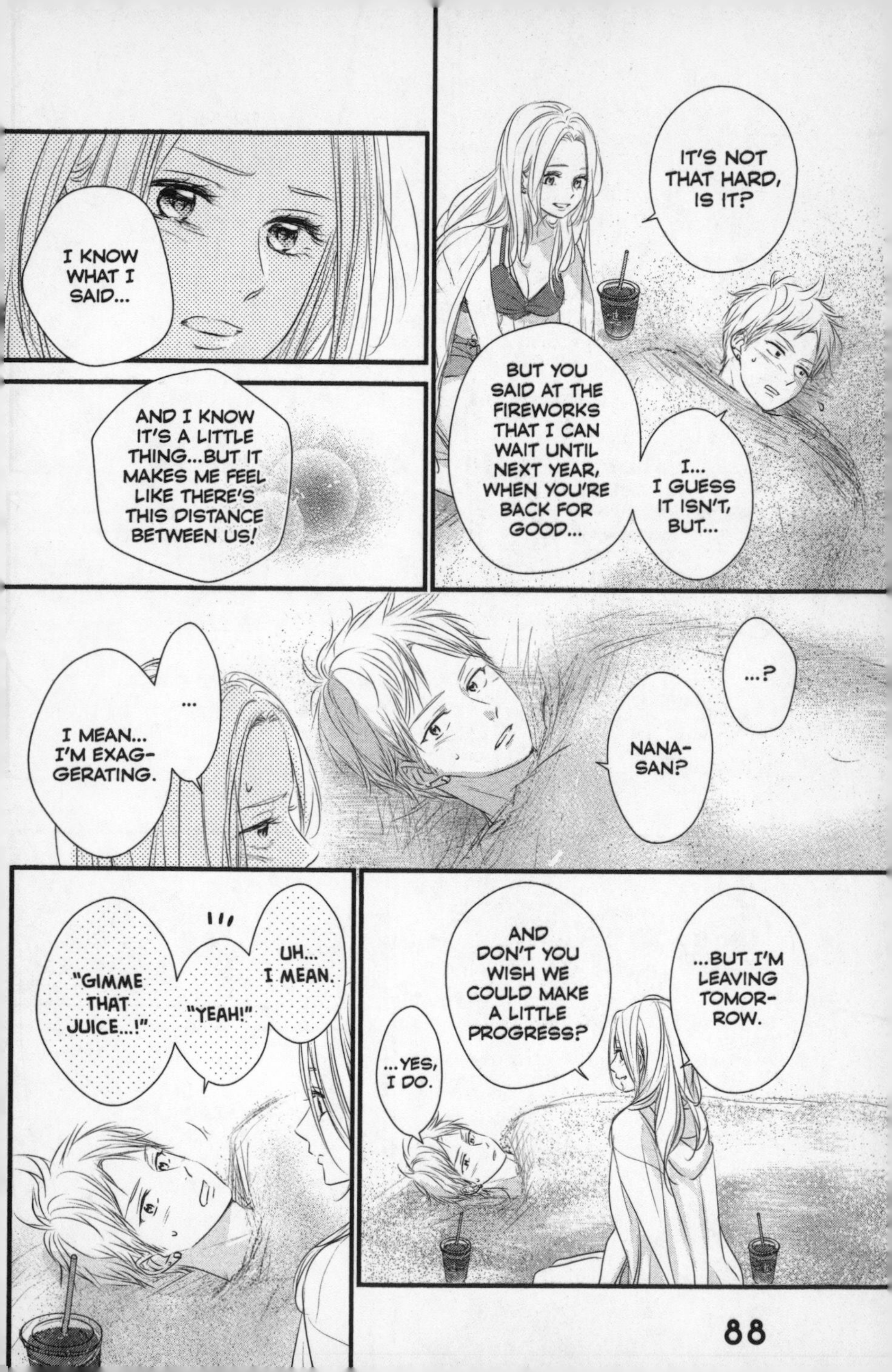
IT'S NOT THAT HARD, IS IT?
I... I GUESS IT ISN'T, BUT...
BUT YOU SAID AT THE FIREWORKS THAT I CAN WAIT UNTIL NEXT YEAR, WHEN YOU'RE BACK FOR GOOD...
I KNOW WHAT I SAID...
AND I KNOW IT'S A LITTLE THING...BUT IT MAKES ME FEEL LIKE THERE'S THIS DISTANCE BETWEEN US!
...?
NANA-SAN?
...
I MEAN... I'M EXAG-GERATING.
...BUT I'M LEAVING TOMOR-ROW.
AND DON'T YOU WISH WE COULD MAKE A LITTLE PROGRESS?
...YES, I DO.
UH... I MEAN.
"YEAH!"
"GIMME THAT JUICE...!"

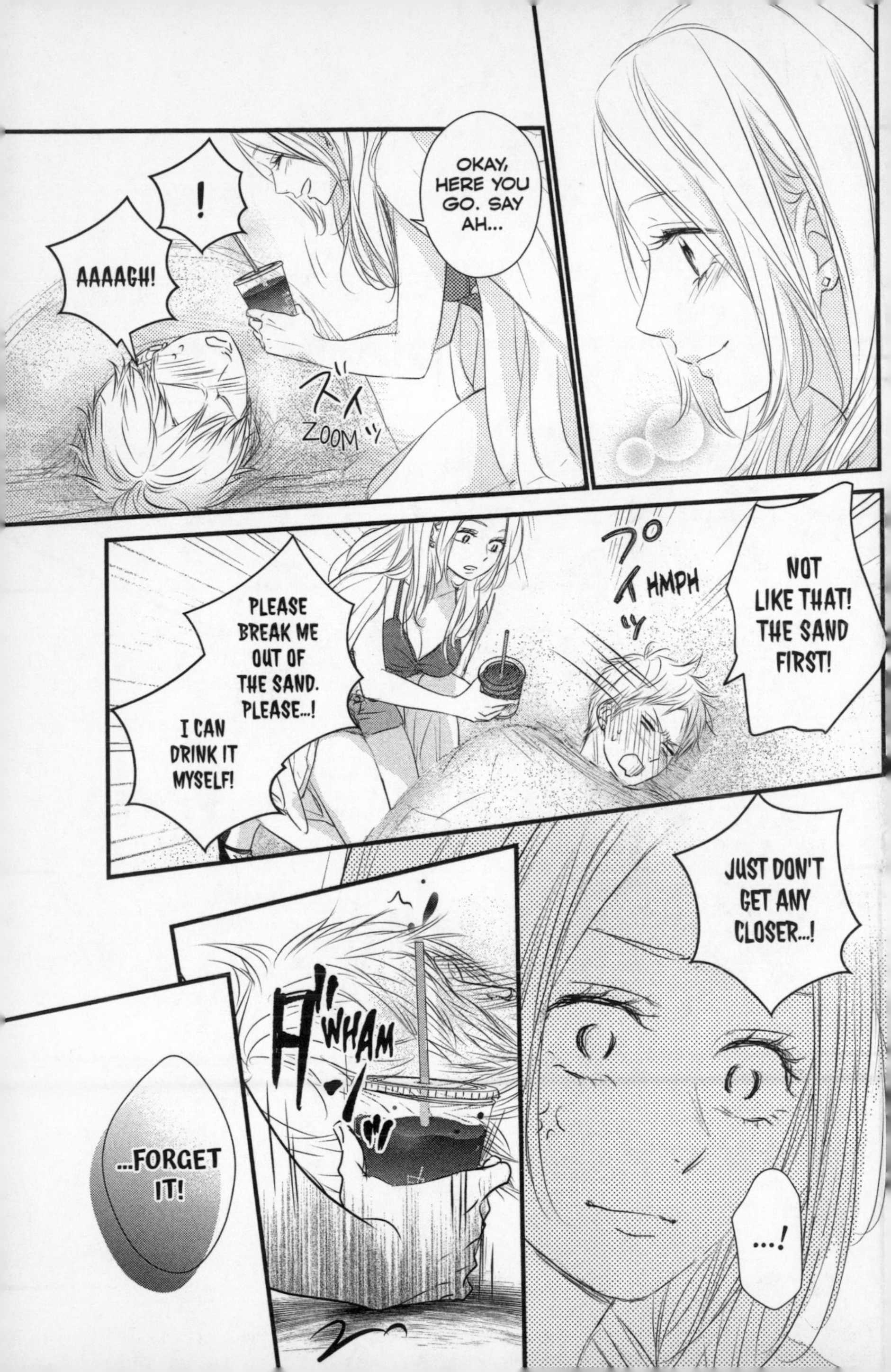
OKAY, HERE YOU GO. SAY AH...
!
AAAAGH!
ZOOM
NOT LIKE THAT! THE SAND FIRST!
HMPH
PLEASE BREAK ME OUT OF THE SAND. PLEASE...!
I CAN DRINK IT MYSELF!
JUST DON'T GET ANY CLOSER...!
...!
WHAM
...FORGET IT!

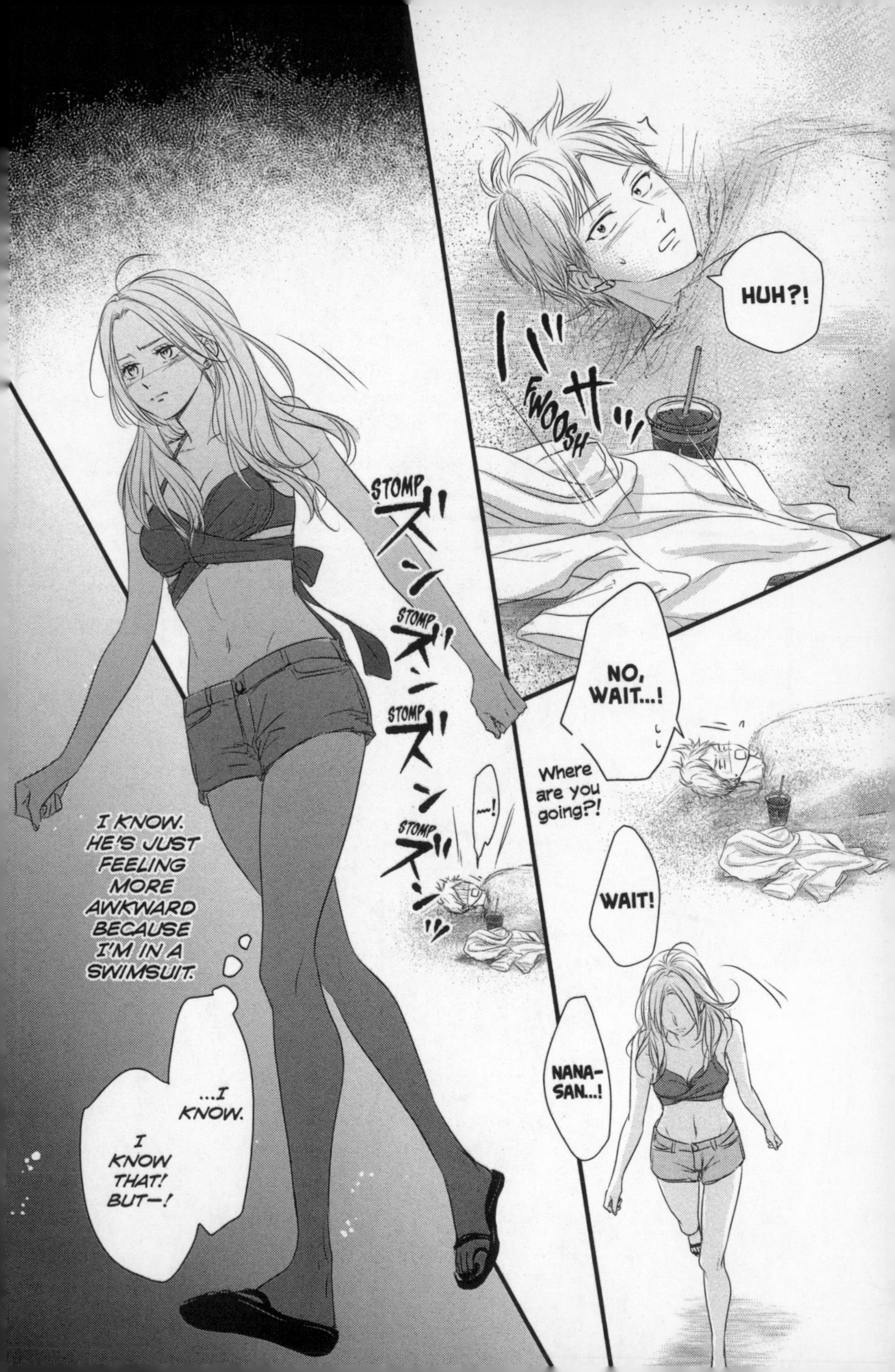
HUH?!
FWOOSH
NO, WAIT...!
Where are you going?!
WAIT!
NANA-SAN...!
STOMP
STOMP
STOMP
STOMP
—!
I KNOW. HE'S JUST FEELING MORE AWKWARD BECAUSE I'M IN A SWIMSUIT.
...I KNOW.
I KNOW THAT! BUT—!

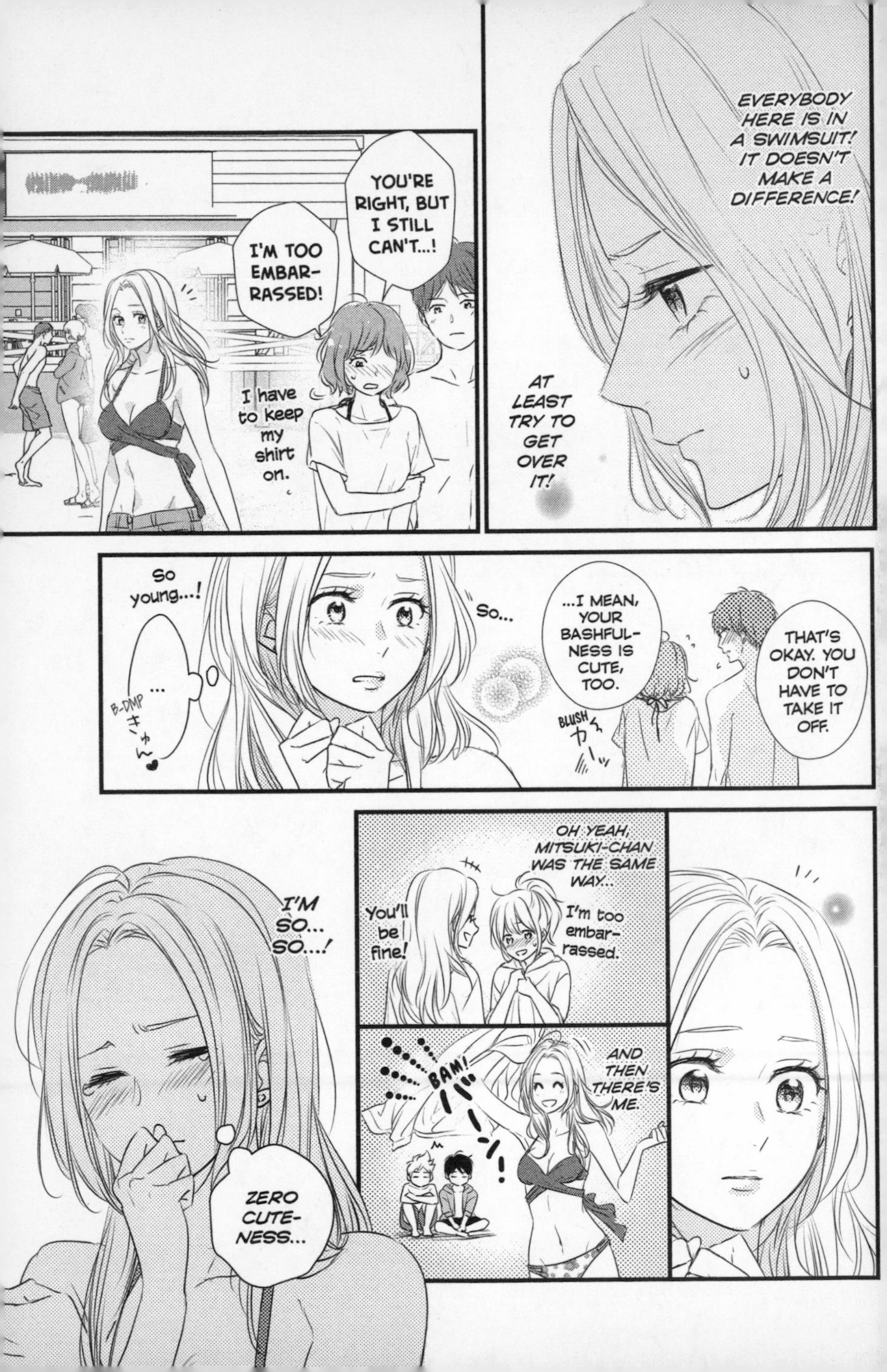
EVERYBODY HERE IS IN A SWIMSUIT! IT DOESN'T MAKE A DIFFERENCE!
AT LEAST TRY TO GET OVER IT!
YOU'RE RIGHT, BUT I STILL CAN'T...!
I'M TOO EMBARRASSED!
I have to keep my shirt on.
THAT'S OKAY. YOU DON'T HAVE TO TAKE IT OFF.
BLUSH
カァッ
...I MEAN, YOUR BASHFULNESS IS CUTE, TOO.
So...
So young...!
...
B-DMP
きゅん
OH YEAH, MITSUKI-CHAN WAS THE SAME WAY...
I'm too embarrassed.
You'll be fine!
AND THEN THERE'S ME.
BAM!
バーン!
I'M SO... SO...!
ZERO CUTENESS...

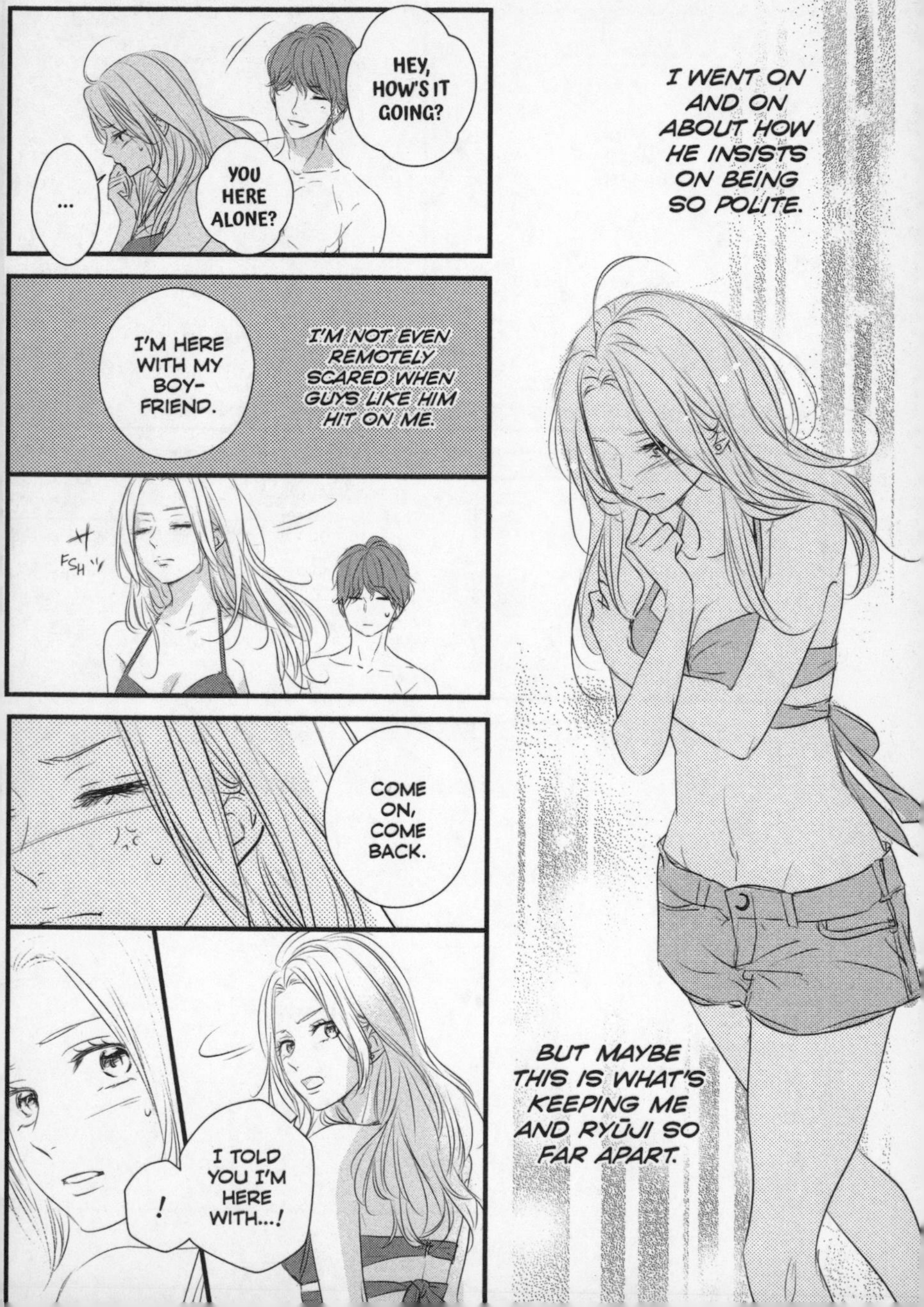
I WENT ON AND ON ABOUT HOW HE INSISTS ON BEING SO POLITE.
BUT MAYBE THIS IS WHAT'S KEEPING ME AND RYŪJI SO FAR APART.
HEY, HOW'S IT GOING?
YOU HERE ALONE?
...
I'M NOT EVEN REMOTELY SCARED WHEN GUYS LIKE HIM HIT ON ME.
I'M HERE WITH MY BOY-FRIEND.
FSH
COME ON, COME BACK.
I TOLD YOU I'M HERE WITH...!
!

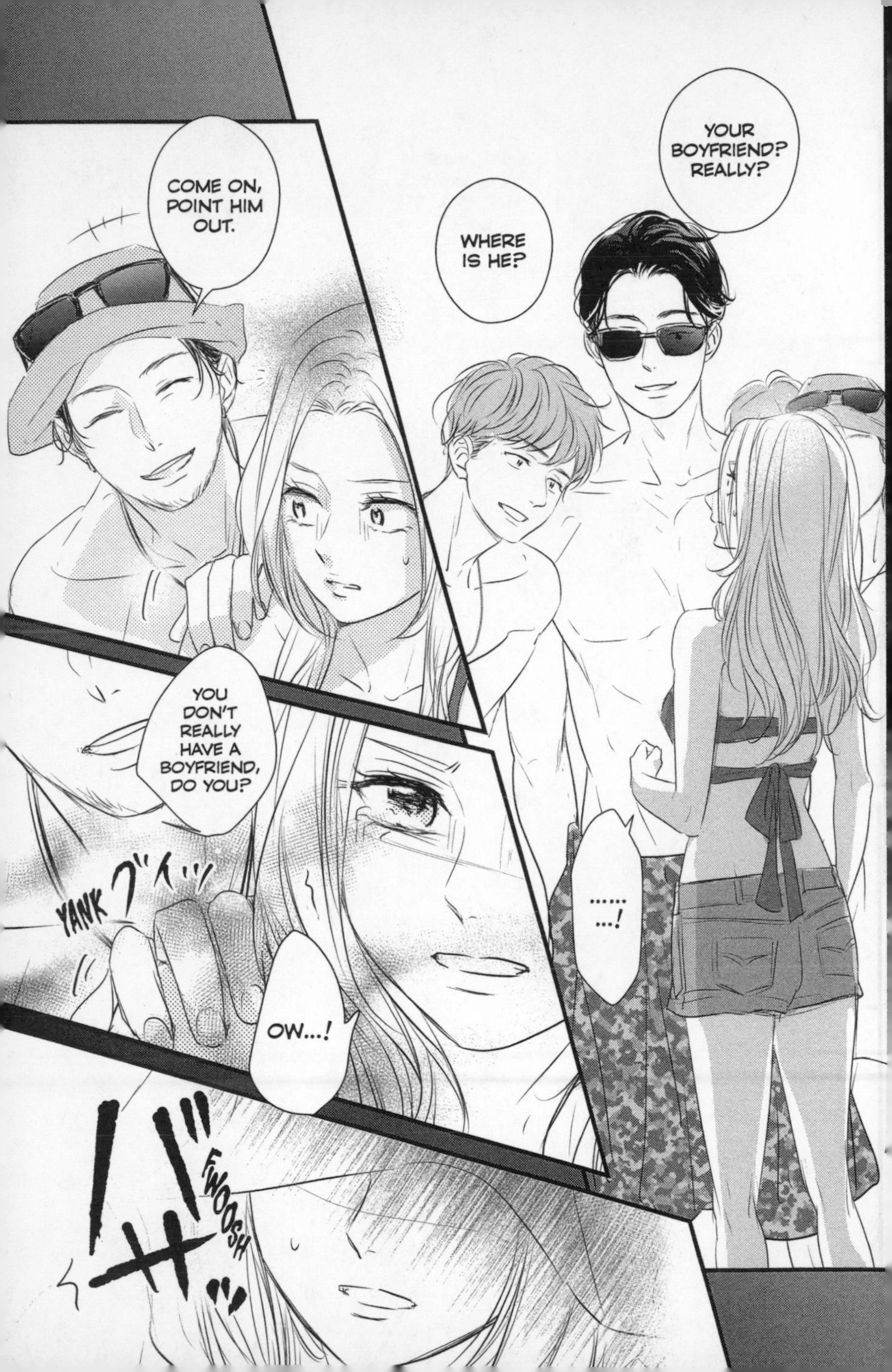
YOUR BOYFRIEND? REALLY?
WHERE IS HE?
…… …!
COME ON, POINT HIM OUT.
YOU DON'T REALLY HAVE A BOYFRIEND, DO YOU?
YANK グイッ
OW…!
FWOOSH バサッ

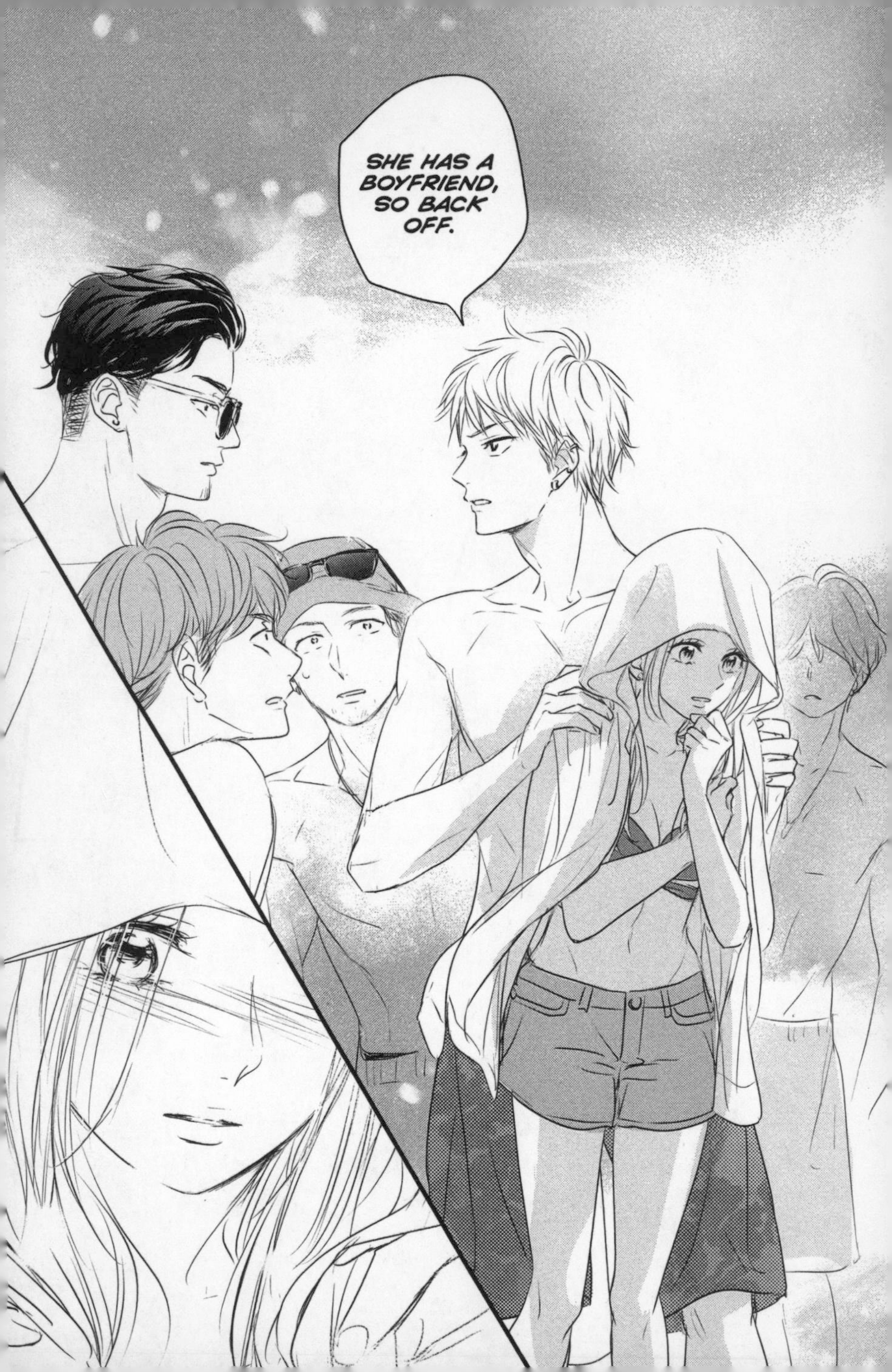
SHE HAS A BOYFRIEND, SO BACK OFF.

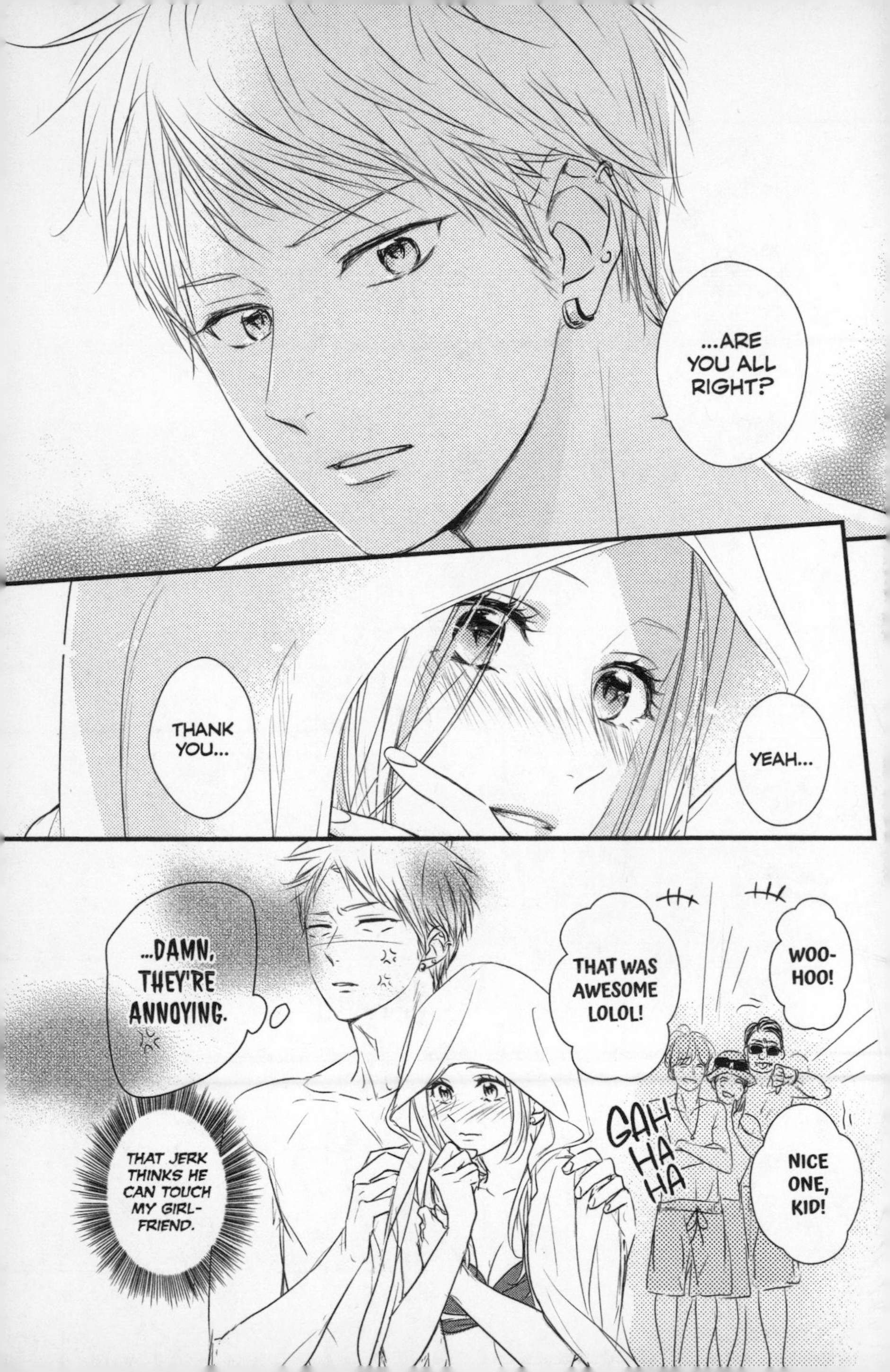
...ARE YOU ALL RIGHT?
YEAH...
THANK YOU...
WOO-HOO!
THAT WAS AWESOME LOLOL!
...DAMN, THEY'RE ANNOYING.
NICE ONE, KID!
GAH HA HA
THAT JERK THINKS HE CAN TOUCH MY GIRL-FRIEND.

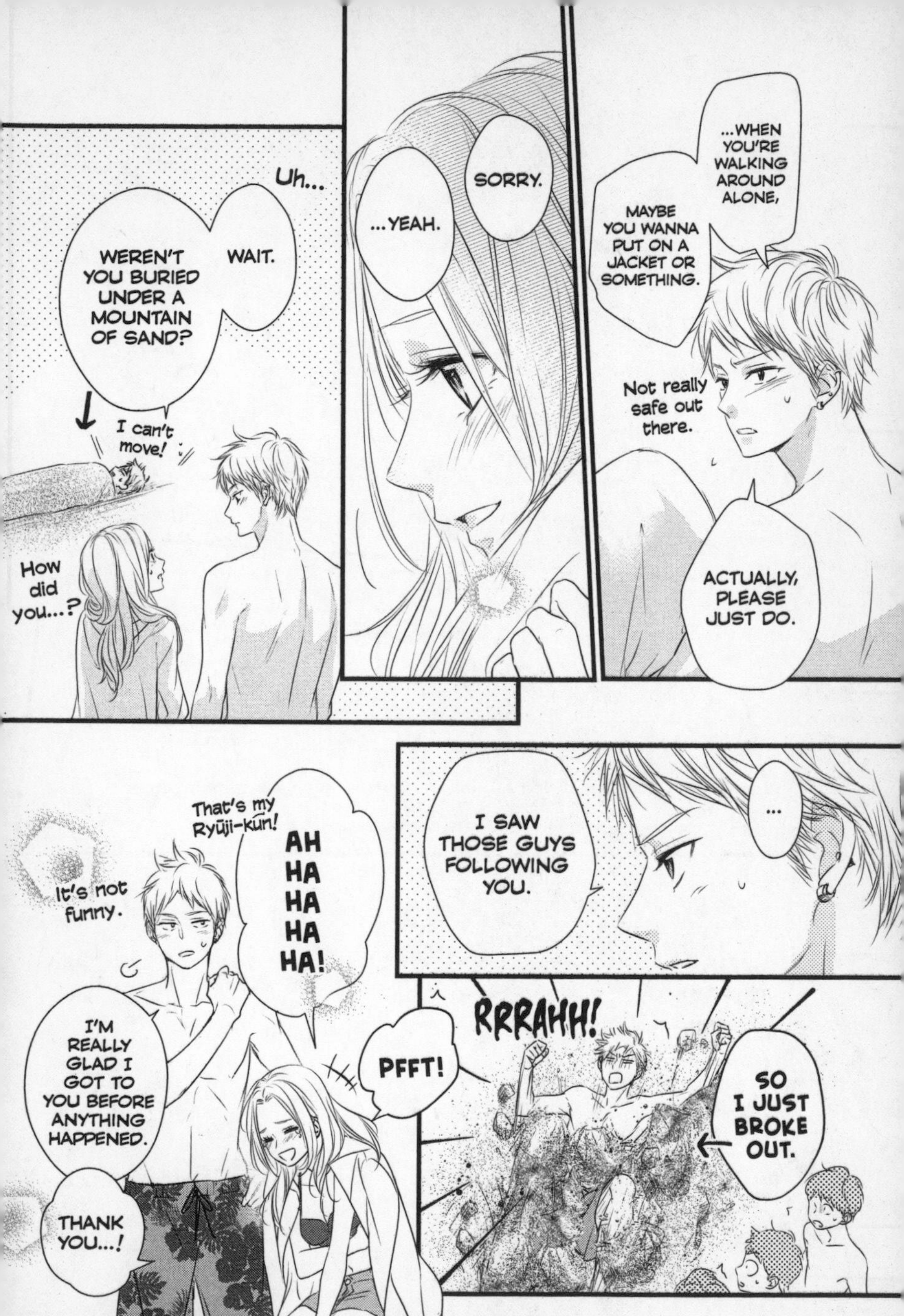
...WHEN YOU'RE WALKING AROUND ALONE,
MAYBE YOU WANNA PUT ON A JACKET OR SOMETHING.
Not really safe out there.
ACTUALLY, PLEASE JUST DO.
SORRY.
...YEAH.
Uh...
WAIT.
WEREN'T YOU BURIED UNDER A MOUNTAIN OF SAND?
I can't move!
How did you...?
...
I SAW THOSE GUYS FOLLOWING YOU.
SO I JUST BROKE OUT.
RRRAHH!
PFFT!
AH HA HA HA HA!
That's my Ryūji-kun!
It's not funny.
I'M REALLY GLAD I GOT TO YOU BEFORE ANYTHING HAPPENED.
THANK YOU...!

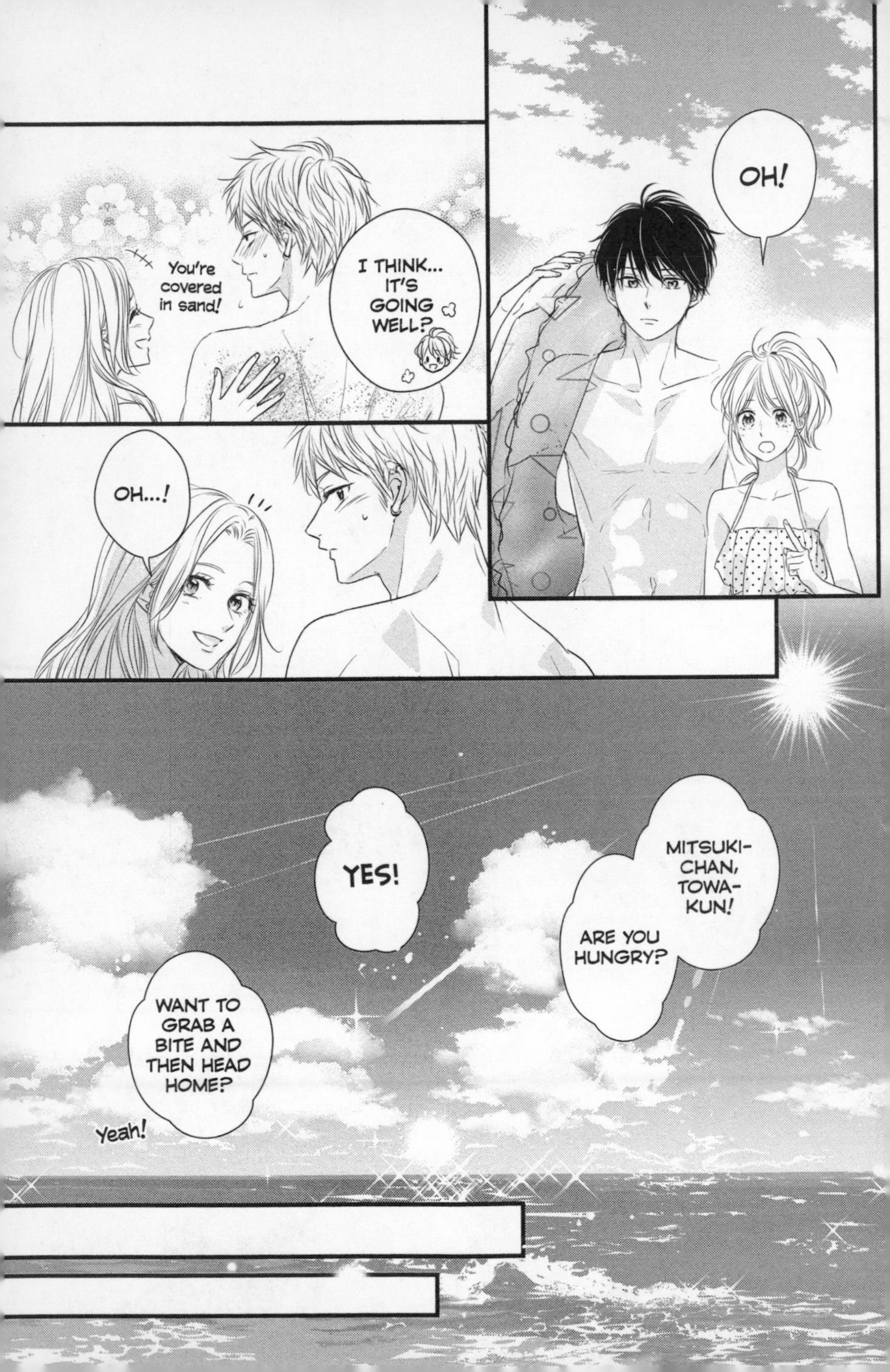
OH!
I THINK... IT'S GOING WELL?
You're covered in sand!
OH...!
MITSUKI-CHAN, TOWA-KUN!
ARE YOU HUNGRY?
YES!
WANT TO GRAB A BITE AND THEN HEAD HOME?
Yeah!

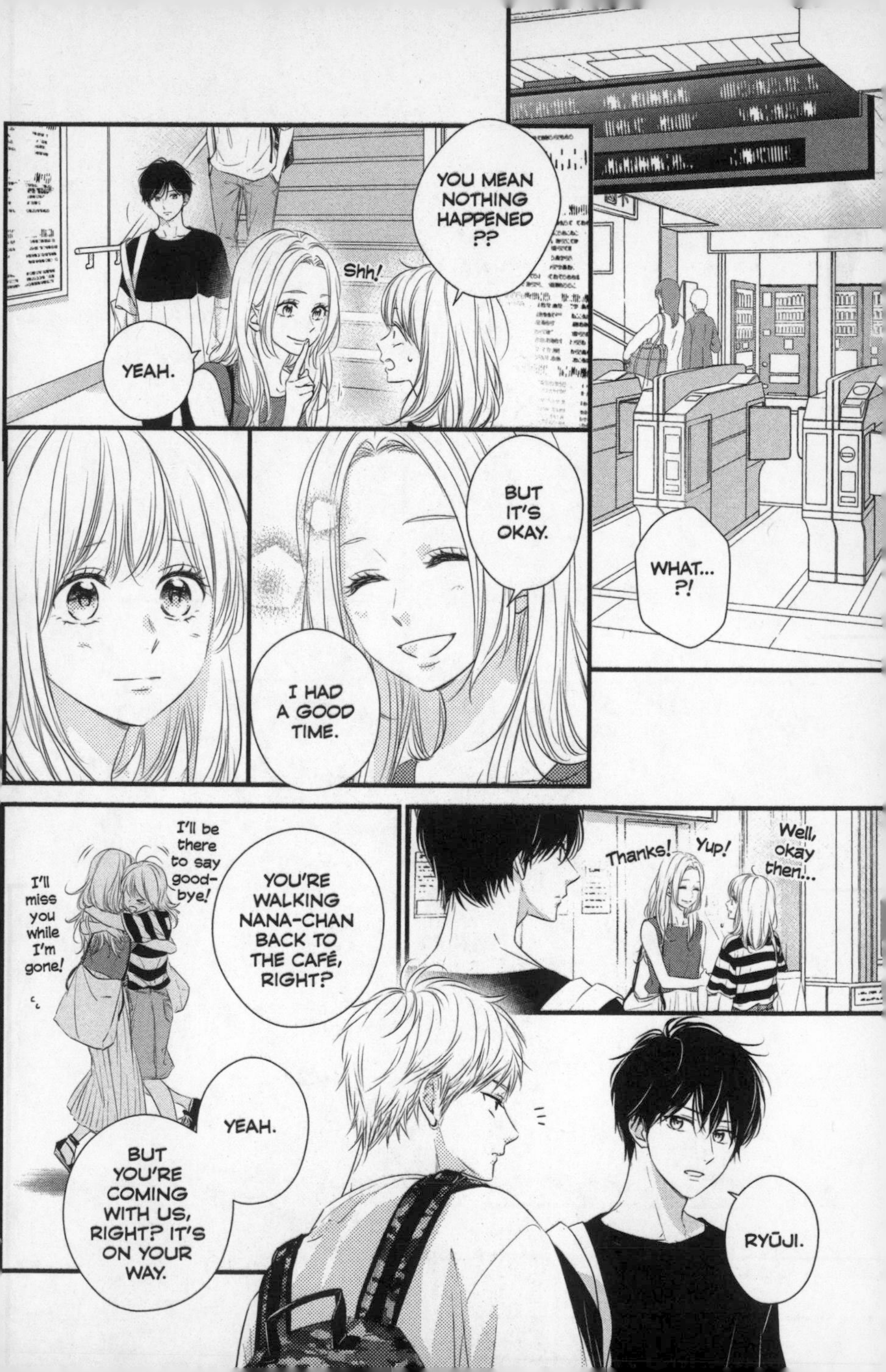
WHAT... ?!
YOU MEAN NOTHING HAPPENED ??
Shh!
YEAH.
BUT IT'S OKAY.
I HAD A GOOD TIME.
Well, okay then...
Yup!
Thanks!
YOU'RE WALKING NANA-CHAN BACK TO THE CAFÉ, RIGHT?
I'll be there to say good-bye!
I'll miss you while I'm gone!
RYŪJI.
YEAH.
BUT YOU'RE COMING WITH US, RIGHT? IT'S ON YOUR WAY.

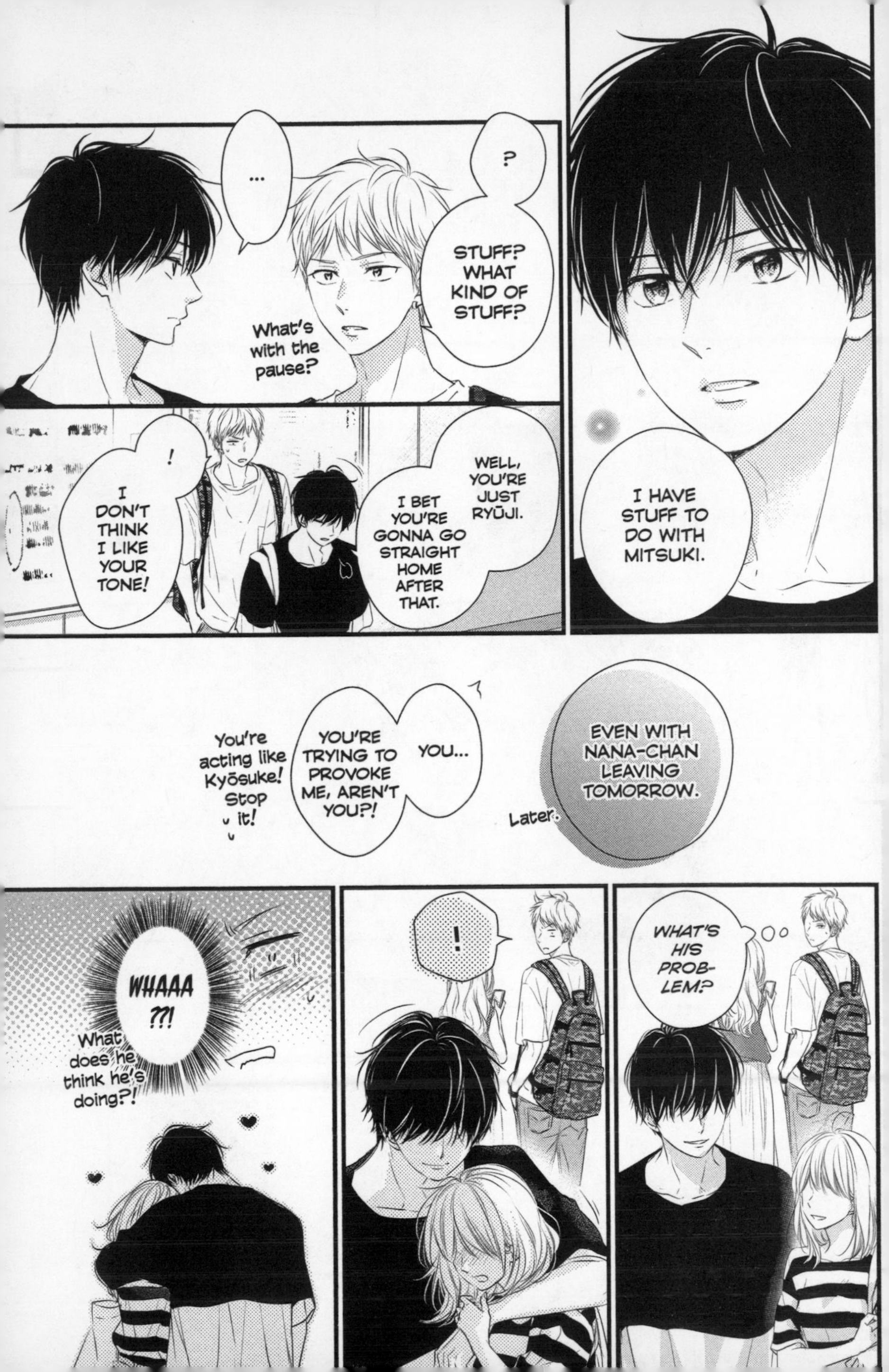
I HAVE STUFF TO DO WITH MITSUKI.
?
STUFF? WHAT KIND OF STUFF?
...
What's with the pause?
WELL, YOU'RE JUST RYŪJI.
I BET YOU'RE GONNA GO STRAIGHT HOME AFTER THAT.
!
I DON'T THINK I LIKE YOUR TONE!
EVEN WITH NANA-CHAN LEAVING TOMORROW.
Later.
YOU...
YOU'RE TRYING TO PROVOKE ME, AREN'T YOU?!
You're acting like Kyōsuke! Stop it!
WHAT'S HIS PROB-LEM?
!
WHAAA ??!
What does he think he's doing?!

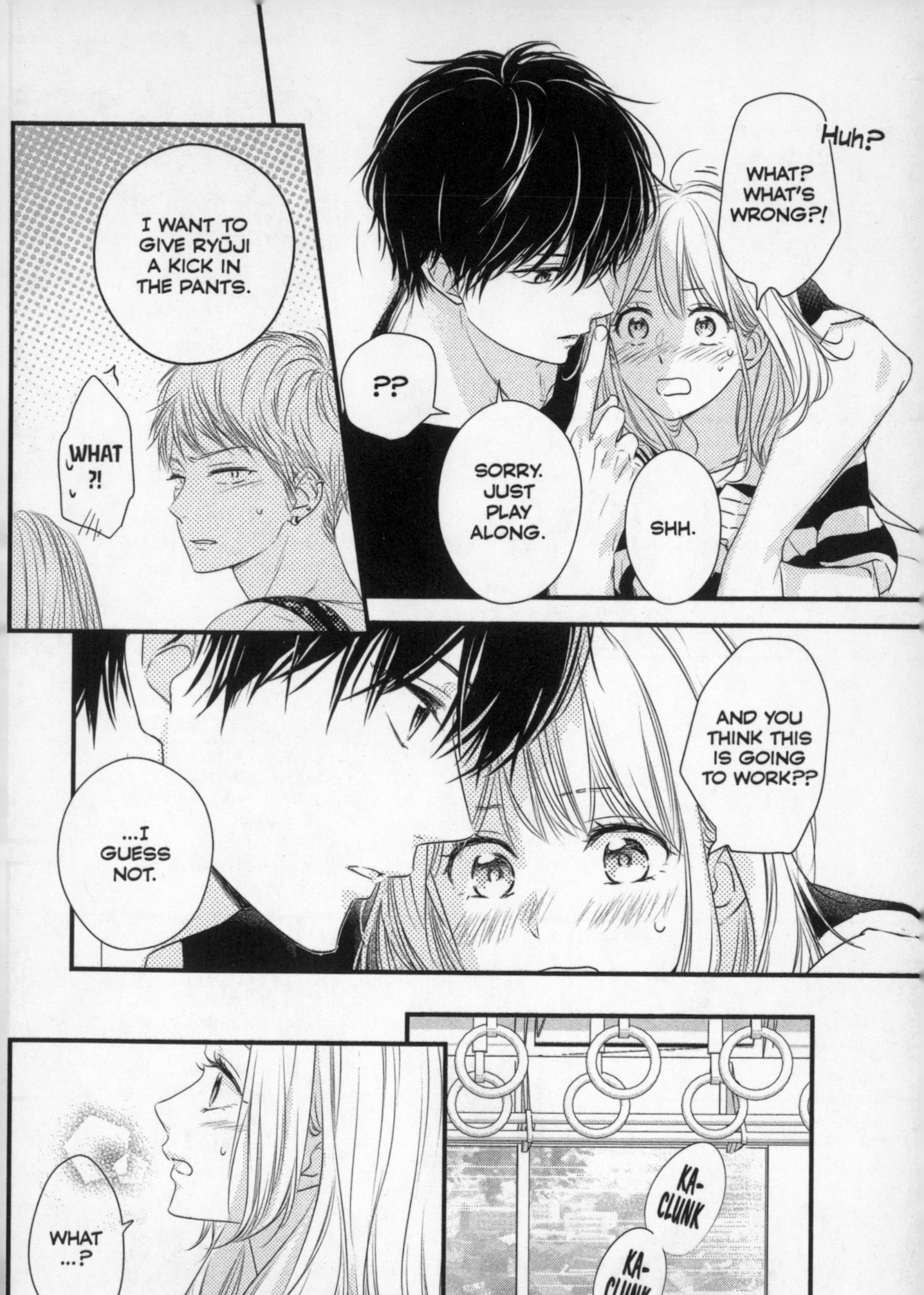
Huh?
WHAT? WHAT'S WRONG?!
??
SHH.
SORRY. JUST PLAY ALONG.
I WANT TO GIVE RYŪJI A KICK IN THE PANTS.
WHAT ?!
AND YOU THINK THIS IS GOING TO WORK??
...I GUESS NOT.
KA-CLUNK
KA-CLUNK
WHAT ...?

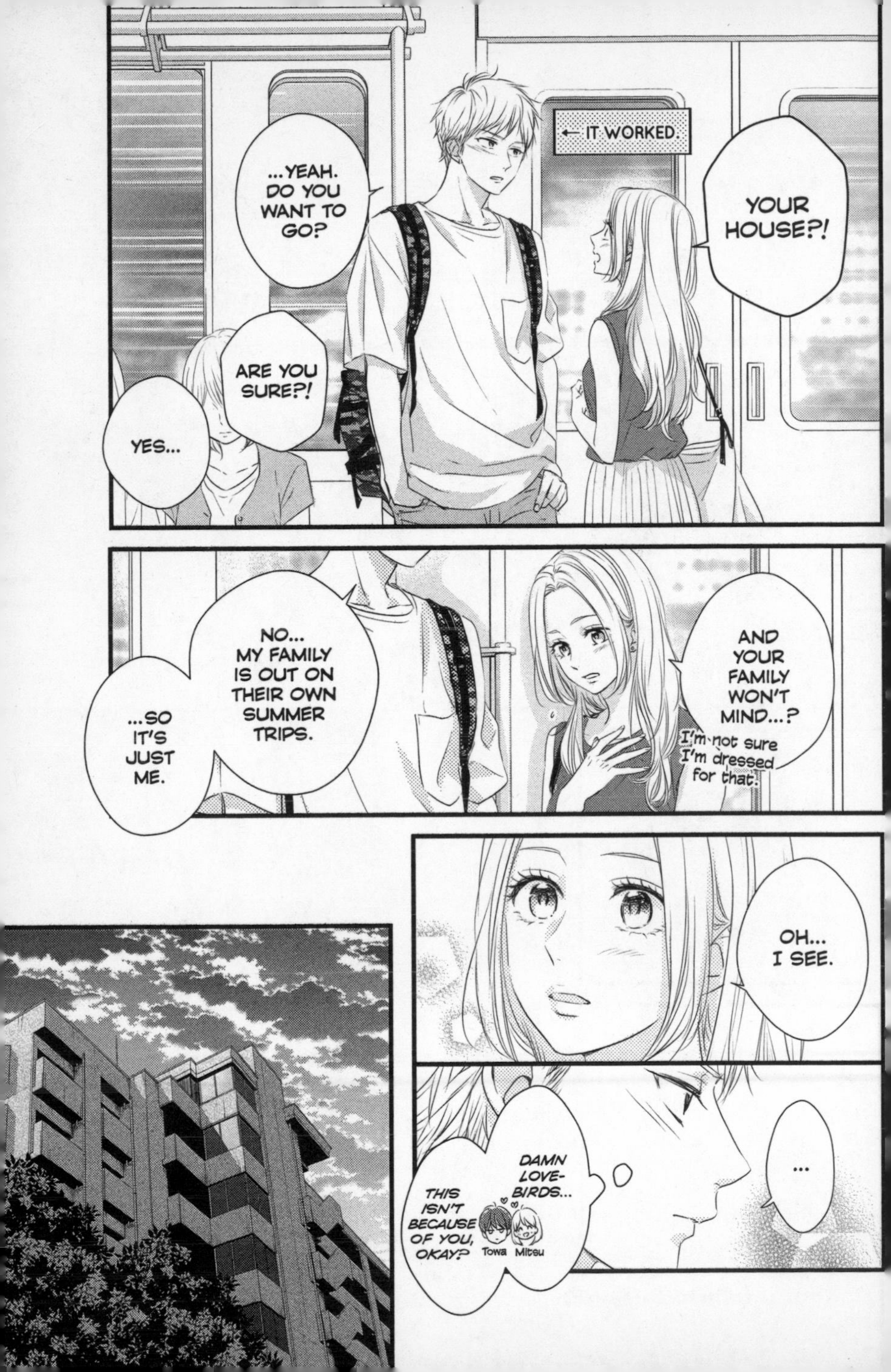
YOUR HOUSE?!
← IT WORKED.
...YEAH. DO YOU WANT TO GO?
ARE YOU SURE?!
YES...
AND YOUR FAMILY WON'T MIND...?
I'm not sure I'm dressed for that.
NO... MY FAMILY IS OUT ON THEIR OWN SUMMER TRIPS.
...SO IT'S JUST ME.
OH... I SEE.
...
DAMN LOVE-BIRDS...
Mitsu
THIS ISN'T BECAUSE OF YOU, OKAY?
Towa

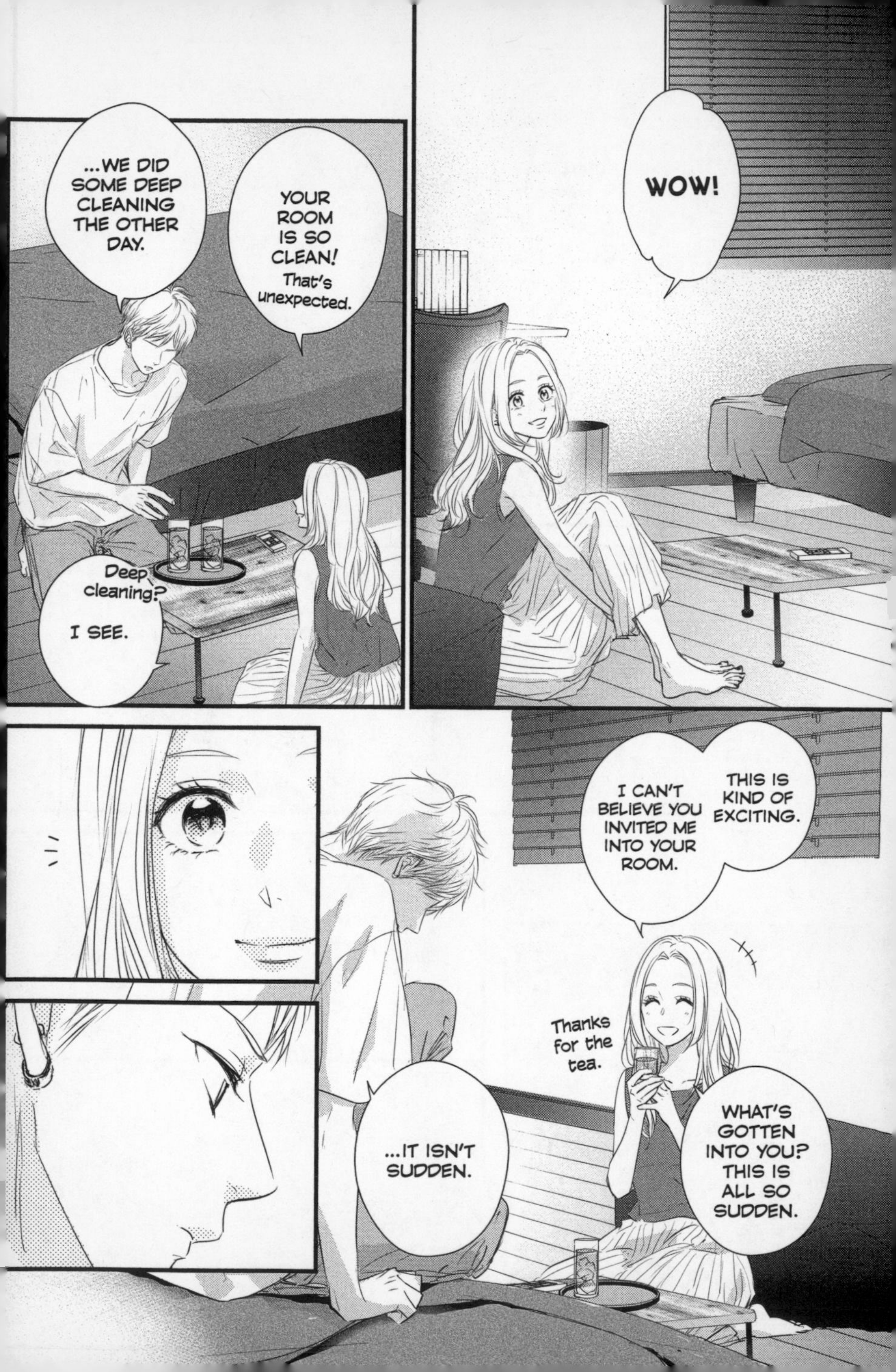
WOW!
YOUR ROOM IS SO CLEAN! That's unexpected.
...WE DID SOME DEEP CLEANING THE OTHER DAY.
Deep cleaning? I SEE.
THIS IS KIND OF EXCITING.
I CAN'T BELIEVE YOU INVITED ME INTO YOUR ROOM.
Thanks for the tea.
WHAT'S GOTTEN INTO YOU? THIS IS ALL SO SUDDEN.
...IT ISN'T SUDDEN.

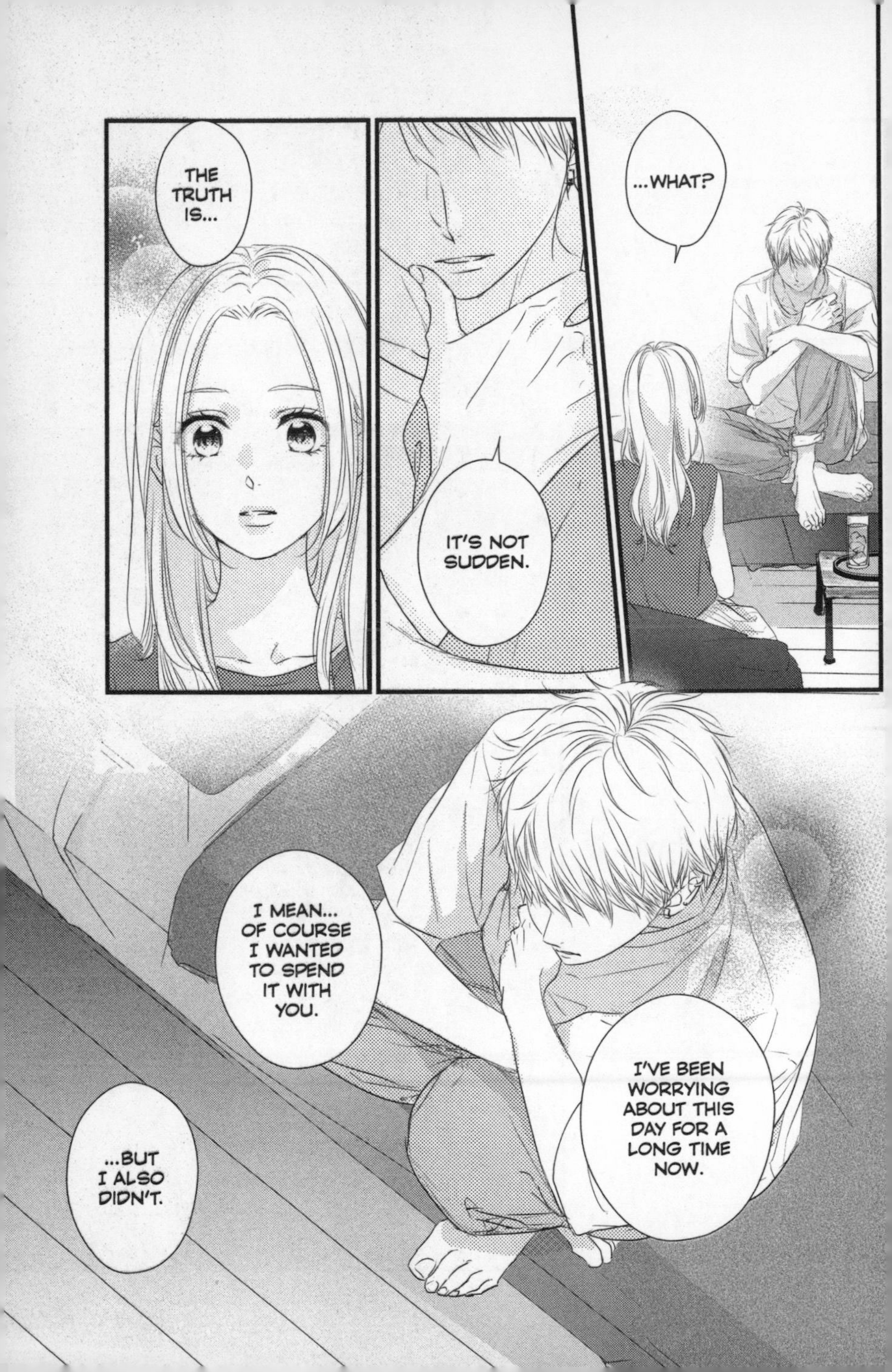
...WHAT?
IT'S NOT SUDDEN.
THE TRUTH IS...
I'VE BEEN WORRYING ABOUT THIS DAY FOR A LONG TIME NOW.
I MEAN... OF COURSE I WANTED TO SPEND IT WITH YOU.
...BUT I ALSO DIDN'T.

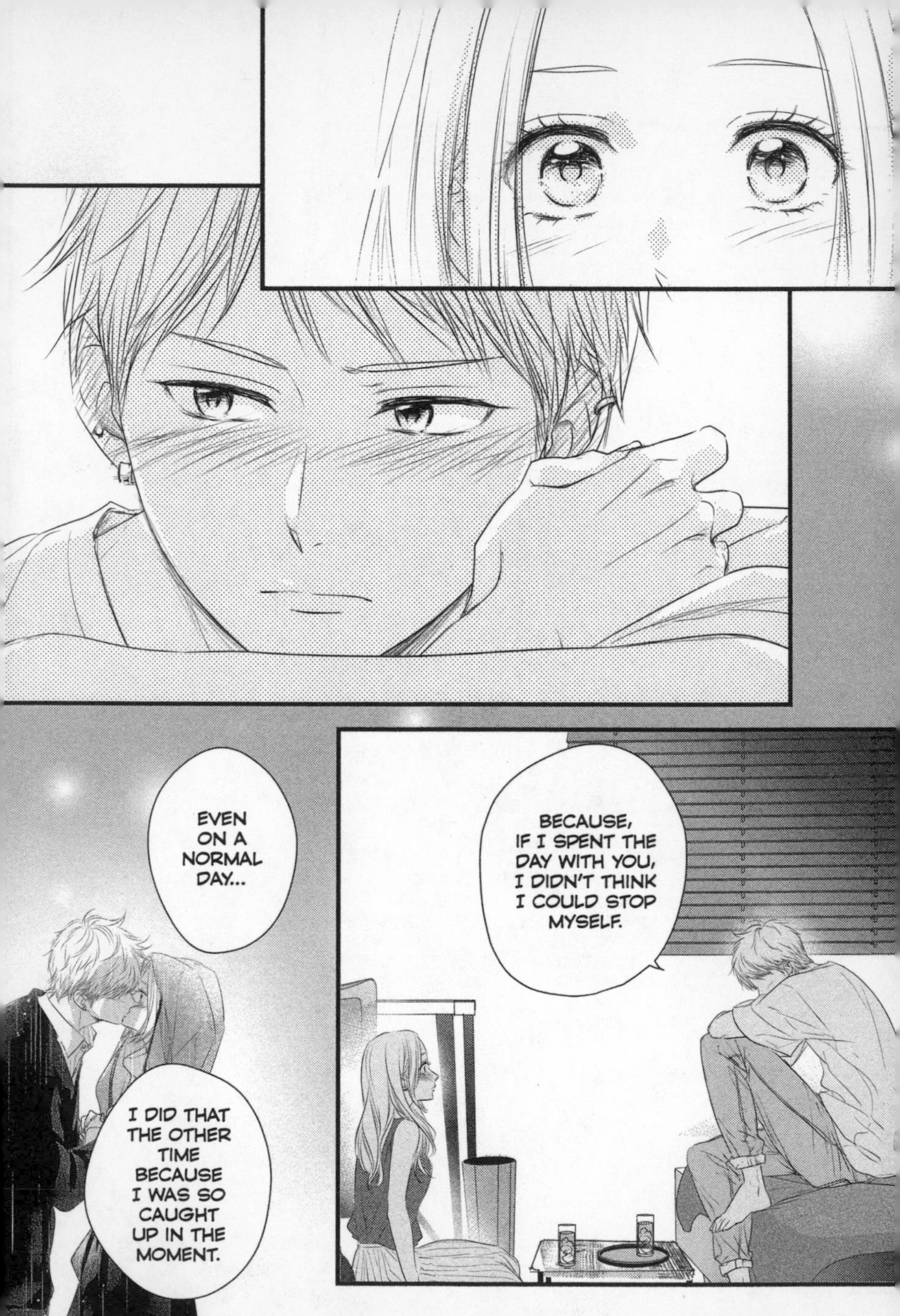
BECAUSE, IF I SPENT THE DAY WITH YOU, I DIDN'T THINK I COULD STOP MYSELF.
EVEN ON A NORMAL DAY...
I DID THAT THE OTHER TIME BECAUSE I WAS SO CAUGHT UP IN THE MOMENT.

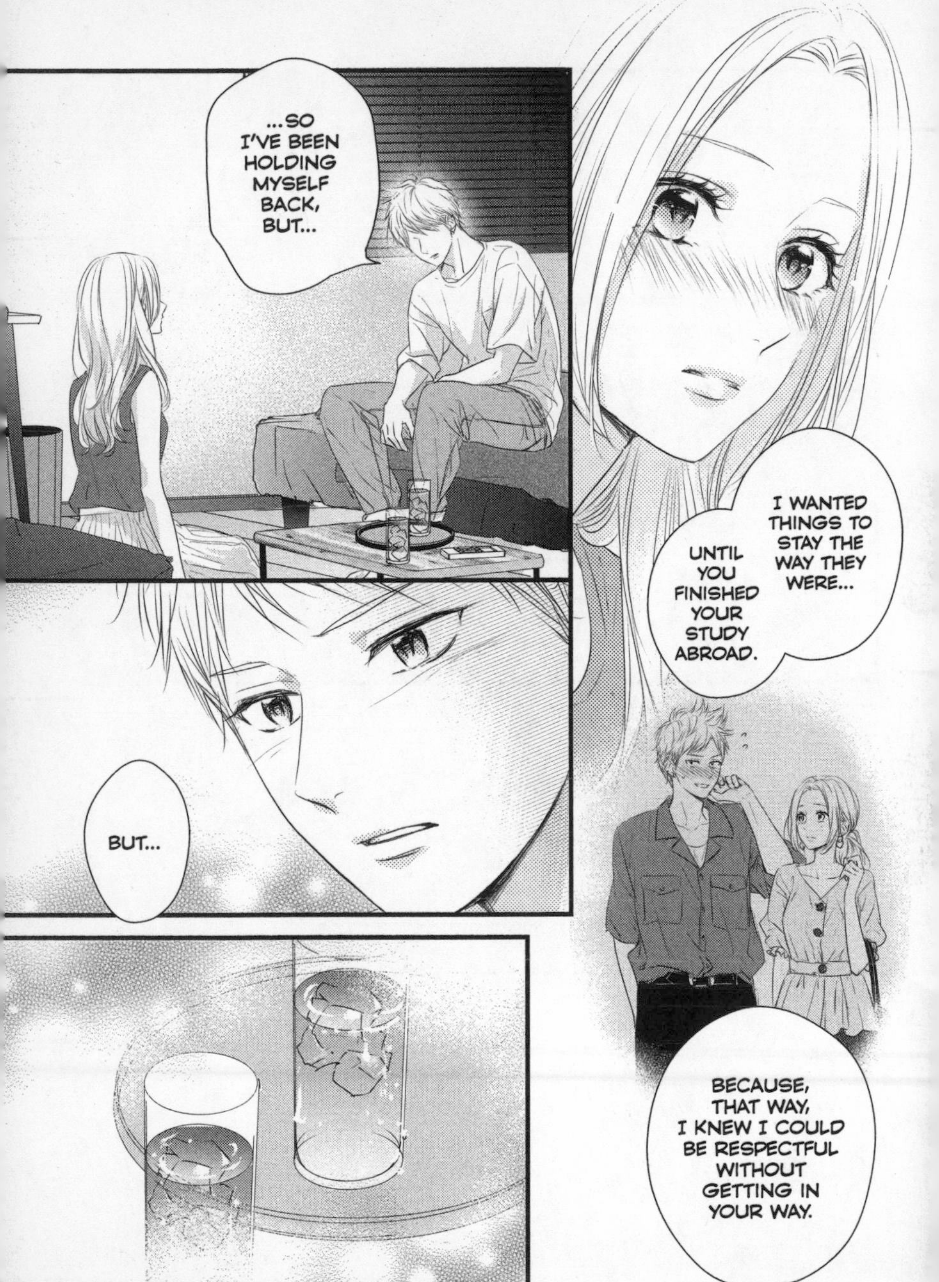
I WANTED THINGS TO STAY THE WAY THEY WERE...
UNTIL YOU FINISHED YOUR STUDY ABROAD.
BECAUSE, THAT WAY, I KNEW I COULD BE RESPECTFUL WITHOUT GETTING IN YOUR WAY.
...SO I'VE BEEN HOLDING MYSELF BACK, BUT...
BUT...

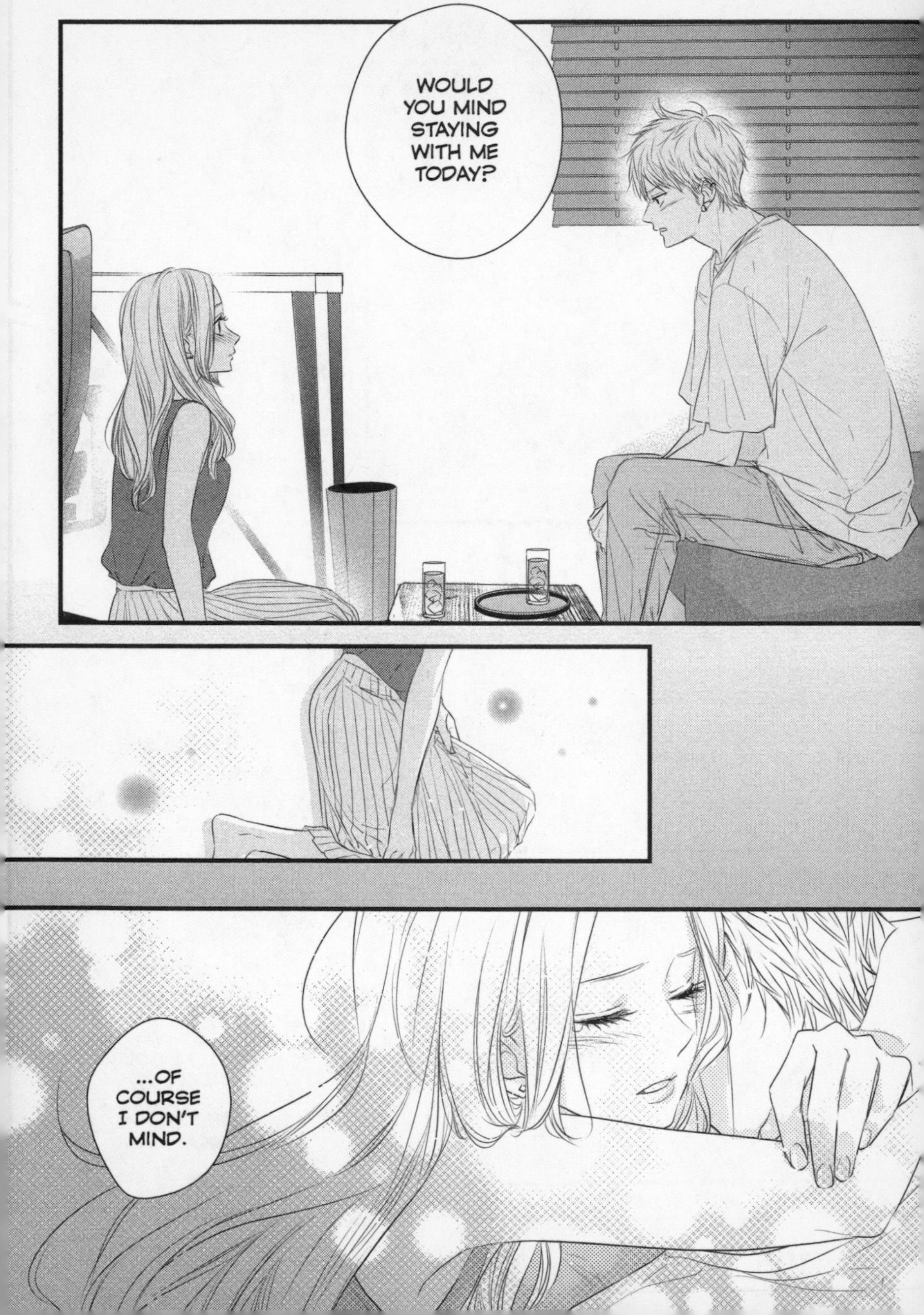
WOULD YOU MIND STAYING WITH ME TODAY?
...OF COURSE I DON'T MIND.

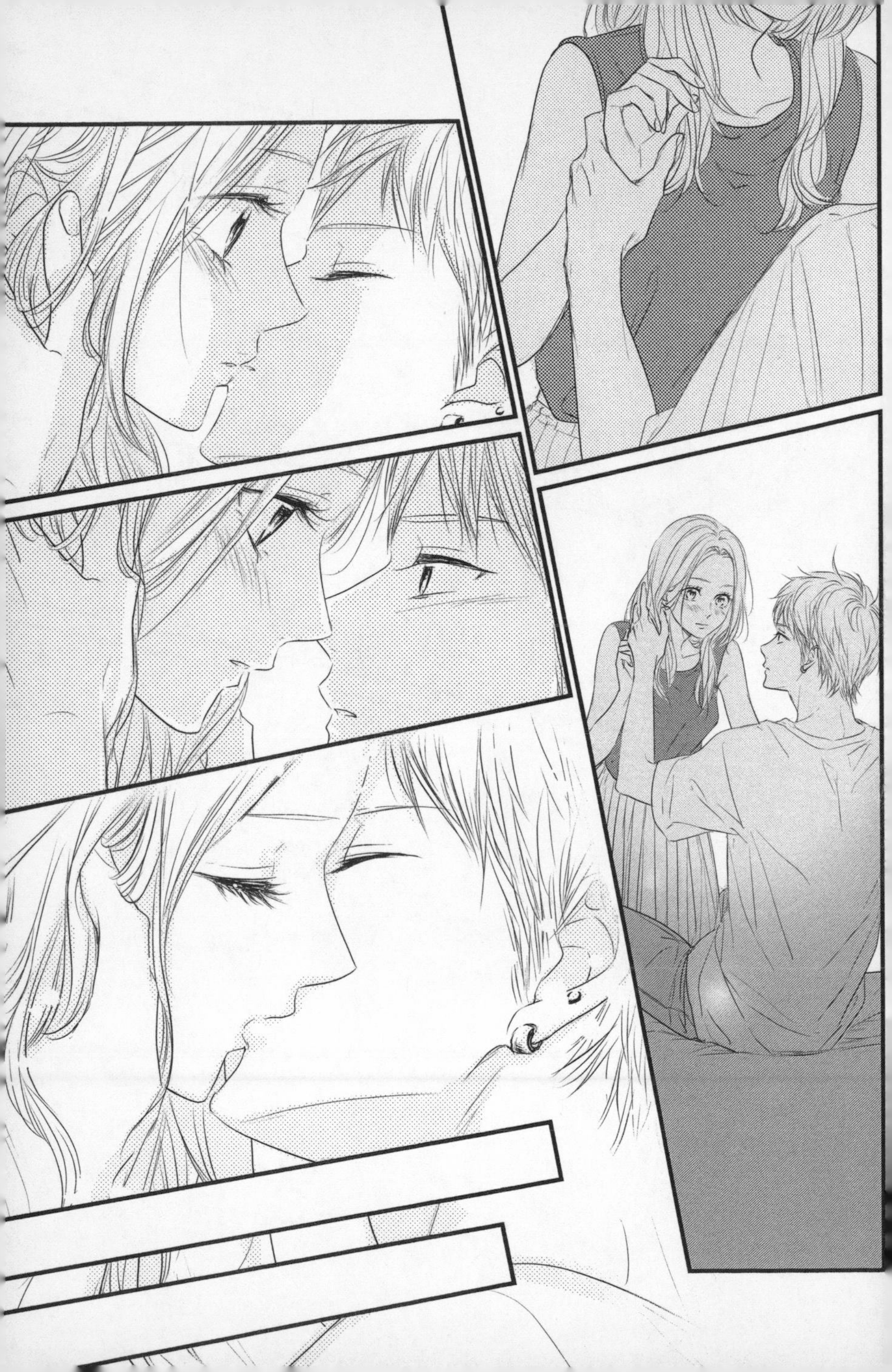

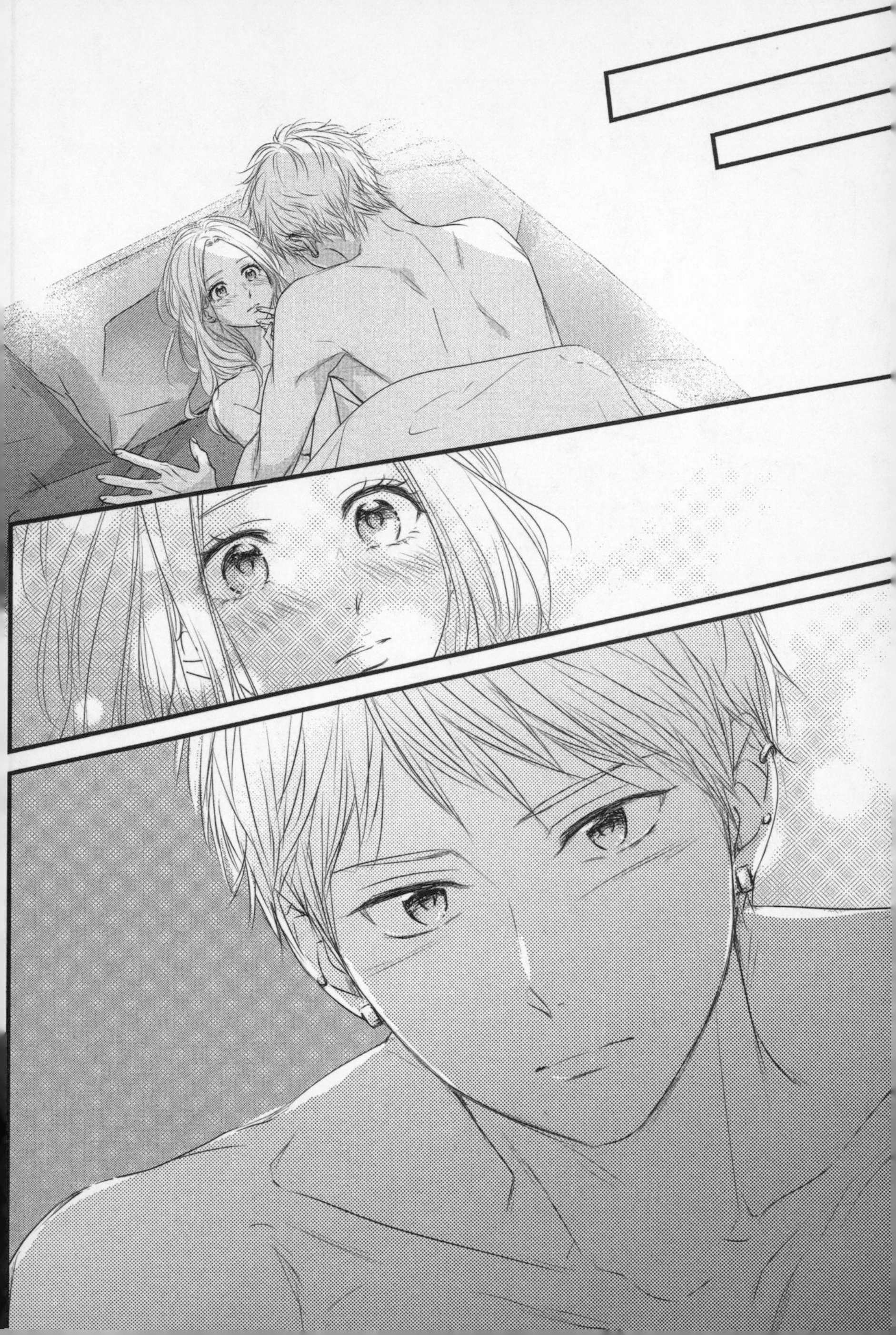

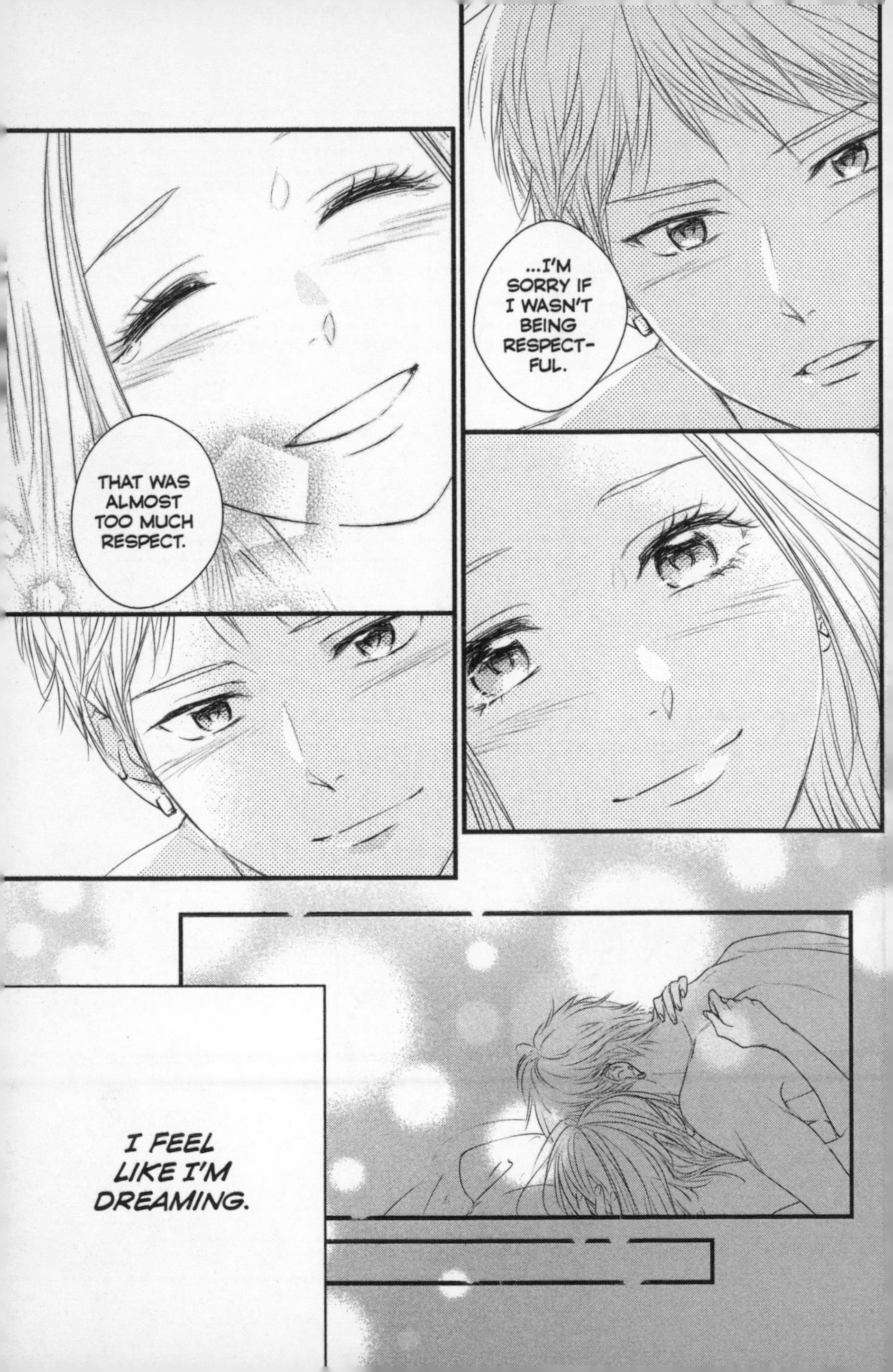
...I'M SORRY IF I WASN'T BEING RESPECT-FUL.
THAT WAS ALMOST TOO MUCH RESPECT.
I FEEL LIKE I'M DREAMING.

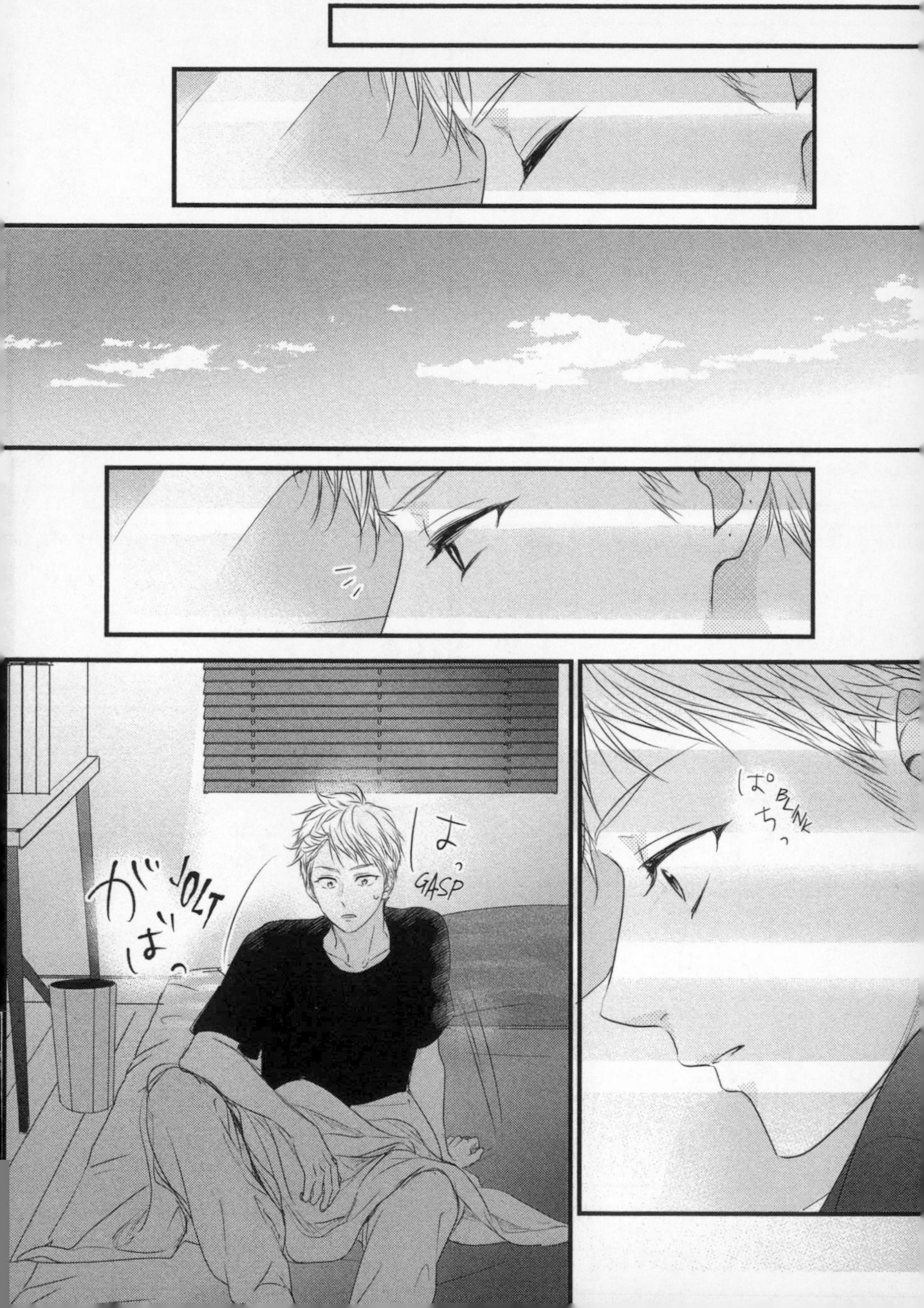
ぱちっ
BLINK
はっ
GASP
がばっ
JOLT

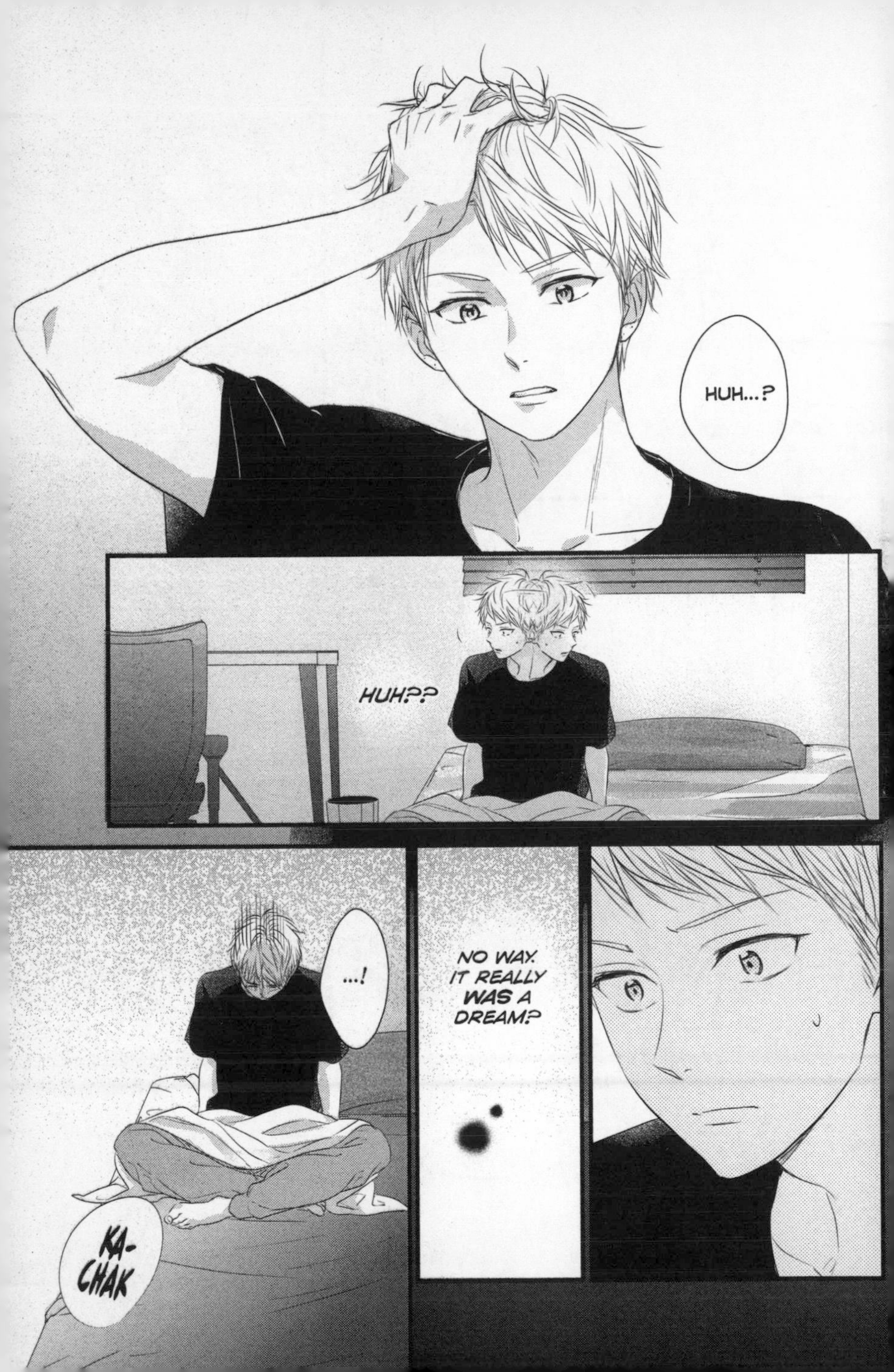
HUH...?
HUH??
NO WAY. IT REALLY WAS A DREAM?
...!
KA-CHAK

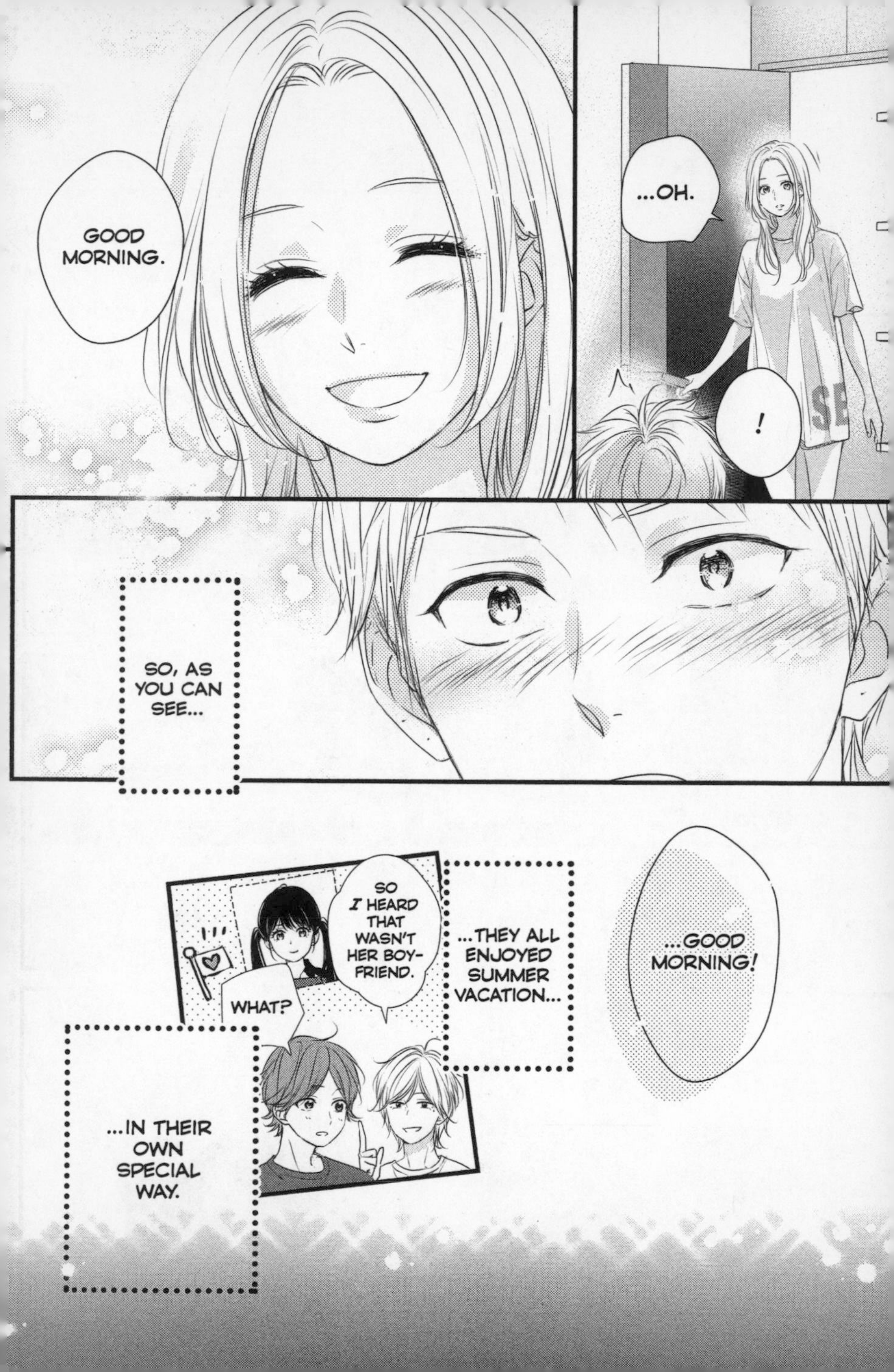
...OH.
!
GOOD MORNING.
SO, AS YOU CAN SEE...
...GOOD MORNING!
...THEY ALL ENJOYED SUMMER VACATION...
SO *I* HEARD THAT WASN'T HER BOY-FRIEND.
WHAT?
...IN THEIR OWN SPECIAL WAY.

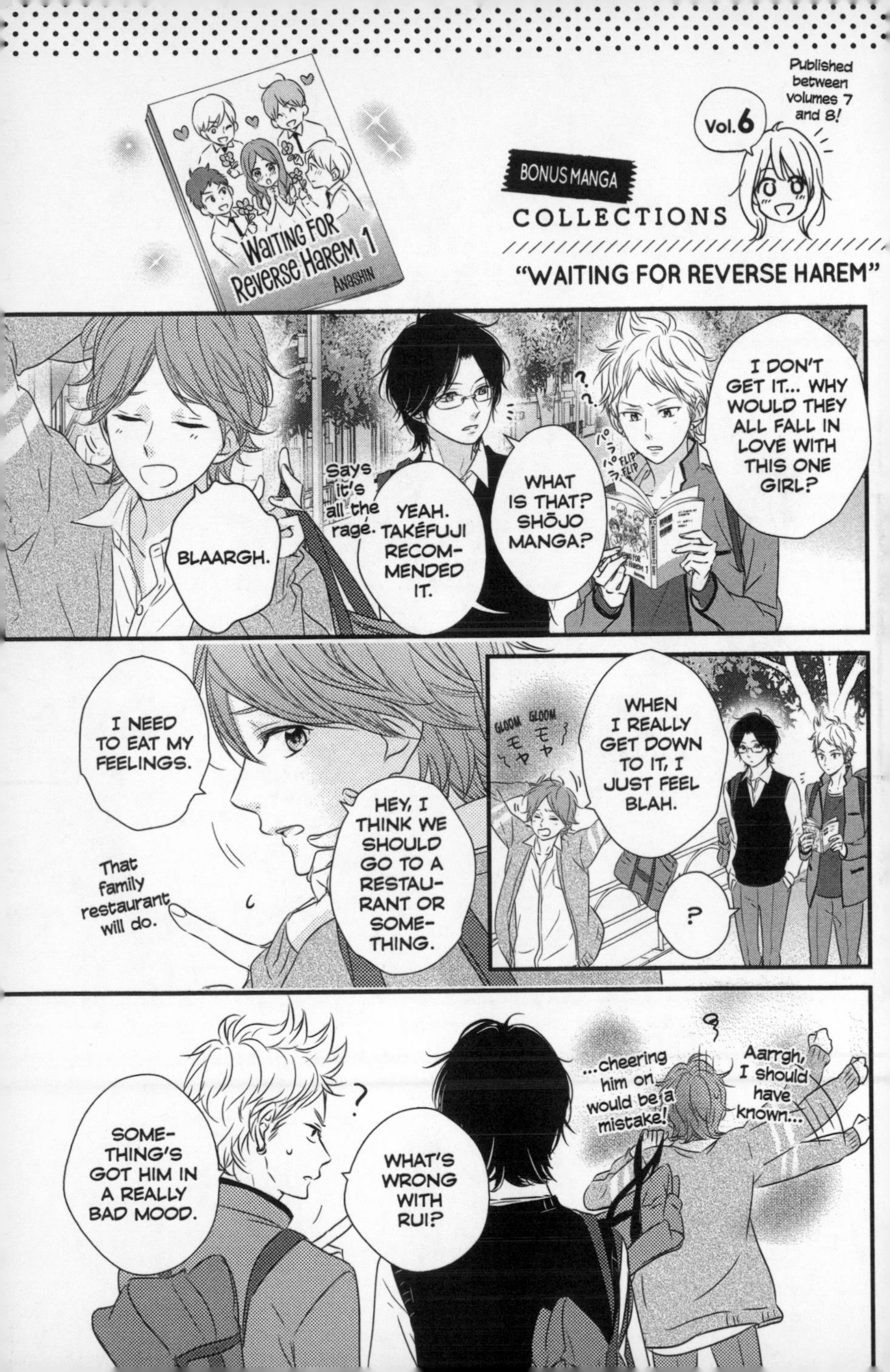
Published between volumes 7 and 8!
Vol.6
BONUS MANGA
COLLECTIONS
"WAITING FOR REVERSE HAREM"
Waiting for Reverse Harem 1
Anashin
I DON'T GET IT... WHY WOULD THEY ALL FALL IN LOVE WITH THIS ONE GIRL?
FLIP FLIP
WHAT IS THAT? SHŌJO MANGA?
YEAH. TAKÉFUJI RECOMMENDED IT.
Says it's all the rage.
BLAARGH.
WHEN I REALLY GET DOWN TO IT, I JUST FEEL BLAH.
GLOOM GLOOM
?
HEY, I THINK WE SHOULD GO TO A RESTAURANT OR SOMETHING.
I NEED TO EAT MY FEELINGS.
That family restaurant will do.
Aarrgh, I should have known...
...cheering him on would be a mistake!
WHAT'S WRONG WITH RUI?
SOMETHING'S GOT HIM IN A REALLY BAD MOOD.

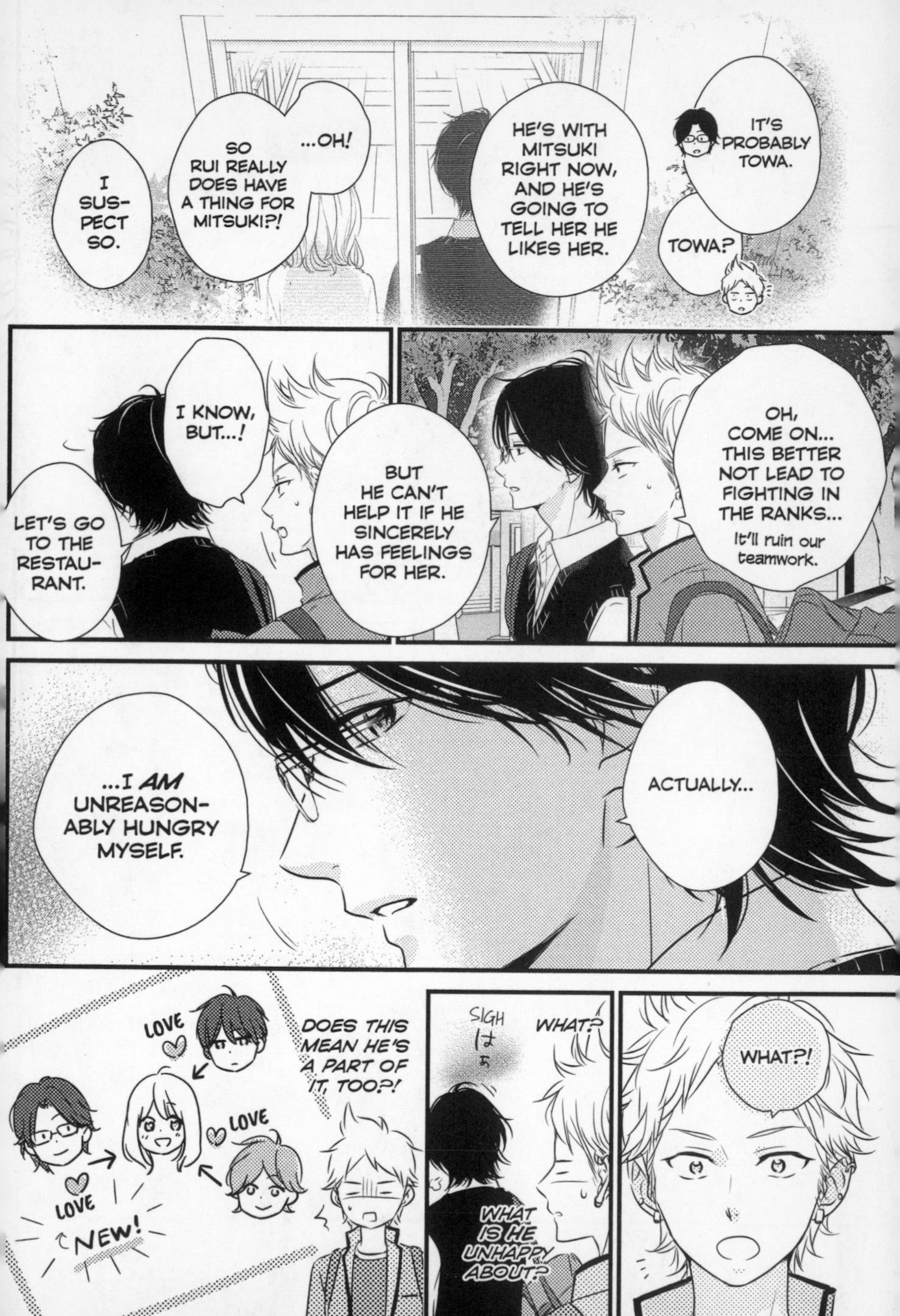
IT'S PROBABLY TOWA.
TOWA?
HE'S WITH MITSUKI RIGHT NOW, AND HE'S GOING TO TELL HER HE LIKES HER.
...OH!
SO RUI REALLY DOES HAVE A THING FOR MITSUKI?!
I SUSPECT SO.
OH, COME ON... THIS BETTER NOT LEAD TO FIGHTING IN THE RANKS...
It'll ruin our teamwork.
BUT HE CAN'T HELP IT IF HE SINCERELY HAS FEELINGS FOR HER.
I KNOW, BUT...!
LET'S GO TO THE RESTAURANT.
ACTUALLY...
...I AM UNREASONABLY HUNGRY MYSELF.
WHAT?!
WHAT?
SIGH
はぁ
WHAT IS HE UNHAPPY ABOUT?
DOES THIS MEAN HE'S A PART OF IT, TOO?!
LOVE
LOVE
LOVE
NEW!

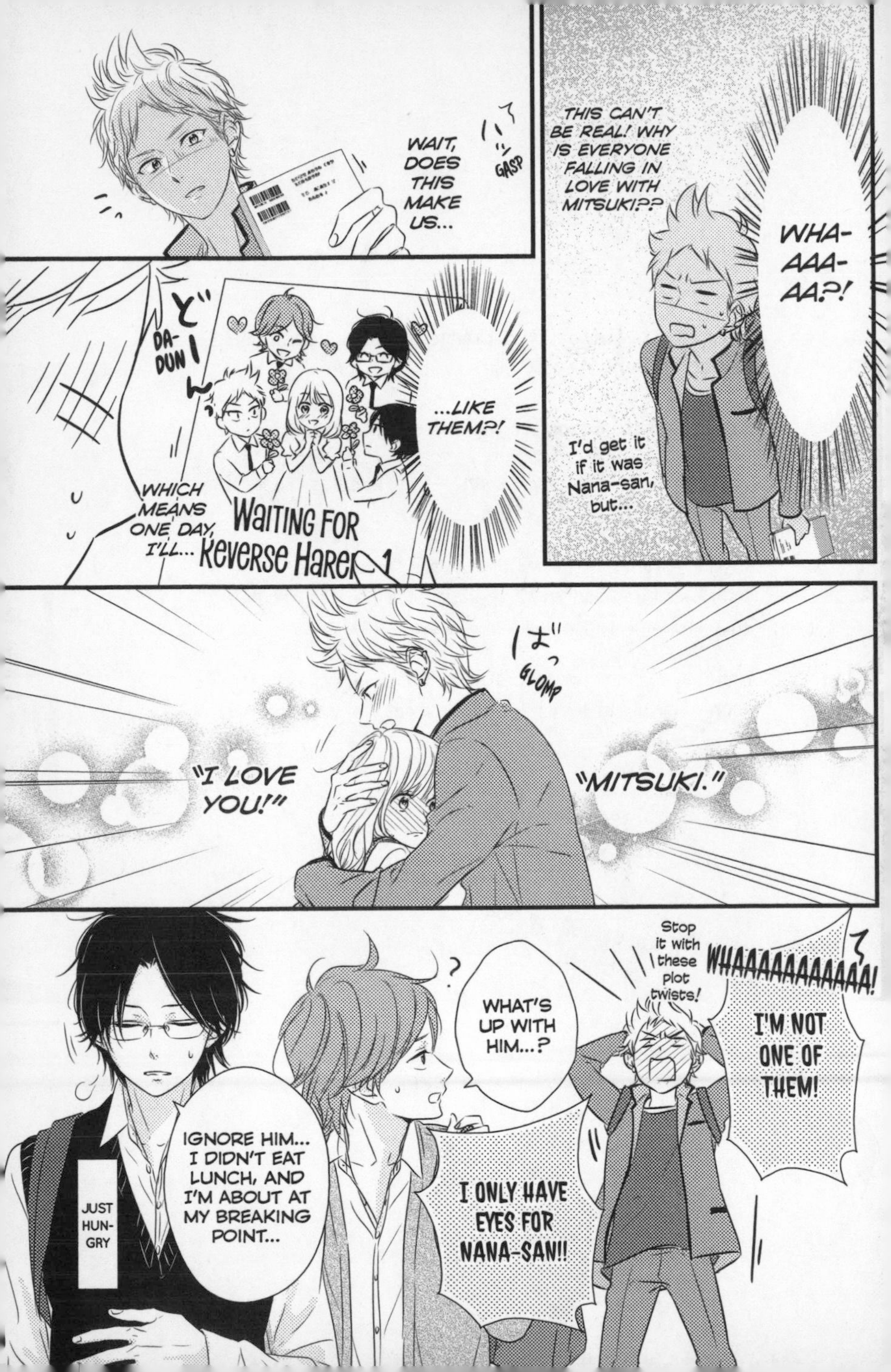
THIS CAN'T BE REAL! WHY IS EVERYONE FALLING IN LOVE WITH MITSUKI!??
WHA-AAA-AA?!
I'd get it if it was Nana-san, but...
ハッ
GASP
WAIT, DOES THIS MAKE US...
...LIKE THEM?!
どーん
DA-DUN
WHICH MEANS ONE DAY, I'LL...
Waiting FOR Reverse Harem 1
ばっ
GLOMP
"MITSUKI."
"I LOVE YOU!"
Stop it with these plot twists!
WHAAAAAAAAAAAA!
I'M NOT ONE OF THEM!
I ONLY HAVE EYES FOR NANA-SAN!!
WHAT'S UP WITH HIM...?
IGNORE HIM... I DIDN'T EAT LUNCH, AND I'M ABOUT AT MY BREAKING POINT...
JUST HUNGRY

## ~ ABOUT THE BONUS MINI-MANGA ~

When I see how my art style changed and how innocent the characters were, it really takes me back in time (ha ha). I drew these bonus mini-chapters after each volume of the series went on sale, before the next full chapter.

So a lot of what happens is connected to what was happening in the main story at that time.

I think you'll enjoy it more if you read these bonus mini-chapters when you're re-reading the series, reading each one between the right volumes.

And they're short, so my goal is to make you snicker more than you would at something in the main story. I hope they make you laugh.

My favorites are... Ryūji's cosplay and Towa's glasses!

vol.2
"What They Don't Have"

vol.3
"Let's Cosplay♪"

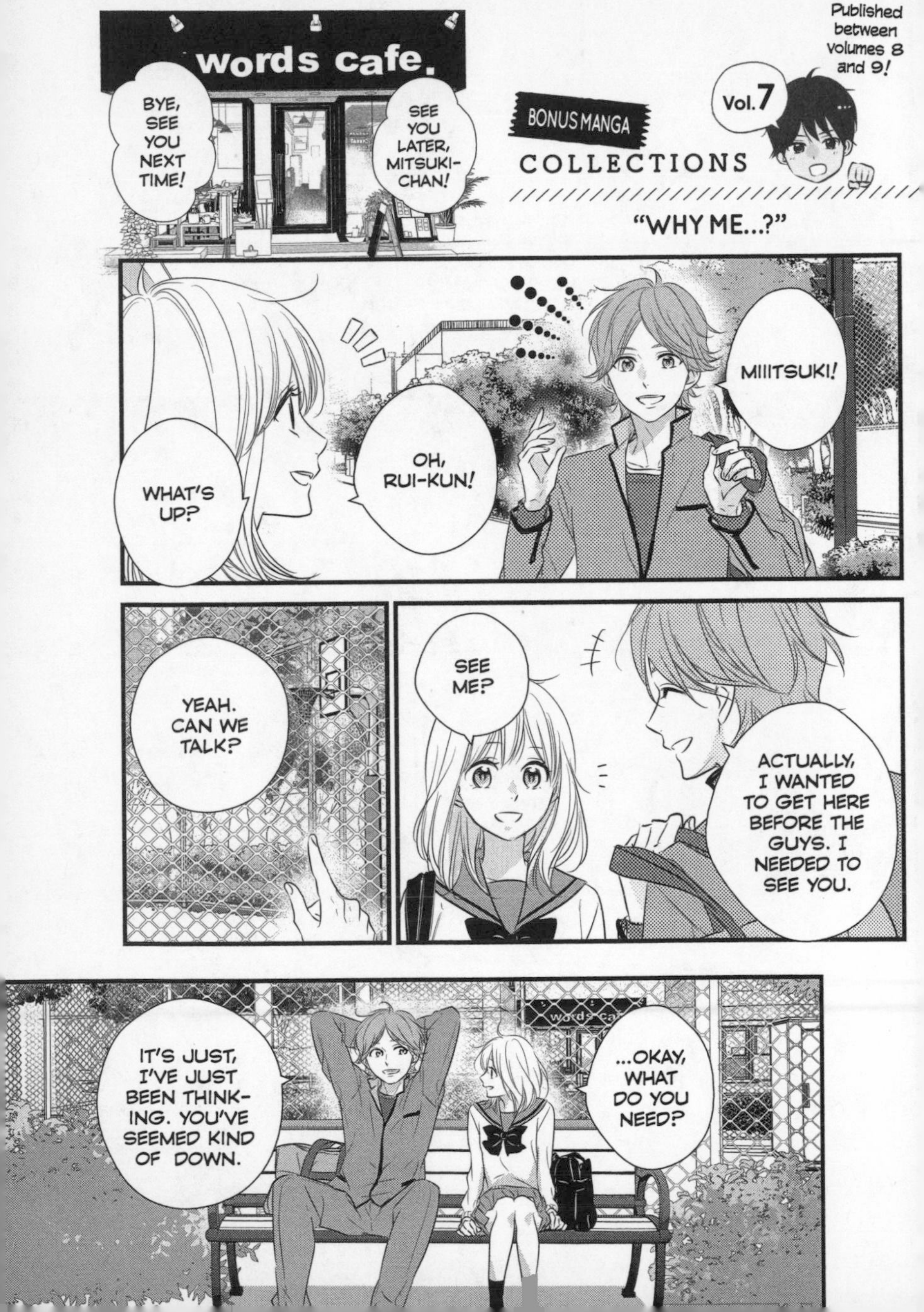
Published between volumes 8 and 9!
Vol.7
BONUS MANGA
COLLECTIONS
"WHY ME...?"
words cafe.
SEE YOU LATER, MITSUKI-CHAN!
BYE, SEE YOU NEXT TIME!
MIIITSUKI!
OH, RUI-KUN!
WHAT'S UP?
ACTUALLY, I WANTED TO GET HERE BEFORE THE GUYS. I NEEDED TO SEE YOU.
SEE ME?
YEAH. CAN WE TALK?
...OKAY, WHAT DO YOU NEED?
IT'S JUST, I'VE JUST BEEN THINKING. YOU'VE SEEMED KIND OF DOWN.

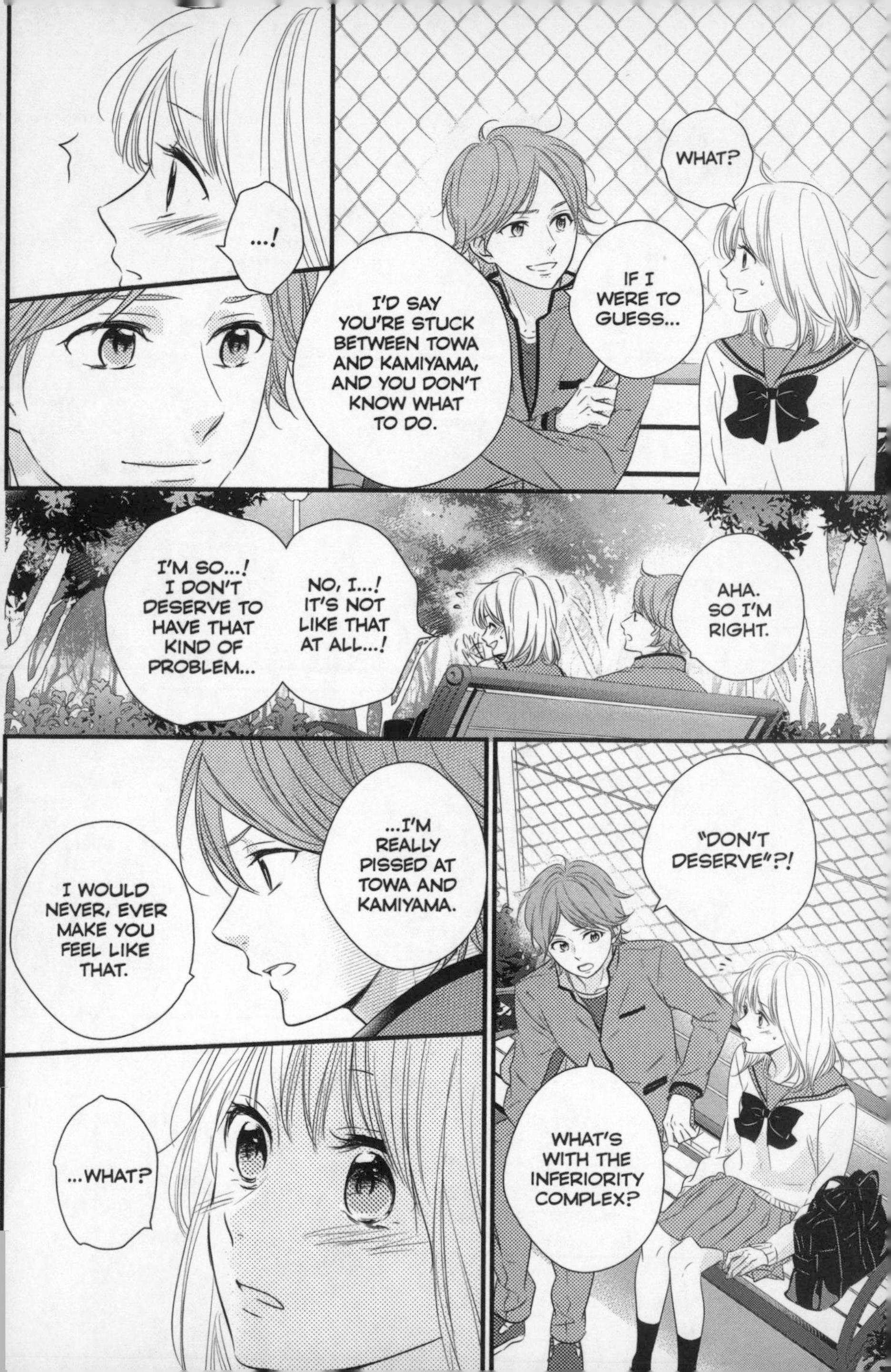
WHAT?
IF I WERE TO GUESS...
I'D SAY YOU'RE STUCK BETWEEN TOWA AND KAMIYAMA, AND YOU DON'T KNOW WHAT TO DO.
...!
AHA. SO I'M RIGHT.
NO, I...! IT'S NOT LIKE THAT AT ALL...!
I'M SO...! I DON'T DESERVE TO HAVE THAT KIND OF PROBLEM...
"DON'T DESERVE"?!
WHAT'S WITH THE INFERIORITY COMPLEX?
...I'M REALLY PISSED AT TOWA AND KAMIYAMA.
I WOULD NEVER, EVER MAKE YOU FEEL LIKE THAT.
...WHAT?

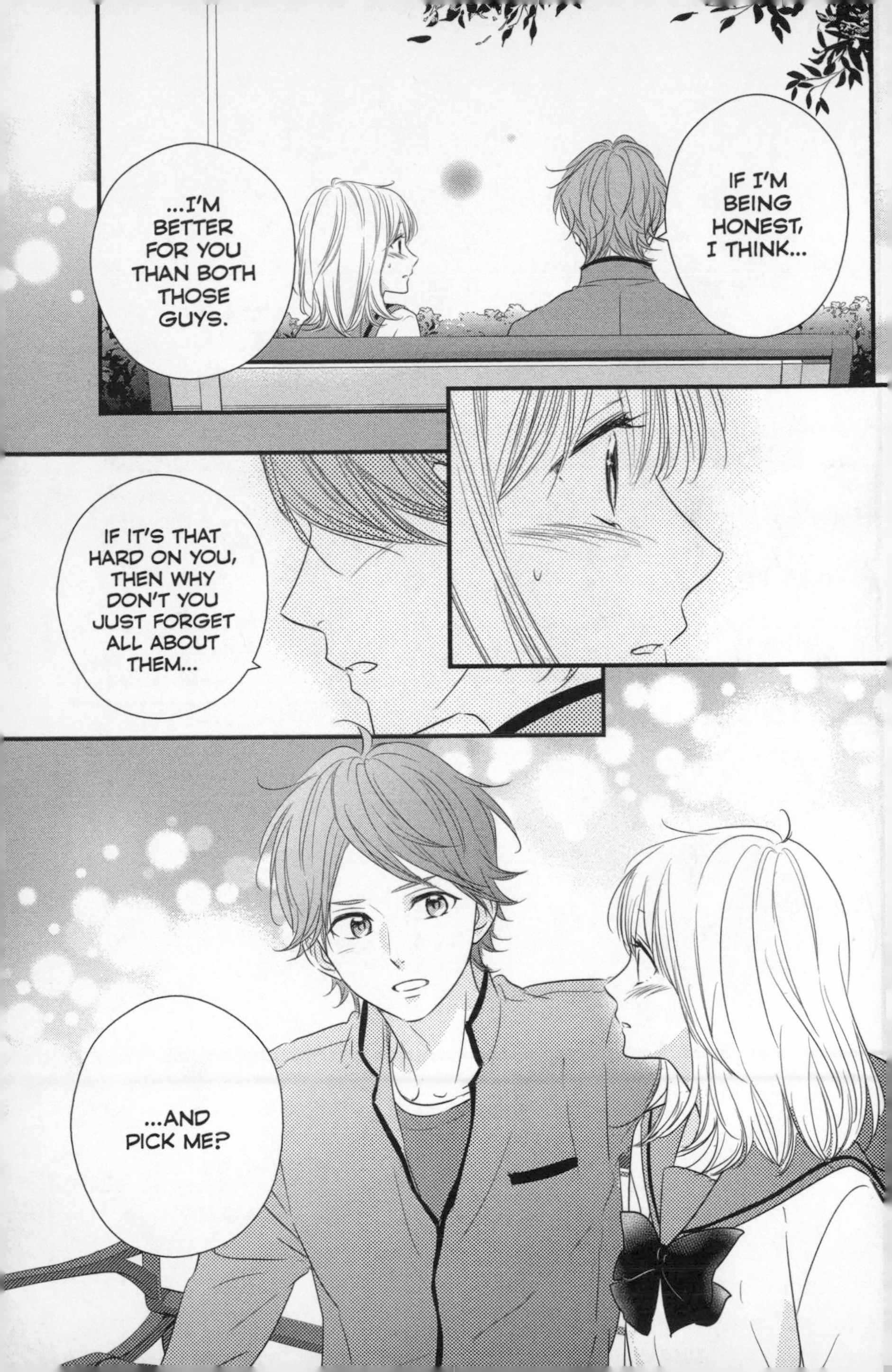
IF I'M BEING HONEST, I THINK...
...I'M BETTER FOR YOU THAN BOTH THOSE GUYS.
IF IT'S THAT HARD ON YOU, THEN WHY DON'T YOU JUST FORGET ALL ABOUT THEM...
...AND PICK ME?

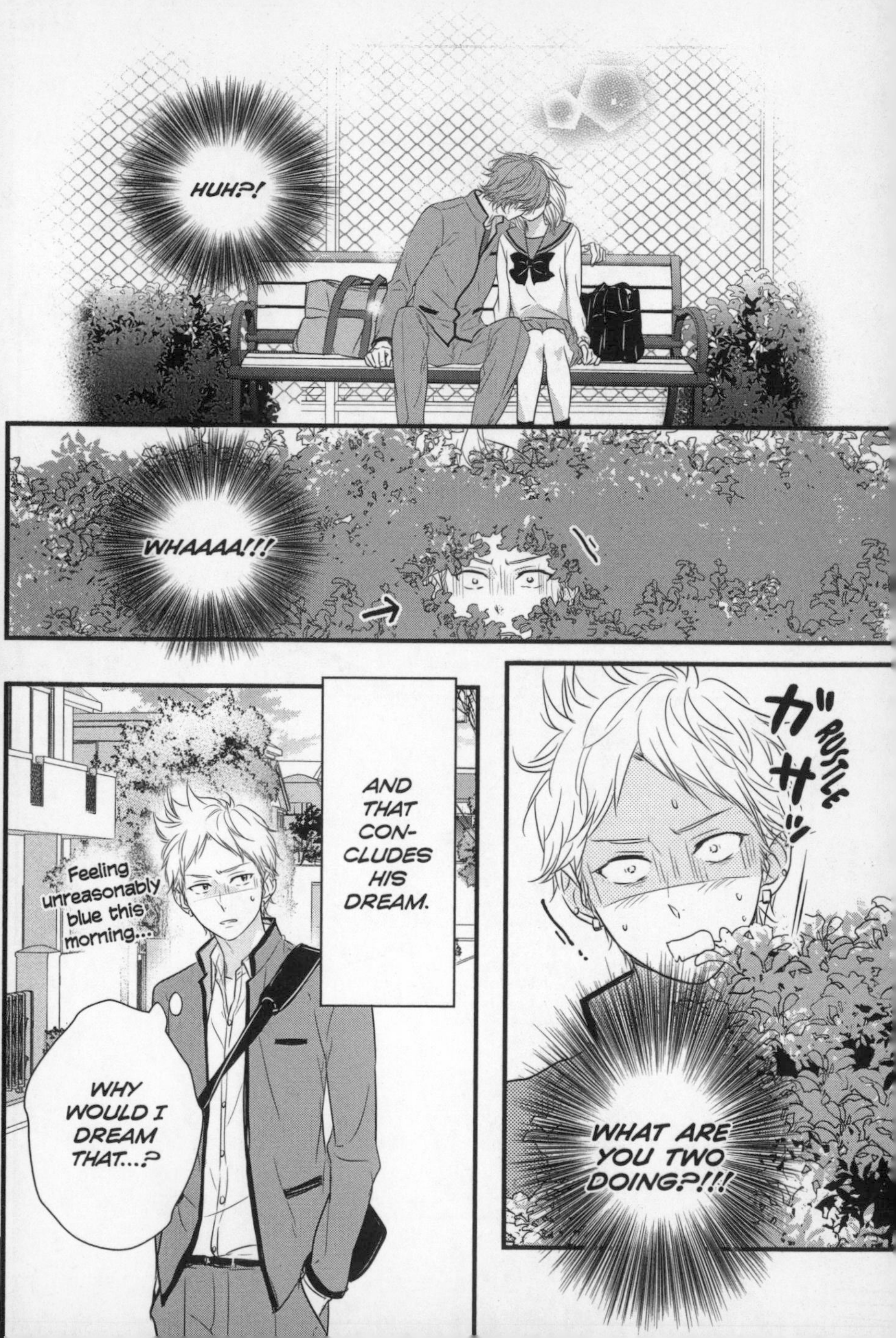
HUH?!
WHAAAA!!!
ガサッ RUSTLE
WHAT ARE YOU TWO DOING?!!!
AND THAT CON-CLUDES HIS DREAM.
Feeling unreasonably blue this morning...
WHY WOULD I DREAM THAT...?

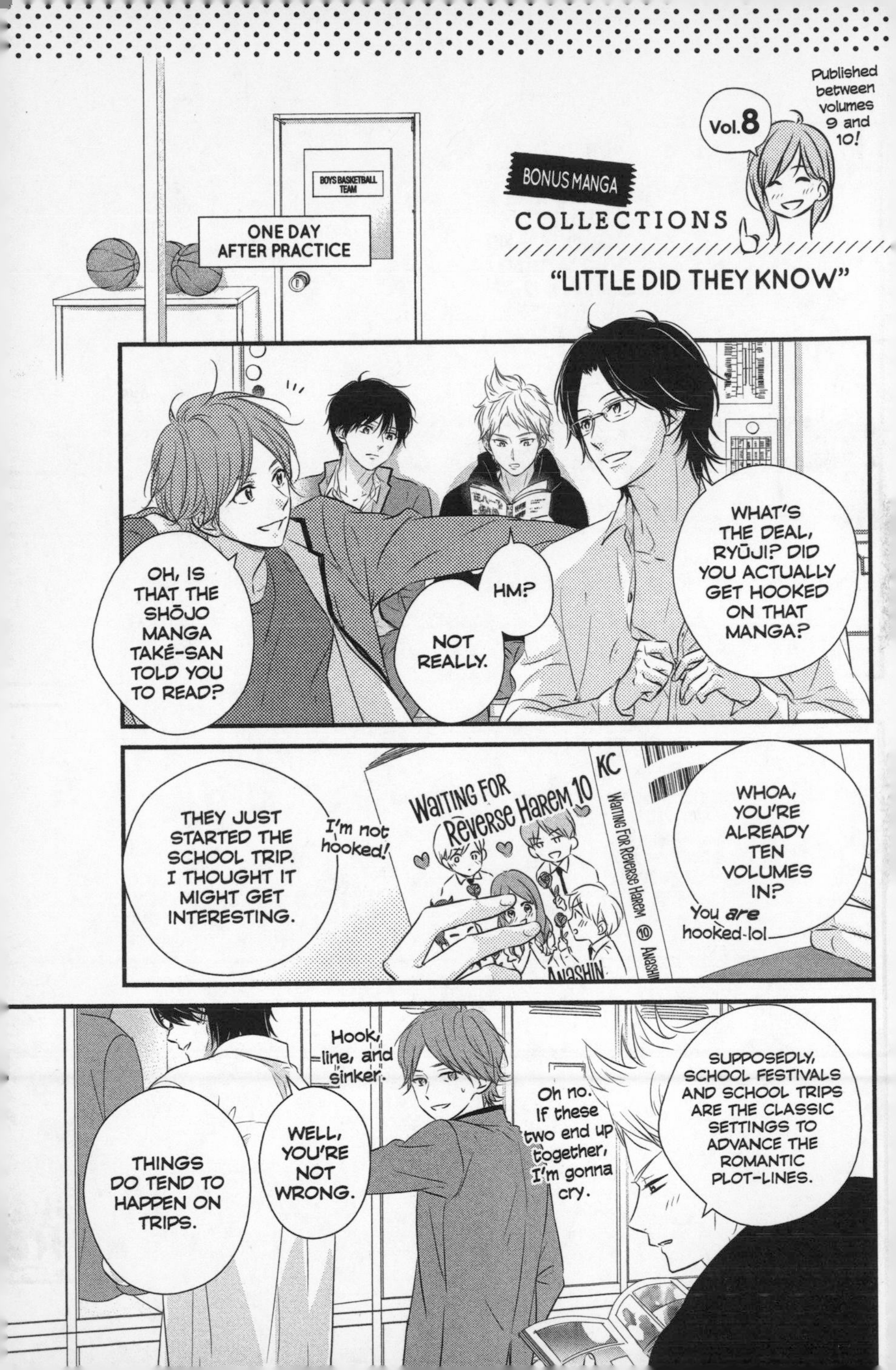
Published between volumes 9 and 10!
Vol.8
BONUS MANGA
COLLECTIONS
"LITTLE DID THEY KNOW"
BOYS BASKETBALL TEAM
ONE DAY AFTER PRACTICE
WHAT'S THE DEAL, RYŪJI? DID YOU ACTUALLY GET HOOKED ON THAT MANGA?
HM?
NOT REALLY.
OH, IS THAT THE SHŌJO MANGA TAKÉ-SAN TOLD YOU TO READ?
KC
Waiting For Reverse Harem 10
Waiting For Reverse Harem 10 Anashin
Anashin
WHOA, YOU'RE ALREADY TEN VOLUMES IN?
You are hooked-lol
I'm not hooked!
THEY JUST STARTED THE SCHOOL TRIP. I THOUGHT IT MIGHT GET INTERESTING.
SUPPOSEDLY, SCHOOL FESTIVALS AND SCHOOL TRIPS ARE THE CLASSIC SETTINGS TO ADVANCE THE ROMANTIC PLOT-LINES.
Oh no. If these two end up together, I'm gonna cry.
Hook, line, and sinker.
WELL, YOU'RE NOT WRONG.
THINGS DO TEND TO HAPPEN ON TRIPS.

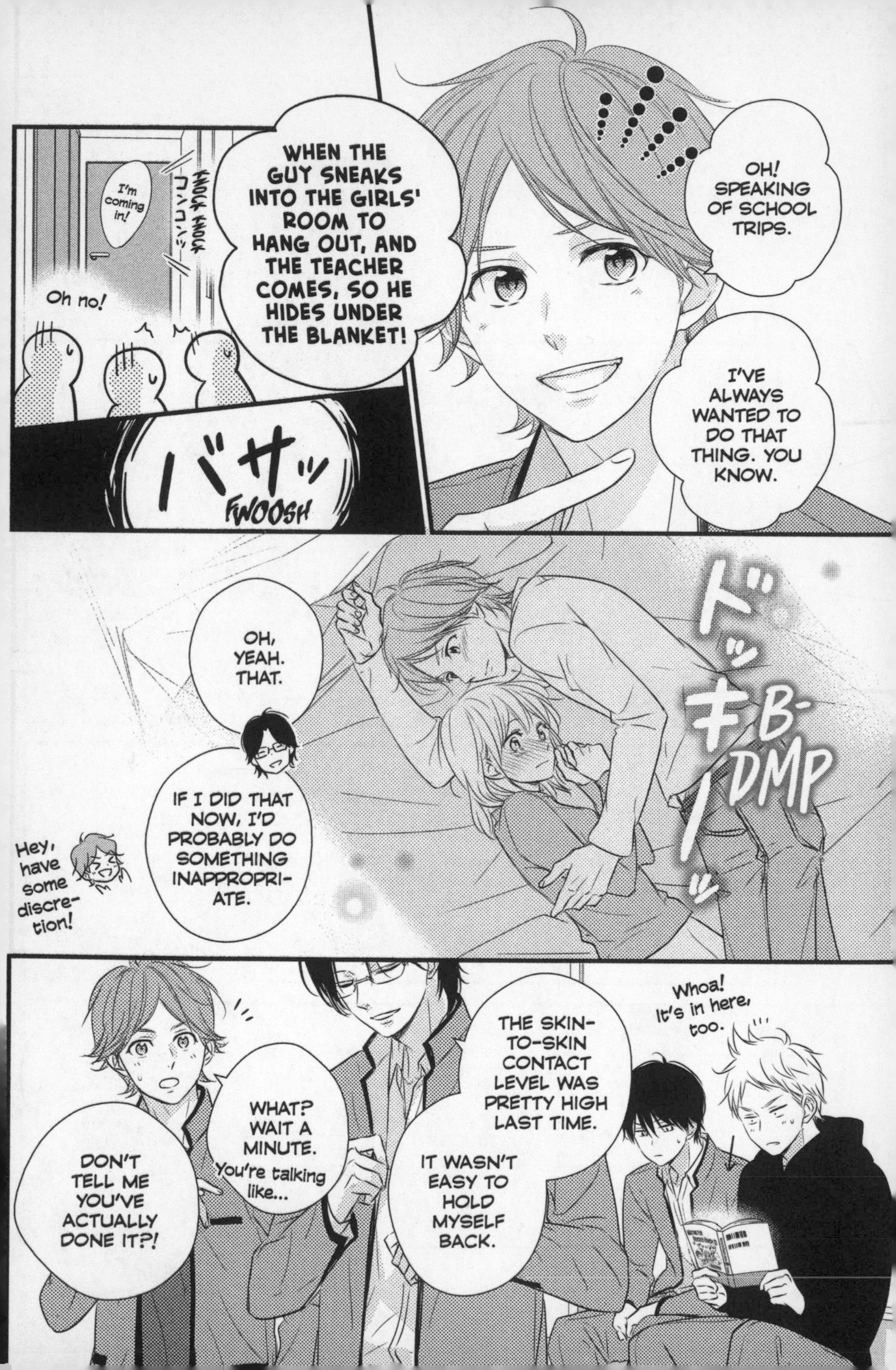
OH! SPEAKING OF SCHOOL TRIPS.
I'VE ALWAYS WANTED TO DO THAT THING. YOU KNOW.
WHEN THE GUY SNEAKS INTO THE GIRLS' ROOM TO HANG OUT, AND THE TEACHER COMES, SO HE HIDES UNDER THE BLANKET!
コンコンッ
KNOCK KNOCK
I'm coming in!
Oh no!
バサッ
FWOOSH
ドッキ
B-DMP
OH, YEAH. THAT.
IF I DID THAT NOW, I'D PROBABLY DO SOMETHING INAPPROPRI-ATE.
Hey, have some discre-tion!
Whoa! It's in here, too.
THE SKIN-TO-SKIN CONTACT LEVEL WAS PRETTY HIGH LAST TIME.
IT WASN'T EASY TO HOLD MYSELF BACK.
WHAT? WAIT A MINUTE.
You're talking like...
DON'T TELL ME YOU'VE ACTUALLY DONE IT?!

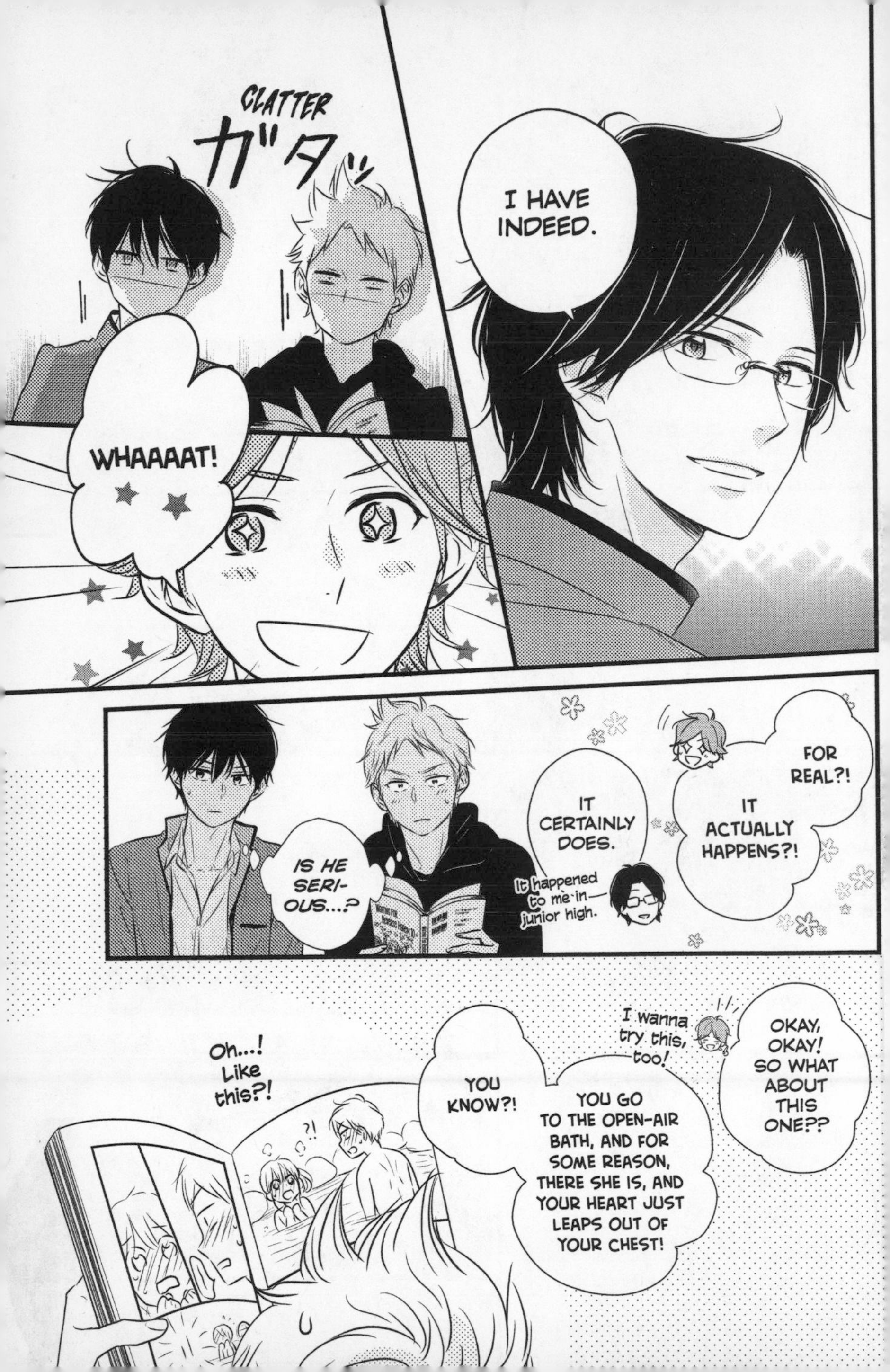
I HAVE INDEED.
CLATTER
ガタッ
WHAAAAT!
FOR REAL?! IT ACTUALLY HAPPENS?!
IT CERTAINLY DOES.
It happened to me in junior high.
IS HE SERI-OUS...?
OKAY, OKAY! SO WHAT ABOUT THIS ONE??
I wanna try this, too!
YOU KNOW?!
YOU GO TO THE OPEN-AIR BATH, AND FOR SOME REASON, THERE SHE IS, AND YOUR HEART JUST LEAPS OUT OF YOUR CHEST!
Oh...! Like this?!

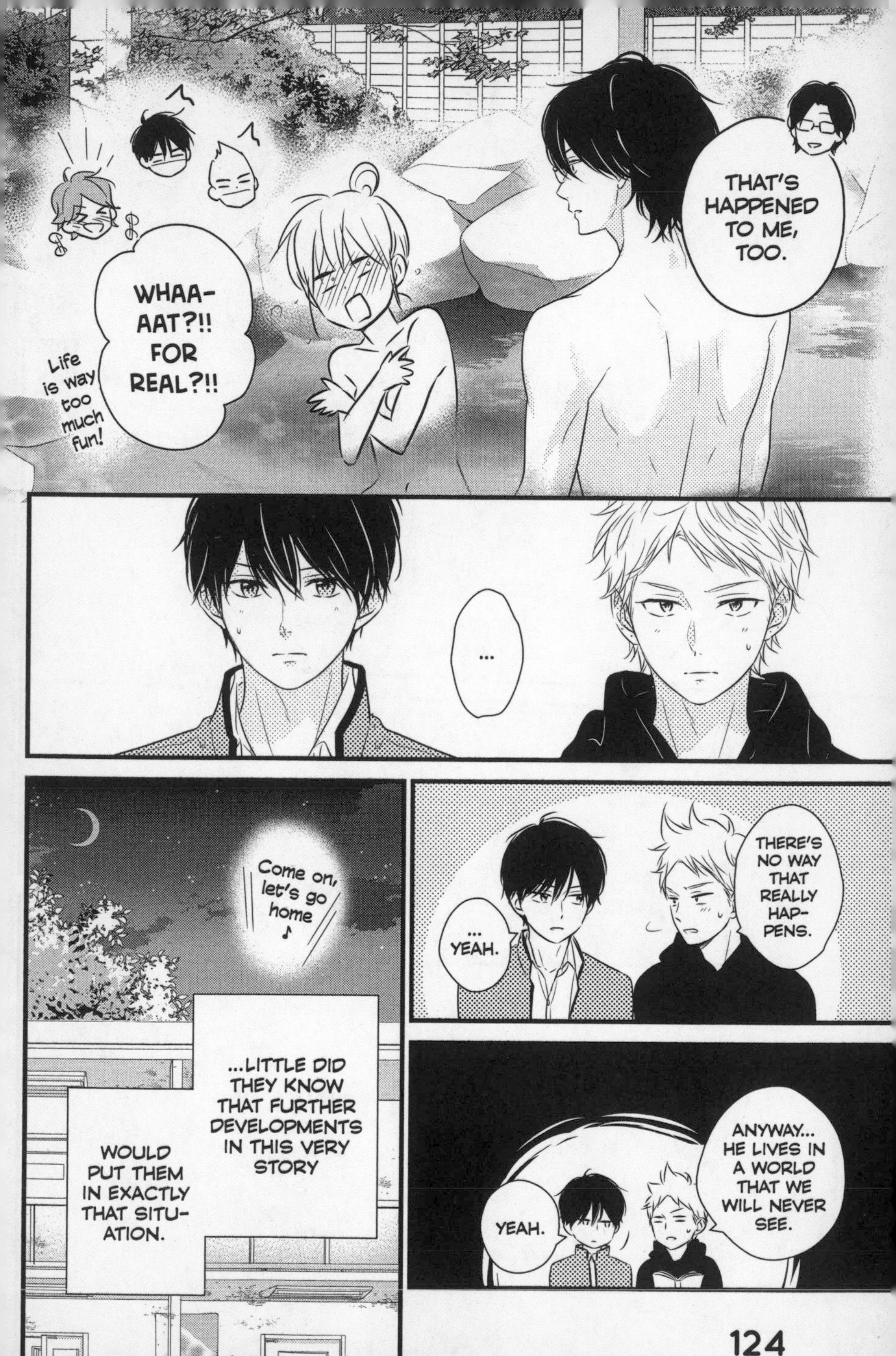
THAT'S HAPPENED TO ME, TOO.
WHAA-AAT?!! FOR REAL?!!
Life is way too much fun!
...
THERE'S NO WAY THAT REALLY HAP-PENS.
... YEAH.
ANYWAY... HE LIVES IN A WORLD THAT WE WILL NEVER SEE.
YEAH.
Come on, let's go home ♪
...LITTLE DID THEY KNOW THAT FURTHER DEVELOPMENTS IN THIS VERY STORY
WOULD PUT THEM IN EXACTLY THAT SITU-ATION.

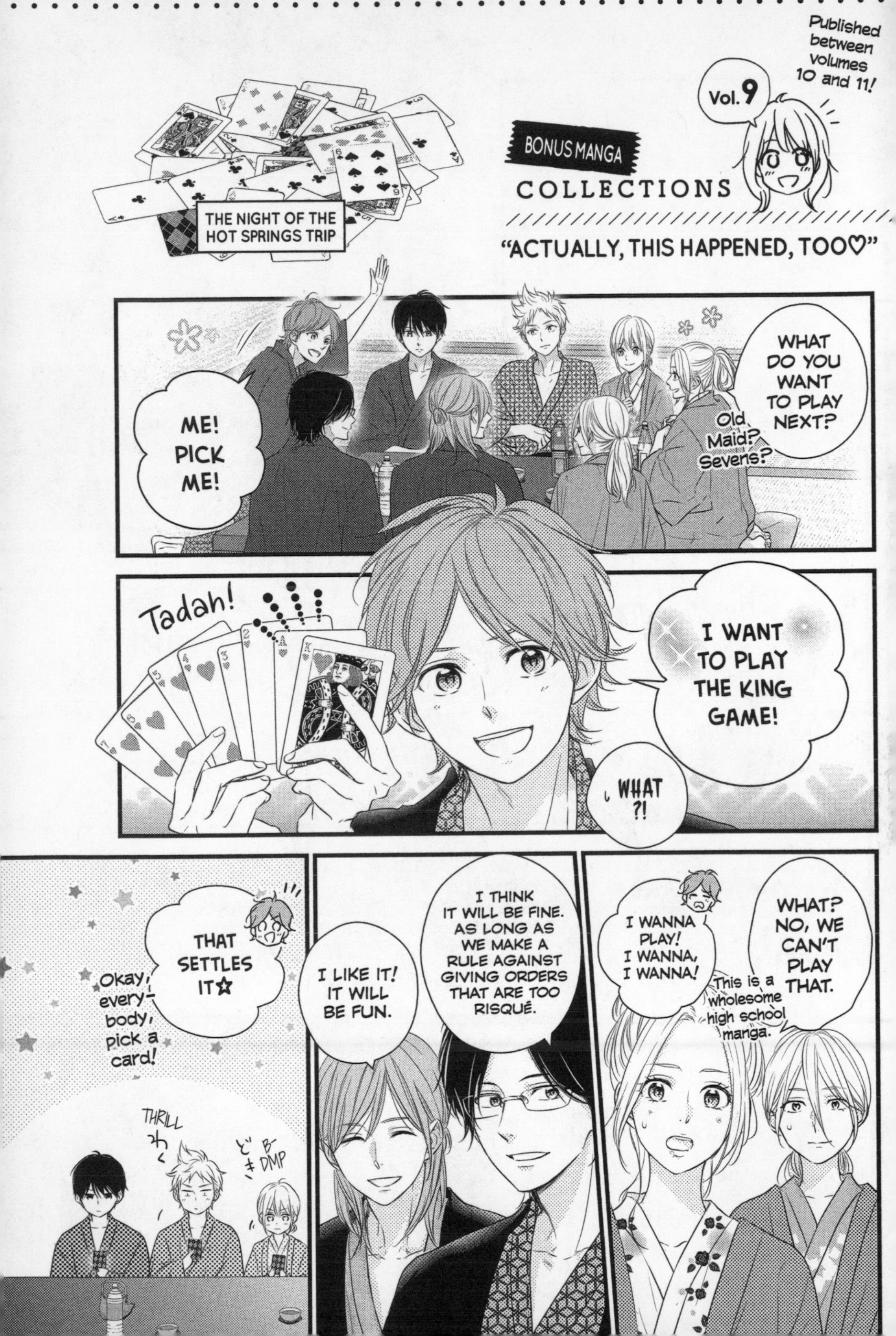
Published between volumes 10 and 11!
Vol. 9
BONUS MANGA
COLLECTIONS
"ACTUALLY, THIS HAPPENED, TOO♡"
THE NIGHT OF THE HOT SPRINGS TRIP
WHAT DO YOU WANT TO PLAY NEXT?
Old Maid? Sevens?
ME! PICK ME!
I WANT TO PLAY THE KING GAME!
WHAT?!
Tadah!
WHAT? NO, WE CAN'T PLAY THAT.
This is a wholesome high school manga.
I WANNA PLAY! I WANNA, I WANNA!
I THINK IT WILL BE FINE. AS LONG AS WE MAKE A RULE AGAINST GIVING ORDERS THAT ARE TOO RISQUÉ.
I LIKE IT! IT WILL BE FUN.
THAT SETTLES IT☆
Okay, everybody, pick a card!
THRILL
B-DMP

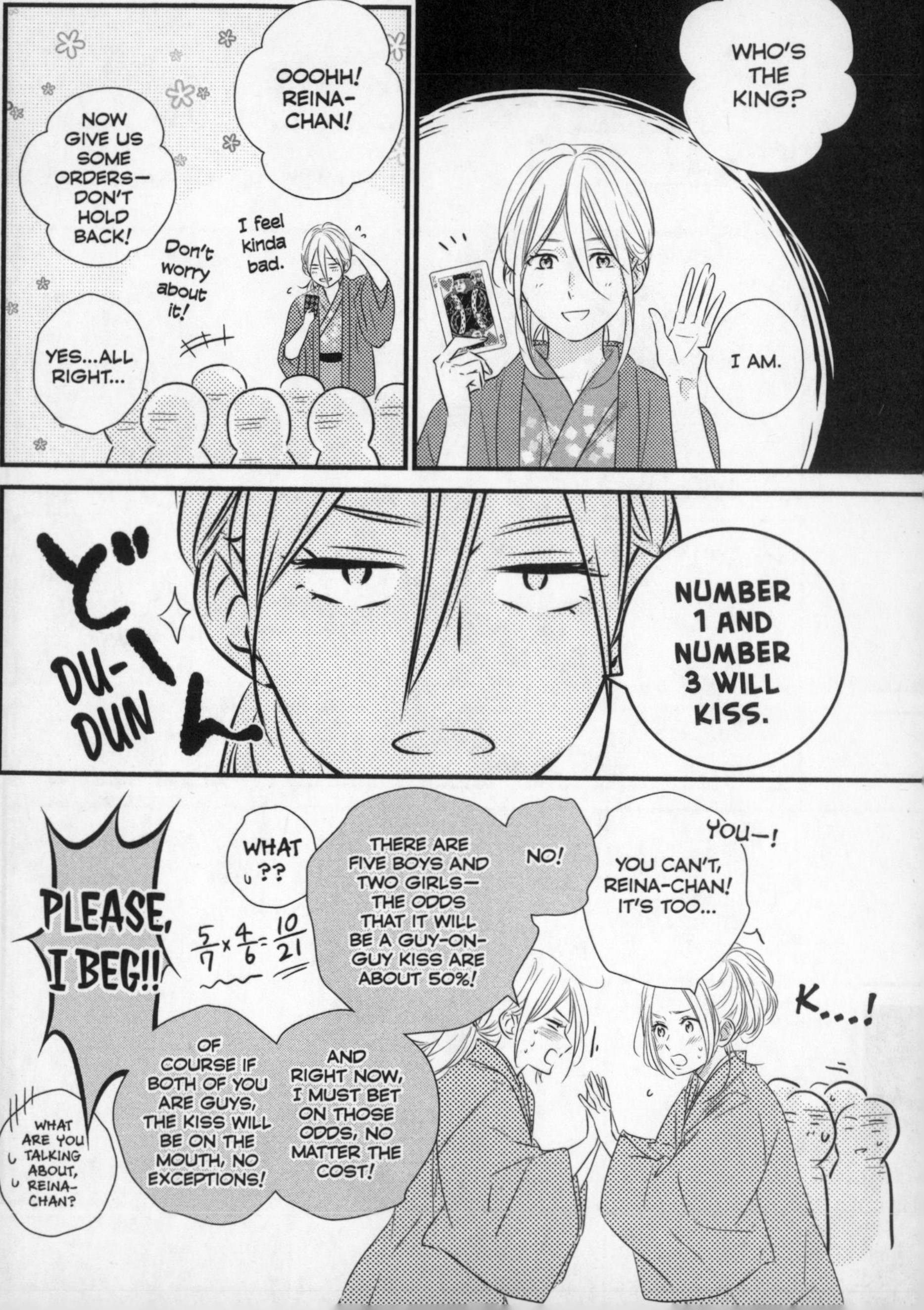

WHO'S THE KING?
I AM.
OOOHH! REINA-CHAN!
NOW GIVE US SOME ORDERS—DON'T HOLD BACK!
I feel kinda bad.
Don't worry about it!
YES...ALL RIGHT...
NUMBER 1 AND NUMBER 3 WILL KISS.
DU-DUN
YOU—!
YOU CAN'T, REINA-CHAN! IT'S TOO...
K...!
NO!
THERE ARE FIVE BOYS AND TWO GIRLS—THE ODDS THAT IT WILL BE A GUY-ON-GUY KISS ARE ABOUT 50%!
WHAT??
$\frac{5}{7} \times \frac{4}{6} = \frac{10}{21}$
PLEASE, I BEG!!
AND RIGHT NOW, I MUST BET ON THOSE ODDS, NO MATTER THE COST!
OF COURSE IF BOTH OF YOU ARE GUYS, THE KISS WILL BE ON THE MOUTH, NO EXCEPTIONS!
WHAT ARE YOU TALKING ABOUT, REINA-CHAN?

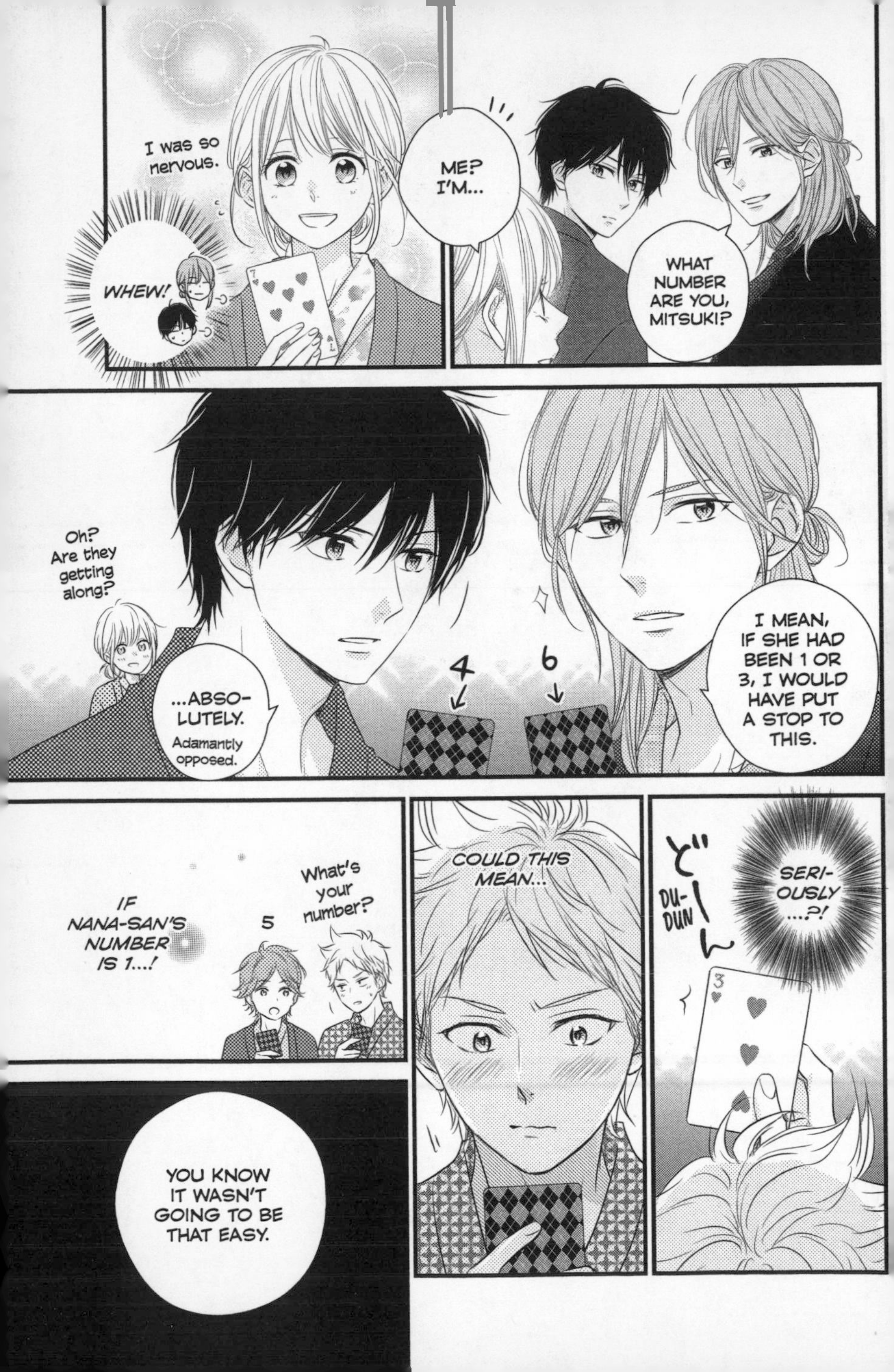
WHAT NUMBER ARE YOU, MITSUKI?
ME? I'M...
I was so nervous.
WHEW!
I MEAN, IF SHE HAD BEEN 1 OR 3, I WOULD HAVE PUT A STOP TO THIS.
6
4
...ABSO-LUTELY.
Adamantly opposed.
Oh? Are they getting along?
SERI-OUSLY ...?!
どーん
DU-DUN
COULD THIS MEAN...
What's your number?
5
IF NANA-SAN'S NUMBER IS 1...!
YOU KNOW IT WASN'T GOING TO BE THAT EASY.

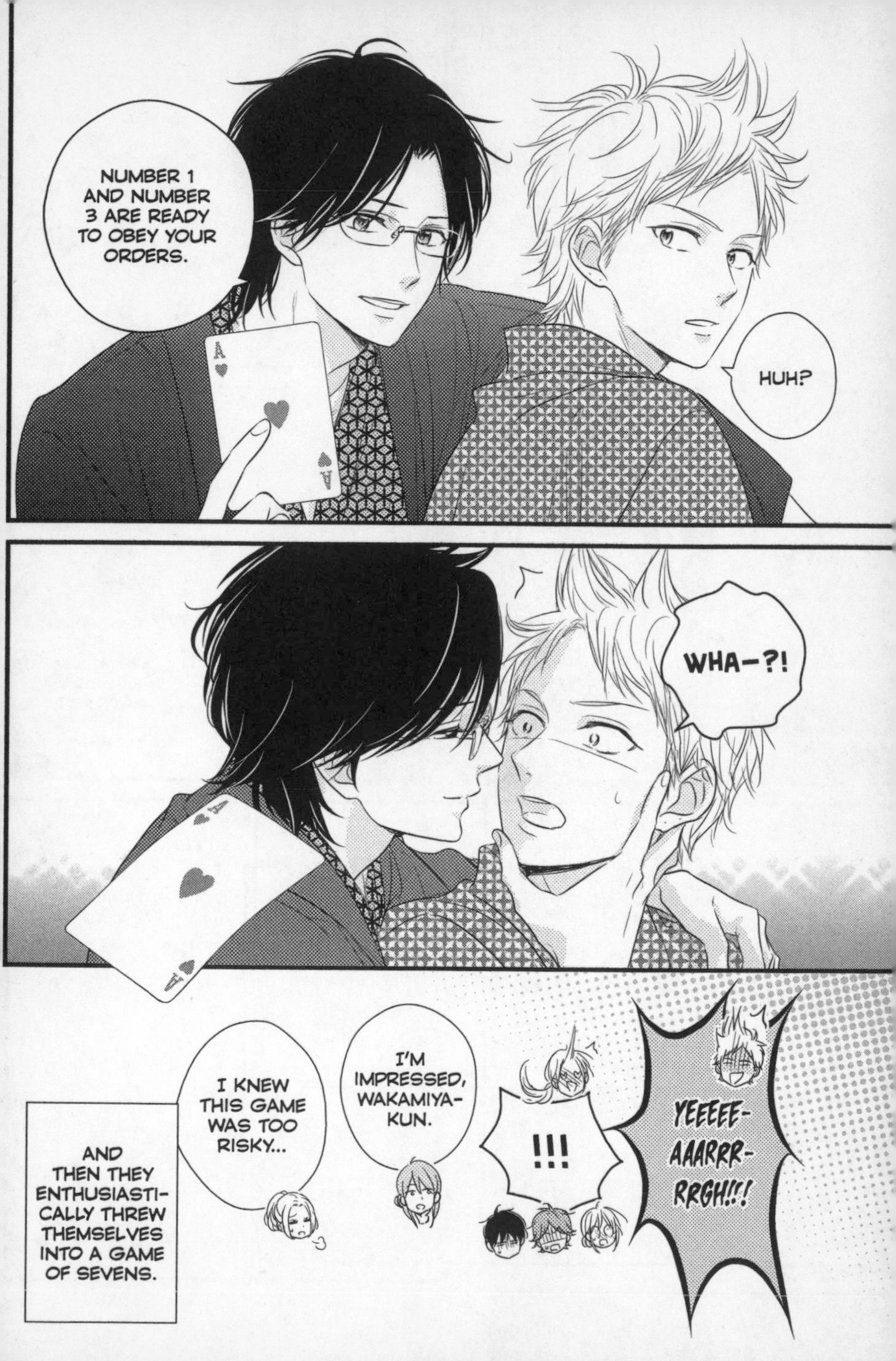
NUMBER 1 AND NUMBER 3 ARE READY TO OBEY YOUR ORDERS.
HUH?
WHA-?!
YEEEEE-AAARRR-RRGH!!?!
!!!
I'M IMPRESSED, WAKAMIYA-KUN.
I KNEW THIS GAME WAS TOO RISKY...
AND THEN THEY ENTHUSIASTICALLY THREW THEMSELVES INTO A GAME OF SEVENS.

And there you have it. The next chapter will be the last. I've been drawing *Waiting for Spring* for six years, and I'm sure a lot has happened in all of your lives, so the fact that you're still reading it, and that you stuck with it for so long—that makes me happier than anything. Thank you so much, I mean it. I hope that this experience gives me the energy to go on, and I hope that you readers will never forget this series...and it's the end, so I can't help feeling a little choked up (ha ha), but I do really mean it when I say that I would love it if you just feel like re-reading it again sometime...!

And when you do, I wish with all my heart that you have a smile on your face, and enjoy the story along with all the characters in *Waiting for Spring*.

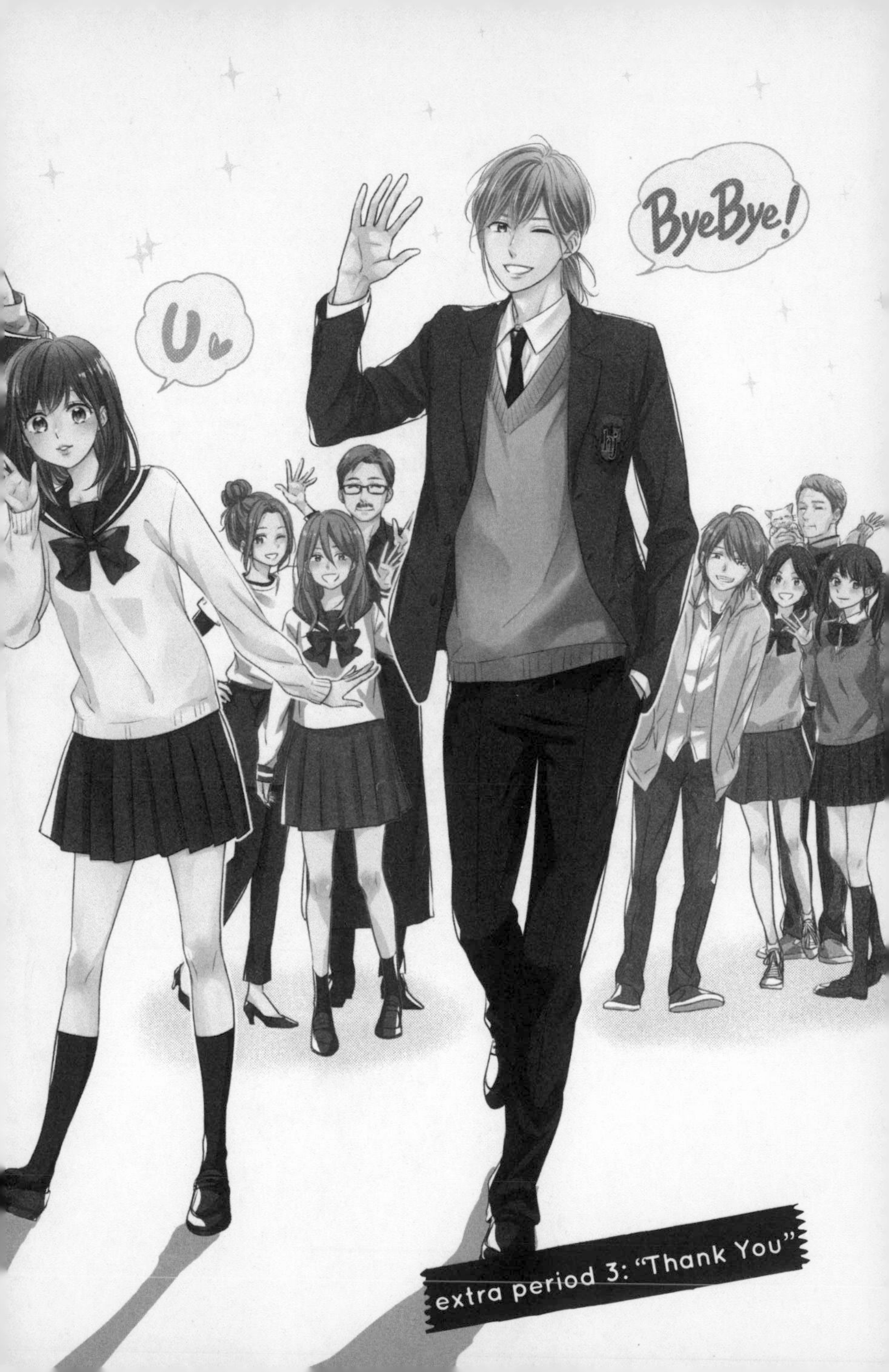
BYEBYE!
U♥
extra period 3: "Thank You"

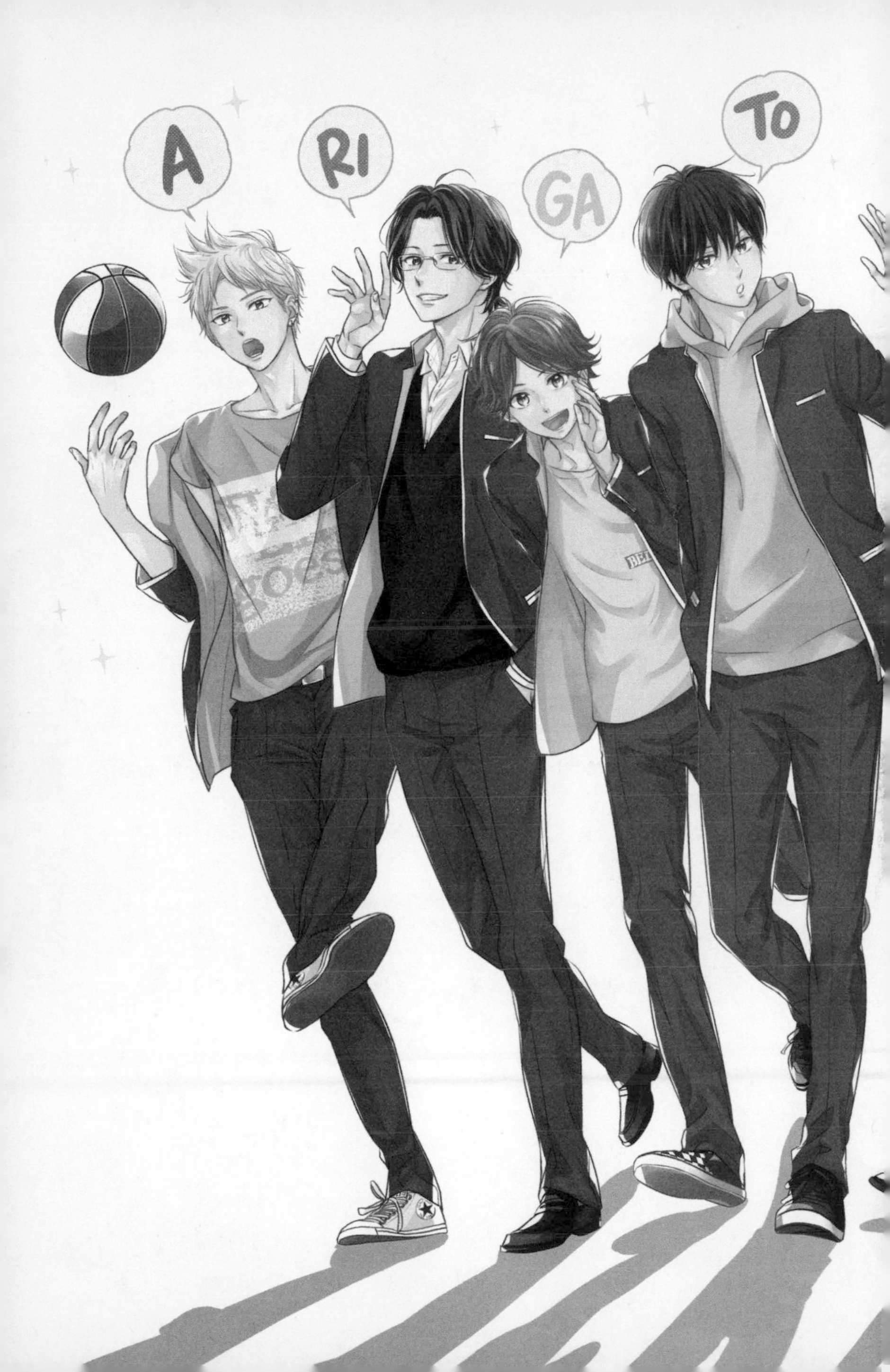
A
RI
GA
TO

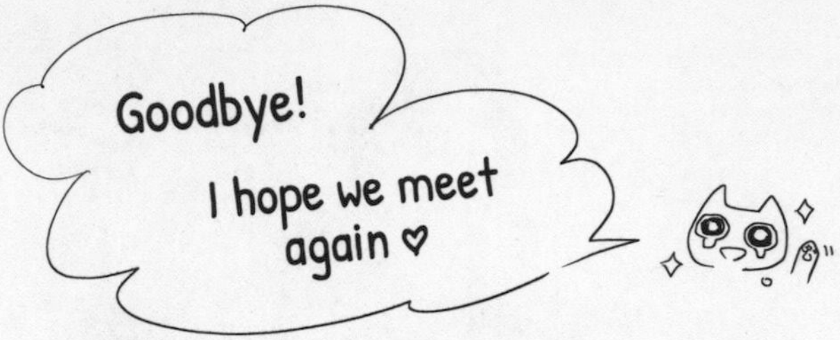
Goodbye!
I hope we meet again ♡

## SPECIAL THANKS

My editors: Suzuki-san, Takahashi-san; the designer: Baba-san
My assistants: Masuda-san, Aki-chan
Everyone at the Dessert editorial department, everyone from Words Cafe
Photographers: Murata-san, Kin-san; Consultant: Yoshioka-san
English Supervisors: Natsuko Konishi-Atwood
Sana Ann Konishi-Atwood
Kia Jean Konishi-Atwood
Everyone who is involved in the creation of this work every month and every volume
My family, my relatives, Bō-chan, Nazu-chan, Shibayama-san,
Everyone at Owase
And each and every person who read this series,
Thank you so much!

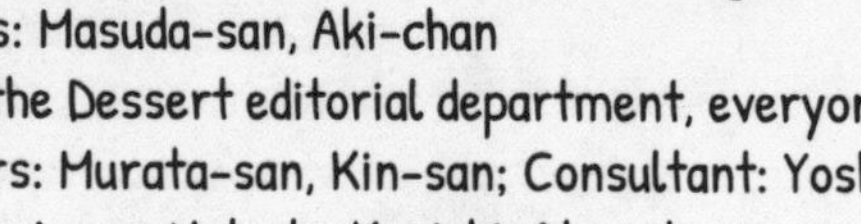
あなしん
Anashin
Spring, 2020

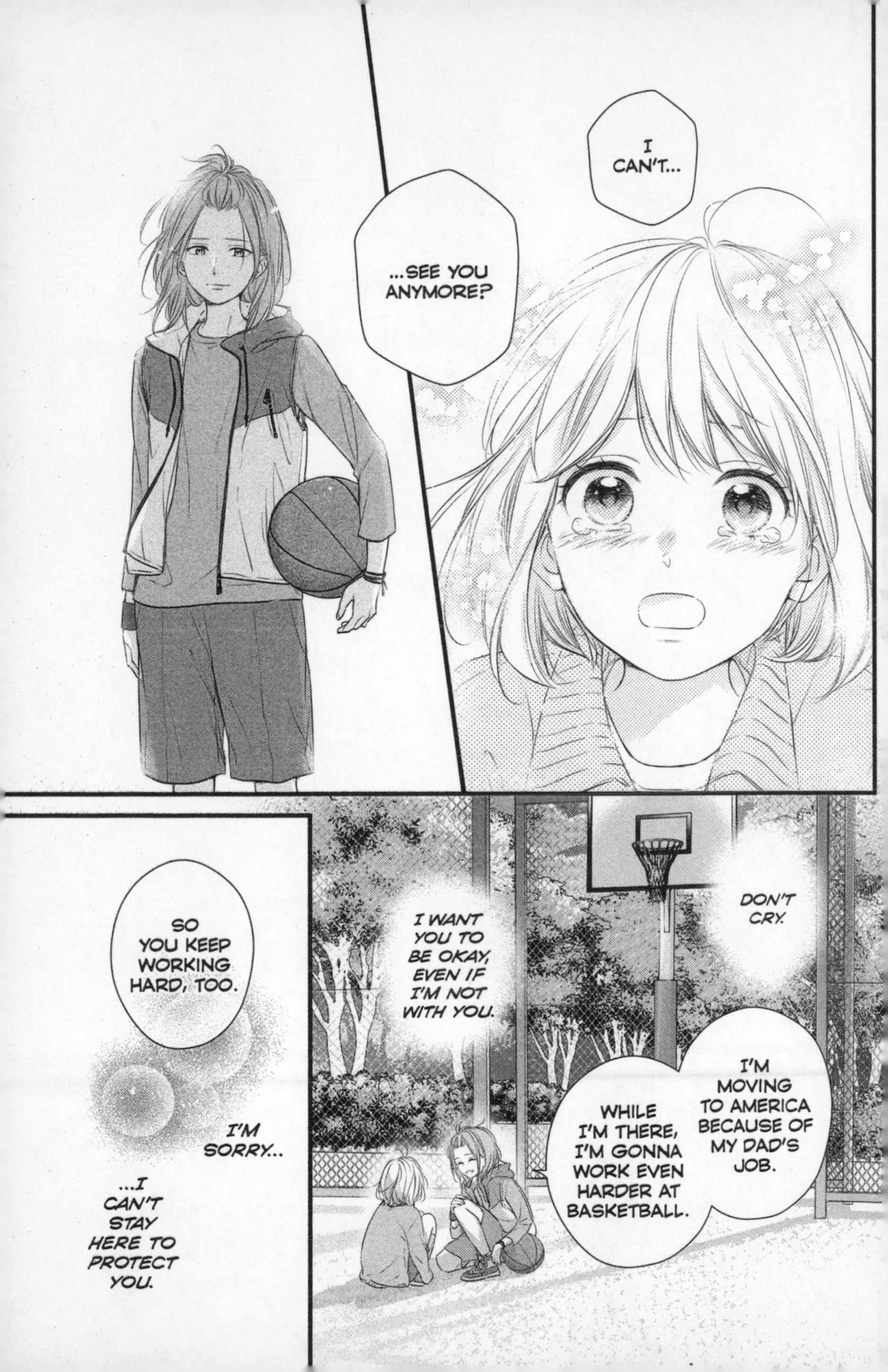
I CAN'T...
...SEE YOU ANYMORE?
DON'T CRY.
I'M MOVING TO AMERICA BECAUSE OF MY DAD'S JOB.
WHILE I'M THERE, I'M GONNA WORK EVEN HARDER AT BASKETBALL.
I WANT YOU TO BE OKAY, EVEN IF I'M NOT WITH YOU.
SO YOU KEEP WORKING HARD, TOO.
I'M SORRY...
...I CAN'T STAY HERE TO PROTECT YOU.

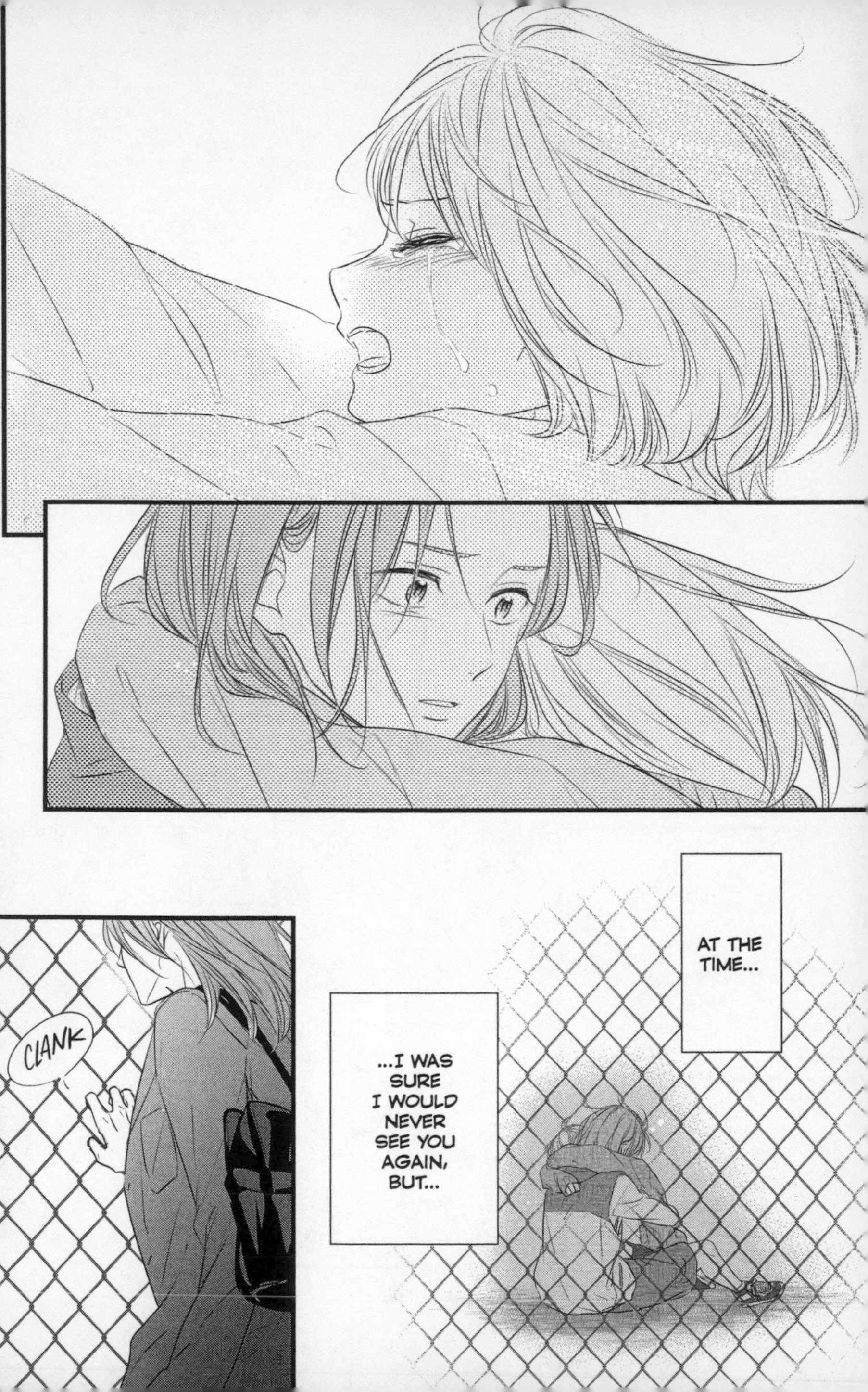
AT THE TIME...
...I WAS SURE I WOULD NEVER SEE YOU AGAIN, BUT...
CLANK

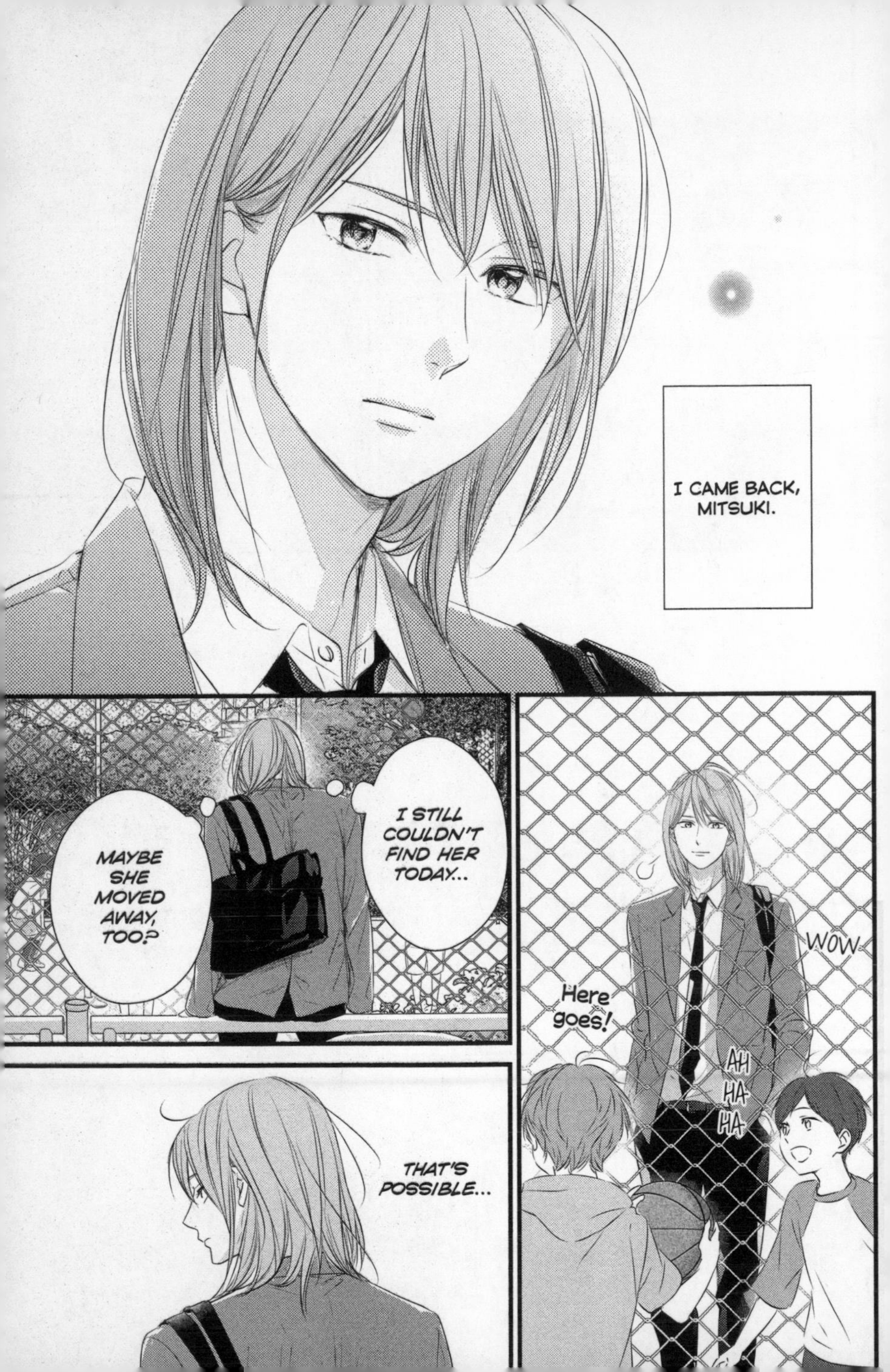
I CAME BACK, MITSUKI.
WOW
Here goes!
AH HA HA
I STILL COULDN'T FIND HER TODAY...
MAYBE SHE MOVED AWAY, TOO?
THAT'S POSSIBLE...

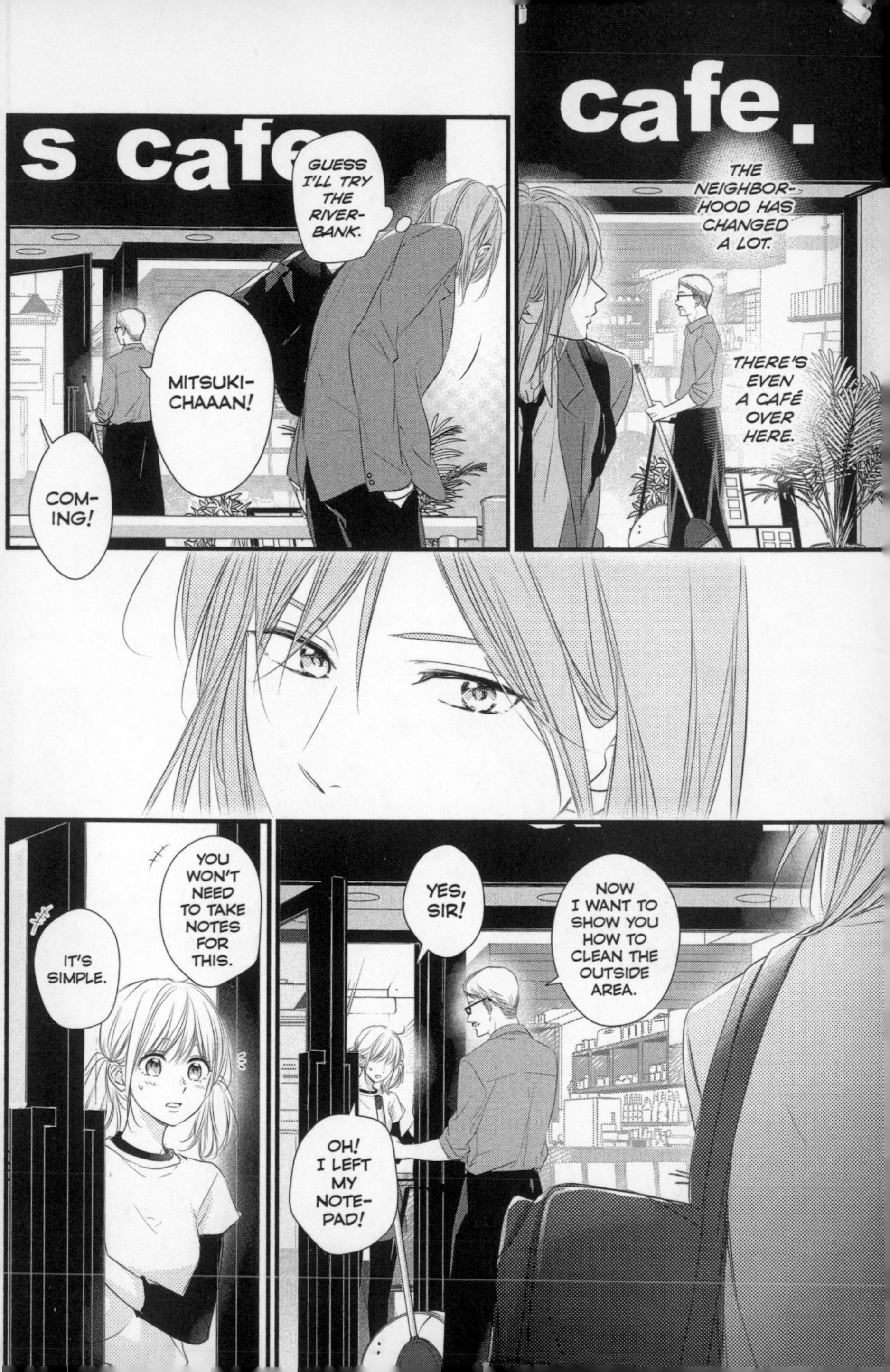
cafe.
THE NEIGHBORHOOD HAS CHANGED A LOT.
THERE'S EVEN A CAFÉ OVER HERE.
s cafe
GUESS I'LL TRY THE RIVERBANK.
MITSUKI-CHAAAN!
COMING!
NOW I WANT TO SHOW YOU HOW TO CLEAN THE OUTSIDE AREA.
YES, SIR!
OH! I LEFT MY NOTEPAD!
YOU WON'T NEED TO TAKE NOTES FOR THIS.
IT'S SIMPLE.

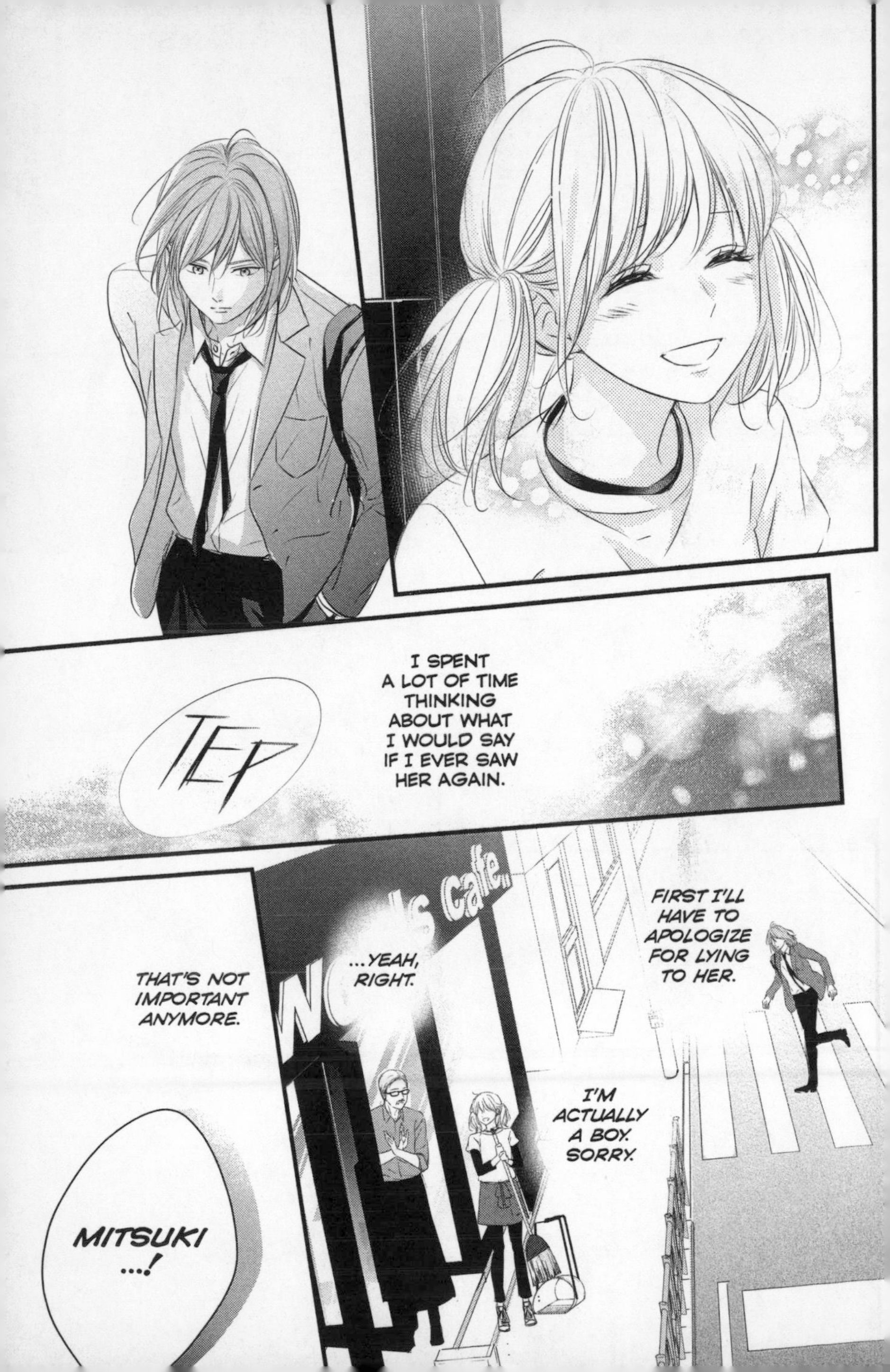
I SPENT A LOT OF TIME THINKING ABOUT WHAT I WOULD SAY IF I EVER SAW HER AGAIN.
TEP
FIRST I'LL HAVE TO APOLOGIZE FOR LYING TO HER.
I'M ACTUALLY A BOY. SORRY.
...YEAH, RIGHT.
THAT'S NOT IMPORTANT ANYMORE.
MITSUKI ...!

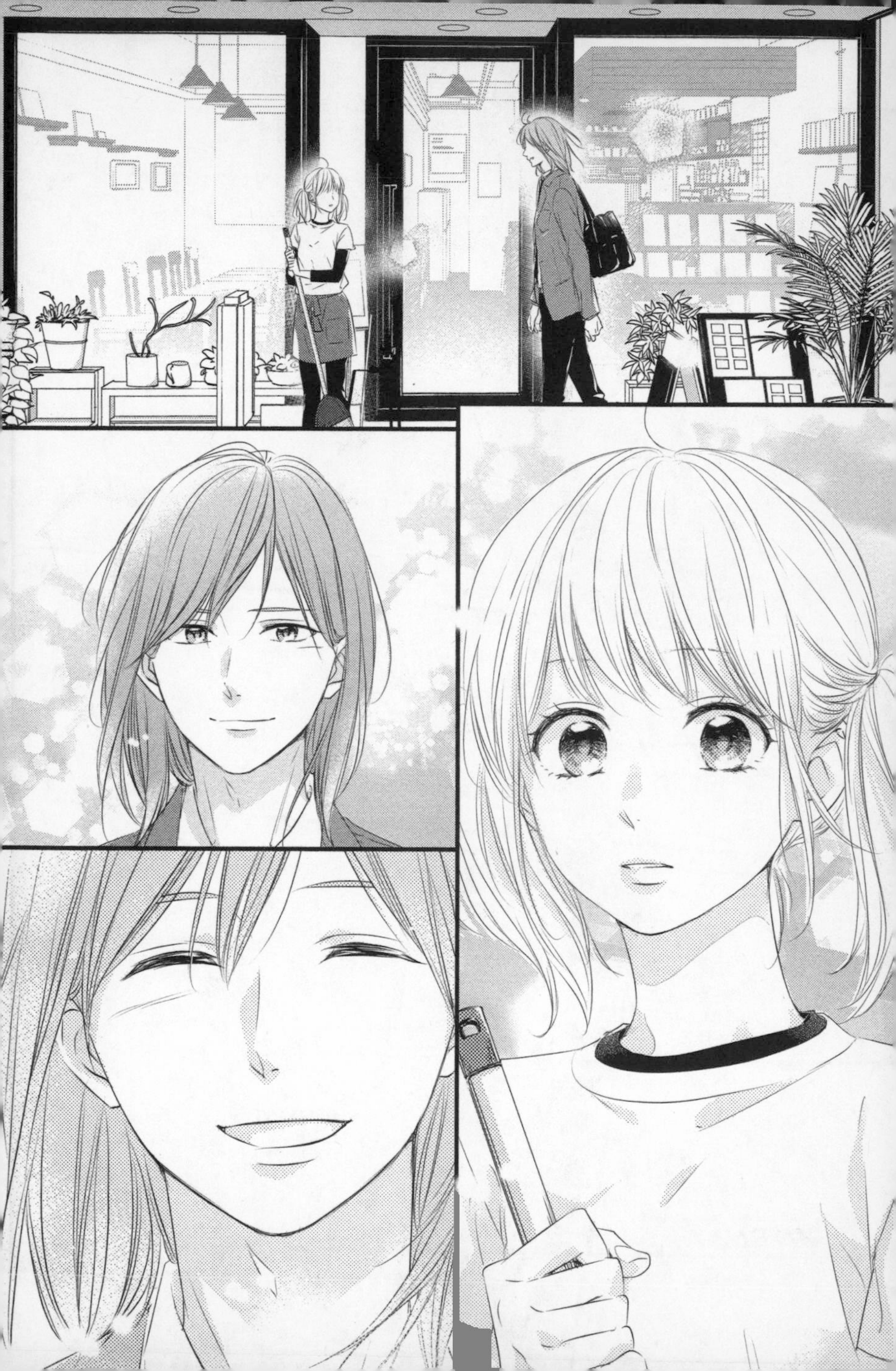

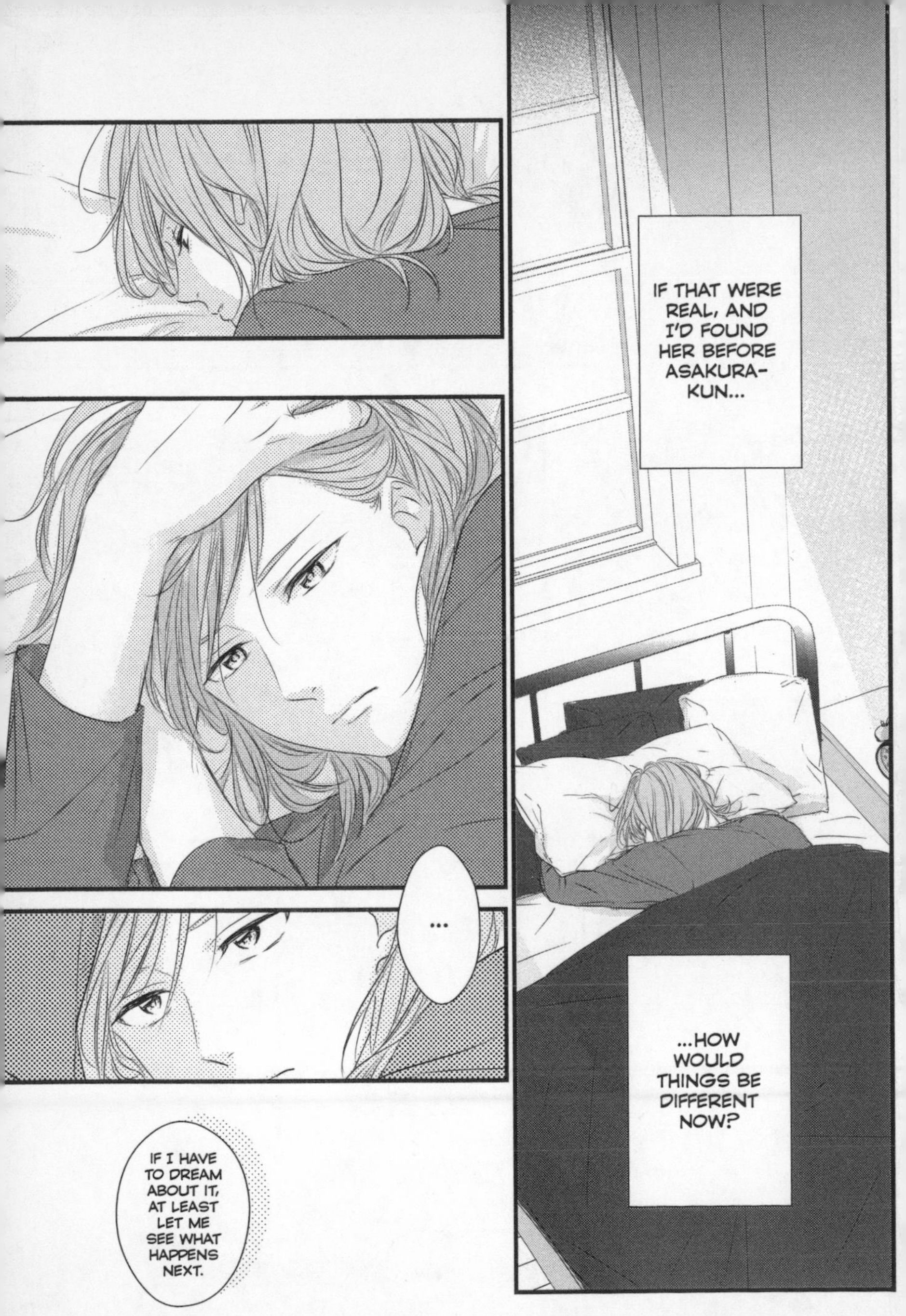
IF THAT WERE REAL, AND I'D FOUND HER BEFORE ASAKURA-KUN...
...HOW WOULD THINGS BE DIFFERENT NOW?
...
IF I HAVE TO DREAM ABOUT IT, AT LEAST LET ME SEE WHAT HAPPENS NEXT.

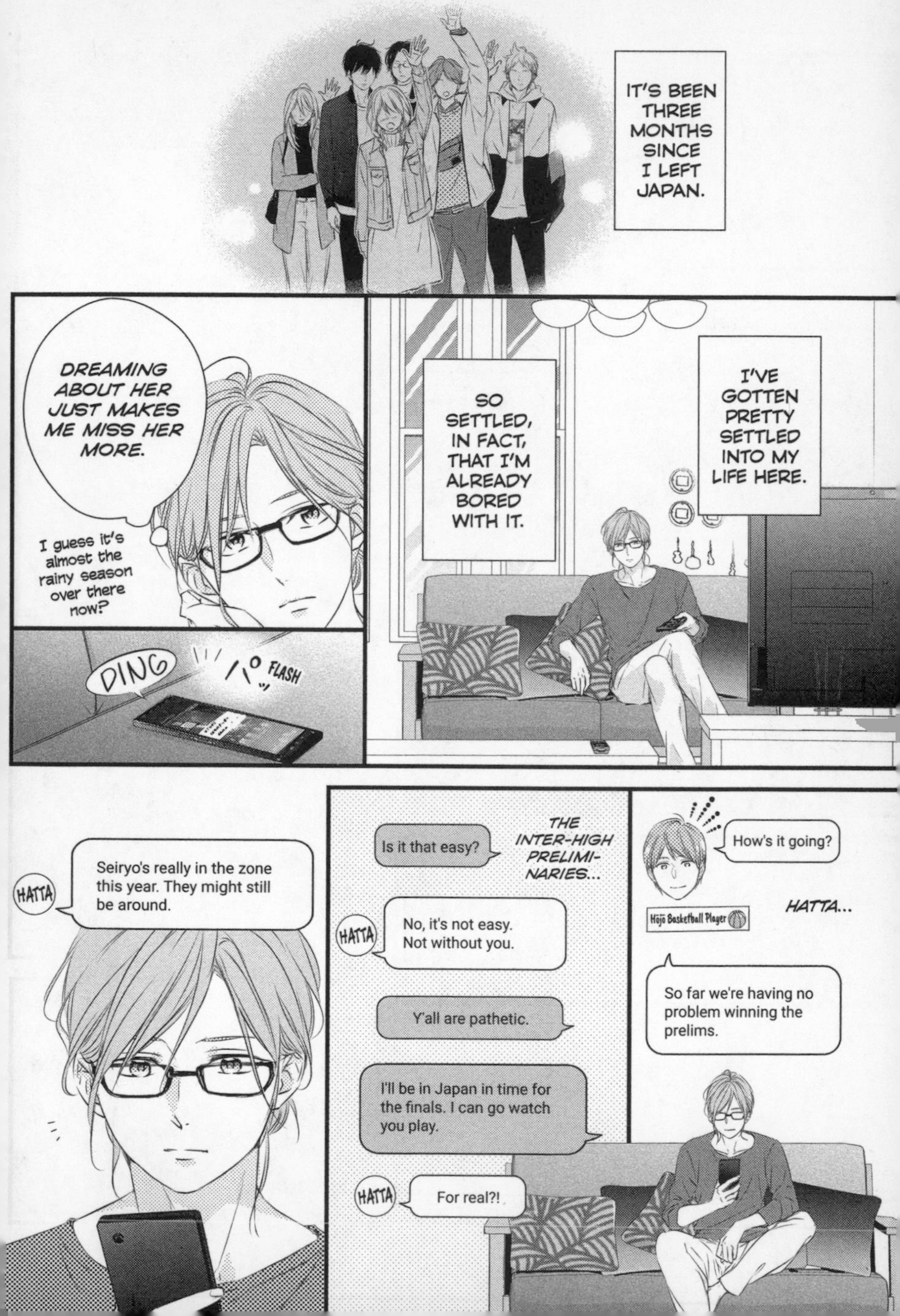

IT'S BEEN THREE MONTHS SINCE I LEFT JAPAN.
I'VE GOTTEN PRETTY SETTLED INTO MY LIFE HERE.
SO SETTLED, IN FACT, THAT I'M ALREADY BORED WITH IT.
DREAMING ABOUT HER JUST MAKES ME MISS HER MORE.
I guess it's almost the rainy season over there now?
DING
FLASH
How's it going?
Hōjō Basketball Player
HATTA...
So far we're having no problem winning the prelims.
THE INTER-HIGH PRELIMINARIES...
Is it that easy?
HATTA
No, it's not easy. Not without you.
Y'all are pathetic.
I'll be in Japan in time for the finals. I can go watch you play.
HATTA
For real?!
HATTA
Seiryo's really in the zone this year. They might still be around.

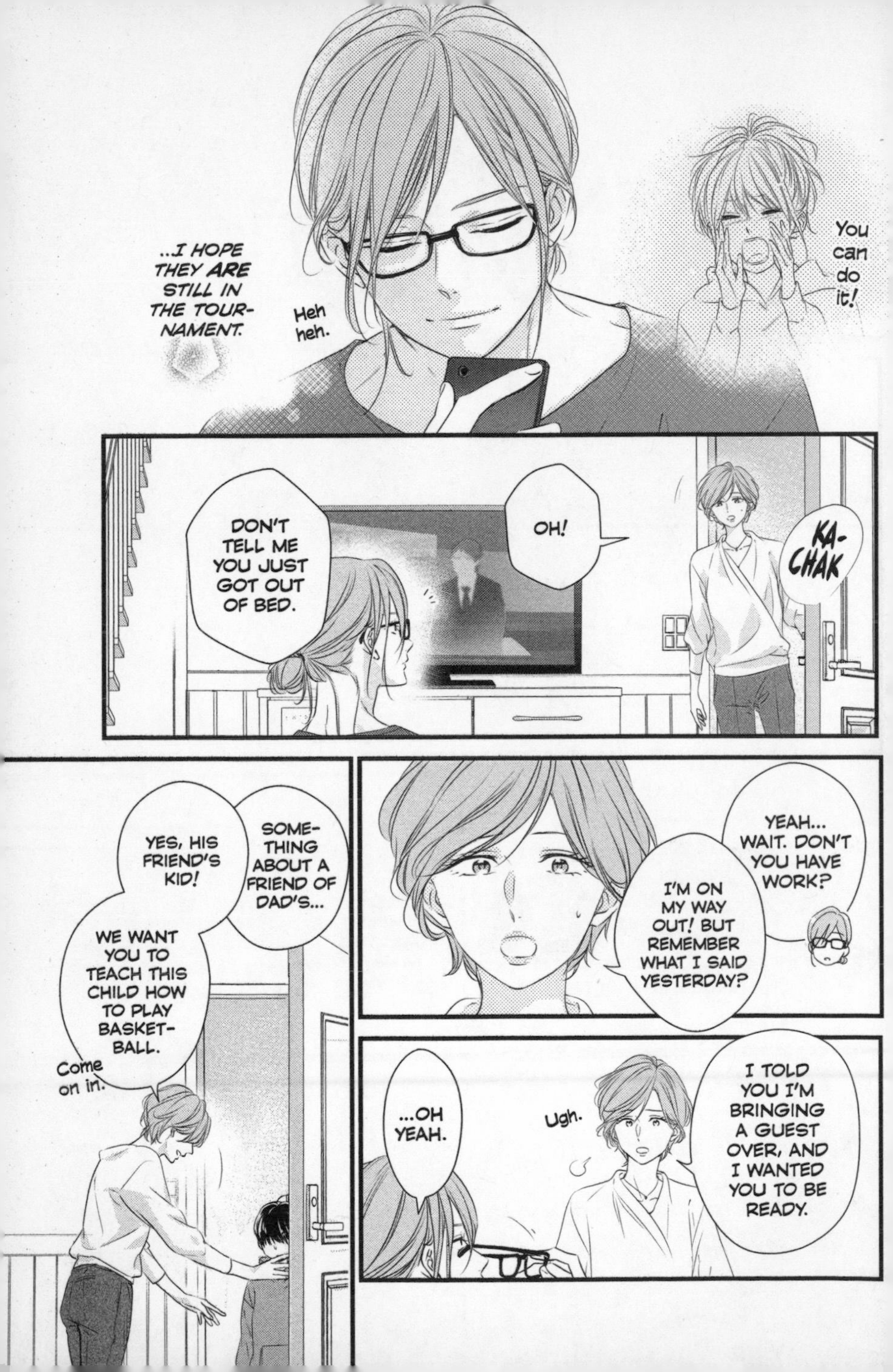
You can do it!
Heh heh.
...I HOPE THEY ARE STILL IN THE TOURNAMENT.
KA-CHAK
OH!
DON'T TELL ME YOU JUST GOT OUT OF BED.
YEAH... WAIT. DON'T YOU HAVE WORK?
I'M ON MY WAY OUT! BUT REMEMBER WHAT I SAID YESTERDAY?
I TOLD YOU I'M BRINGING A GUEST OVER, AND I WANTED YOU TO BE READY.
Ugh.
...OH YEAH.
SOMETHING ABOUT A FRIEND OF DAD'S...
YES, HIS FRIEND'S KID!
WE WANT YOU TO TEACH THIS CHILD HOW TO PLAY BASKETBALL.
Come on in.

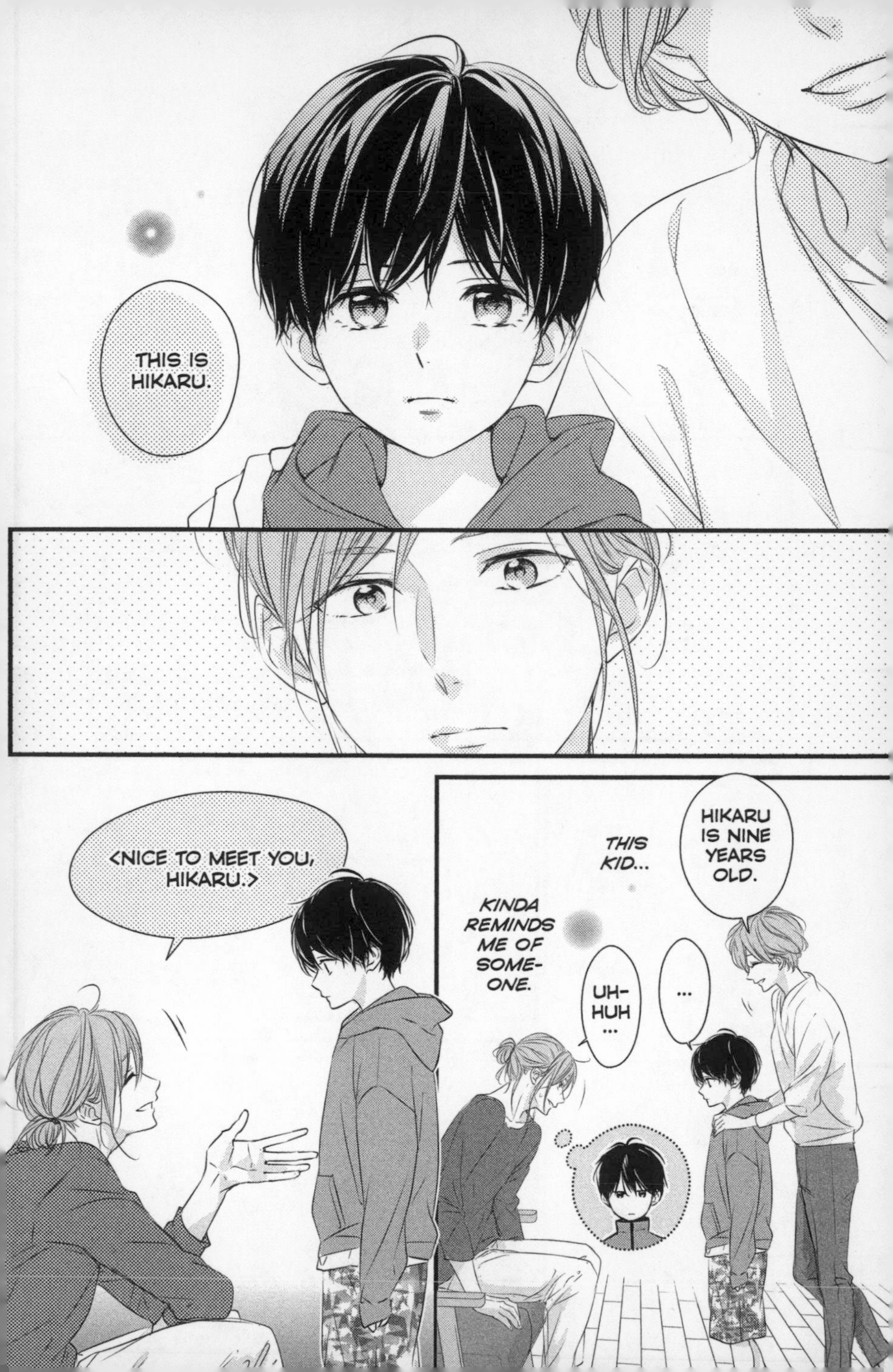
THIS IS HIKARU.
HIKARU IS NINE YEARS OLD.
...
UH-HUH...
THIS KID...
KINDA REMINDS ME OF SOME-ONE.
<NICE TO MEET YOU, HIKARU.>

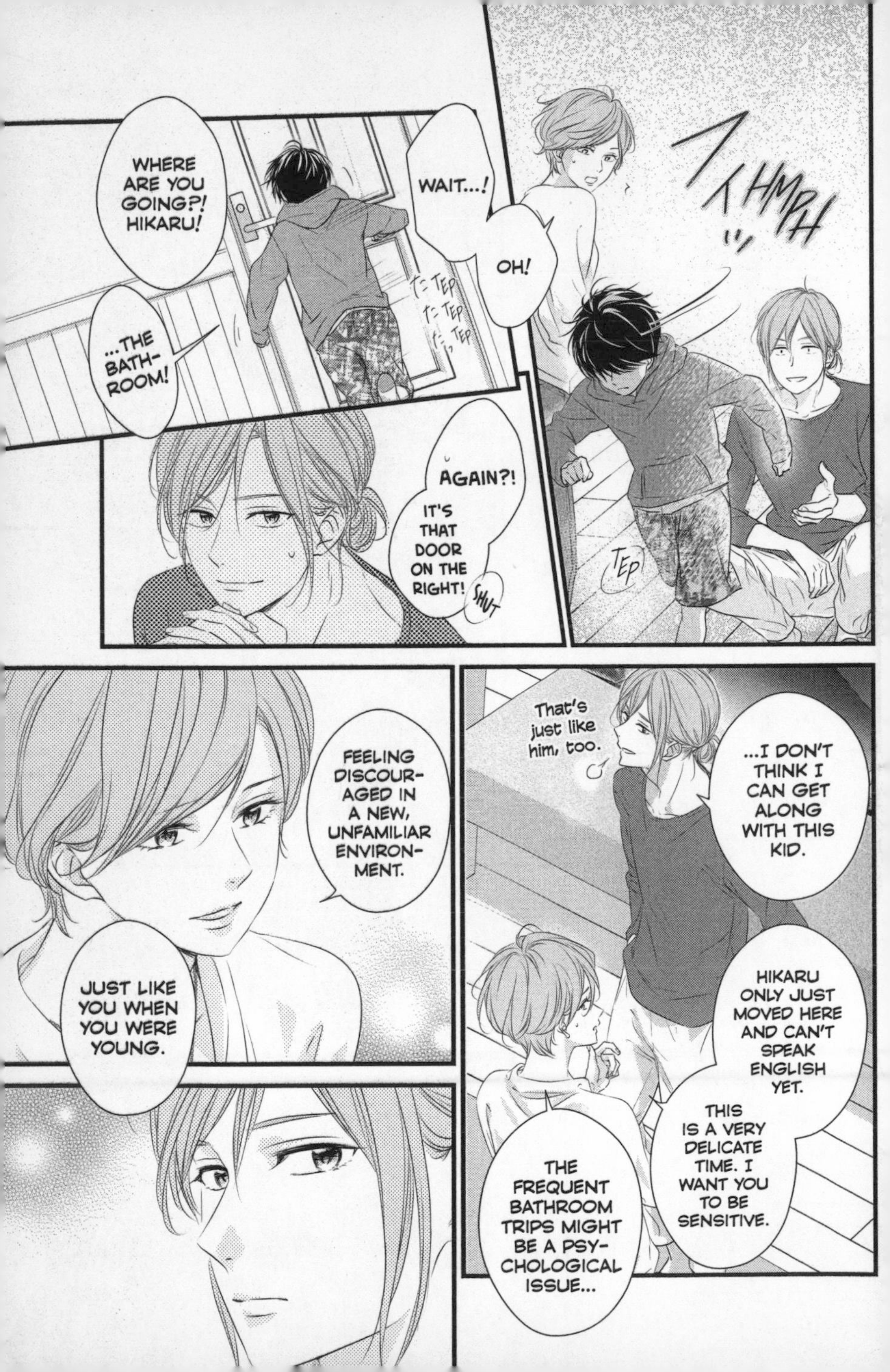
WAIT...!
OH!
HMPH
TEP
WHERE ARE YOU GOING?! HIKARU!
TEP TEP TEP
...THE BATH-ROOM!
AGAIN?!
IT'S THAT DOOR ON THE RIGHT!
SHUT
That's just like him, too.
...I DON'T THINK I CAN GET ALONG WITH THIS KID.
HIKARU ONLY JUST MOVED HERE AND CAN'T SPEAK ENGLISH YET.
THIS IS A VERY DELICATE TIME. I WANT YOU TO BE SENSITIVE.
THE FREQUENT BATHROOM TRIPS MIGHT BE A PSY-CHOLOGICAL ISSUE...
FEELING DISCOUR-AGED IN A NEW, UNFAMILIAR ENVIRON-MENT.
JUST LIKE YOU WHEN YOU WERE YOUNG.

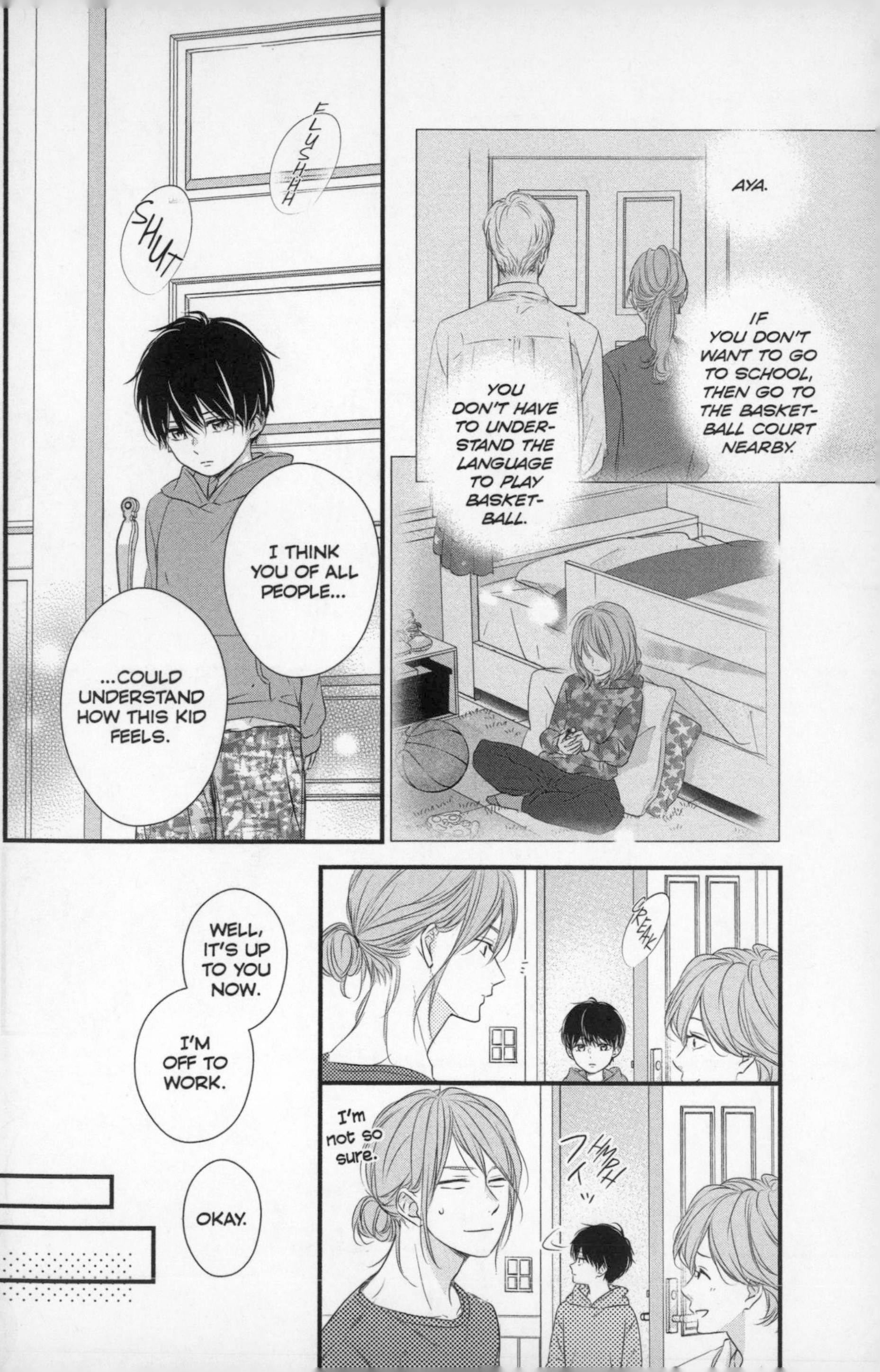
AYA.
IF YOU DON'T WANT TO GO TO SCHOOL, THEN GO TO THE BASKETBALL COURT NEARBY.
YOU DON'T HAVE TO UNDERSTAND THE LANGUAGE TO PLAY BASKETBALL.
FLUSHHH
SHUT
I THINK YOU OF ALL PEOPLE...
...COULD UNDERSTAND HOW THIS KID FEELS.
CREAK
WELL, IT'S UP TO YOU NOW.
I'M OFF TO WORK.
HMPH
I'm not so sure.
OKAY.

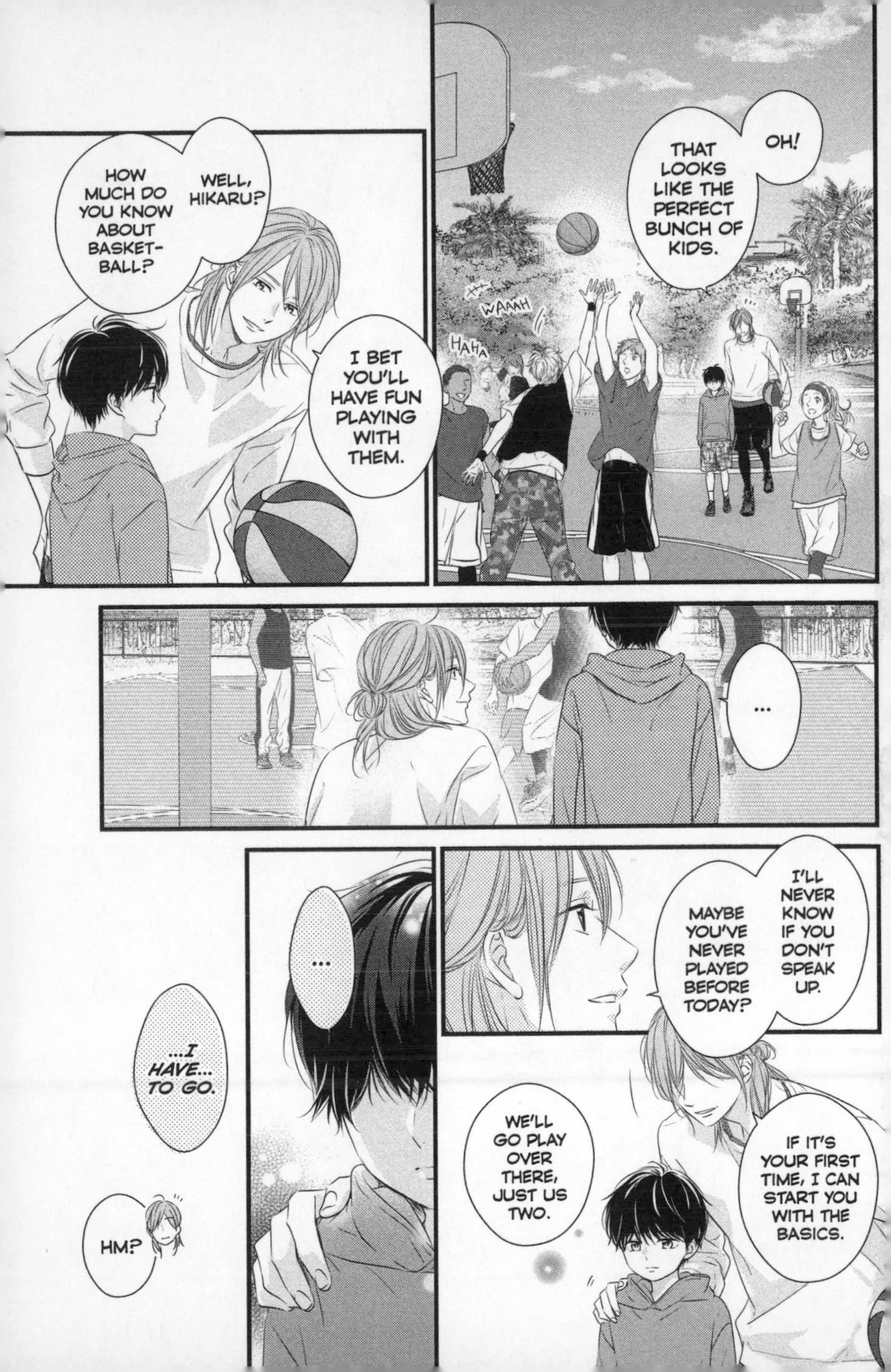

OH!
THAT LOOKS LIKE THE PERFECT BUNCH OF KIDS.
WAAAH
HAHA
WELL, HIKARU?
HOW MUCH DO YOU KNOW ABOUT BASKET-BALL?
I BET YOU'LL HAVE FUN PLAYING WITH THEM.
...
I'LL NEVER KNOW IF YOU DON'T SPEAK UP.
MAYBE YOU'VE NEVER PLAYED BEFORE TODAY?
IF IT'S YOUR FIRST TIME, I CAN START YOU WITH THE BASICS.
WE'LL GO PLAY OVER THERE, JUST US TWO.
...
...I HAVE... TO GO.
HM?

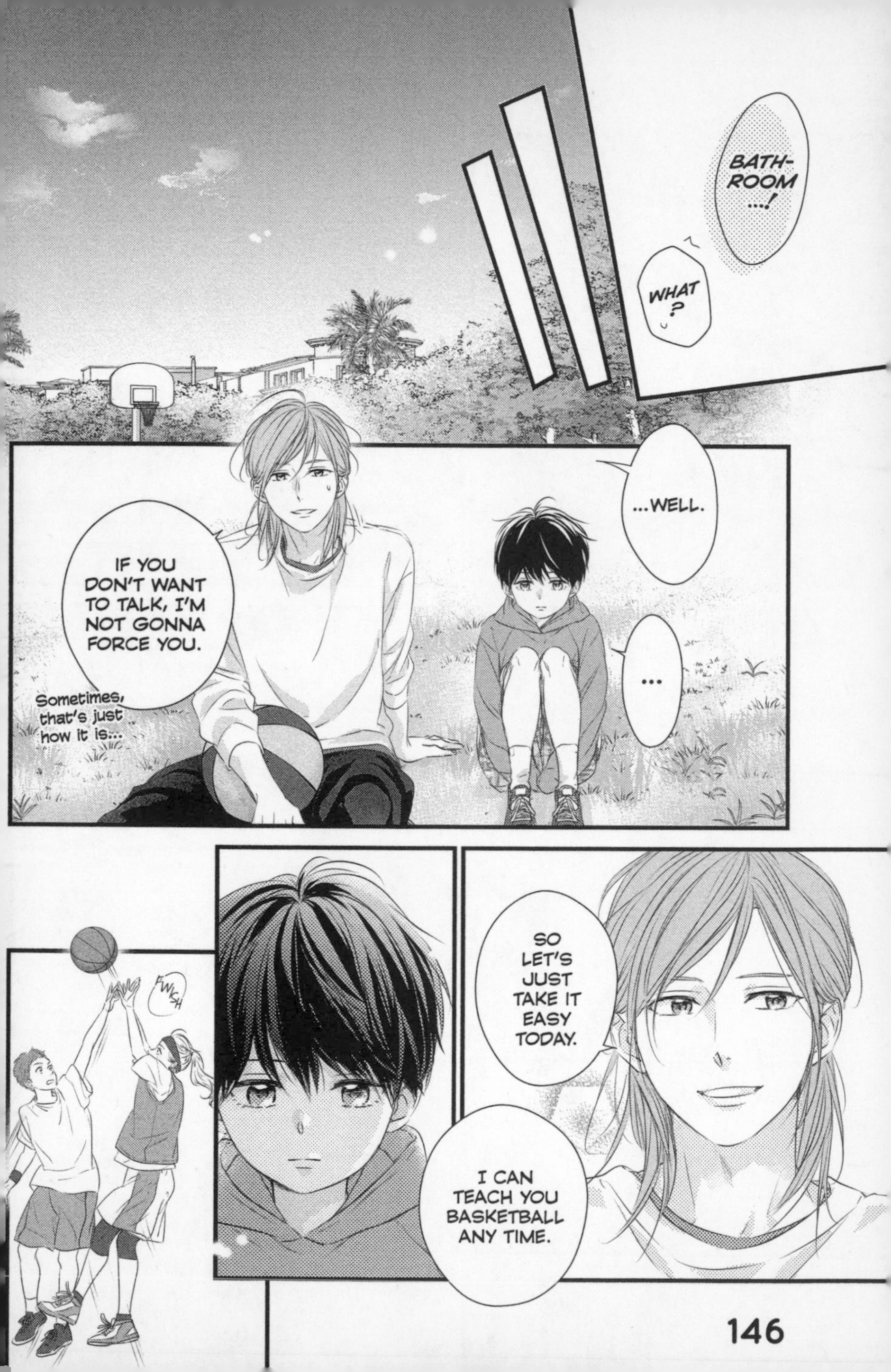
BATH-ROOM ...!
WHAT ?
...WELL.
...
IF YOU DON'T WANT TO TALK, I'M NOT GONNA FORCE YOU.
Sometimes, that's just how it is...
SO LET'S JUST TAKE IT EASY TODAY.
I CAN TEACH YOU BASKETBALL ANY TIME.
FWISH

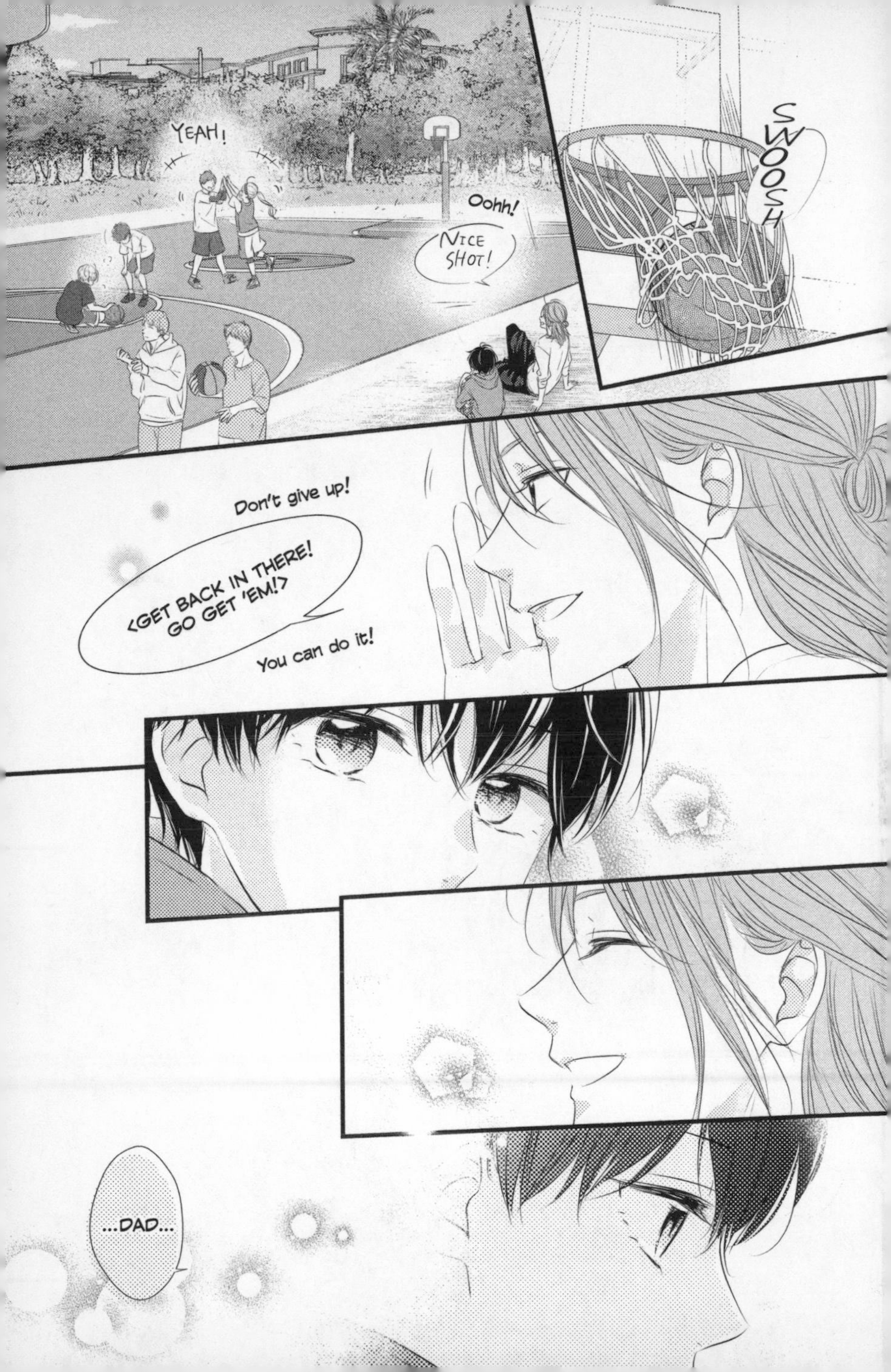
SWOOSH
Oohh!
NICE SHOT!
YEAH!
Don't give up!
<GET BACK IN THERE! GO GET 'EM!>
You can do it!
...DAD...

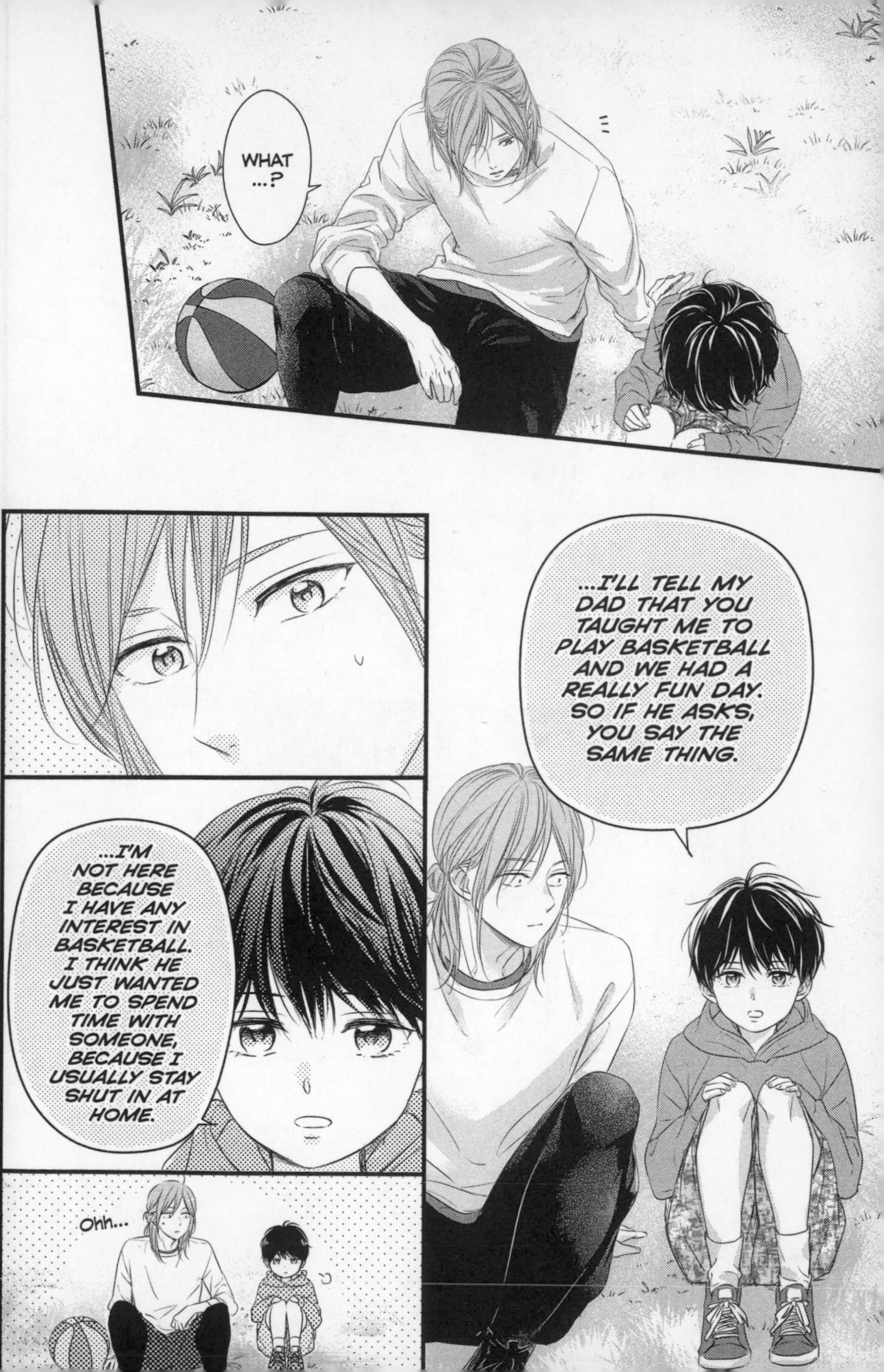
WHAT ...?
...I'LL TELL MY DAD THAT YOU TAUGHT ME TO PLAY BASKETBALL AND WE HAD A REALLY FUN DAY. SO IF HE ASKS, YOU SAY THE SAME THING.
...I'M NOT HERE BECAUSE I HAVE ANY INTEREST IN BASKETBALL. I THINK HE JUST WANTED ME TO SPEND TIME WITH SOMEONE, BECAUSE I USUALLY STAY SHUT IN AT HOME.
Ohh...

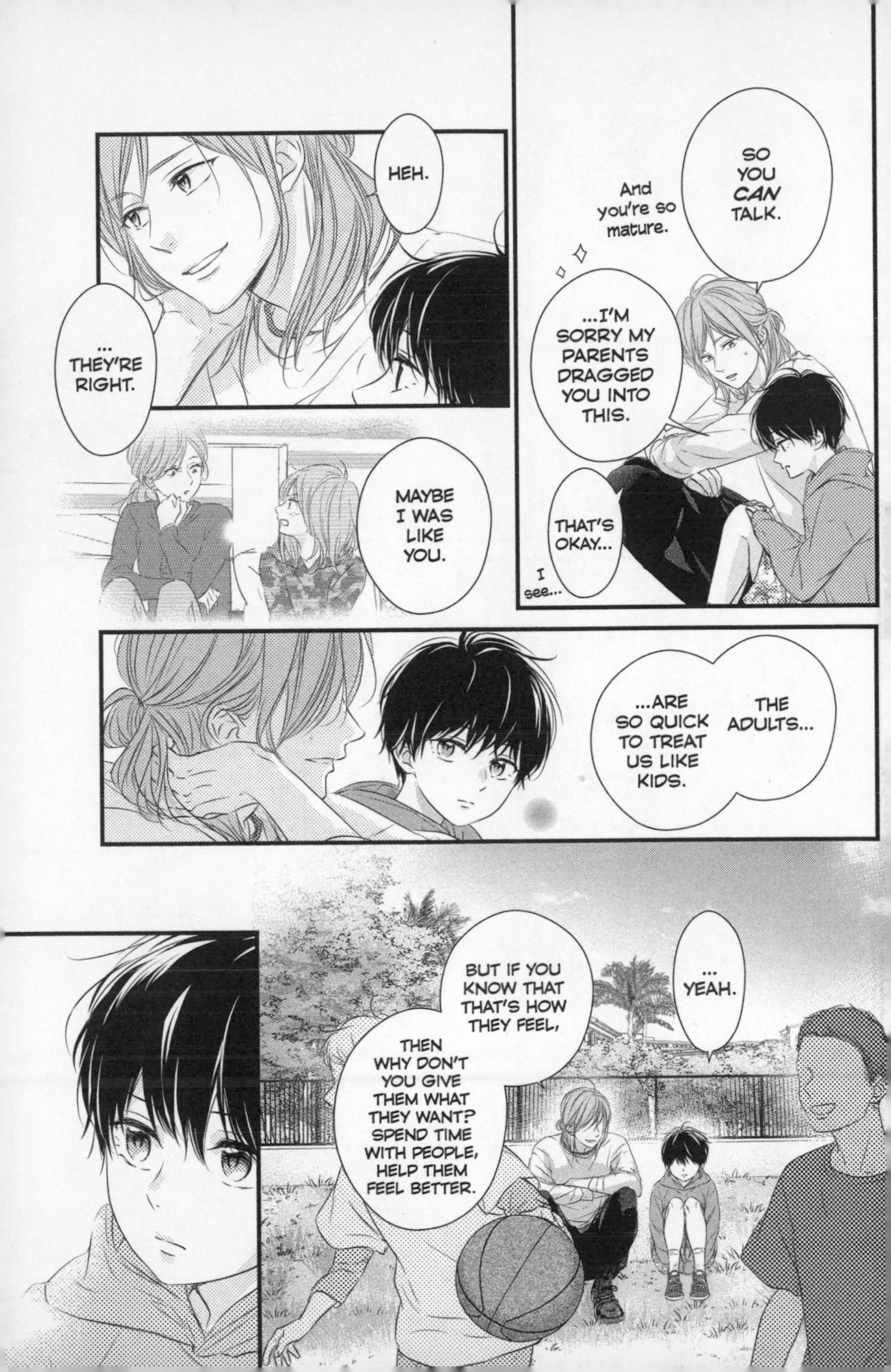
SO YOU CAN TALK.
And you're so mature.
...I'M SORRY MY PARENTS DRAGGED YOU INTO THIS.
THAT'S OKAY...
I see...
HEH.
... THEY'RE RIGHT.
MAYBE I WAS LIKE YOU.
THE ADULTS...
...ARE SO QUICK TO TREAT US LIKE KIDS.
... YEAH.
BUT IF YOU KNOW THAT THAT'S HOW THEY FEEL,
THEN WHY DON'T YOU GIVE THEM WHAT THEY WANT? SPEND TIME WITH PEOPLE, HELP THEM FEEL BETTER.

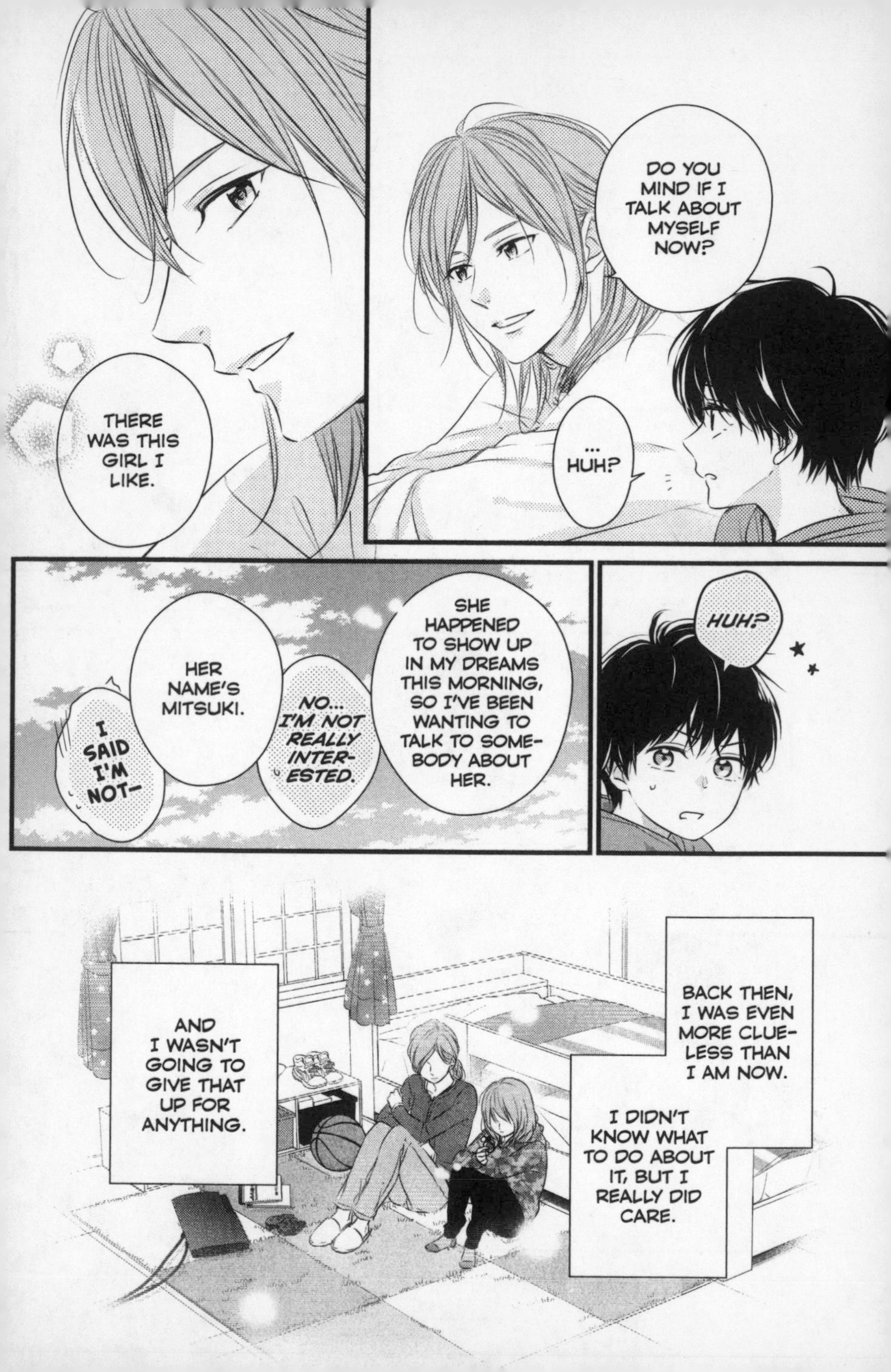
DO YOU MIND IF I TALK ABOUT MYSELF NOW?
... HUH?
THERE WAS THIS GIRL I LIKE.
HUH?
SHE HAPPENED TO SHOW UP IN MY DREAMS THIS MORNING, SO I'VE BEEN WANTING TO TALK TO SOME-BODY ABOUT HER.
NO... I'M NOT REALLY INTER-ESTED.
HER NAME'S MITSUKI.
I SAID I'M NOT-
BACK THEN, I WAS EVEN MORE CLUE-LESS THAN I AM NOW.
I DIDN'T KNOW WHAT TO DO ABOUT IT, BUT I REALLY DID CARE.
AND I WASN'T GOING TO GIVE THAT UP FOR ANYTHING.

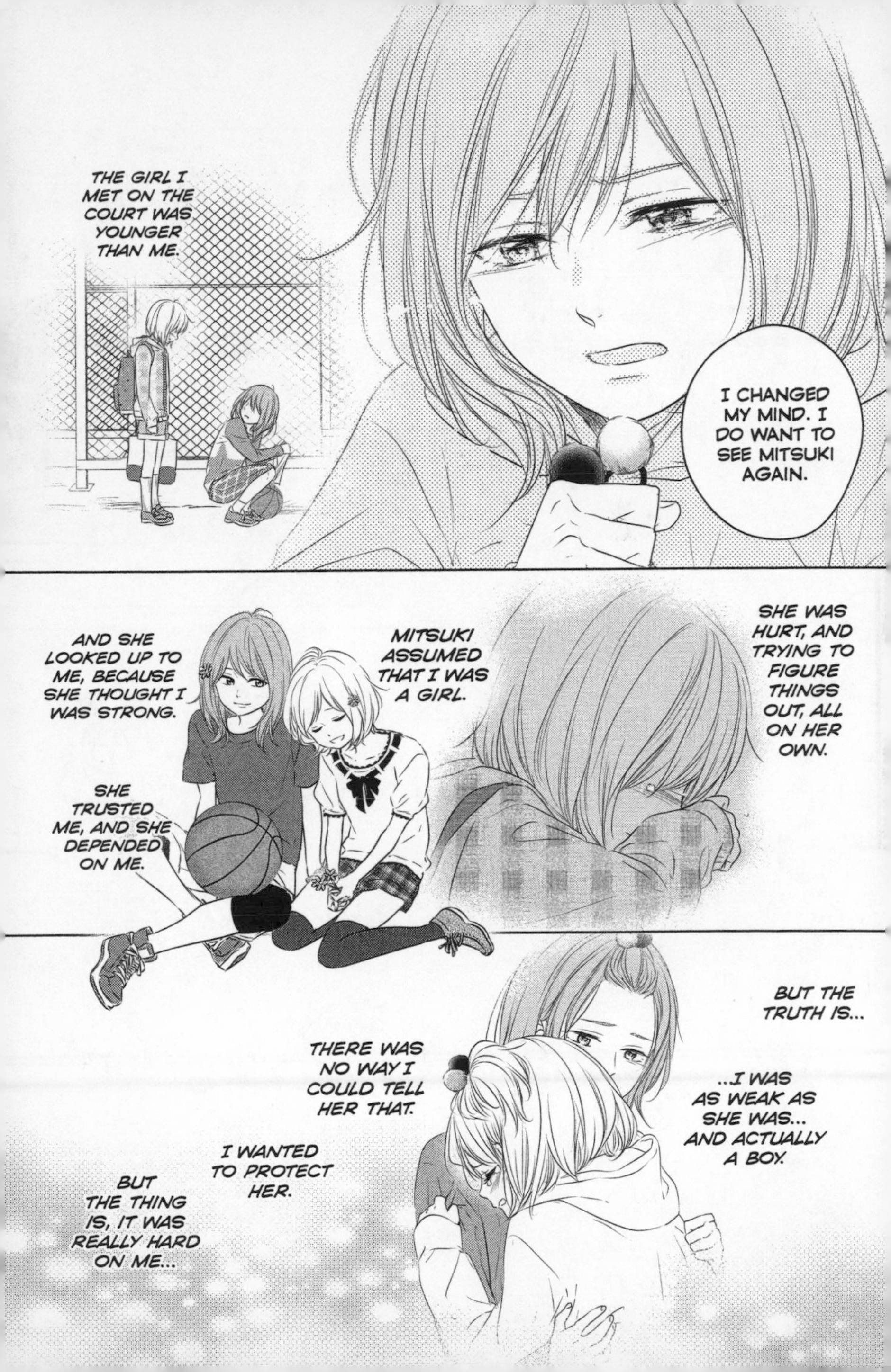
THE GIRL I MET ON THE COURT WAS YOUNGER THAN ME.
I CHANGED MY MIND. I DO WANT TO SEE MITSUKI AGAIN.
SHE WAS HURT, AND TRYING TO FIGURE THINGS OUT, ALL ON HER OWN.
MITSUKI ASSUMED THAT I WAS A GIRL.
AND SHE LOOKED UP TO ME, BECAUSE SHE THOUGHT I WAS STRONG.
SHE TRUSTED ME, AND SHE DEPENDED ON ME.
BUT THE TRUTH IS...
...I WAS AS WEAK AS SHE WAS... AND ACTUALLY A BOY.
THERE WAS NO WAY I COULD TELL HER THAT.
I WANTED TO PROTECT HER.
BUT THE THING IS, IT WAS REALLY HARD ON ME...

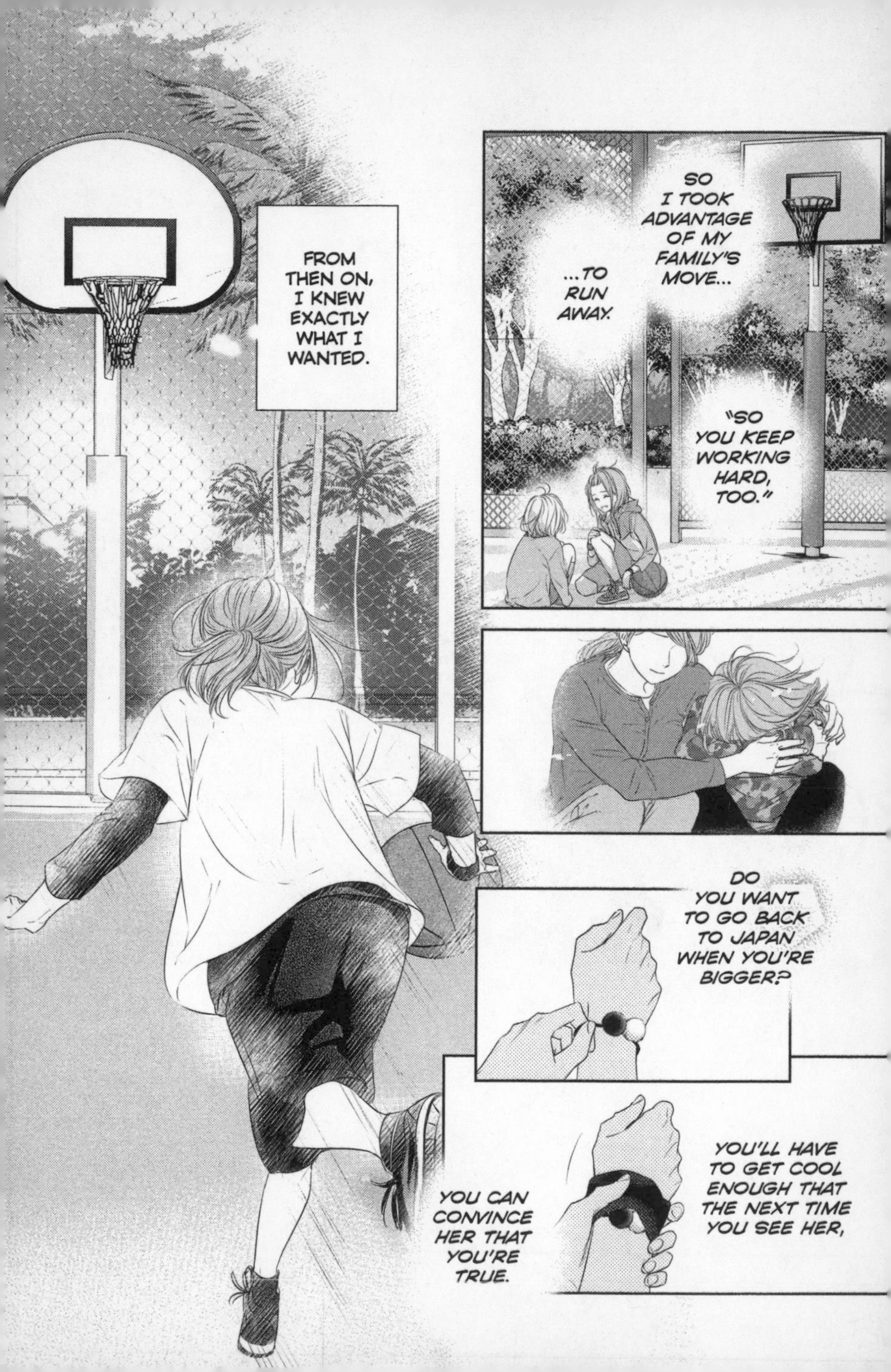
SO I TOOK ADVANTAGE OF MY FAMILY'S MOVE...
...TO RUN AWAY.
"SO YOU KEEP WORKING HARD, TOO."
DO YOU WANT TO GO BACK TO JAPAN WHEN YOU'RE BIGGER?
YOU'LL HAVE TO GET COOL ENOUGH THAT THE NEXT TIME YOU SEE HER,
YOU CAN CONVINCE HER THAT YOU'RE TRUE.
FROM THEN ON, I KNEW EXACTLY WHAT I WANTED.

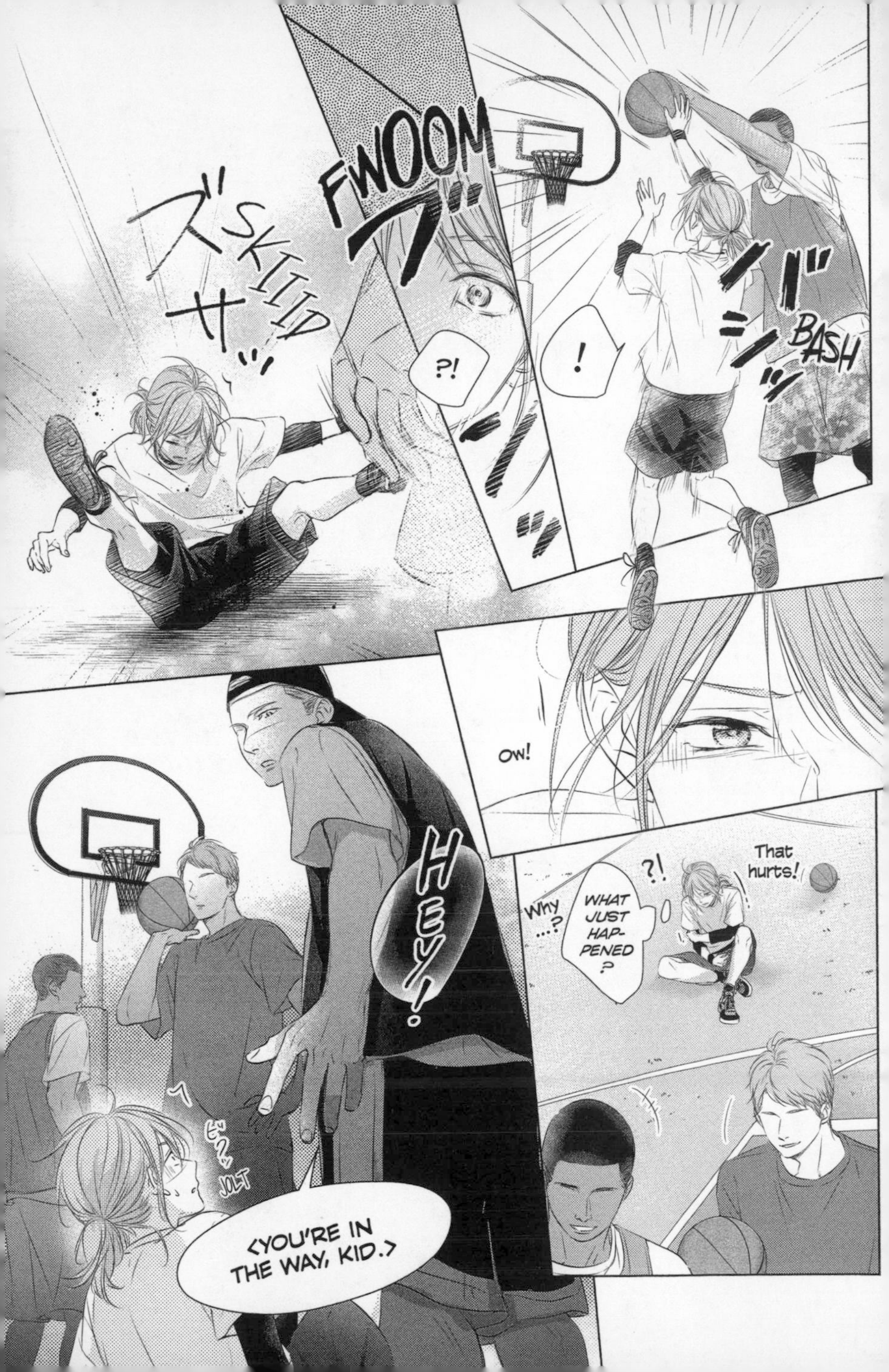
BASH
!
FWOOM
?!
SKIIID
OW!
That hurts!
?!
WHAT JUST HAPPENED?
Why ...?
HEY!
JOLT
<YOU'RE IN THE WAY, KID.>

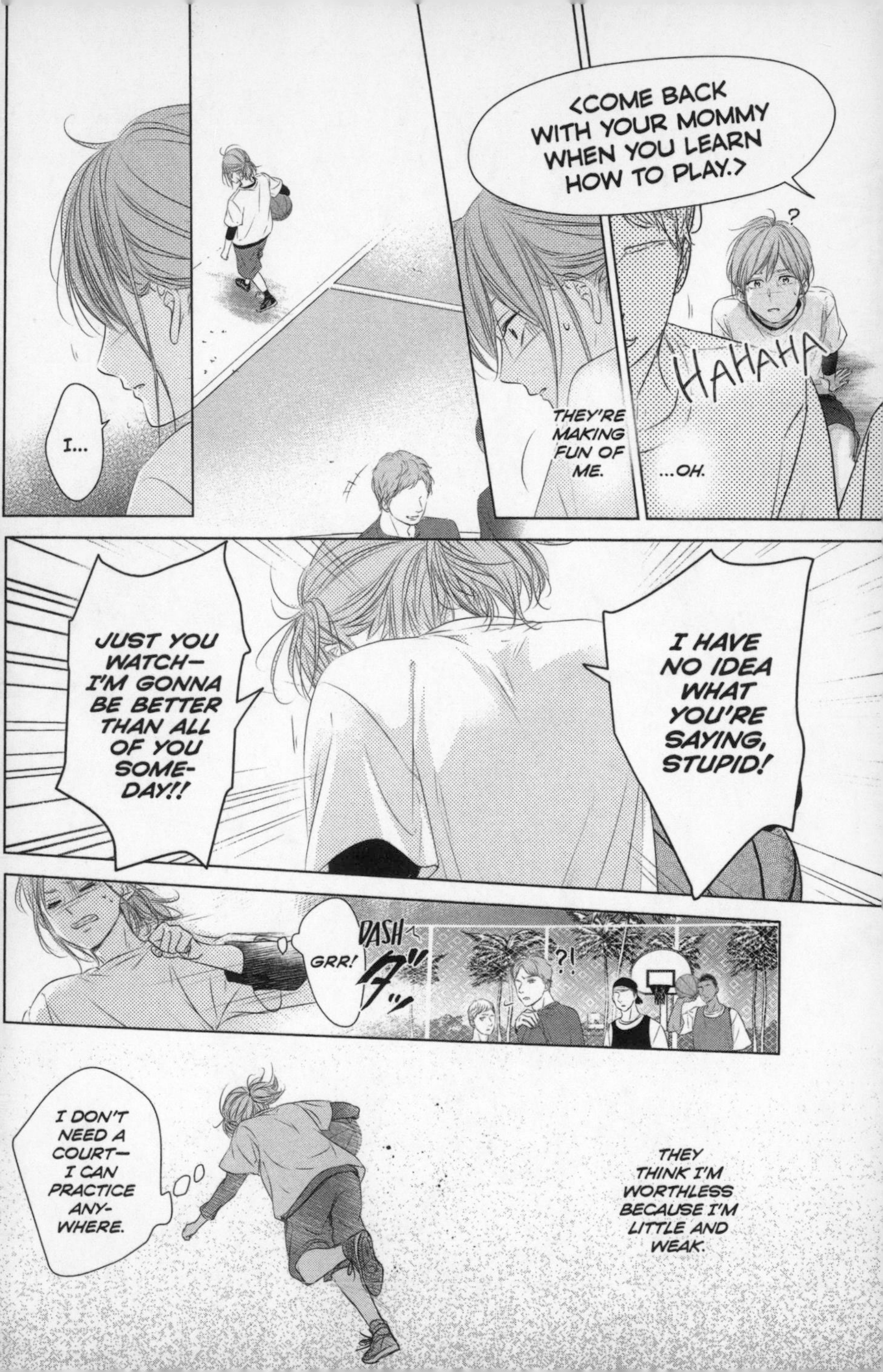
<COME BACK WITH YOUR MOMMY WHEN YOU LEARN HOW TO PLAY.>
?
HAHAHA
...OH.
THEY'RE MAKING FUN OF ME.
I...
I HAVE NO IDEA WHAT YOU'RE SAYING, STUPID!
JUST YOU WATCH—I'M GONNA BE BETTER THAN ALL OF YOU SOME-DAY!!
?!
DASH
GRR!
THEY THINK I'M WORTHLESS BECAUSE I'M LITTLE AND WEAK.
I DON'T NEED A COURT—I CAN PRACTICE ANY-WHERE.

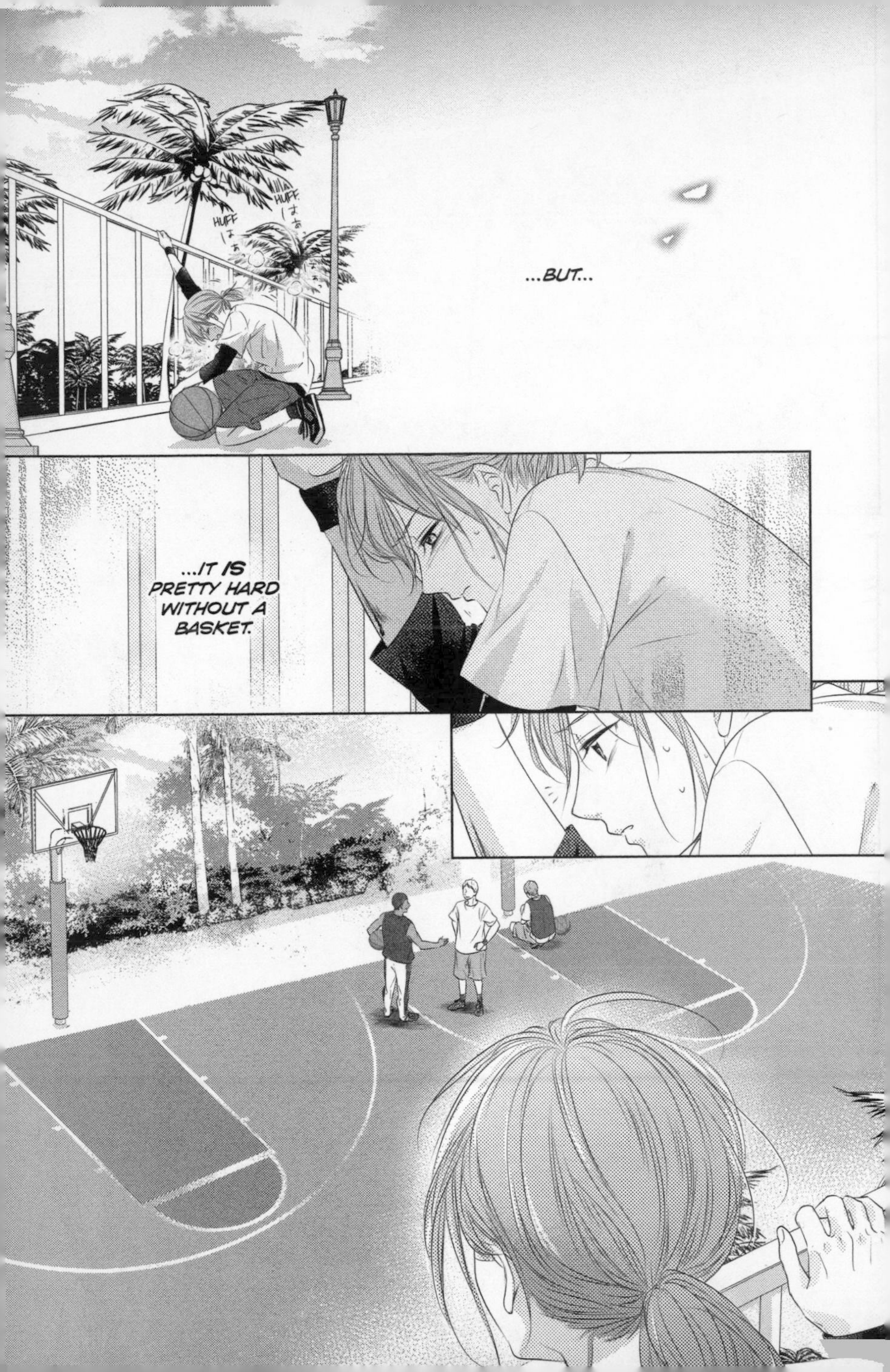
...BUT...
HUFF はぁ
HUFF はぁ
...IT IS PRETTY HARD WITHOUT A BASKET.

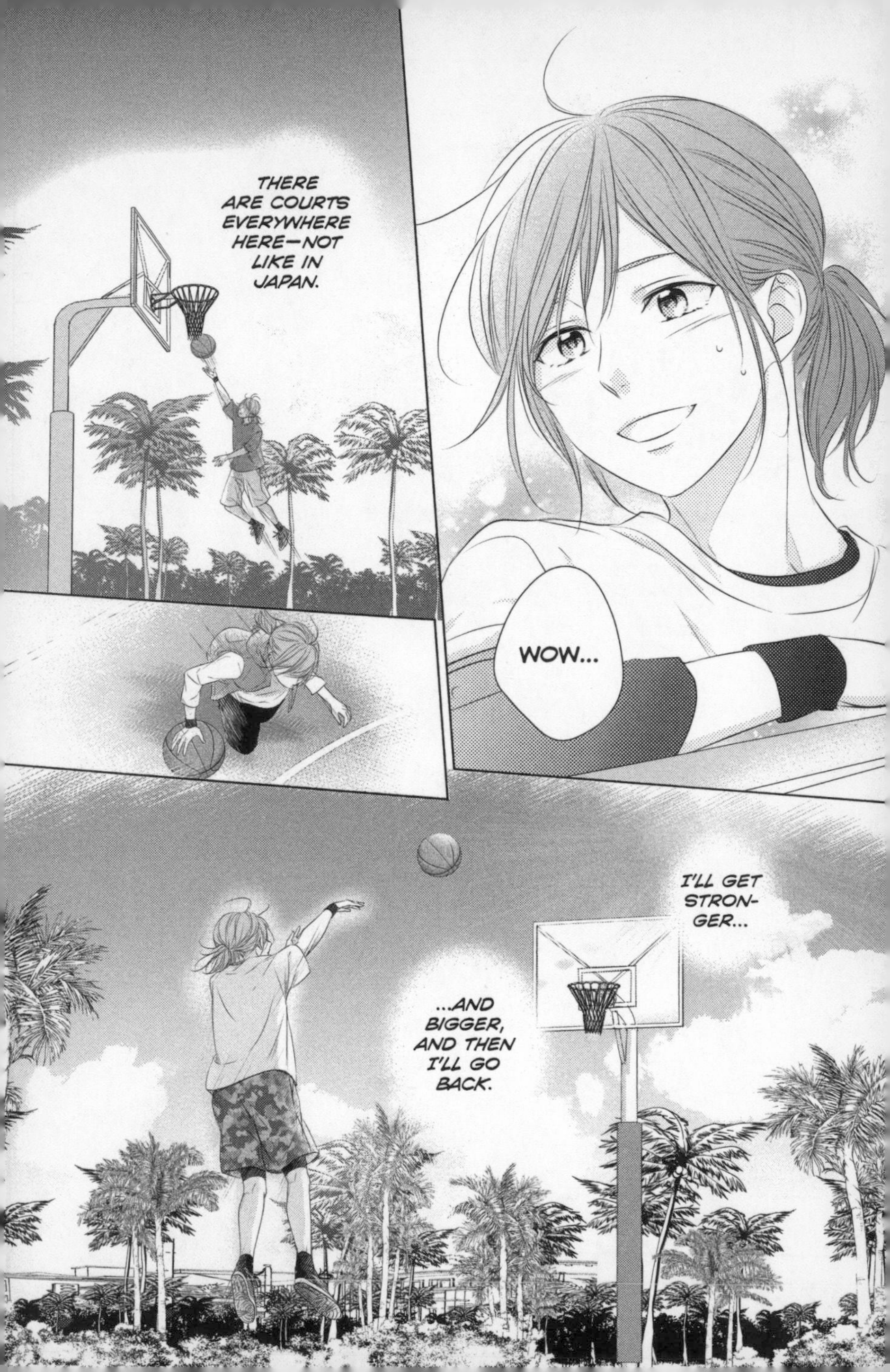
WOW...
THERE ARE COURTS EVERYWHERE HERE—NOT LIKE IN JAPAN.
I'LL GET STRONGER...
...AND BIGGER, AND THEN I'LL GO BACK.

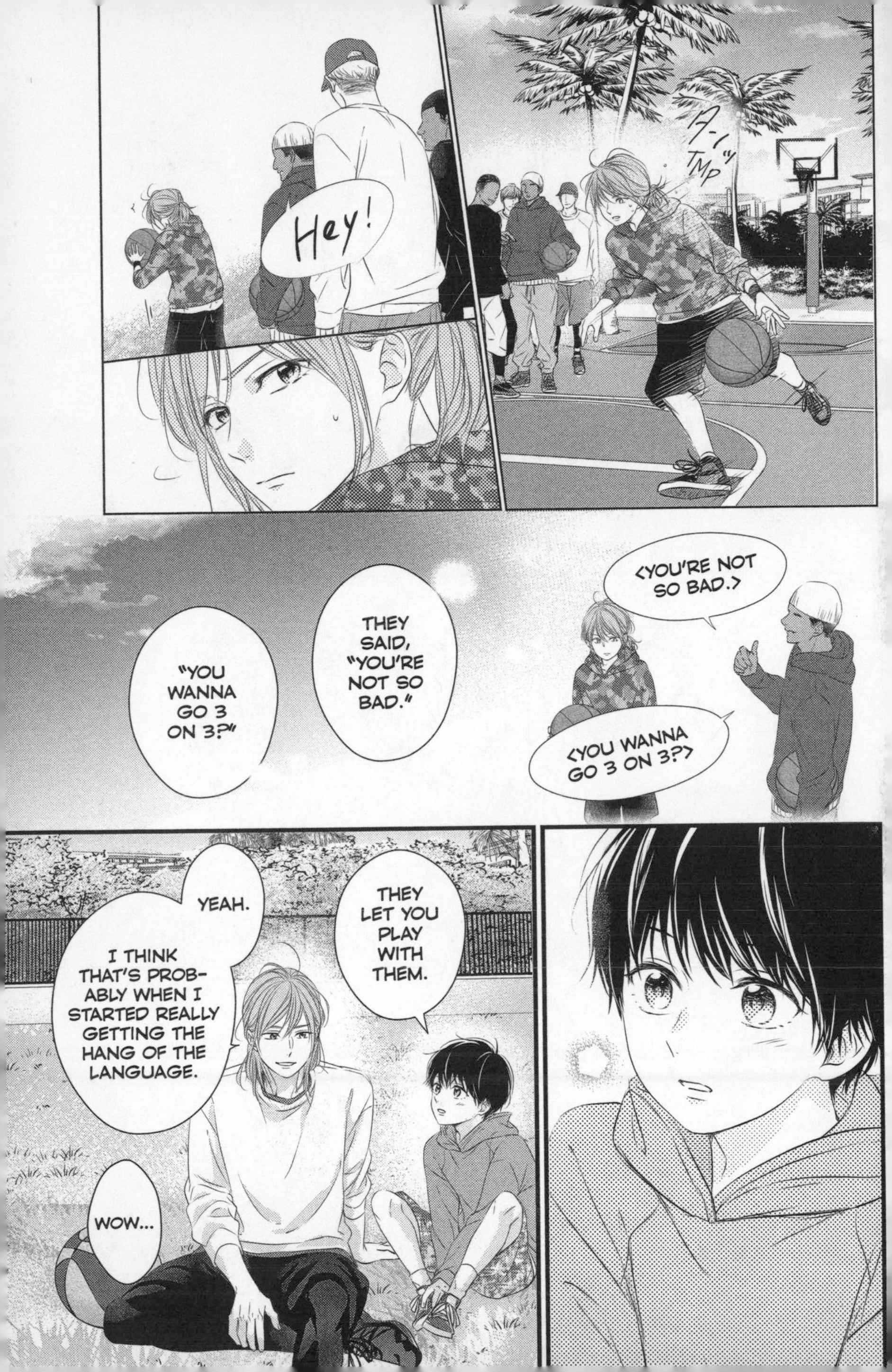
TMP
Hey!
<YOU'RE NOT SO BAD.>
<YOU WANNA GO 3 ON 3?>
THEY SAID, "YOU'RE NOT SO BAD."
"YOU WANNA GO 3 ON 3?"
THEY LET YOU PLAY WITH THEM.
YEAH.
I THINK THAT'S PROB-ABLY WHEN I STARTED REALLY GETTING THE HANG OF THE LANGUAGE.
WOW...

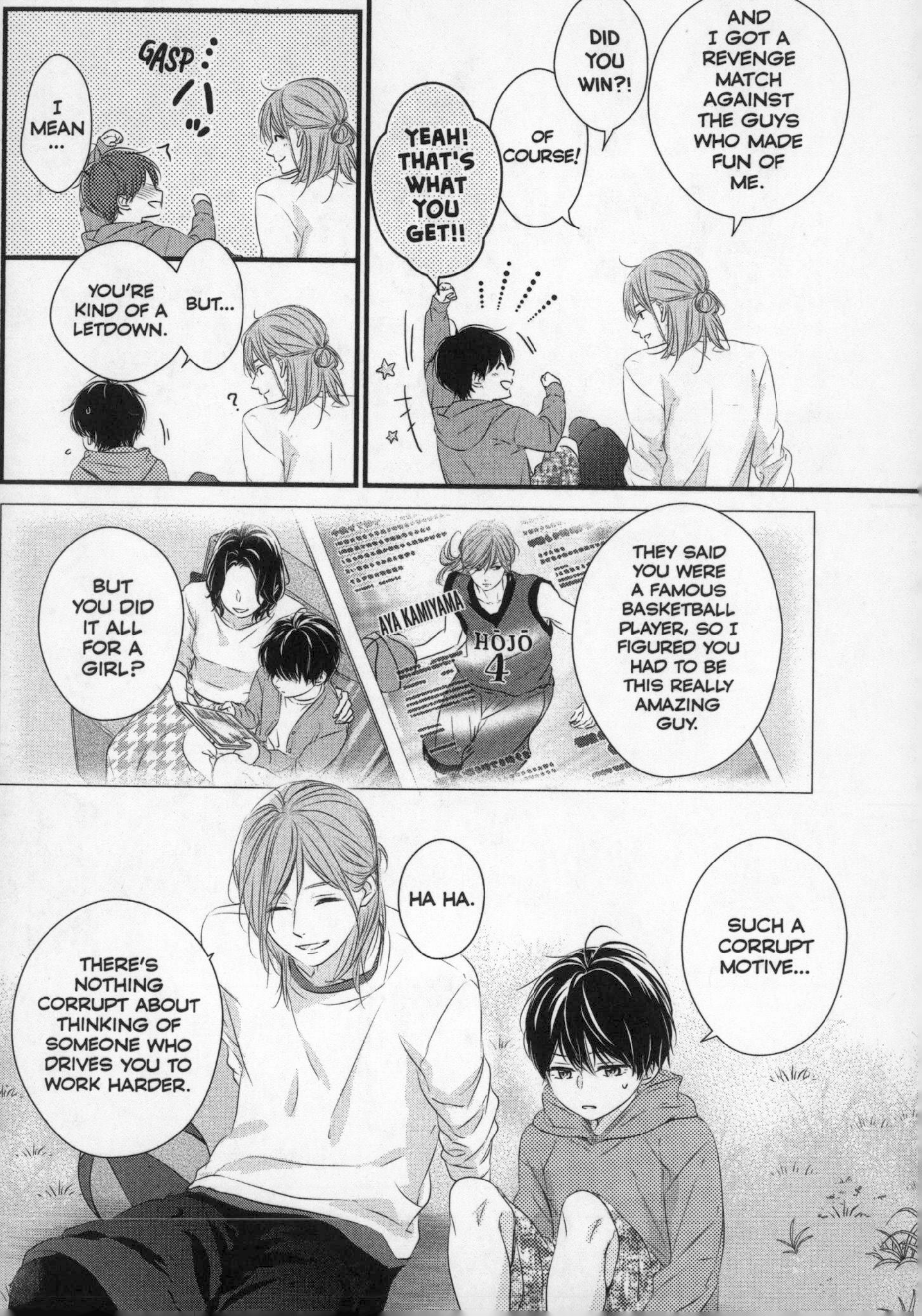
AND I GOT A REVENGE MATCH AGAINST THE GUYS WHO MADE FUN OF ME.
DID YOU WIN?!
OF COURSE!
YEAH! THAT'S WHAT YOU GET!!
GASP
I MEAN ...
BUT...
YOU'RE KIND OF A LETDOWN.
THEY SAID YOU WERE A FAMOUS BASKETBALL PLAYER, SO I FIGURED YOU HAD TO BE THIS REALLY AMAZING GUY.
AYA KAMIYAMA
HŌJŌ
4
BUT YOU DID IT ALL FOR A GIRL?
SUCH A CORRUPT MOTIVE...
HA HA.
THERE'S NOTHING CORRUPT ABOUT THINKING OF SOMEONE WHO DRIVES YOU TO WORK HARDER.

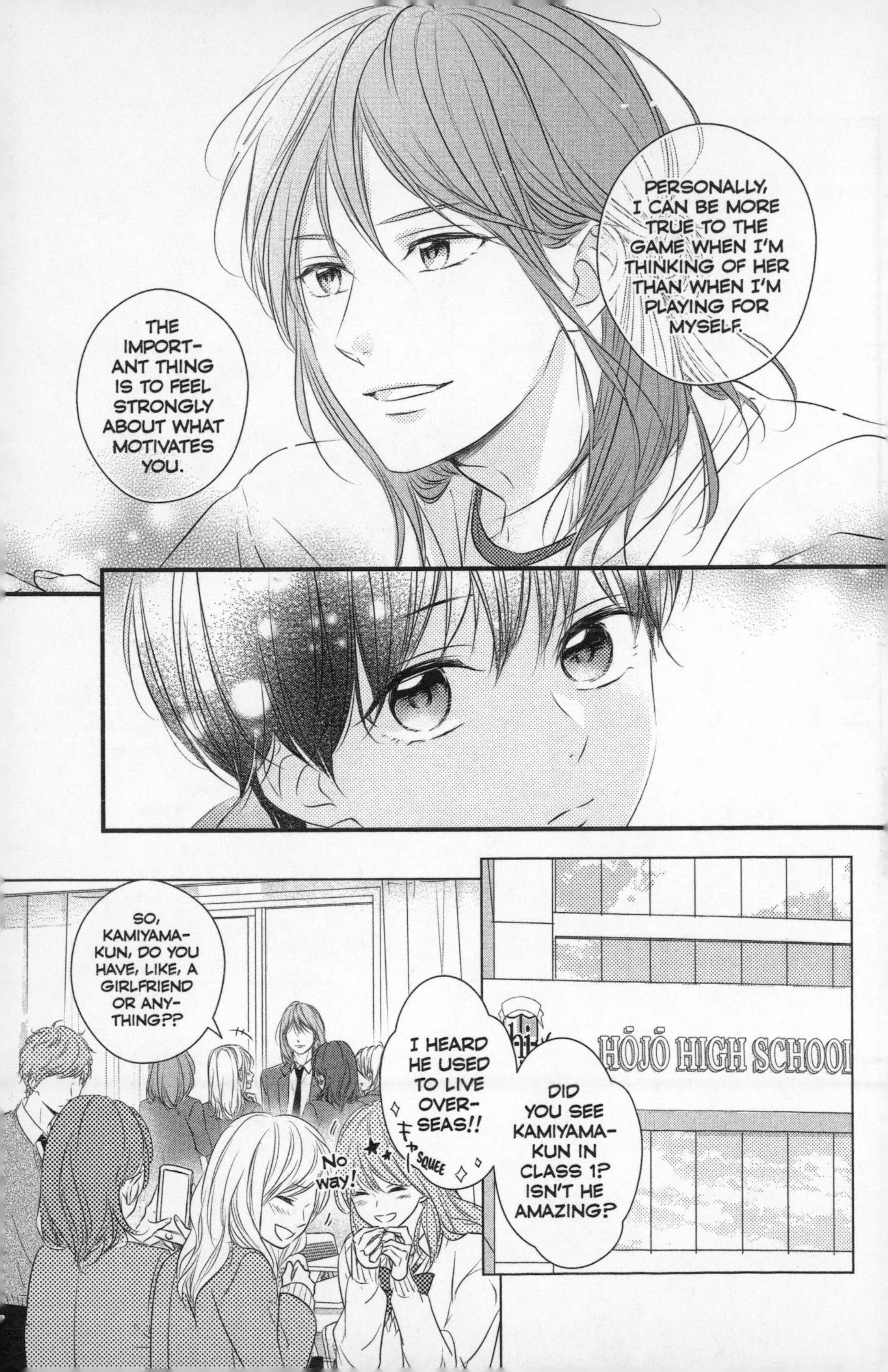
PERSONALLY, I CAN BE MORE TRUE TO THE GAME WHEN I'M THINKING OF HER THAN WHEN I'M PLAYING FOR MYSELF.
THE IMPORTANT THING IS TO FEEL STRONGLY ABOUT WHAT MOTIVATES YOU.
HŌJŌ HIGH SCHOOL
DID YOU SEE KAMIYAMA-KUN IN CLASS 1? ISN'T HE AMAZING?
I HEARD HE USED TO LIVE OVERSEAS!!
SQUEE
SO, KAMIYAMA-KUN, DO YOU HAVE, LIKE, A GIRLFRIEND OR ANYTHING??
No way!

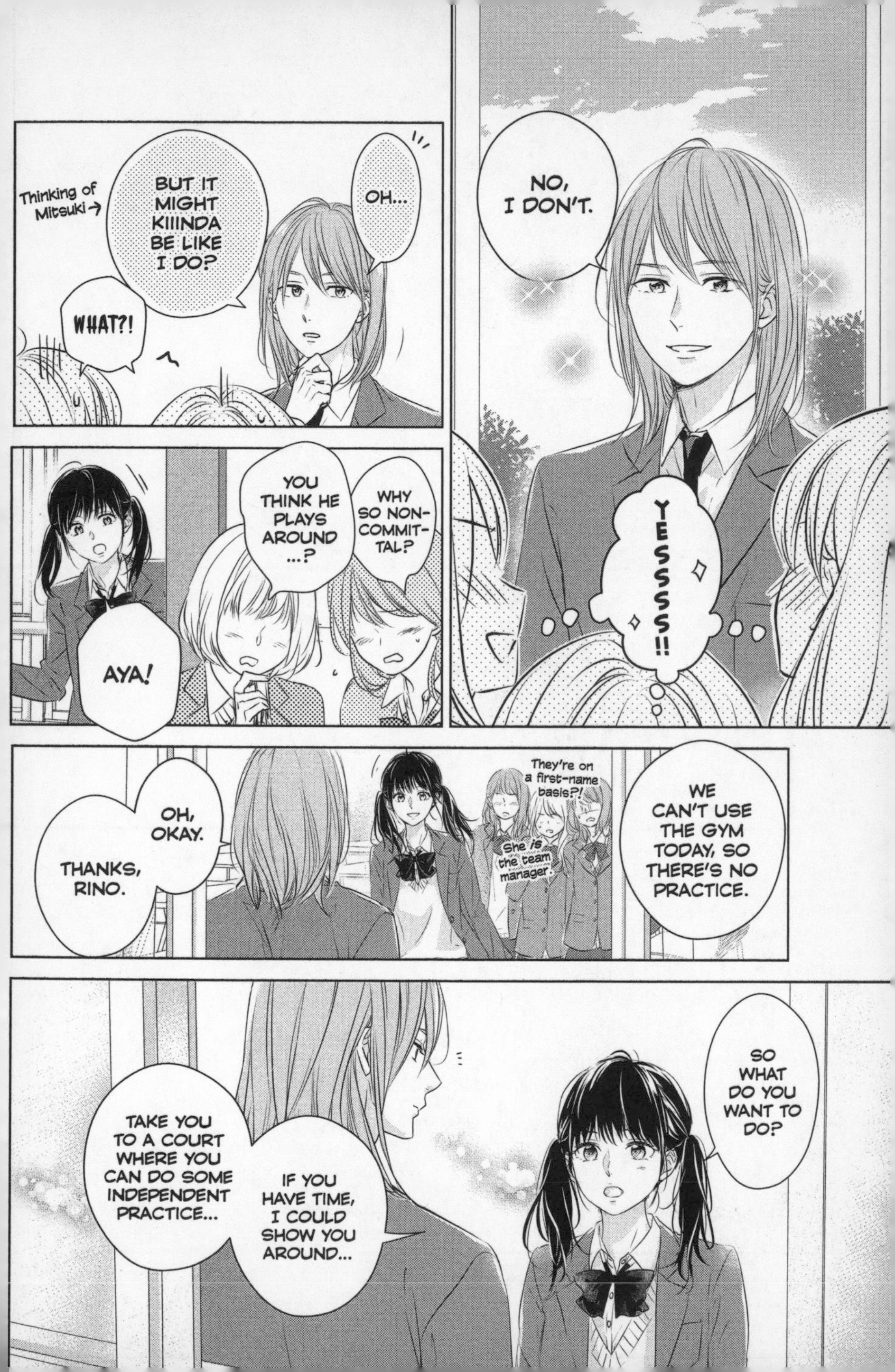
NO, I DON'T.
YESSSS!!
OH...
BUT IT MIGHT KIIINDA BE LIKE I DO?
Thinking of Mitsuki →
WHAT?!
WHY SO NON-COMMIT-TAL?
YOU THINK HE PLAYS AROUND ...?
AYA!
WE CAN'T USE THE GYM TODAY, SO THERE'S NO PRACTICE.
They're on a first-name basis?!
She is the team manager.
OH, OKAY.
THANKS, RINO.
SO WHAT DO YOU WANT TO DO?
IF YOU HAVE TIME, I COULD SHOW YOU AROUND...
TAKE YOU TO A COURT WHERE YOU CAN DO SOME INDEPENDENT PRACTICE...

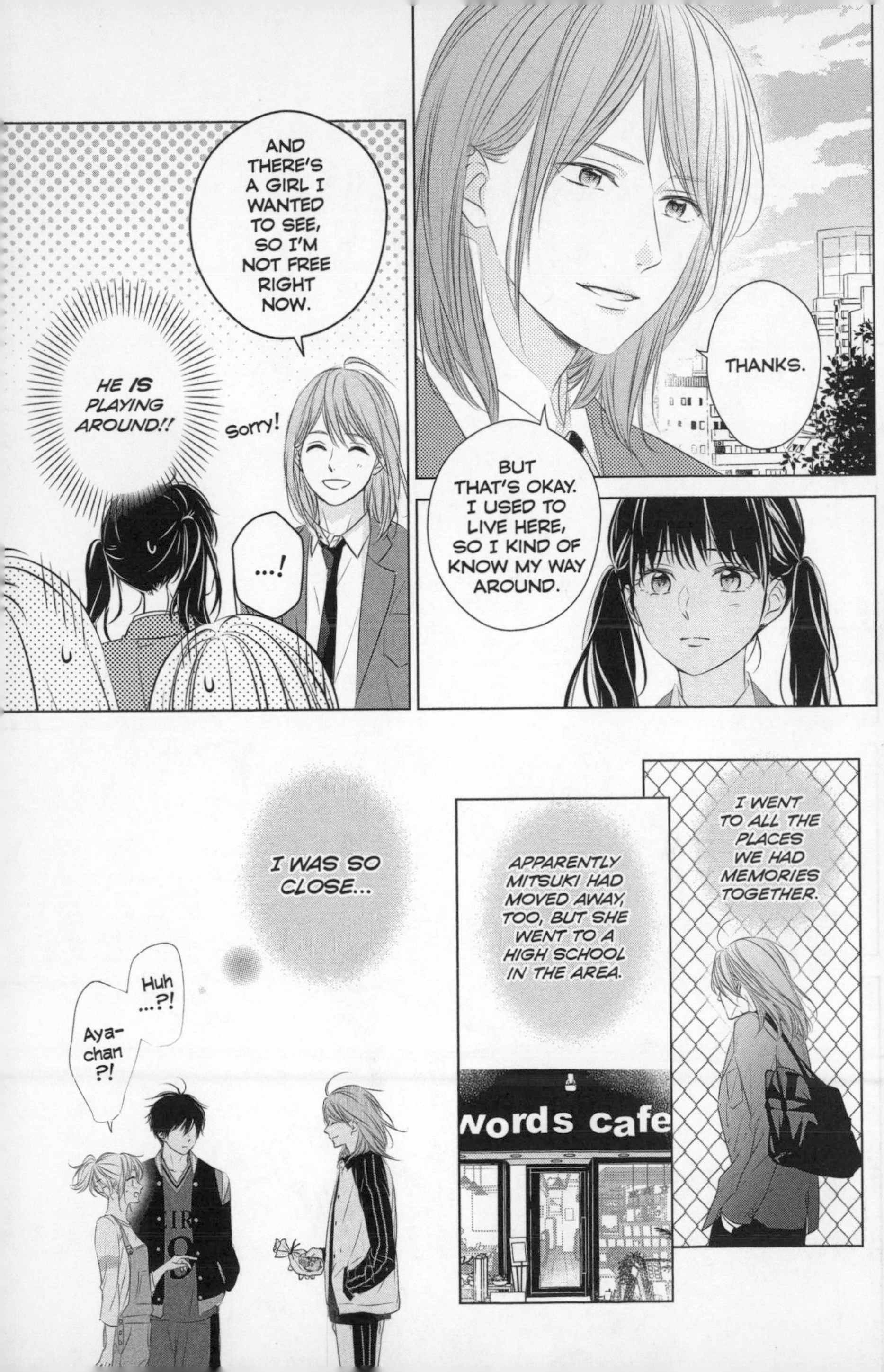
THANKS.
BUT THAT'S OKAY. I USED TO LIVE HERE, SO I KIND OF KNOW MY WAY AROUND.
AND THERE'S A GIRL I WANTED TO SEE, SO I'M NOT FREE RIGHT NOW.
Sorry!
HE IS PLAYING AROUND!!
...!
I WENT TO ALL THE PLACES WE HAD MEMORIES TOGETHER.
APPARENTLY MITSUKI HAD MOVED AWAY, TOO, BUT SHE WENT TO A HIGH SCHOOL IN THE AREA.
words cafe
I WAS SO CLOSE...
Huh ...?!
Aya-chan ?!

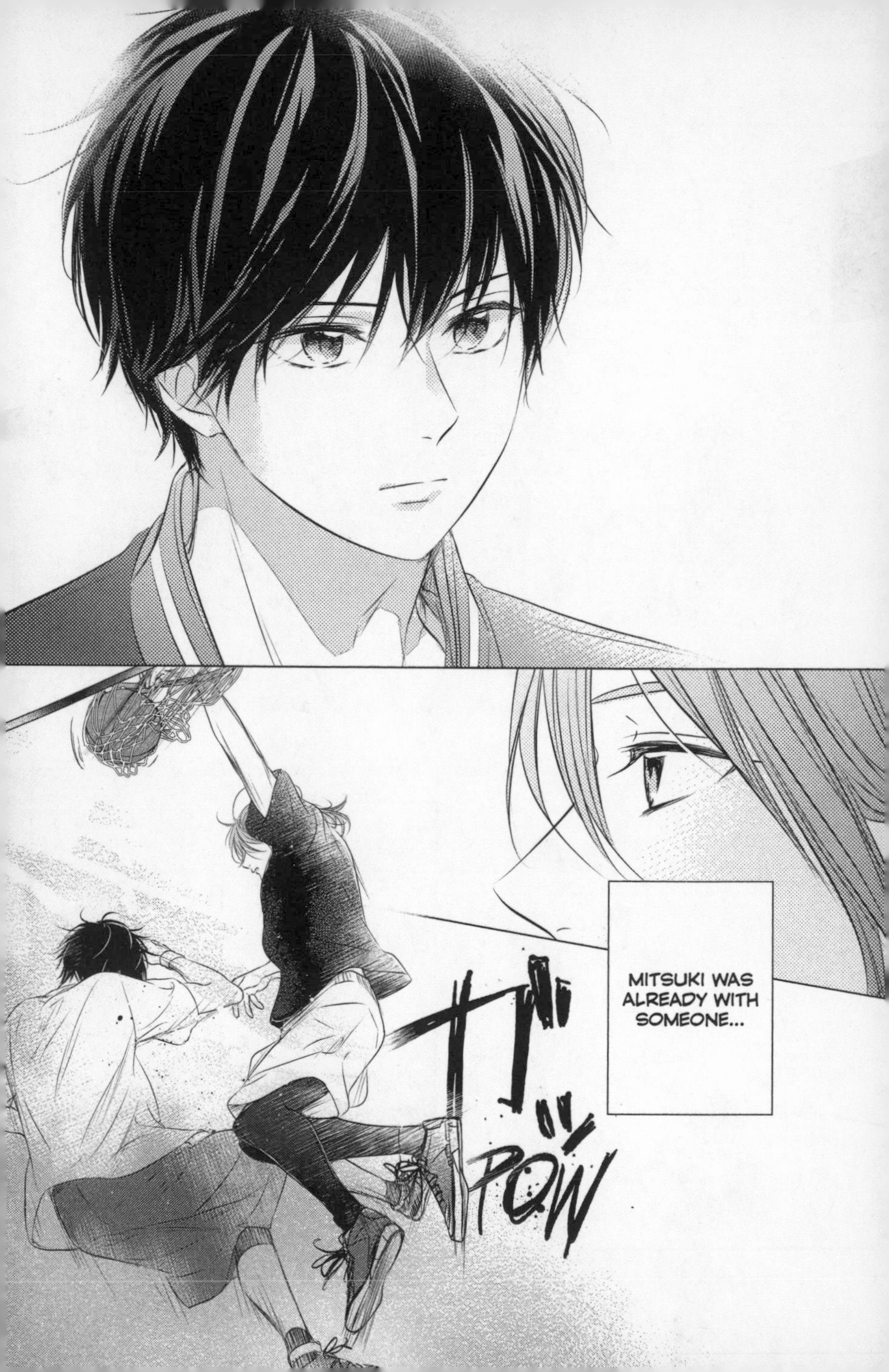
MITSUKI WAS ALREADY WITH SOMEONE...
POW

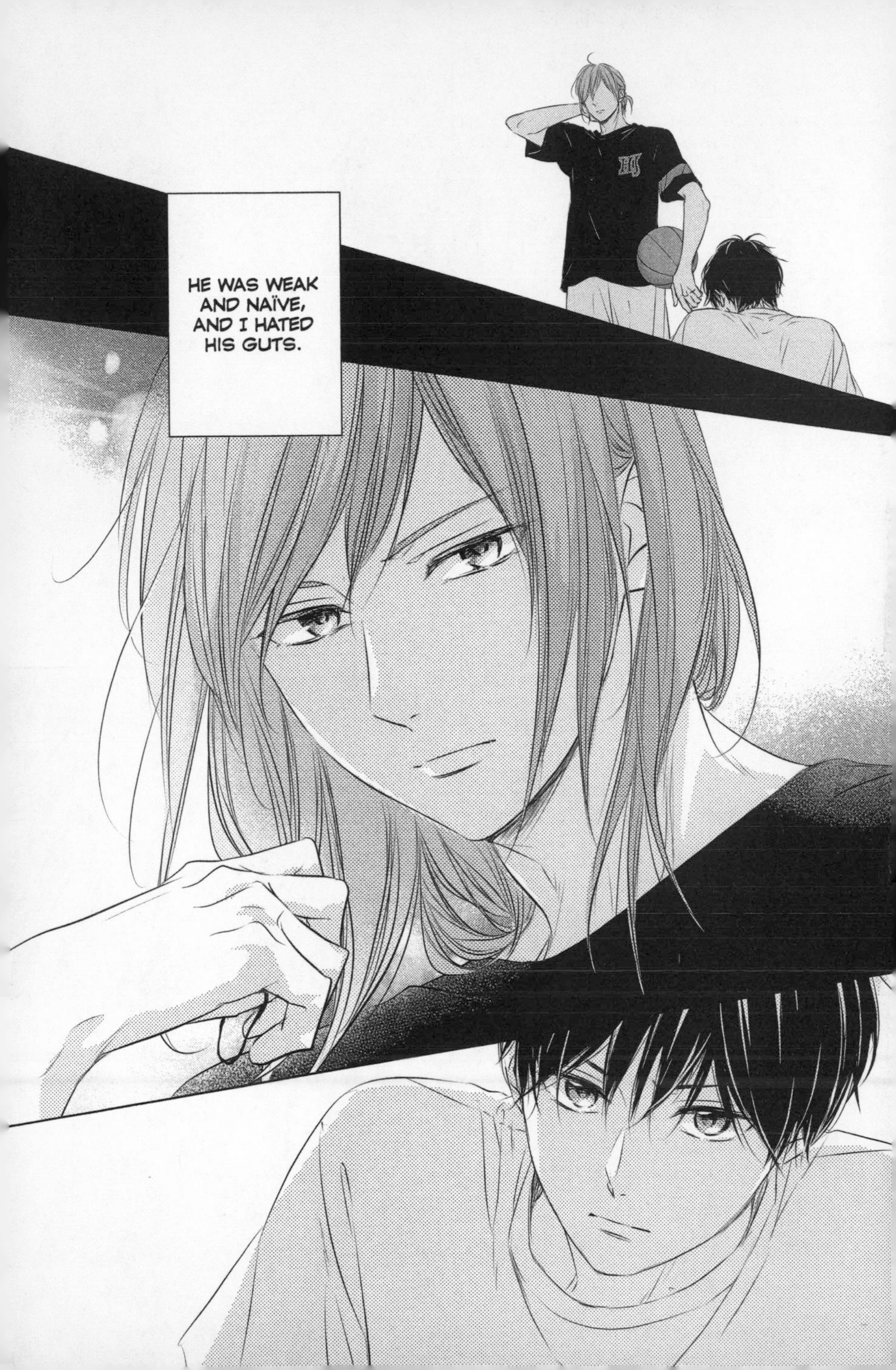
HE WAS WEAK AND NAÏVE, AND I HATED HIS GUTS.

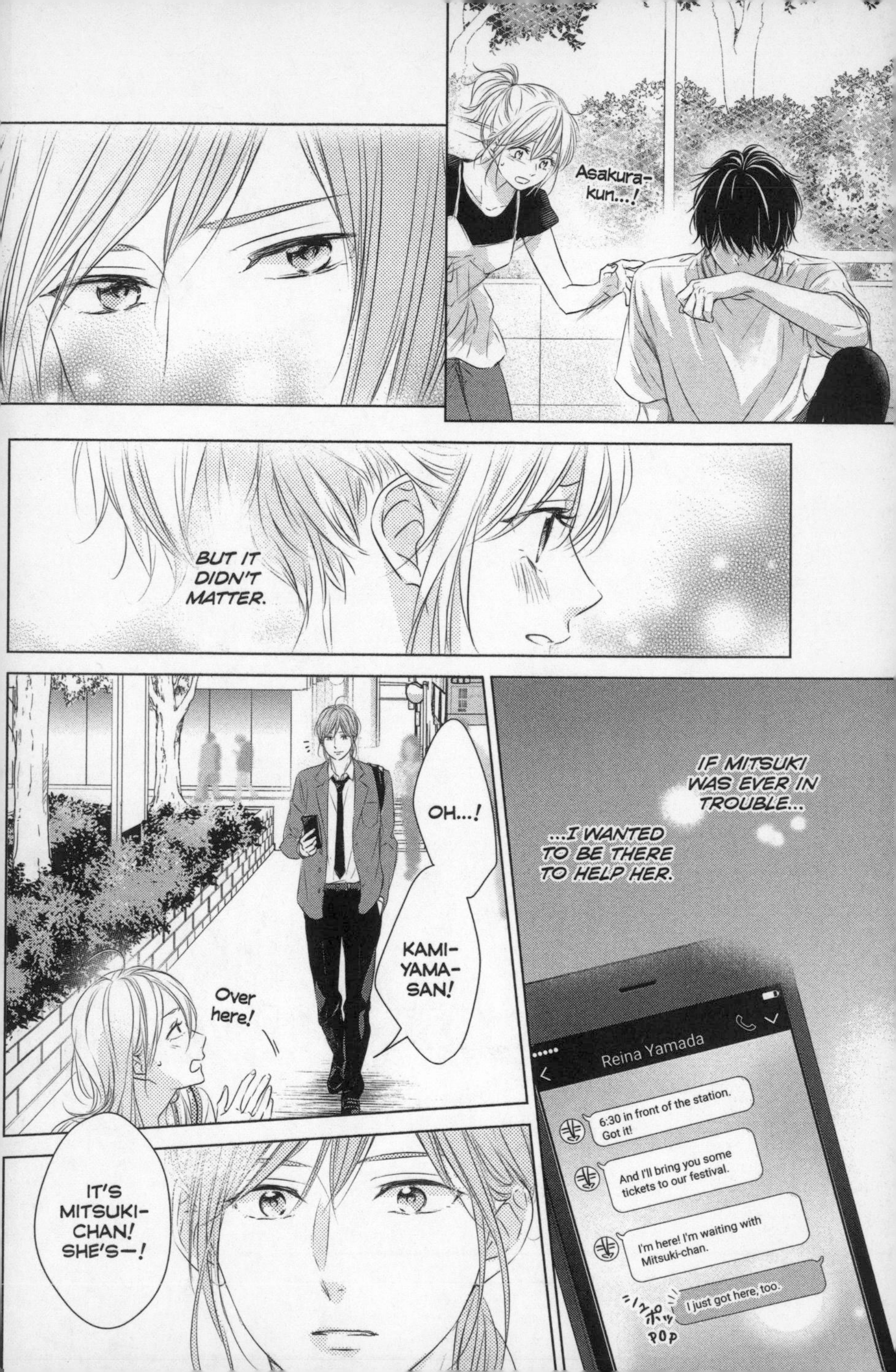
Asakura-kun...!
BUT IT DIDN'T MATTER.
IF MITSUKI WAS EVER IN TROUBLE...
...I WANTED TO BE THERE TO HELP HER.
Reina Yamada
6:30 in front of the station. Got it!
And I'll bring you some tickets to our festival.
I'm here! I'm waiting with Mitsuki-chan.
I just got here, too.
ニュポッ
POP
OH...!
KAMI-YAMA-SAN!
Over here!
IT'S MITSUKI-CHAN! SHE'S—!

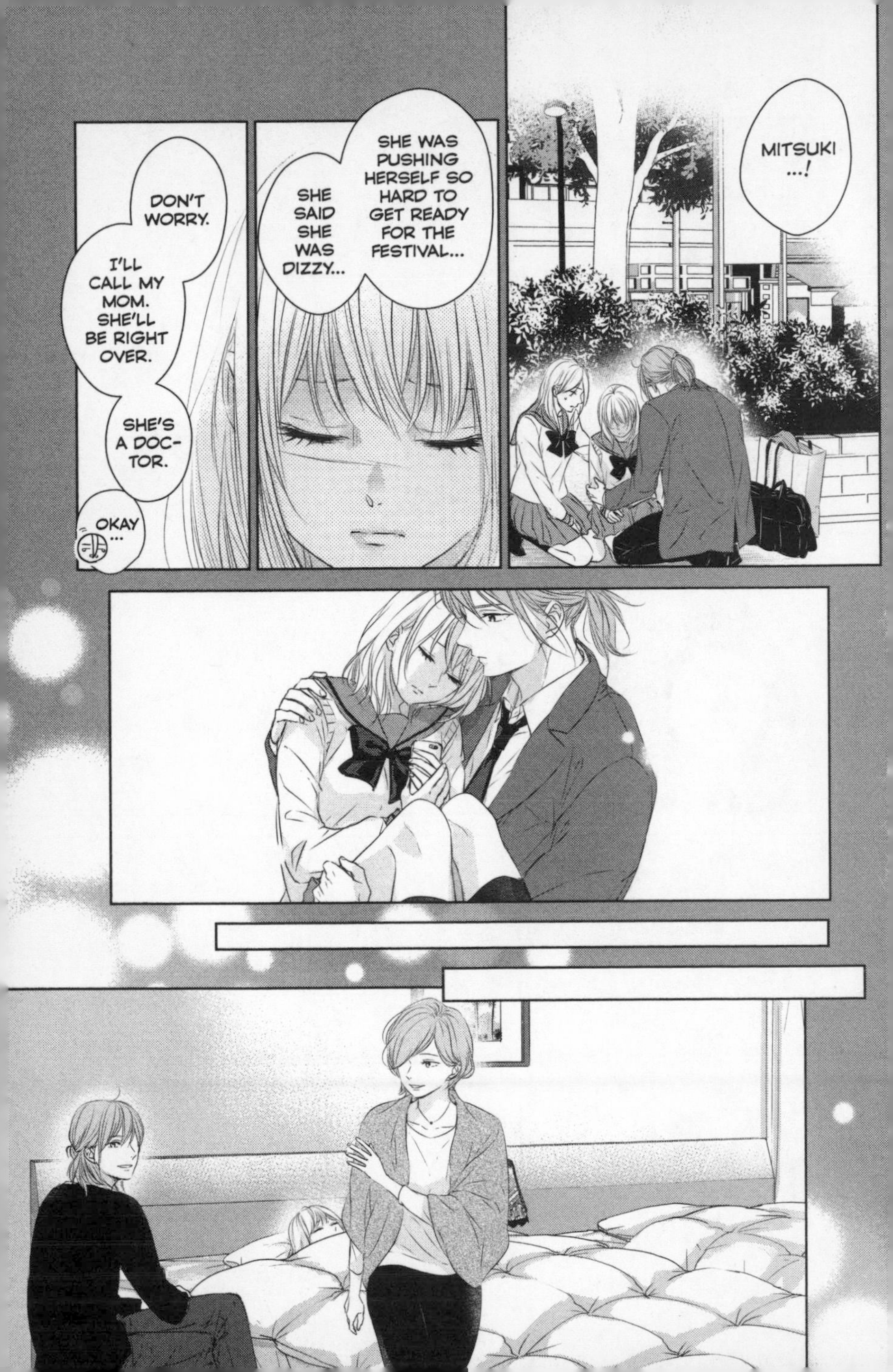
MITSUKI ...!
SHE WAS PUSHING HERSELF SO HARD TO GET READY FOR THE FESTIVAL...
SHE SAID SHE WAS DIZZY...
DON'T WORRY.
I'LL CALL MY MOM. SHE'LL BE RIGHT OVER.
SHE'S A DOC-TOR.
OKAY ...

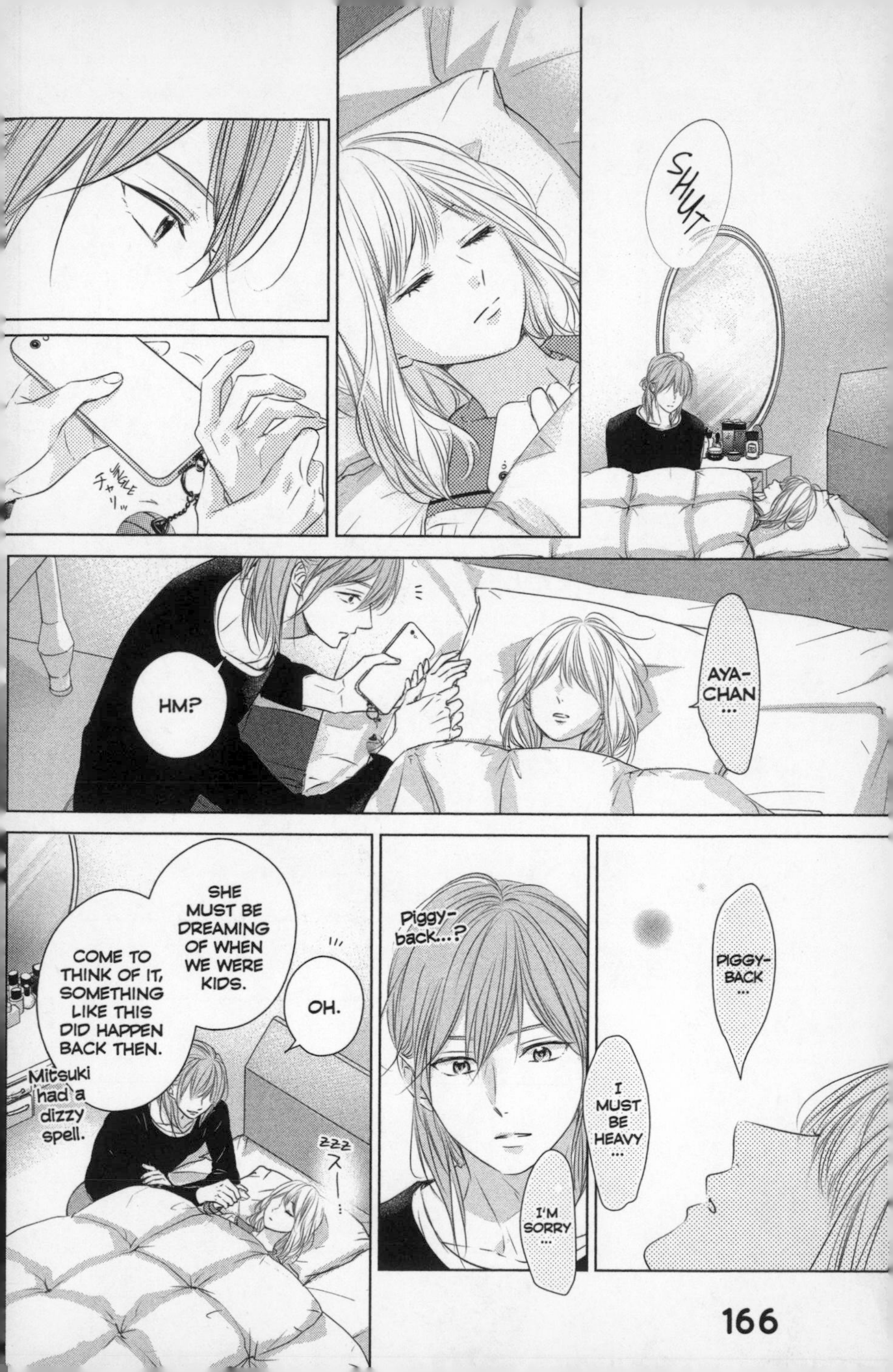
SHUT
JINGLE
チャリッ
AYA-CHAN...
HM?
PIGGY-BACK...
I MUST BE HEAVY...
I'M SORRY...
Piggy-back...?
OH.
SHE MUST BE DREAMING OF WHEN WE WERE KIDS.
COME TO THINK OF IT, SOMETHING LIKE THIS DID HAPPEN BACK THEN.
Mitsuki had a dizzy spell.
zzz
スー…

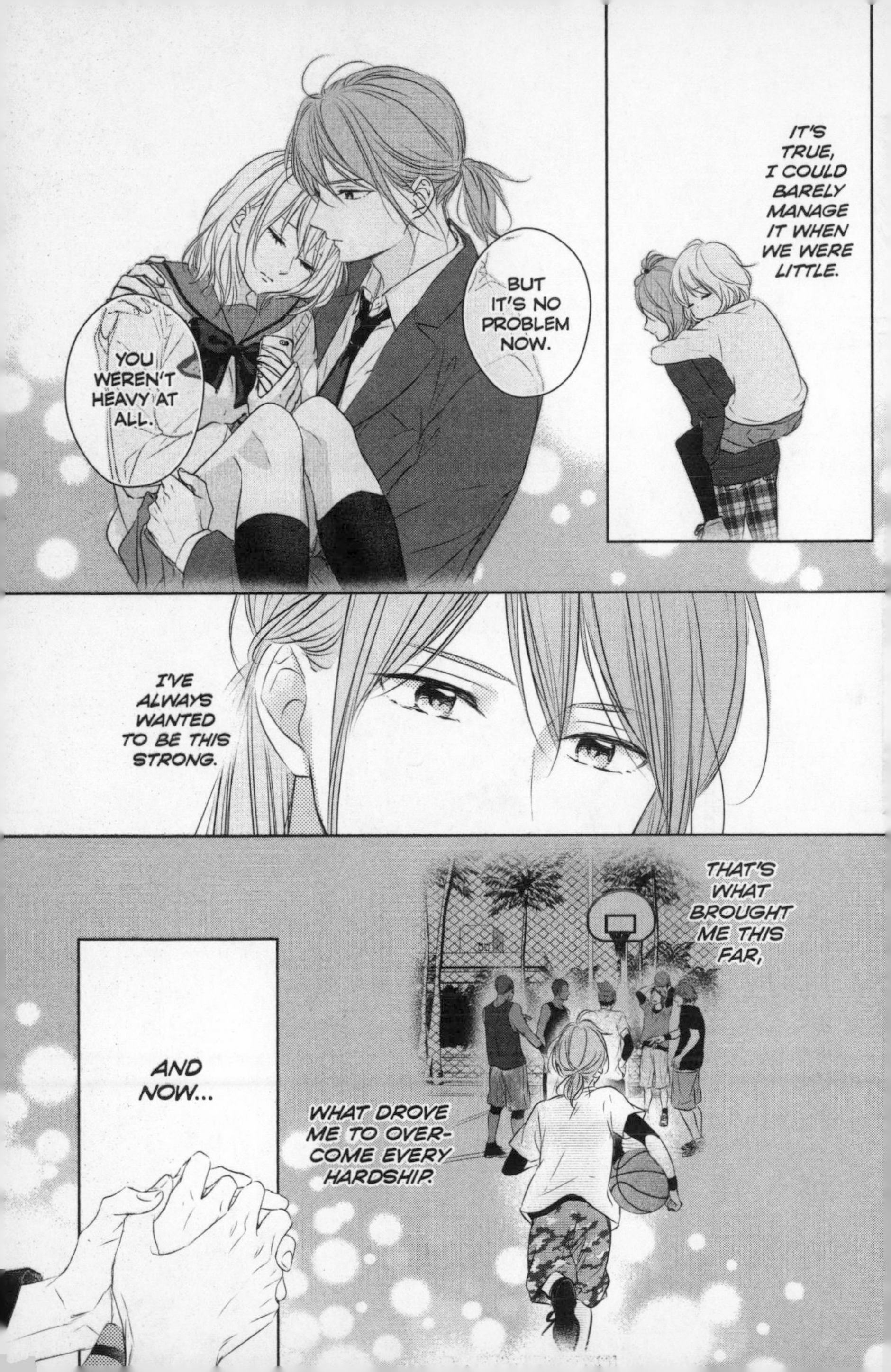
IT'S TRUE, I COULD BARELY MANAGE IT WHEN WE WERE LITTLE.
BUT IT'S NO PROBLEM NOW.
YOU WEREN'T HEAVY AT ALL.
I'VE ALWAYS WANTED TO BE THIS STRONG.
THAT'S WHAT BROUGHT ME THIS FAR,
WHAT DROVE ME TO OVER-COME EVERY HARDSHIP.
AND NOW...

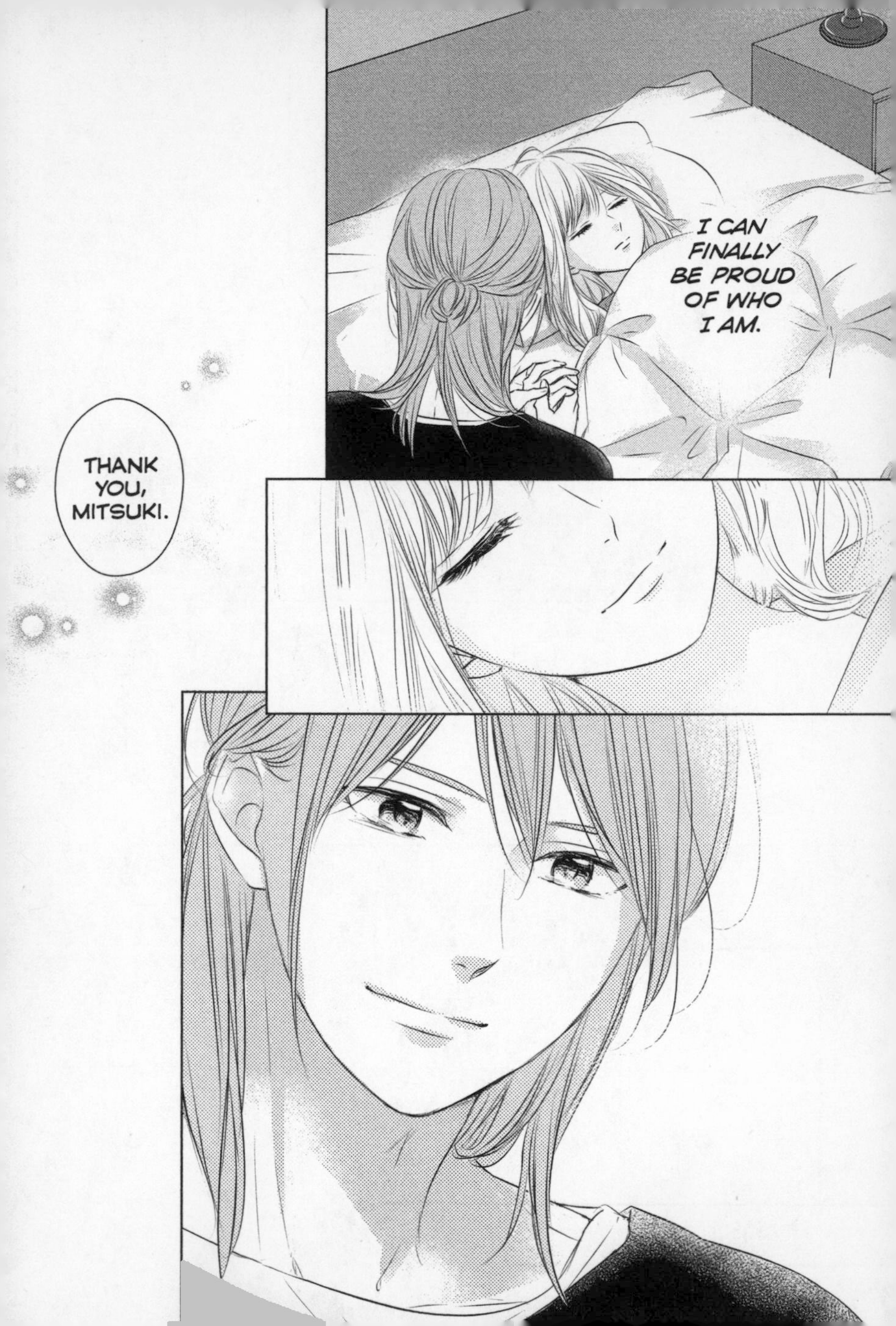
I CAN FINALLY BE PROUD OF WHO I AM.
THANK YOU, MITSUKI.

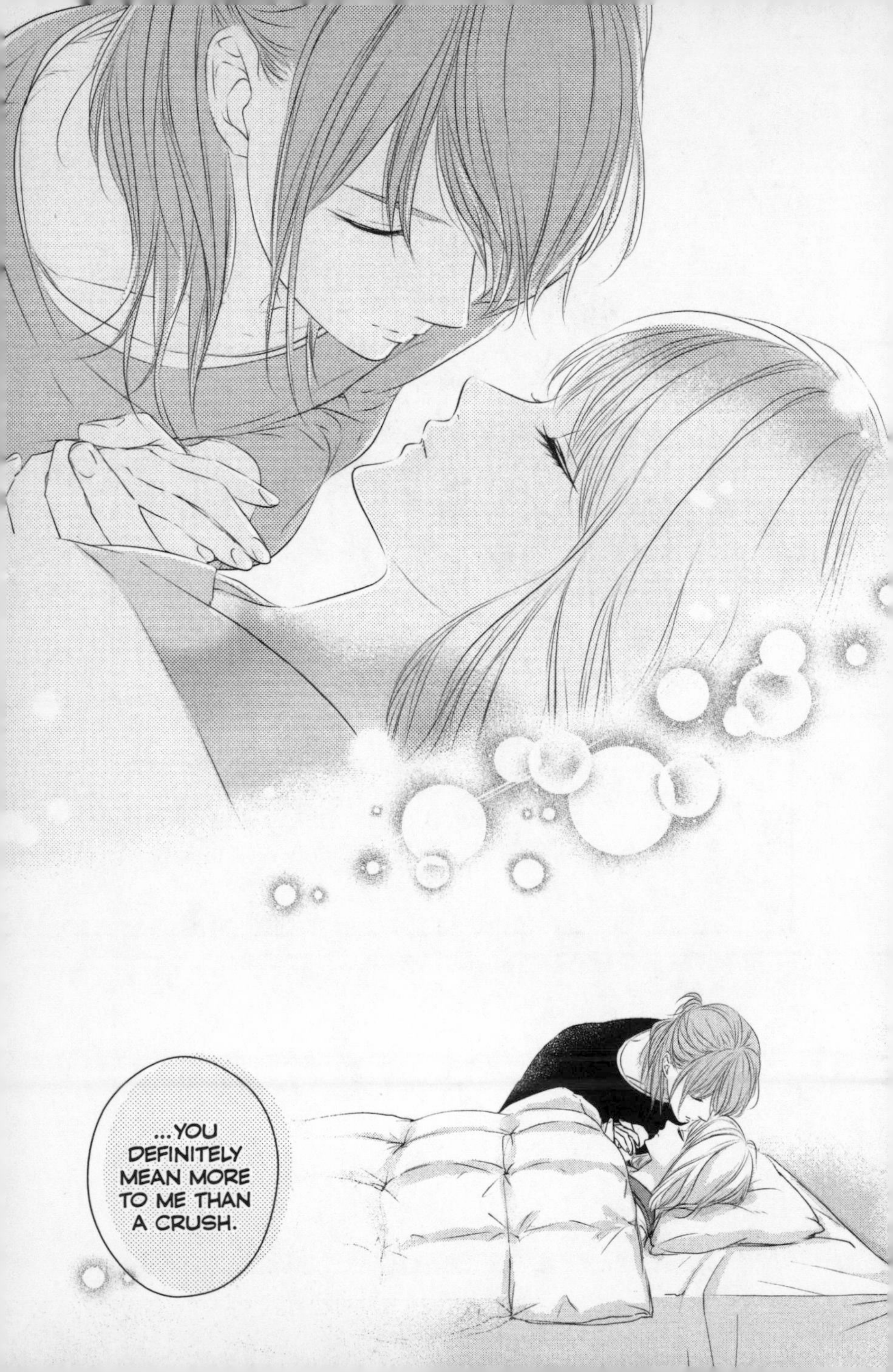
...YOU DEFINITELY MEAN MORE TO ME THAN A CRUSH.

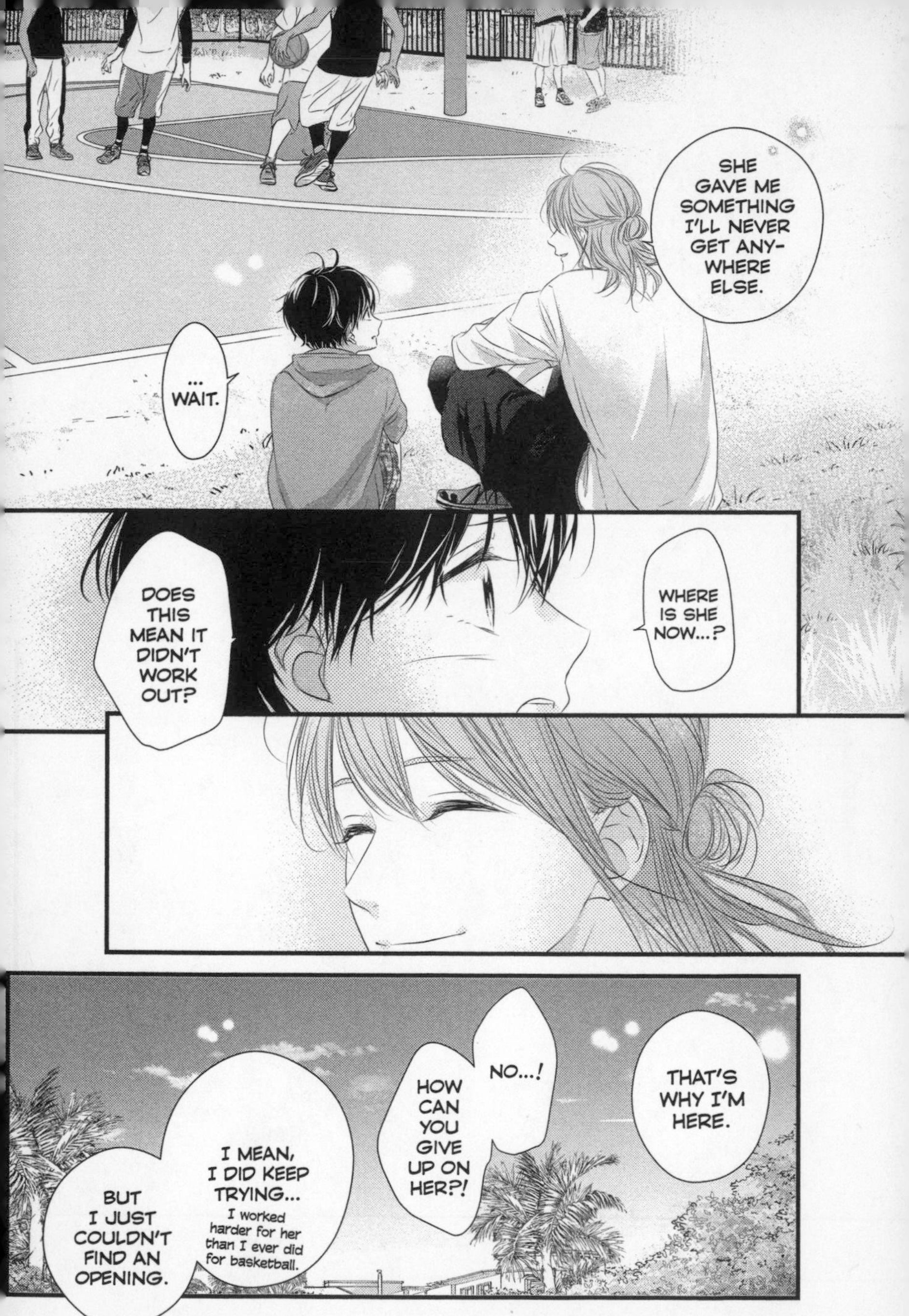
SHE GAVE ME SOMETHING I'LL NEVER GET ANY-WHERE ELSE.
... WAIT.
WHERE IS SHE NOW...?
DOES THIS MEAN IT DIDN'T WORK OUT?
THAT'S WHY I'M HERE.
NO...!
HOW CAN YOU GIVE UP ON HER?!
I MEAN, I DID KEEP TRYING...
I worked harder for her than I ever did for basketball.
BUT I JUST COULDN'T FIND AN OPENING.

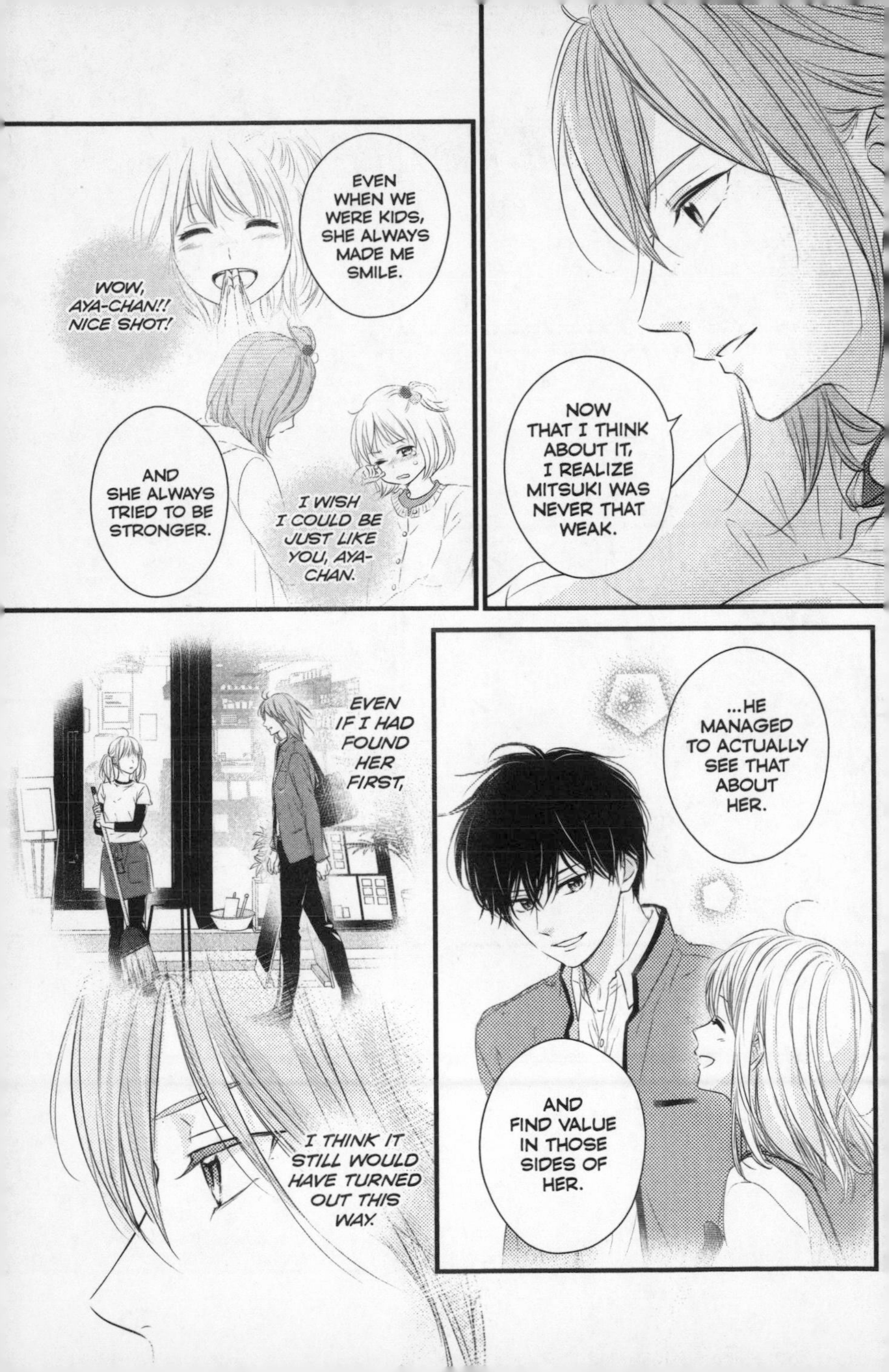
NOW THAT I THINK ABOUT IT, I REALIZE MITSUKI WAS NEVER THAT WEAK.
EVEN WHEN WE WERE KIDS, SHE ALWAYS MADE ME SMILE.
WOW, AYA-CHAN!! NICE SHOT!
AND SHE ALWAYS TRIED TO BE STRONGER.
I WISH I COULD BE JUST LIKE YOU, AYA-CHAN.
...HE MANAGED TO ACTUALLY SEE THAT ABOUT HER.
AND FIND VALUE IN THOSE SIDES OF HER.
EVEN IF I HAD FOUND HER FIRST,
I THINK IT STILL WOULD HAVE TURNED OUT THIS WAY.

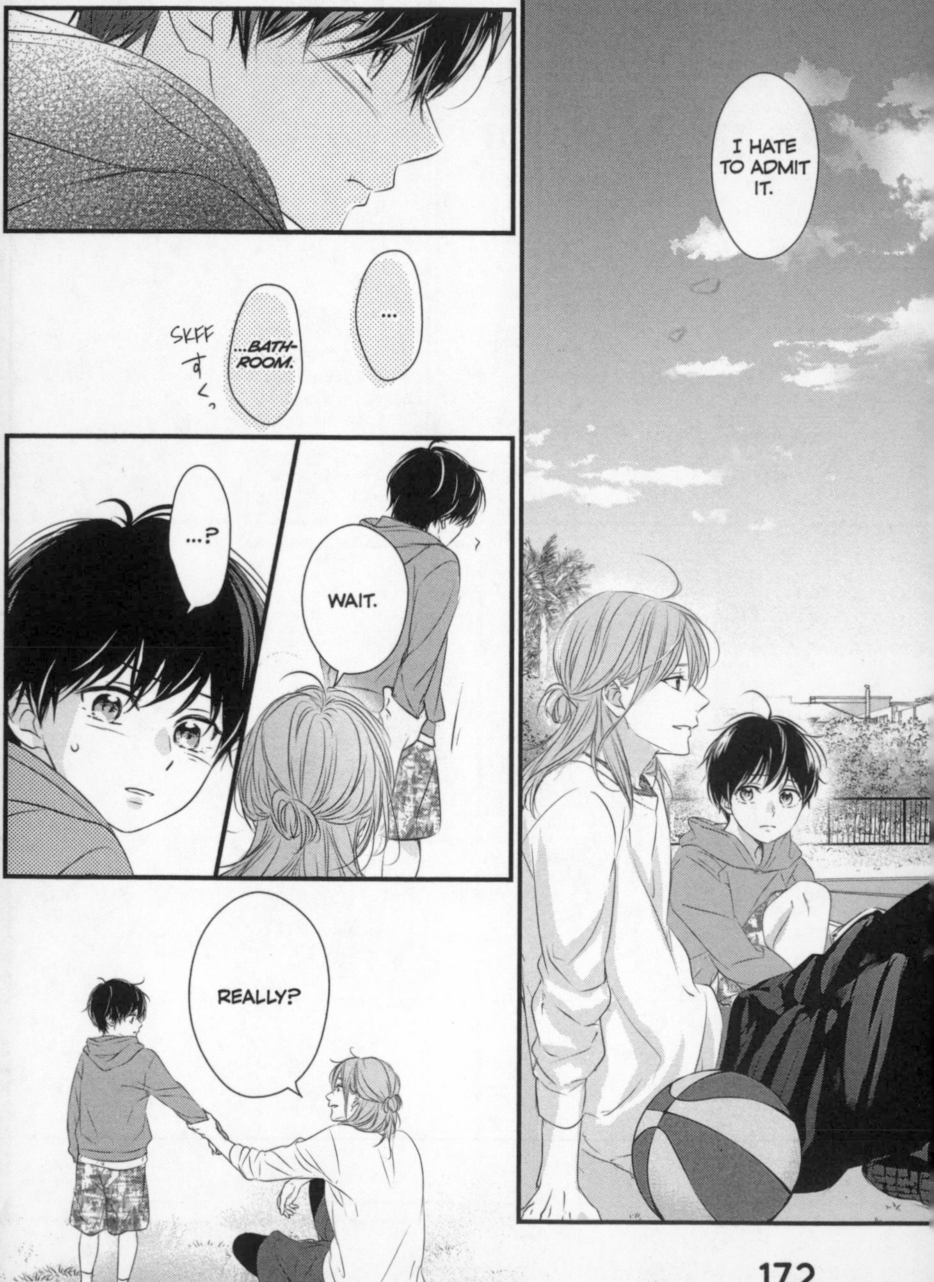
I HATE TO ADMIT IT.
...
...BATH-ROOM.
SKFF
すくっ
WAIT.
...?
REALLY?

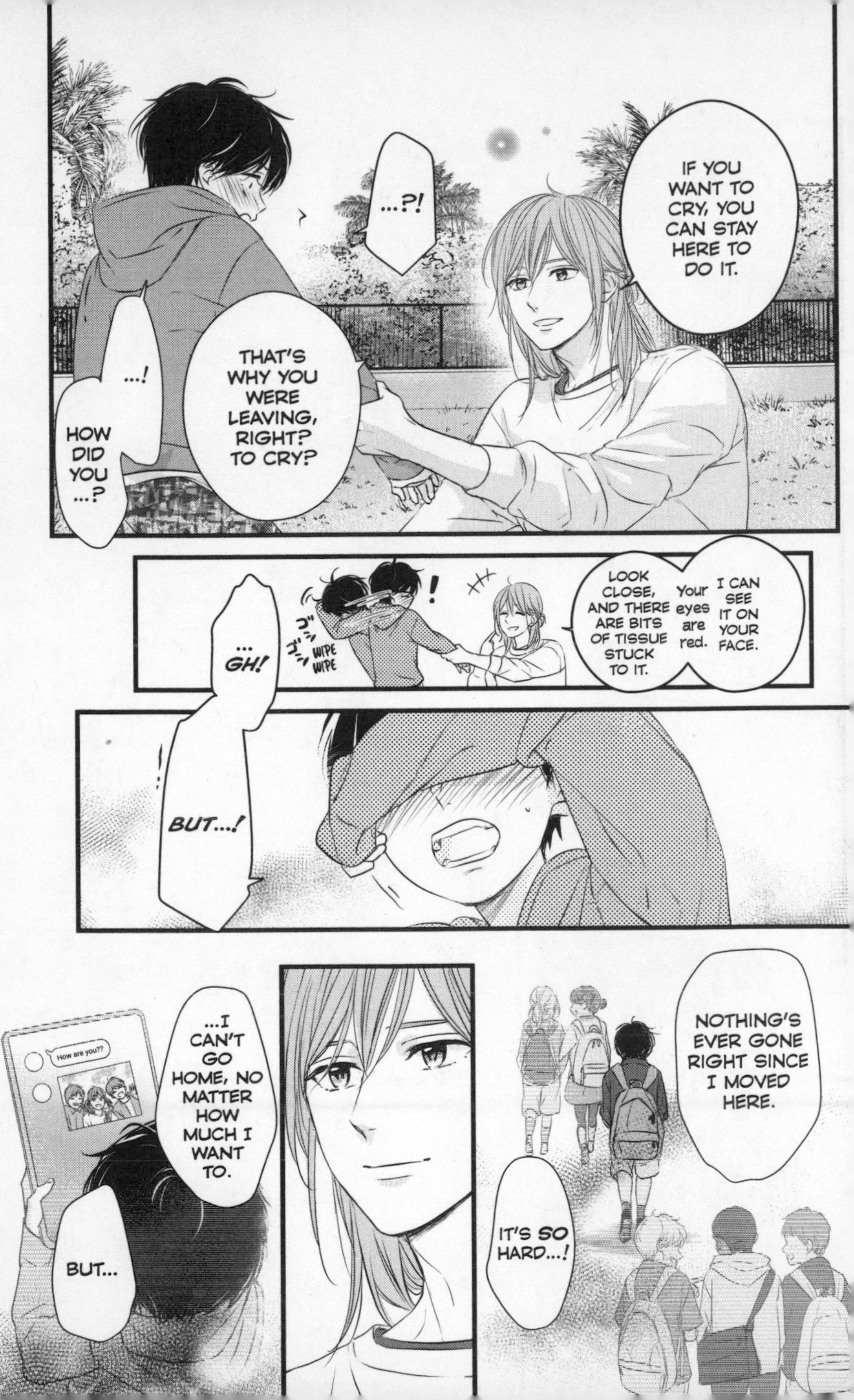
IF YOU WANT TO CRY, YOU CAN STAY HERE TO DO IT.
...?!
THAT'S WHY YOU WERE LEAVING, RIGHT? TO CRY?
...!
HOW DID YOU ...?
I CAN SEE IT ON YOUR FACE.
Your eyes are red.
LOOK CLOSE, AND THERE ARE BITS OF TISSUE STUCK TO IT.
!
WIPE WIPE
... GH!
BUT...!
NOTHING'S EVER GONE RIGHT SINCE I MOVED HERE.
IT'S SO HARD...!
...I CAN'T GO HOME, NO MATTER HOW MUCH I WANT TO.
How are you??
BUT...

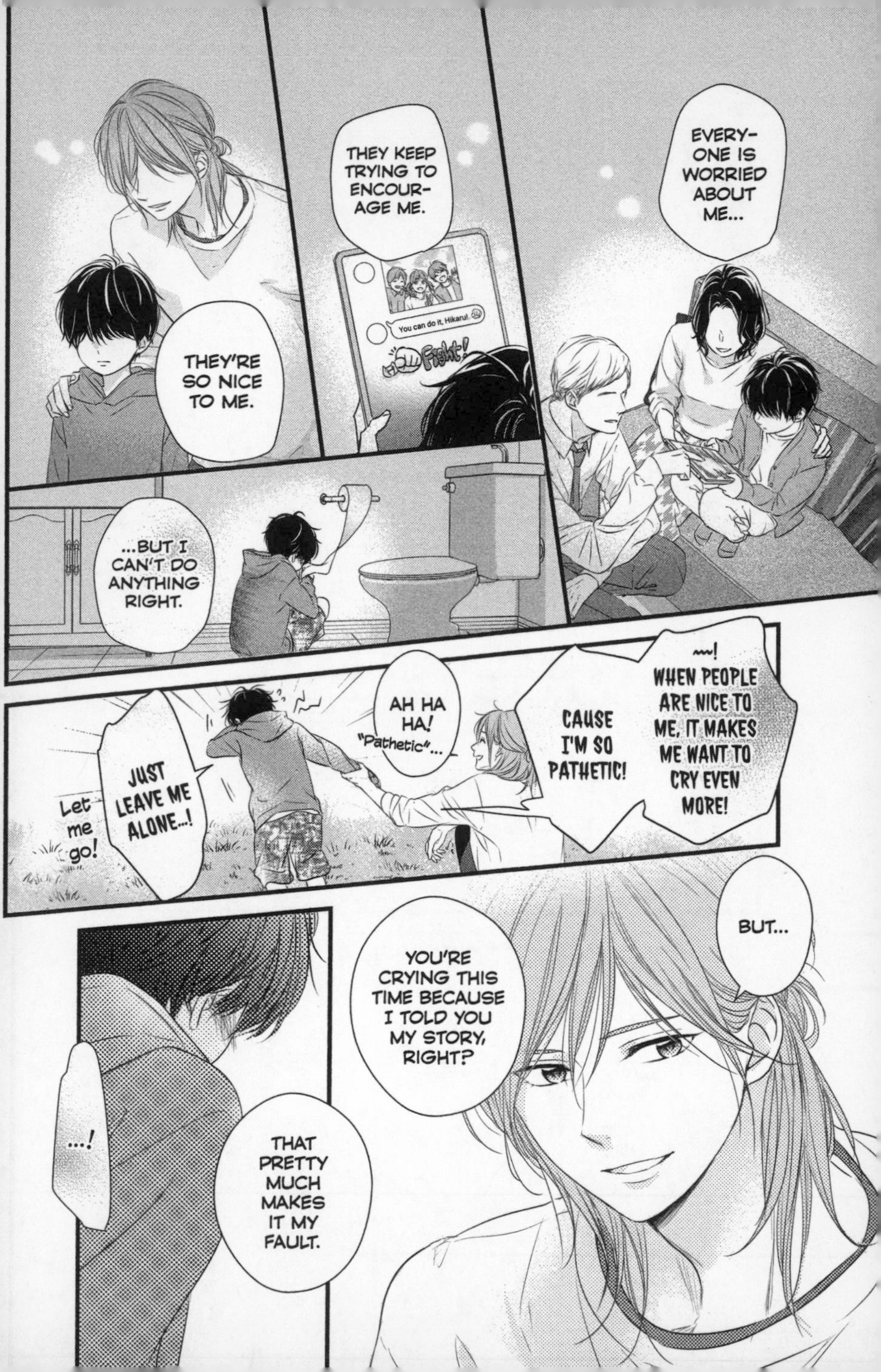
EVERY-ONE IS WORRIED ABOUT ME...
THEY KEEP TRYING TO ENCOURAGE ME.
You can do it, Hikaru!
Fight!
THEY'RE SO NICE TO ME.
...BUT I CAN'T DO ANYTHING RIGHT.
~! WHEN PEOPLE ARE NICE TO ME, IT MAKES ME WANT TO CRY EVEN MORE!
CAUSE I'M SO PATHETIC!
AH HA HA! "Pathetic"...
JUST LEAVE ME ALONE...!
Let me go!
BUT...
YOU'RE CRYING THIS TIME BECAUSE I TOLD YOU MY STORY, RIGHT?
THAT PRETTY MUCH MAKES IT MY FAULT.
...!

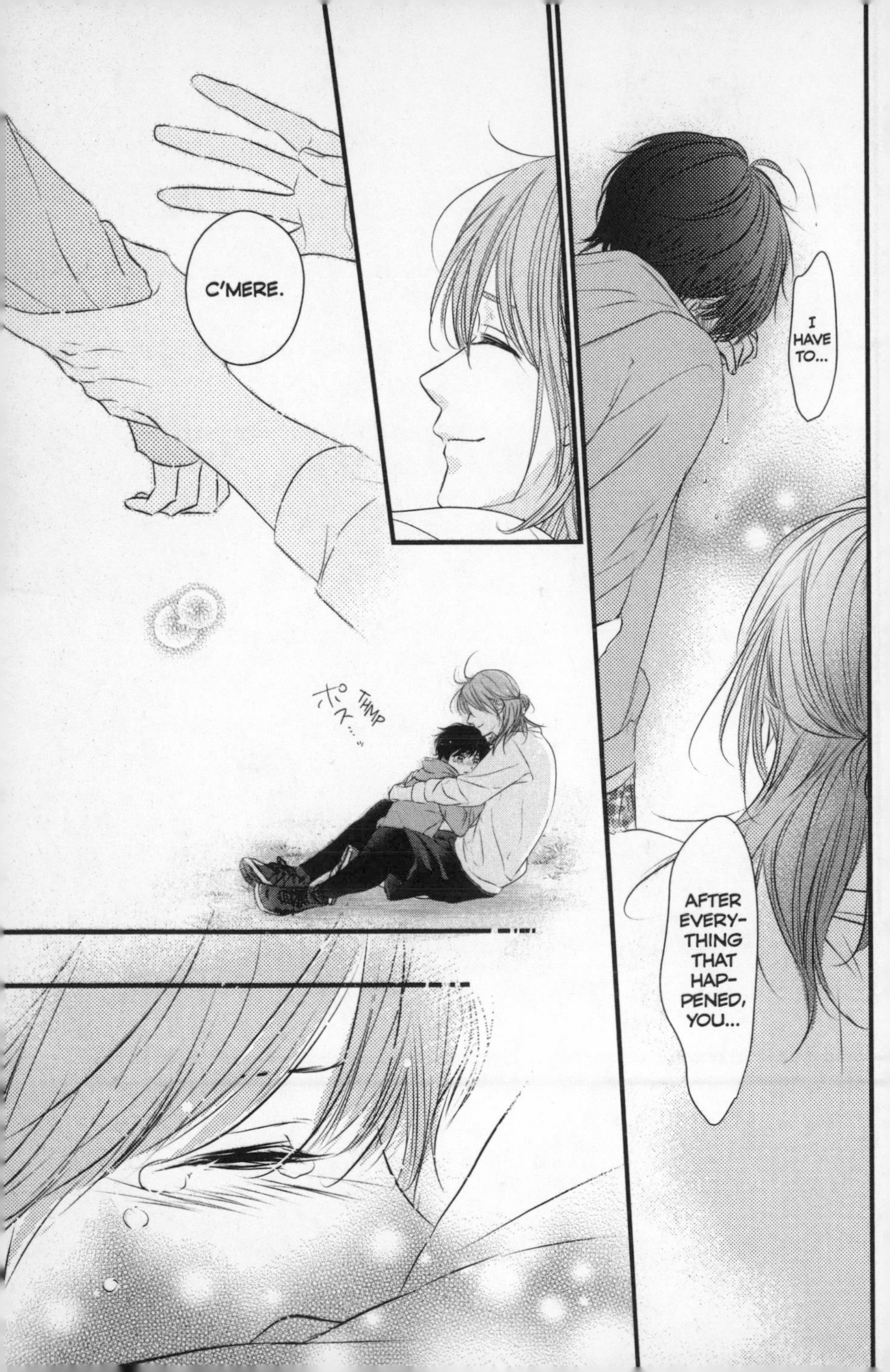
I HAVE TO...
AFTER EVERYTHING THAT HAPPENED, YOU...
C'MERE.
ポス…
THMP

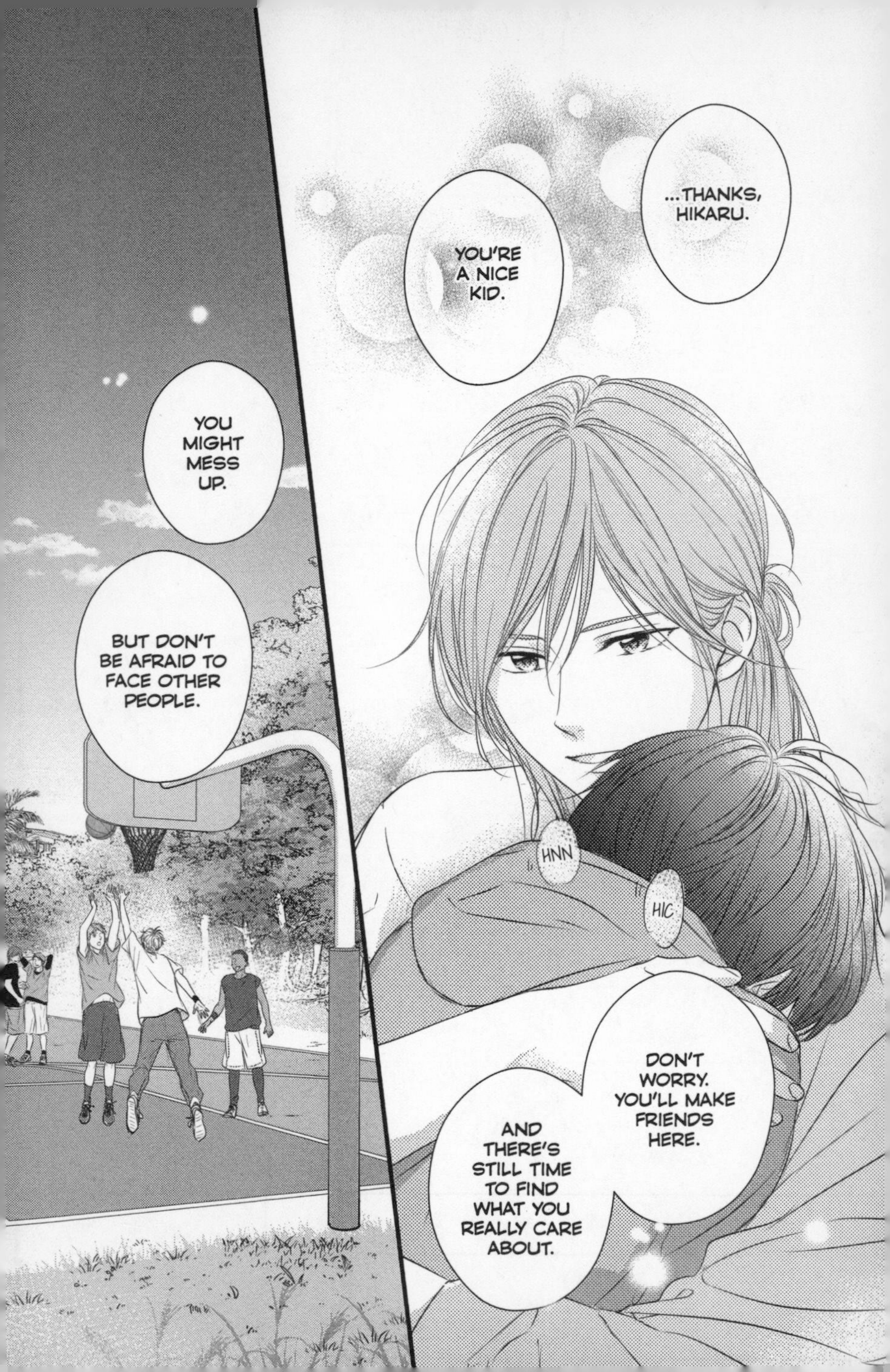
...THANKS, HIKARU.
YOU'RE A NICE KID.
HNN
HIC
DON'T WORRY. YOU'LL MAKE FRIENDS HERE.
AND THERE'S STILL TIME TO FIND WHAT YOU REALLY CARE ABOUT.
YOU MIGHT MESS UP.
BUT DON'T BE AFRAID TO FACE OTHER PEOPLE.

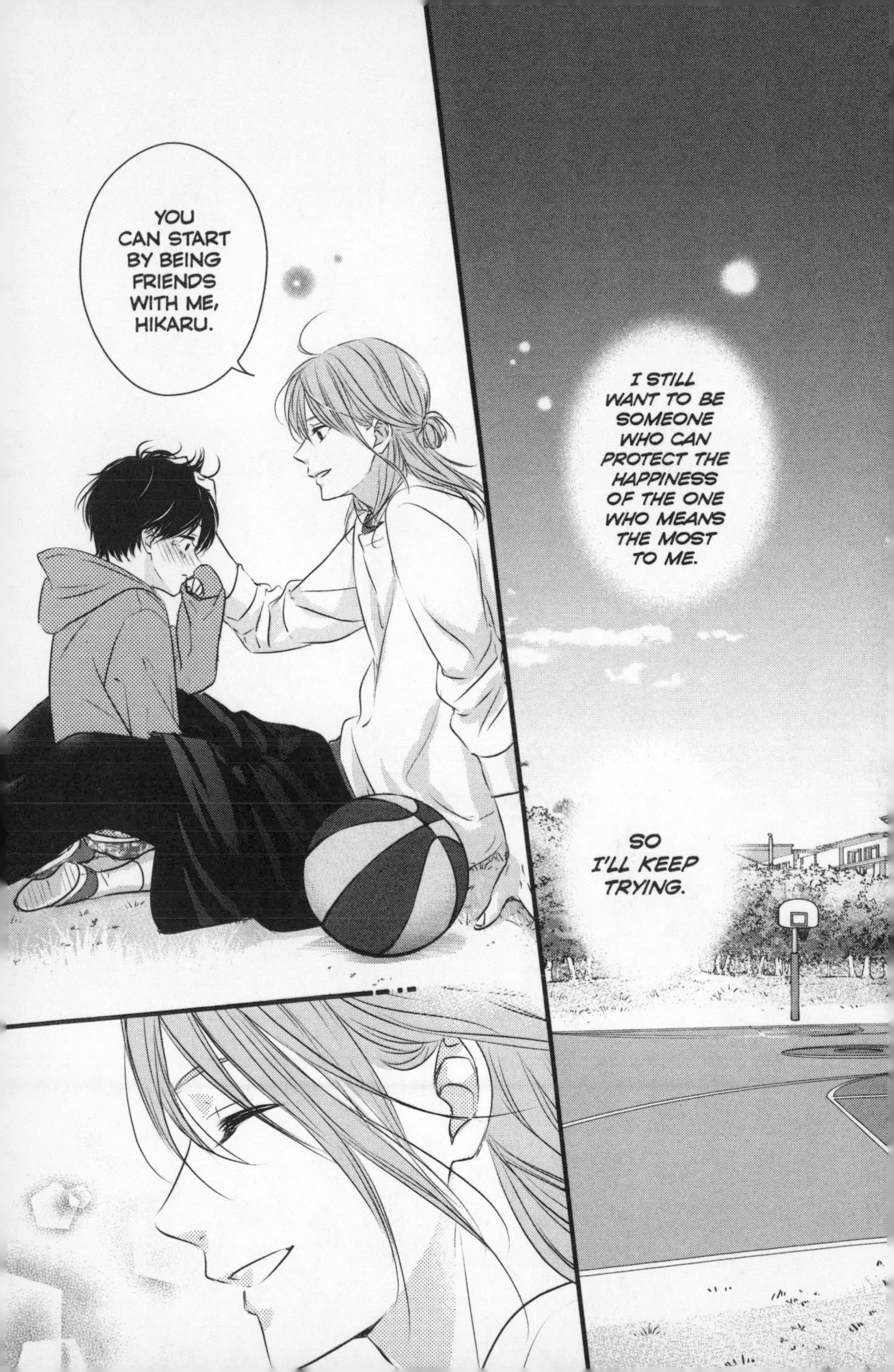
I STILL WANT TO BE SOMEONE WHO CAN PROTECT THE HAPPINESS OF THE ONE WHO MEANS THE MOST TO ME.
SO I'LL KEEP TRYING.
YOU CAN START BY BEING FRIENDS WITH ME, HIKARU.

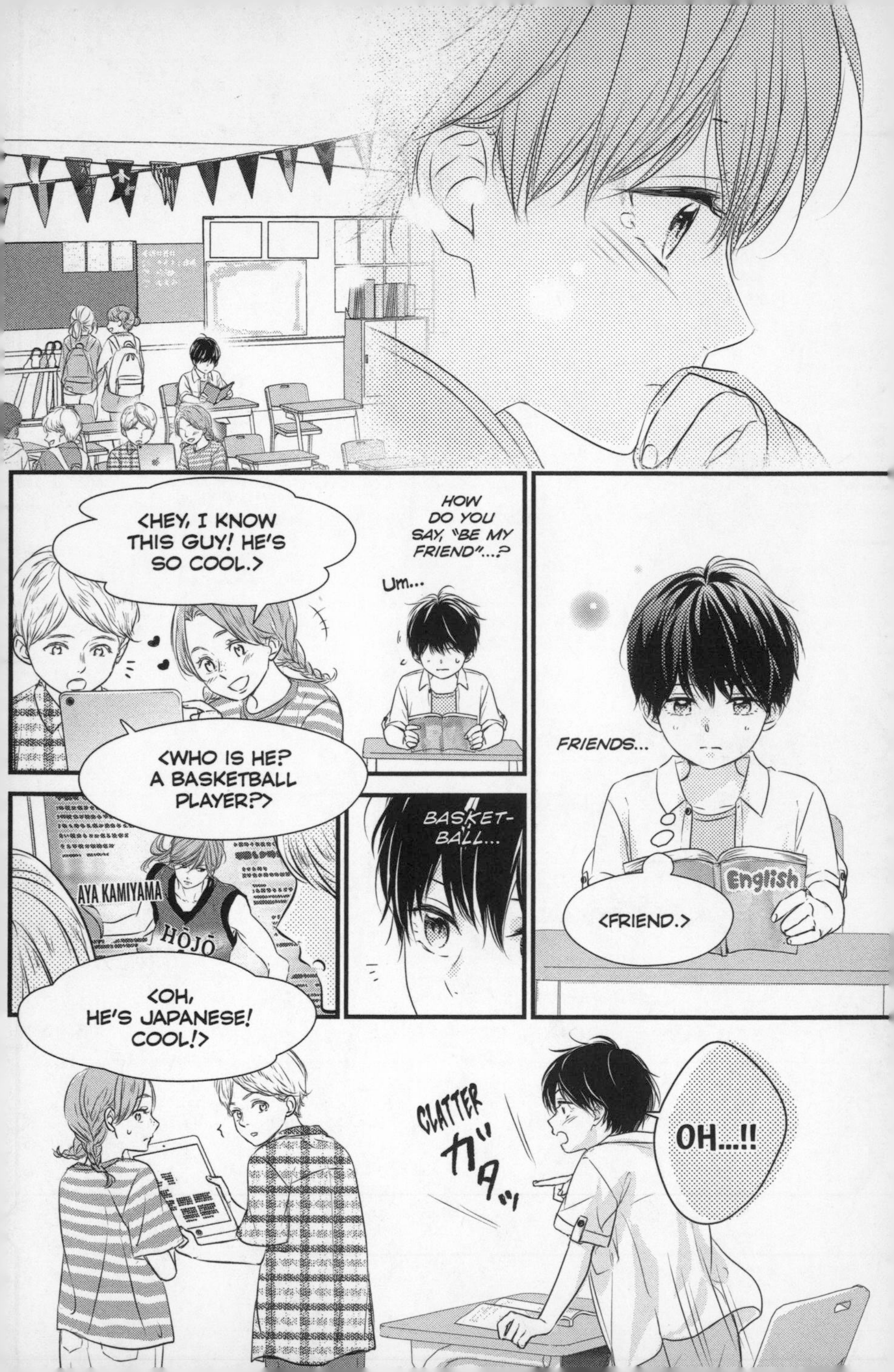
FRIENDS...
<FRIEND.>
English
HOW DO YOU SAY, "BE MY FRIEND"...?
Um...
<HEY, I KNOW THIS GUY! HE'S SO COOL.>
<WHO IS HE? A BASKETBALL PLAYER?>
BASKET-BALL...
AYA KAMIYAMA
HŌJŌ
<OH, HE'S JAPANESE! COOL!>
OH...!!
CLATTER
ガタッ

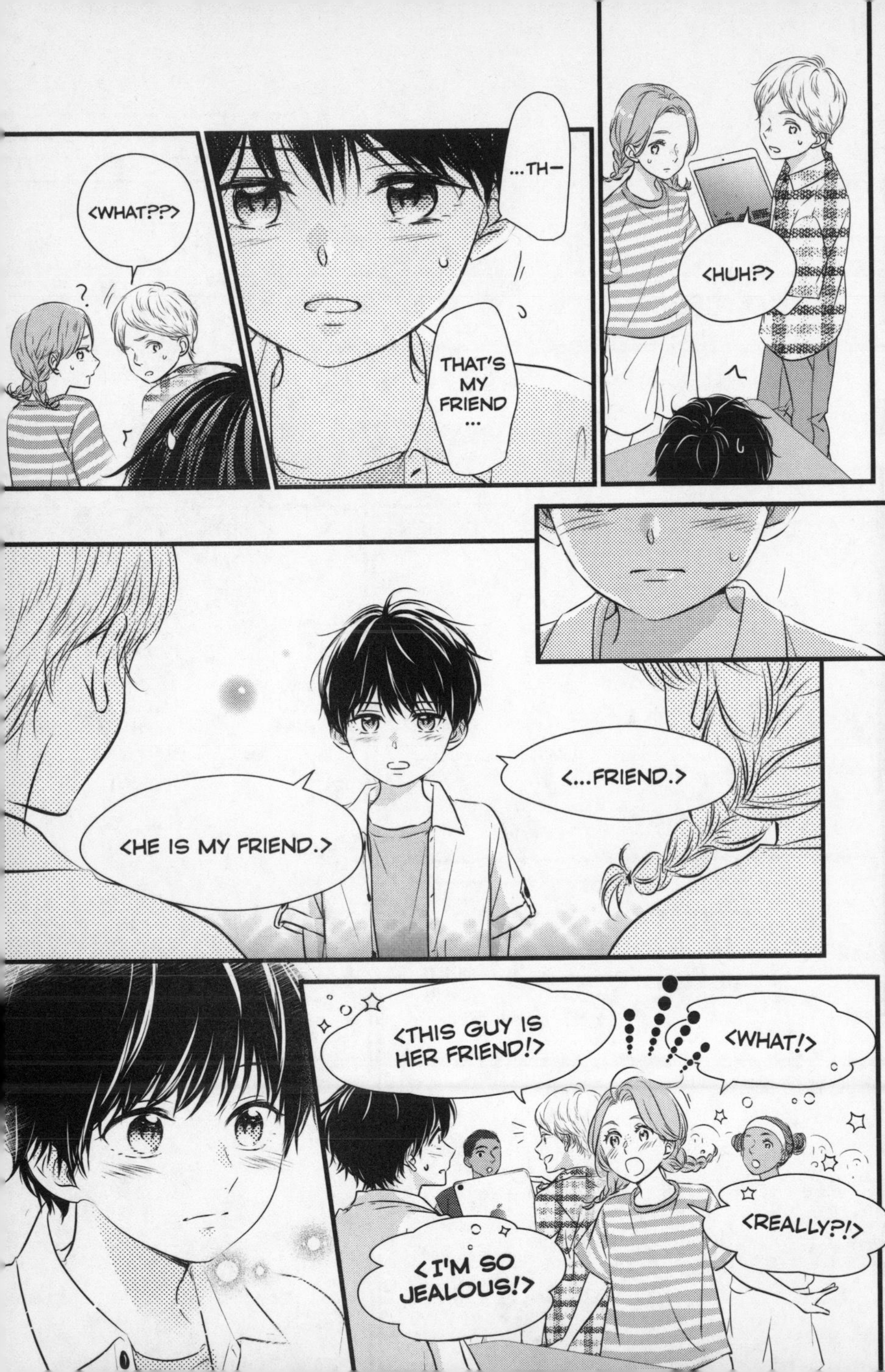
<HUH?>
...TH—
THAT'S MY FRIEND ...
<WHAT??>
<...FRIEND.>
<HE IS MY FRIEND.>
<WHAT!>
<THIS GUY IS HER FRIEND!>
<REALLY?!>
<I'M SO JEALOUS!>

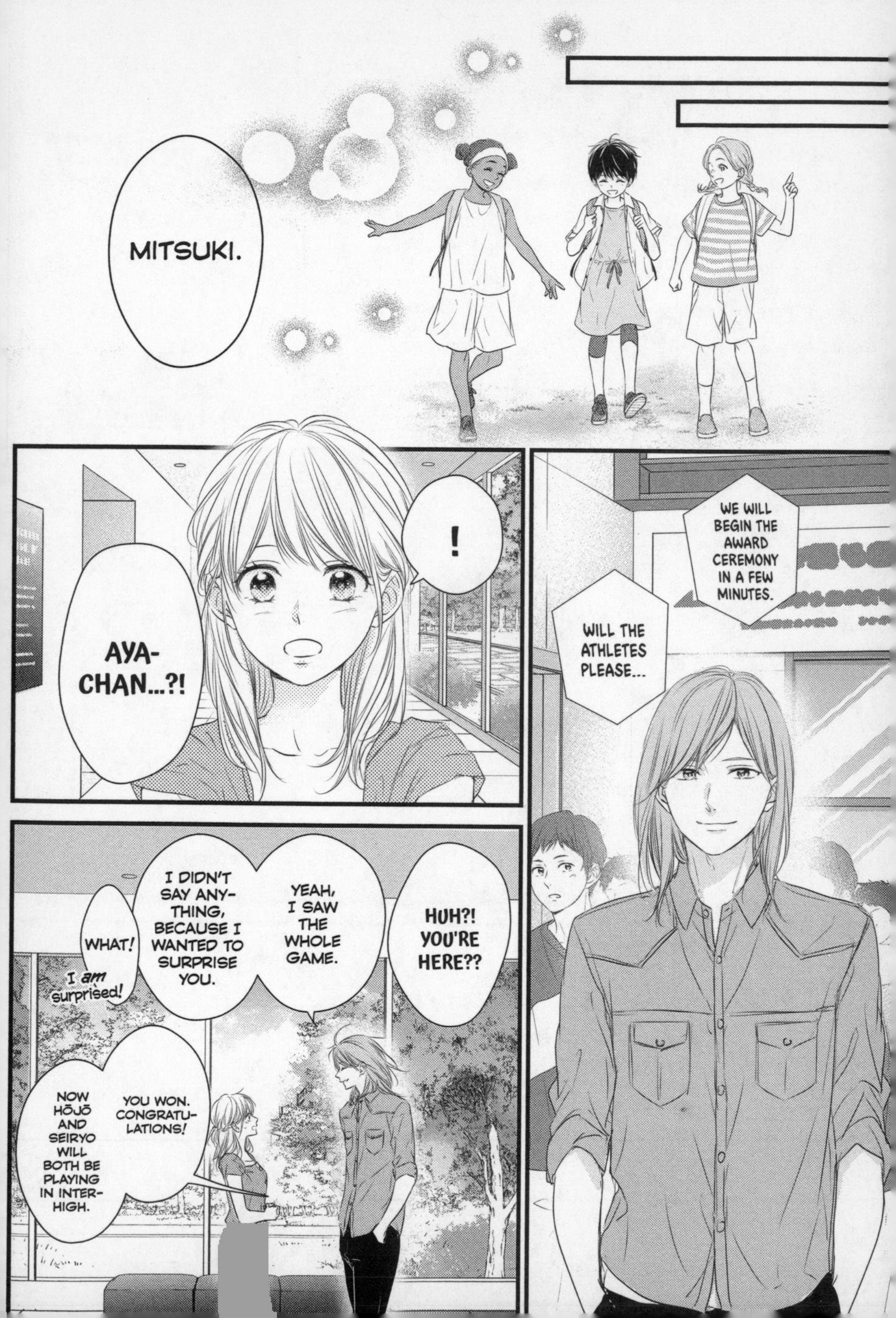
MITSUKI.
WE WILL BEGIN THE AWARD CEREMONY IN A FEW MINUTES.
WILL THE ATHLETES PLEASE...
!
AYA-CHAN...?!
HUH?! YOU'RE HERE??
YEAH, I SAW THE WHOLE GAME.
I DIDN'T SAY ANYTHING, BECAUSE I WANTED TO SURPRISE YOU.
WHAT!
I *am* surprised!
YOU WON. CONGRATULATIONS!
NOW HŌJŌ AND SEIRYO WILL BOTH BE PLAYING IN INTER-HIGH.

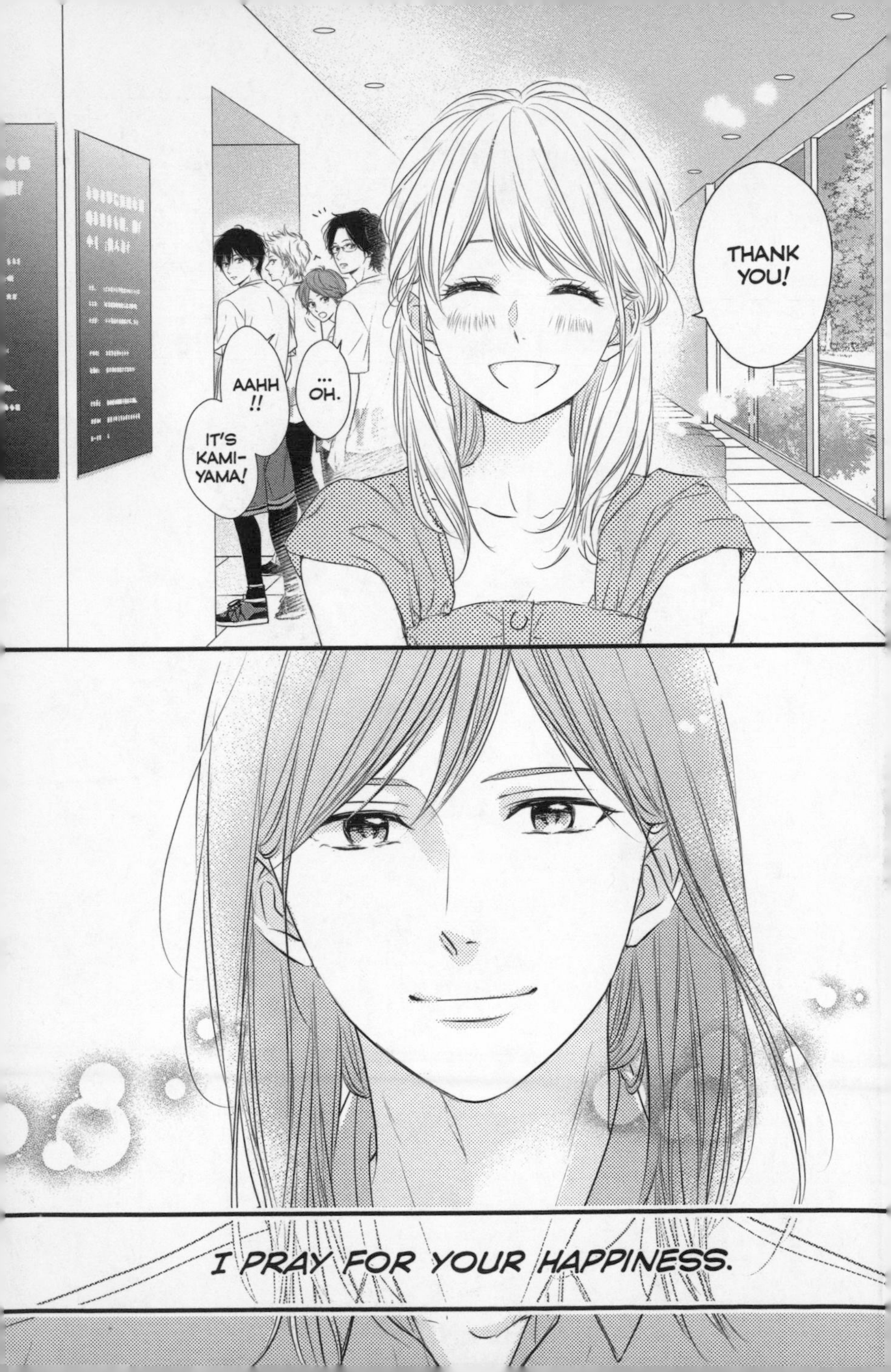
THANK YOU!
...OH.
AAHH!!
IT'S KAMI-YAMA!
I PRAY FOR YOUR HAPPINESS.

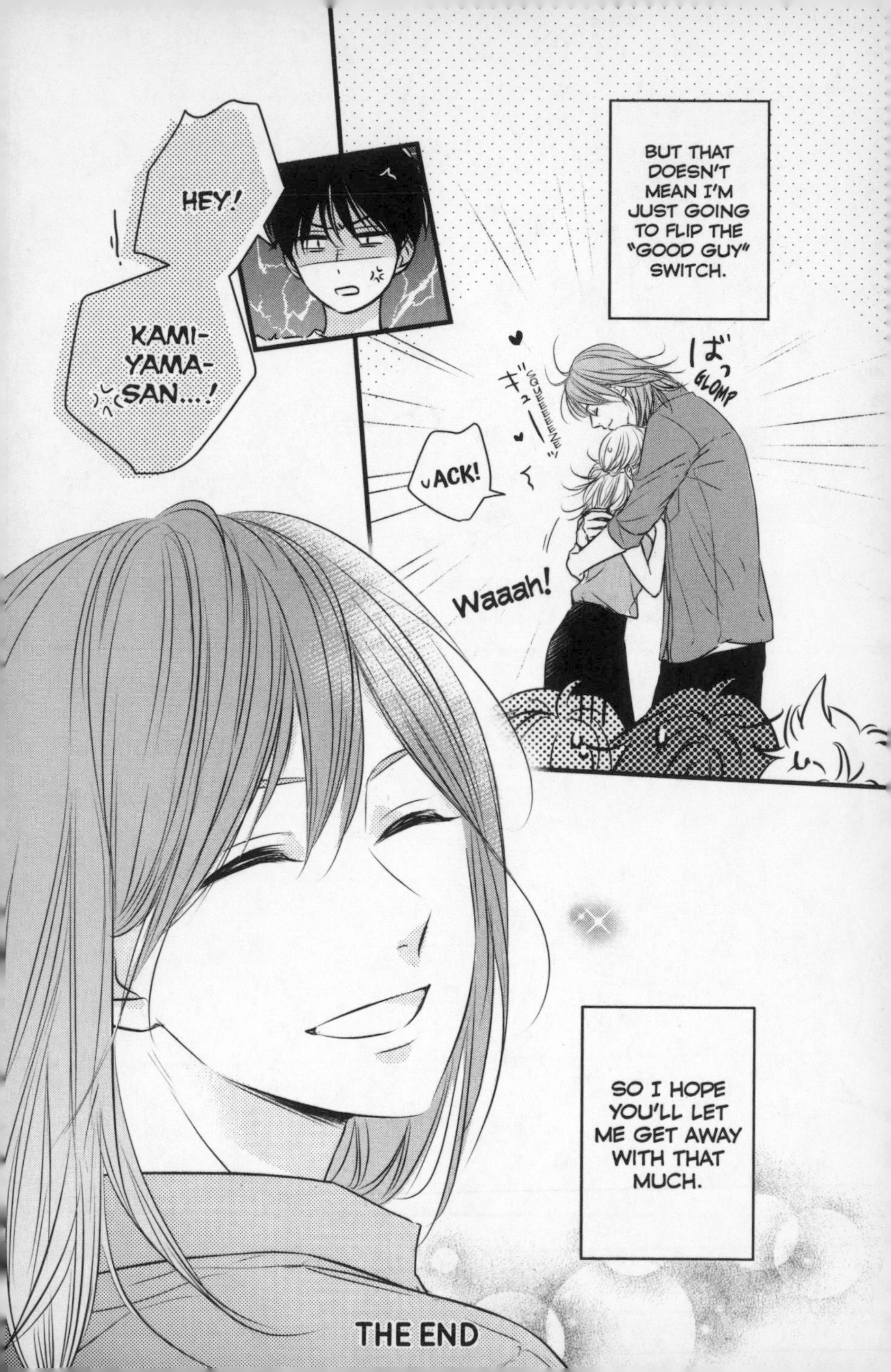
BUT THAT DOESN'T MEAN I'M JUST GOING TO FLIP THE "GOOD GUY" SWITCH.
ばっ
GLOMP
ギュ～ッ
SQUEEEEZE
ACK!
Waaah!
HEY!
KAMI-YAMA-SAN...!
SO I HOPE YOU'LL LET ME GET AWAY WITH THAT MUCH.
THE END

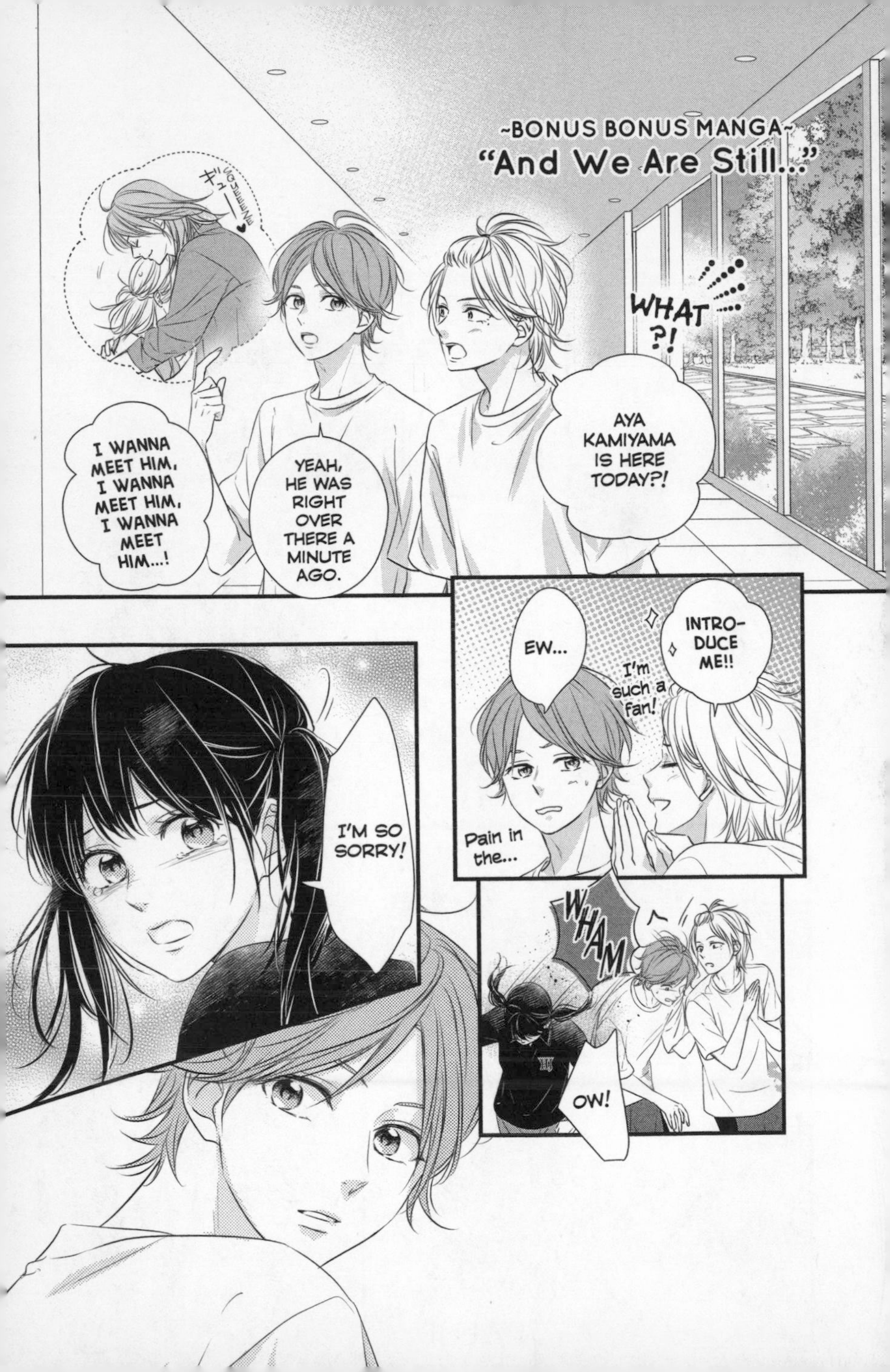
~BONUS BONUS MANGA~
"And We Are Still..."
WHAT ?!
AYA KAMIYAMA IS HERE TODAY?!
YEAH, HE WAS RIGHT OVER THERE A MINUTE AGO.
I WANNA MEET HIM, I WANNA MEET HIM, I WANNA MEET HIM...!
INTRO-DUCE ME!!
I'm such a fan!
EW...
Pain in the...
WHAM
OW!
I'M SO SORRY!

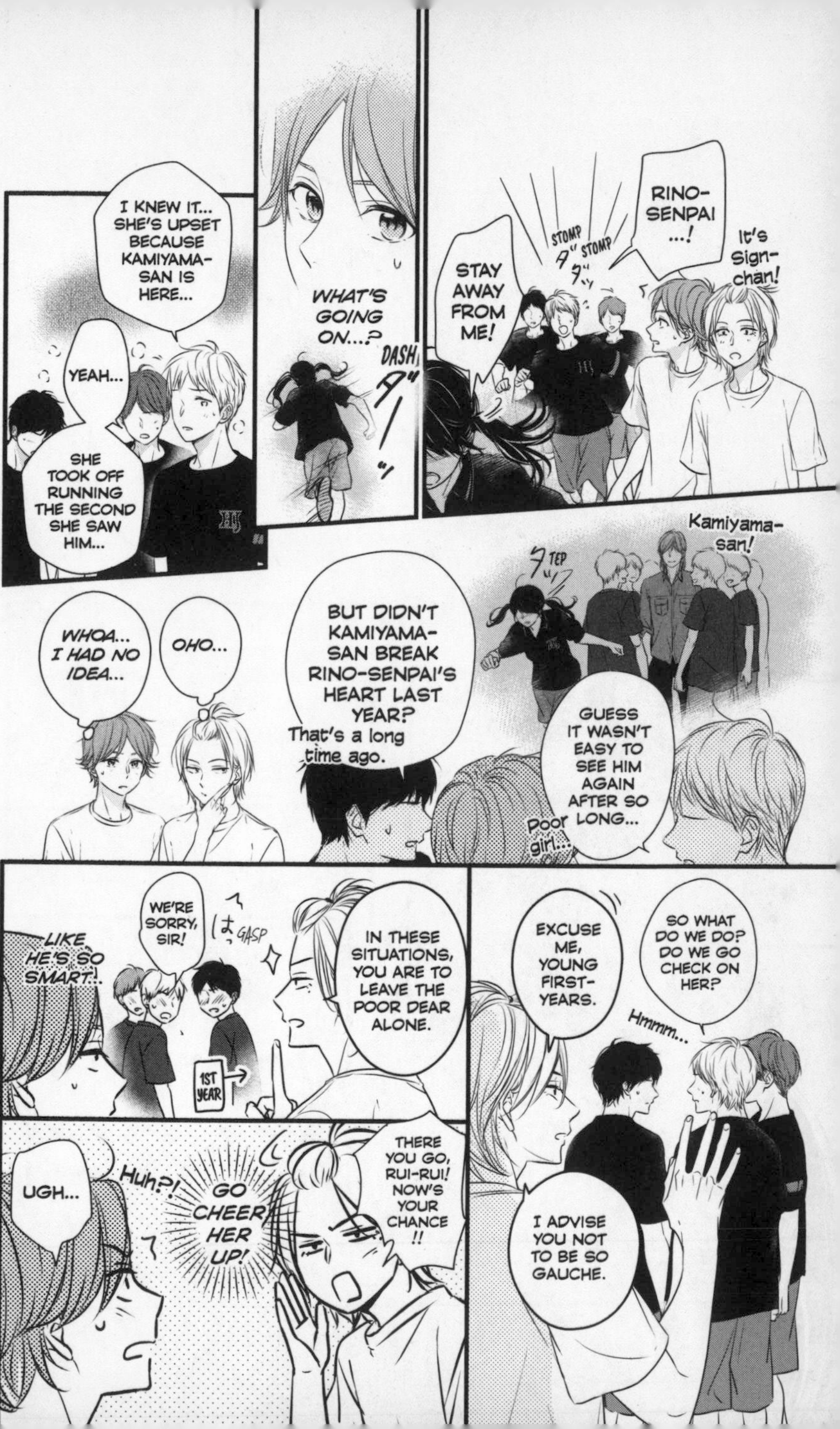
RINO-SENPAI ...!
It's Sign-chan!
STOMP
STOMP
STAY AWAY FROM ME!
WHAT'S GOING ON...?
DASH
I KNEW IT... SHE'S UPSET BECAUSE KAMIYAMA-SAN IS HERE...
YEAH...
SHE TOOK OFF RUNNING THE SECOND SHE SAW HIM...
Kamiyama-san!
TEP
GUESS IT WASN'T EASY TO SEE HIM AGAIN AFTER SO LONG...
Poor girl...
BUT DIDN'T KAMIYAMA-SAN BREAK RINO-SENPAI'S HEART LAST YEAR?
That's a long time ago.
OHO...
WHOA... I HAD NO IDEA...
SO WHAT DO WE DO? DO WE GO CHECK ON HER?
Hmmm...
EXCUSE ME, YOUNG FIRST-YEARS.
I ADVISE YOU NOT TO BE SO GAUCHE.
IN THESE SITUATIONS, YOU ARE TO LEAVE THE POOR DEAR ALONE.
GASP
WE'RE SORRY, SIR!
1ST YEAR
LIKE HE'S SO SMART...
THERE YOU GO, RUI-RUI! NOW'S YOUR CHANCE !!
GO CHEER HER UP!
Huh?!
UGH...

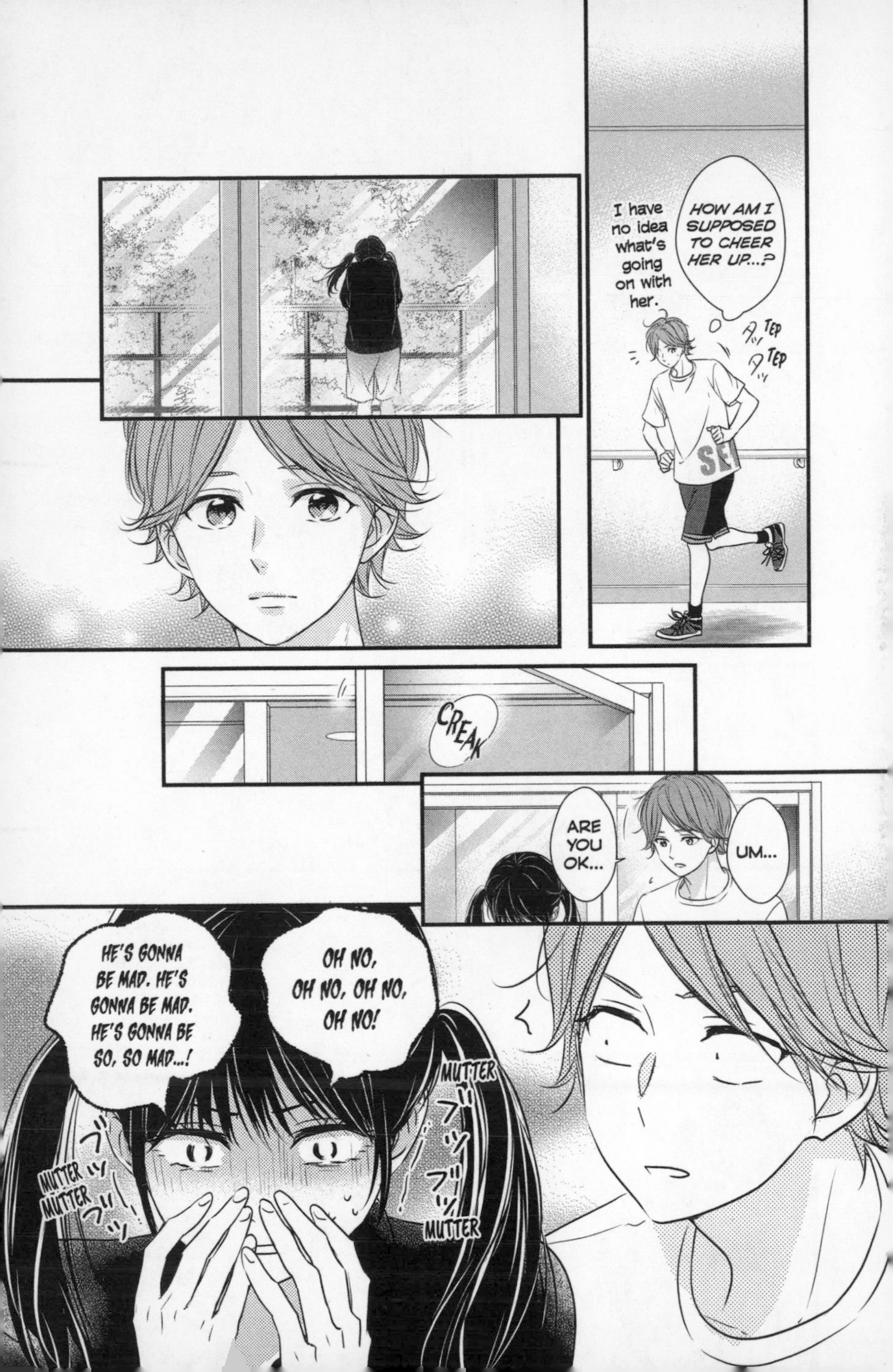
HOW AM I SUPPOSED TO CHEER HER UP...?
I have no idea what's going on with her.
TEP TEP
CREAK
UM...
ARE YOU OK...
OH NO, OH NO, OH NO, OH NO!
HE'S GONNA BE MAD. HE'S GONNA BE MAD. HE'S GONNA BE SO, SO MAD...!
MUTTER
MUTTER MUTTER
MUTTER

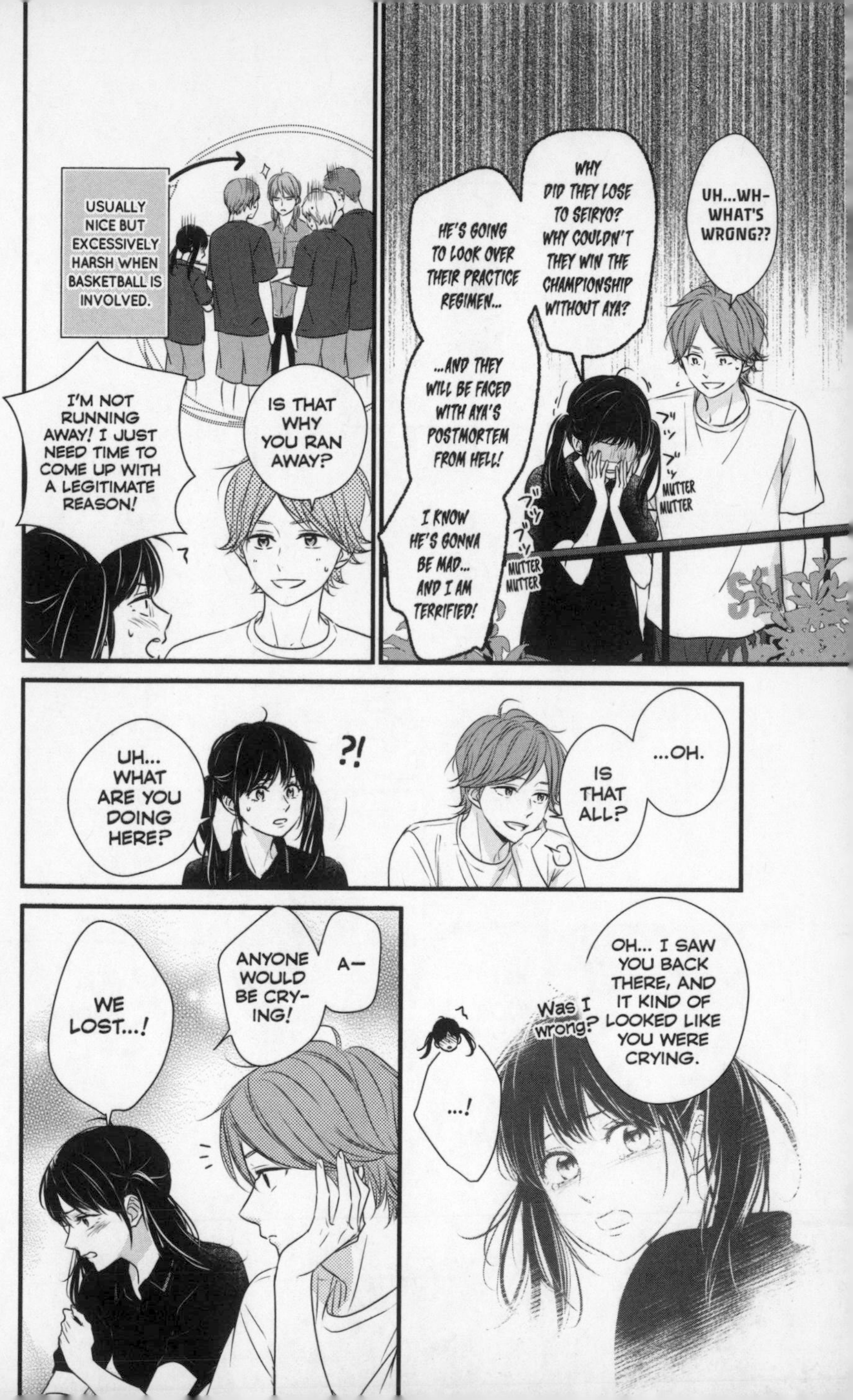
UH...WH-WHAT'S WRONG??
WHY DID THEY LOSE TO SEIRYO? WHY COULDN'T THEY WIN THE CHAMPIONSHIP WITHOUT AYA?
HE'S GOING TO LOOK OVER THEIR PRACTICE REGIMEN...
...AND THEY WILL BE FACED WITH AYA'S POSTMORTEM FROM HELL!
MUTTER MUTTER
I KNOW HE'S GONNA BE MAD... AND I AM TERRIFIED!
MUTTER MUTTER
USUALLY NICE BUT EXCESSIVELY HARSH WHEN BASKETBALL IS INVOLVED.
IS THAT WHY YOU RAN AWAY?
I'M NOT RUNNING AWAY! I JUST NEED TIME TO COME UP WITH A LEGITIMATE REASON!
...OH.
IS THAT ALL?
?!
UH... WHAT ARE YOU DOING HERE?
OH... I SAW YOU BACK THERE, AND IT KIND OF LOOKED LIKE YOU WERE CRYING.
Was I wrong?
...!
A—
ANYONE WOULD BE CRY-ING!
WE LOST...!

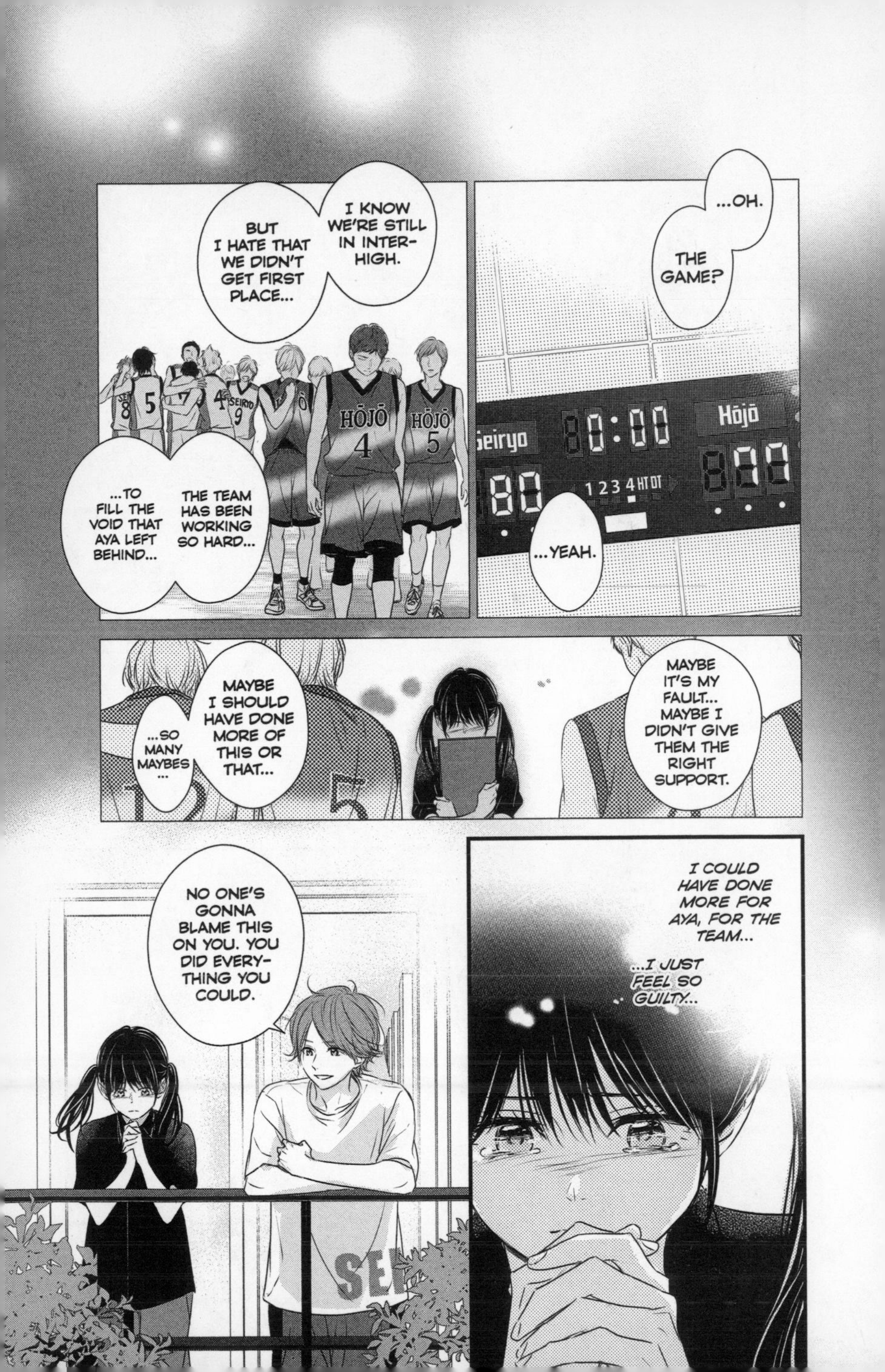
...OH.
THE GAME?
Seiryo
Hōjō
...YEAH.
I KNOW WE'RE STILL IN INTER-HIGH.
BUT I HATE THAT WE DIDN'T GET FIRST PLACE...
HŌJŌ
THE TEAM HAS BEEN WORKING SO HARD...
...TO FILL THE VOID THAT AYA LEFT BEHIND...
MAYBE IT'S MY FAULT... MAYBE I DIDN'T GIVE THEM THE RIGHT SUPPORT.
MAYBE I SHOULD HAVE DONE MORE OF THIS OR THAT...
...SO MANY MAYBES...
I COULD HAVE DONE MORE FOR AYA, FOR THE TEAM...
...I JUST FEEL SO GUILTY...
NO ONE'S GONNA BLAME THIS ON YOU. YOU DID EVERY-THING YOU COULD.

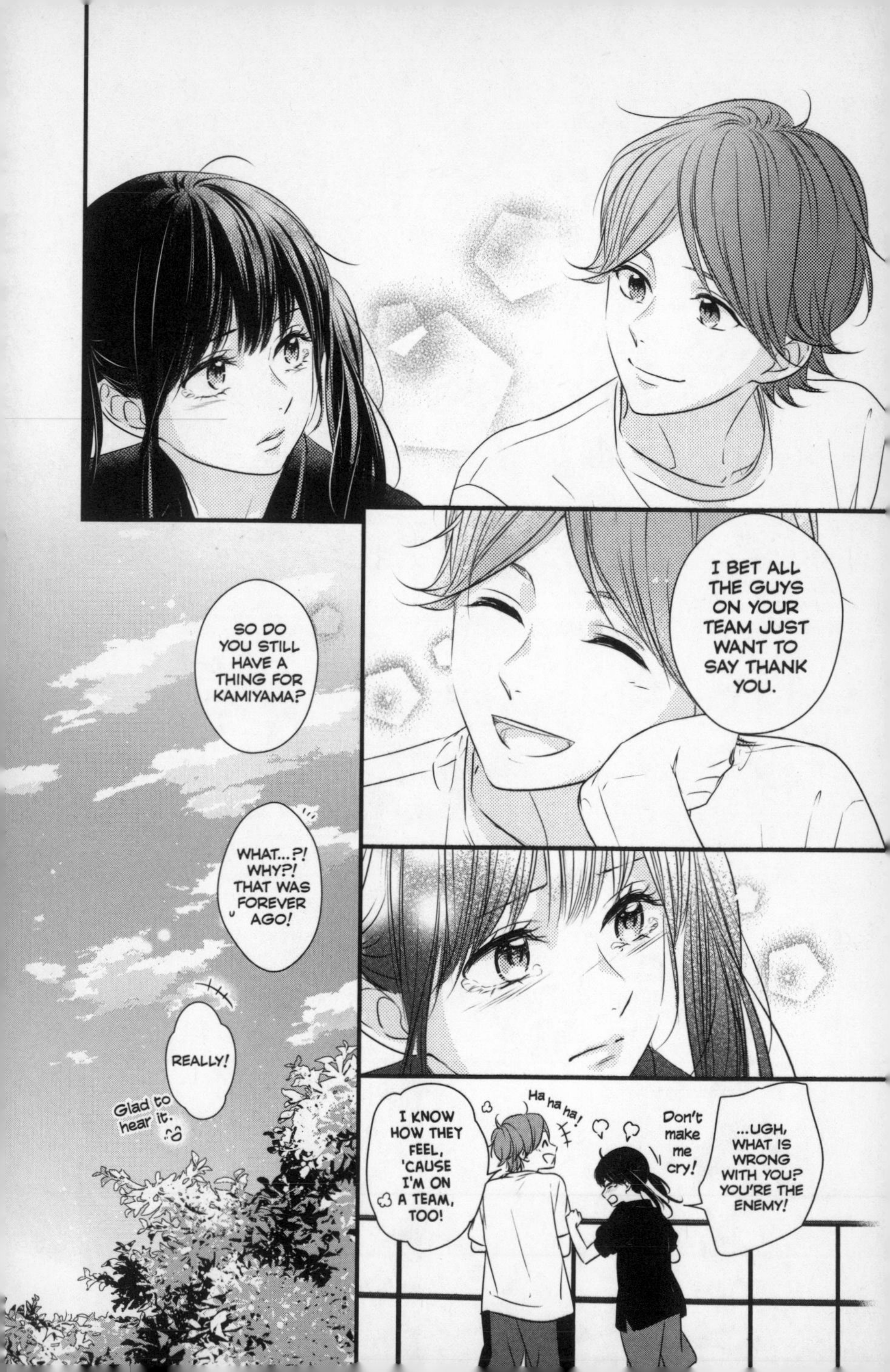
I BET ALL THE GUYS ON YOUR TEAM JUST WANT TO SAY THANK YOU.
...UGH, WHAT IS WRONG WITH YOU? YOU'RE THE ENEMY!
Don't make me cry!
Ha ha ha!
I KNOW HOW THEY FEEL, 'CAUSE I'M ON A TEAM, TOO!
SO DO YOU STILL HAVE A THING FOR KAMIYAMA?
WHAT...?! WHY?! THAT WAS FOREVER AGO!
REALLY!
Glad to hear it.

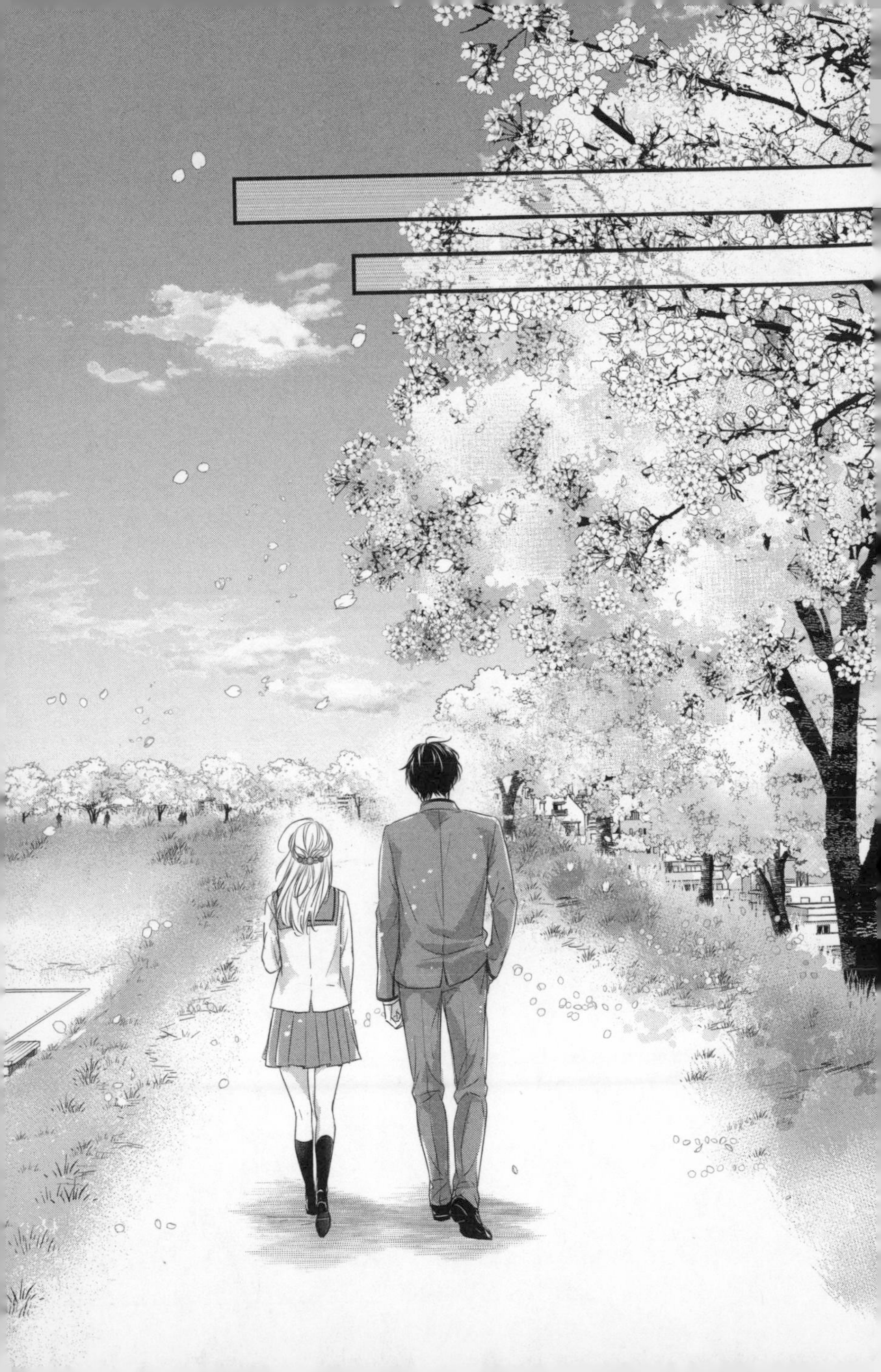

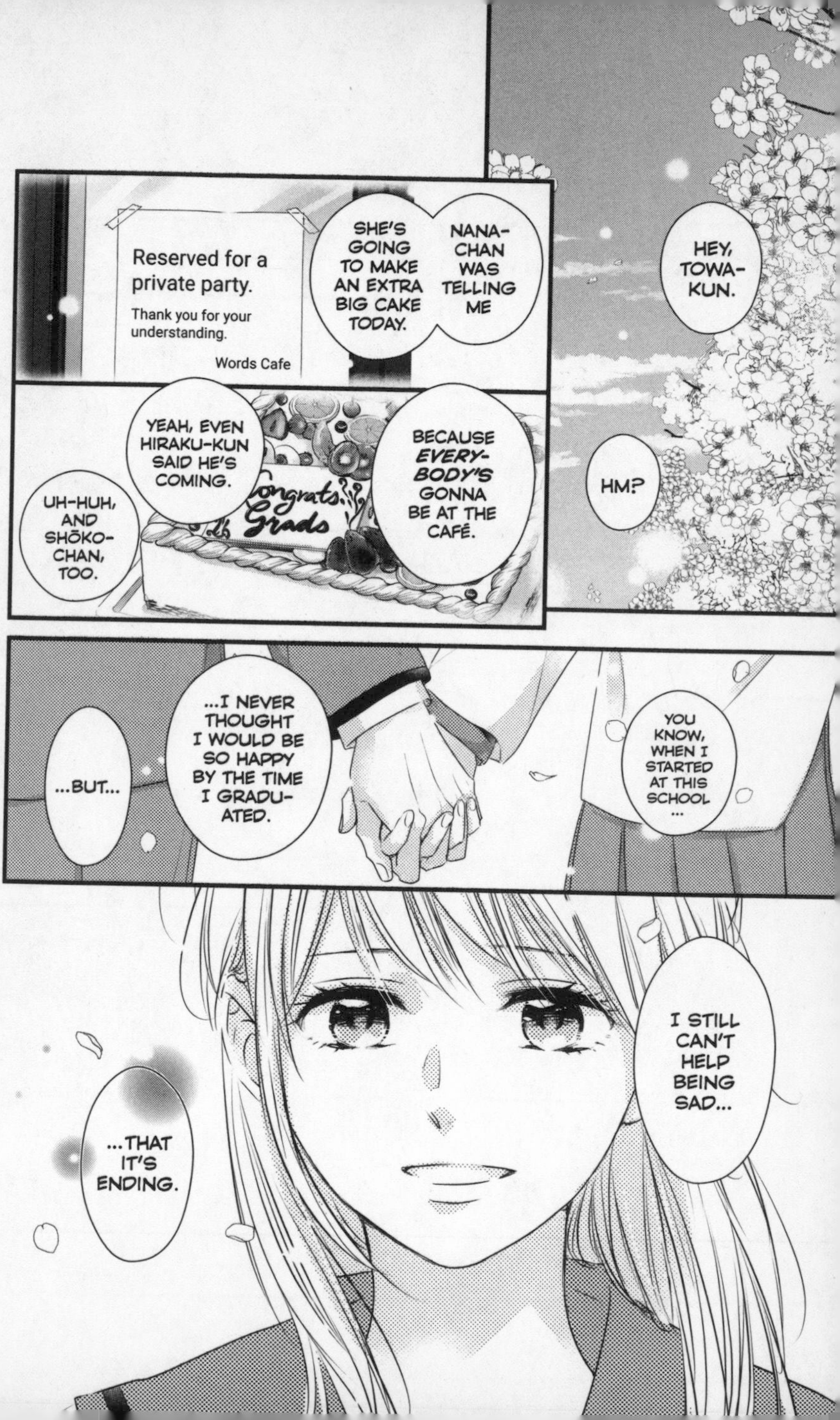
HEY, TOWA-KUN.
HM?
Reserved for a private party.
Thank you for your understanding.
Words Cafe
NANA-CHAN WAS TELLING ME
SHE'S GOING TO MAKE AN EXTRA BIG CAKE TODAY.
BECAUSE *EVERY-BODY'S* GONNA BE AT THE CAFÉ.
Congrats Grads
YEAH, EVEN HIRAKU-KUN SAID HE'S COMING.
UH-HUH, AND SHŌKO-CHAN, TOO.
YOU KNOW, WHEN I STARTED AT THIS SCHOOL...
...I NEVER THOUGHT I WOULD BE SO HAPPY BY THE TIME I GRADUATED.
...BUT...
I STILL CAN'T HELP BEING SAD...
...THAT IT'S ENDING.

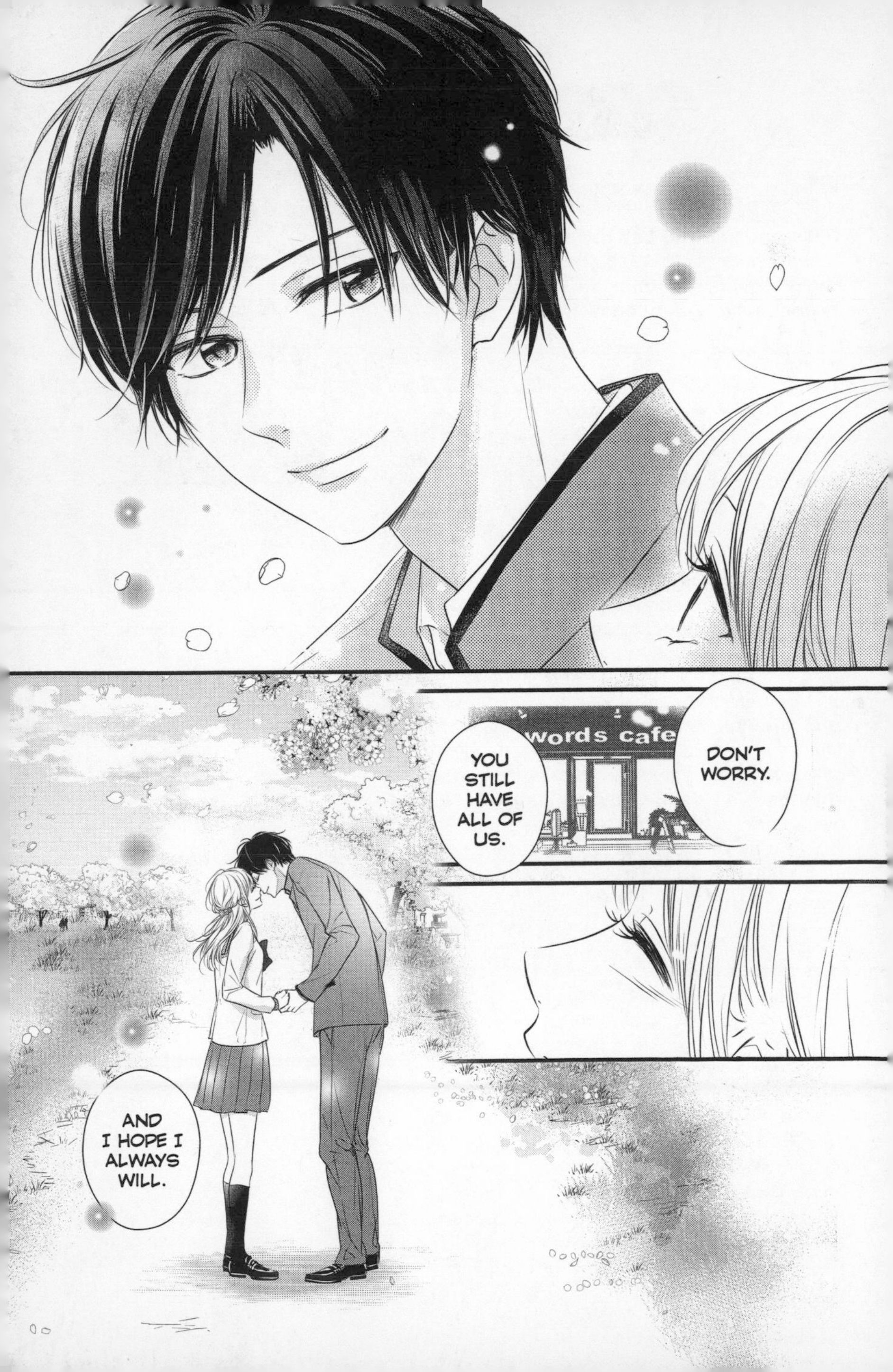
DON'T WORRY.
words cafe
YOU STILL HAVE ALL OF US.
AND I HOPE I ALWAYS WILL.

## Translation Notes

**Gyaru, yankii, and Lolita, page 11**

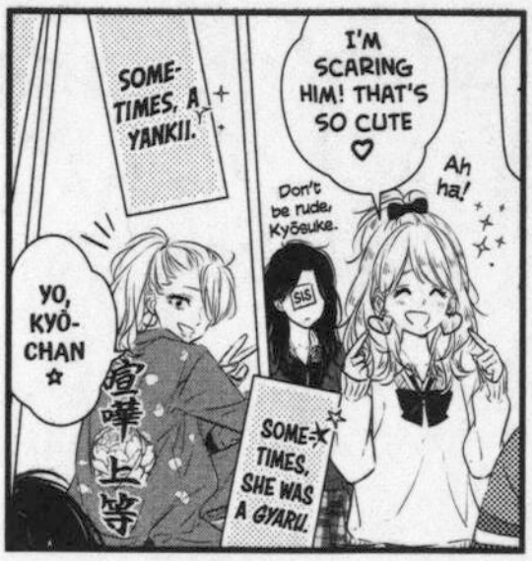
I'M SCARING HIM! THAT'S SO CUTE ♡
Ah ha!
SOME-TIMES, A YANKII.
Don't be rude, Kyōsuke.
SIS
YO, KYŌ-CHAN ☆
SOME-TIMES, SHE WAS A GYARU.

*Gyaru*, though initially borrowed from the English term "girl" and "gal," has since become a subculture of Japanese street fashion. *Gyaru* typically bleach and dye their hair lighter and wear a lot of make up and gaudy accessories. The excessive and fun femininity that *gyaru* put on is at once an indulgent performance and also a statement that catches one's eyes. Because of this, *gyaru* are sometimes thought of as vain, shallow, or airheaded. In the Japanese, the term *yankii*, which is also a borrowed term from the English, "yankee," referring to the original inspiration from the post-WWII American GI culture of bad boys and rock 'n roll, most often translates to "juvenile delinquent." *Yankii* reject social norms, manners, and expectations with flair. Stereotypically, *yankii* are known for their rebellious attitude—all of which comes through their affected language, big hairstyles, and flashy clothing. Their long coats with intricate embroidery are called *tokkōfuku*, or "suicide squad clothes." The now well-known Lolita style is similarly a performance of donning femininity, worn by individuals who project a particular brand of youthfulness and cuteness, wearing frills, ribbons, and patterns one might find on a doll.

**Rui's pose, page 57**

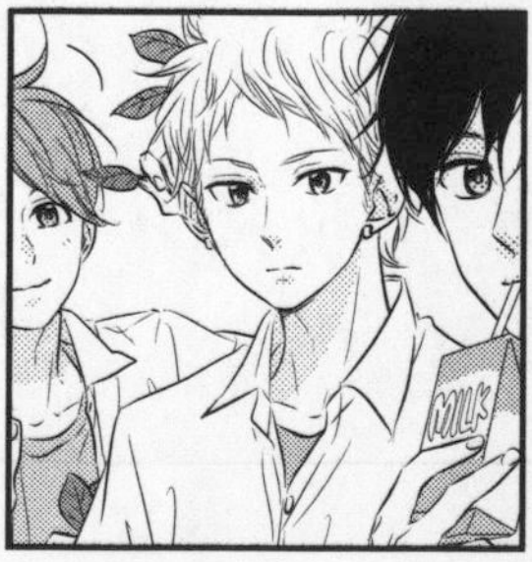
MILK

In Japanese folklore, the tanuki, or raccoon dog, is known for taking other forms that it will use to trick people. In pop culture, this action is performed by striking a certain pose, and the leaf on the head is a clue that reveals a person is in fact a transformed tanuki. While only Rui knows why he was putting leaves in his friend's hair, when he ends up with one on his own head and poses in this manner, he resembles a tanuki that has transformed into something else, such as a waiter.

GASP
はっ

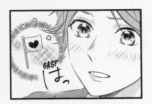

**A sign, page 73**

In the original Japanese, Rui thinks of this event as a "flag" (hence the flag in his imagination), which is used in Japanese entertainment to describe an action or event that acts as foreshadowing. Most commonly, flags signal future romantic developments between characters.

Tadah!

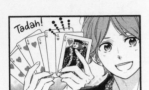

**The King Game, page 125**

A game similar to Truth or Dare, without the truth. The players draw lots, which either have a number or the word "king" (in this case, cards are used instead). The king then commands his subjects to do ridiculous things, such as, "Number 1 will give Number 3 a hug," or "Number 4 will now dance on the table."

Waiting for Spring

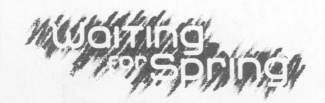

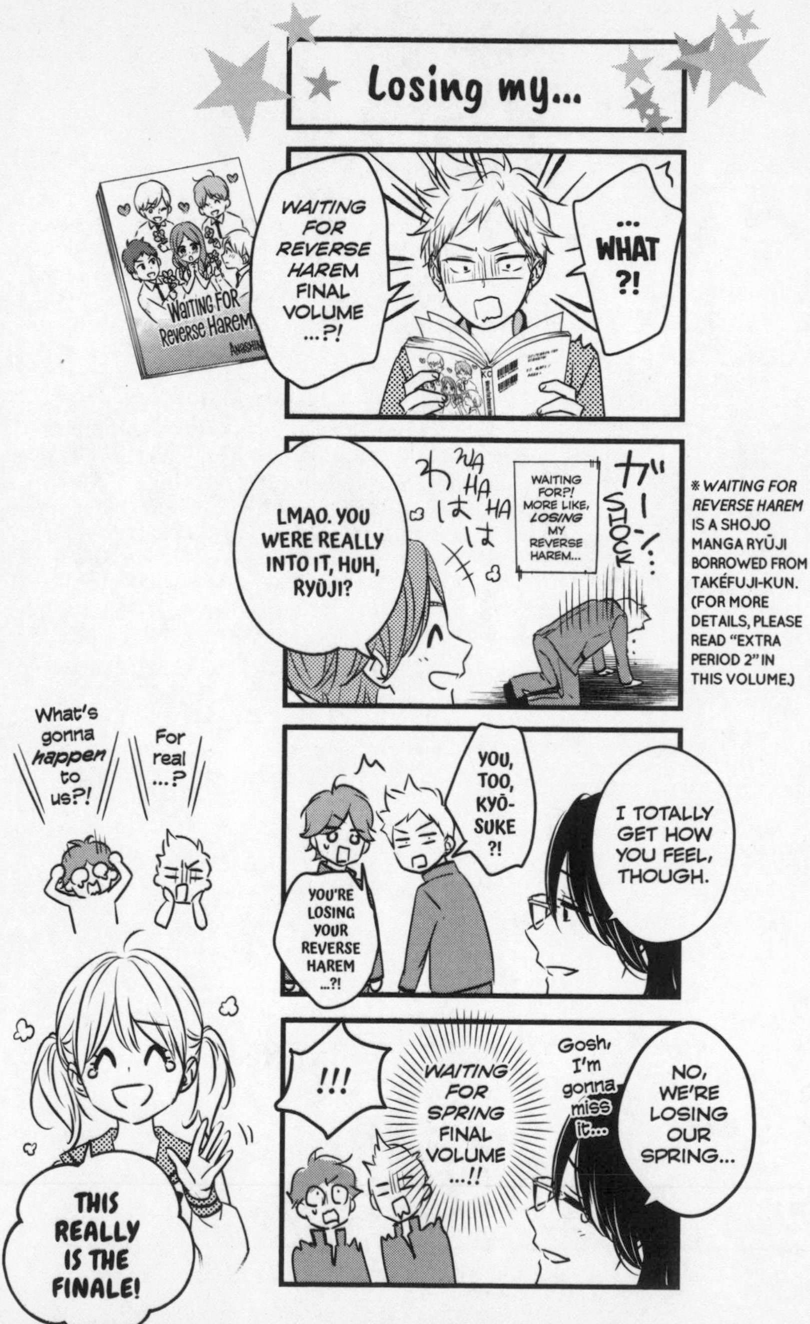
Losing my...
...WHAT?!
WAITING FOR REVERSE HAREM FINAL VOLUME ...?!
Waiting FOR Reverse Harem
ガーン SHOCK
WAITING FOR?! MORE LIKE, LOSING MY REVERSE HAREM...
わはは WA HA HA
LMAO. YOU WERE REALLY INTO IT, HUH, RYŪJI?
※ WAITING FOR REVERSE HAREM IS A SHOJO MANGA RYŪJI BORROWED FROM TAKÉFUJI-KUN. (FOR MORE DETAILS, PLEASE READ "EXTRA PERIOD 2" IN THIS VOLUME.)
I TOTALLY GET HOW YOU FEEL, THOUGH.
YOU, TOO, KYŌ-SUKE?!
YOU'RE LOSING YOUR REVERSE HAREM ...?!
For real ...?
What's gonna happen to us?!
NO, WE'RE LOSING OUR SPRING...
Gosh, I'm gonna miss it...
WAITING FOR SPRING FINAL VOLUME ...!!
!!!
THIS REALLY IS THE FINALE!

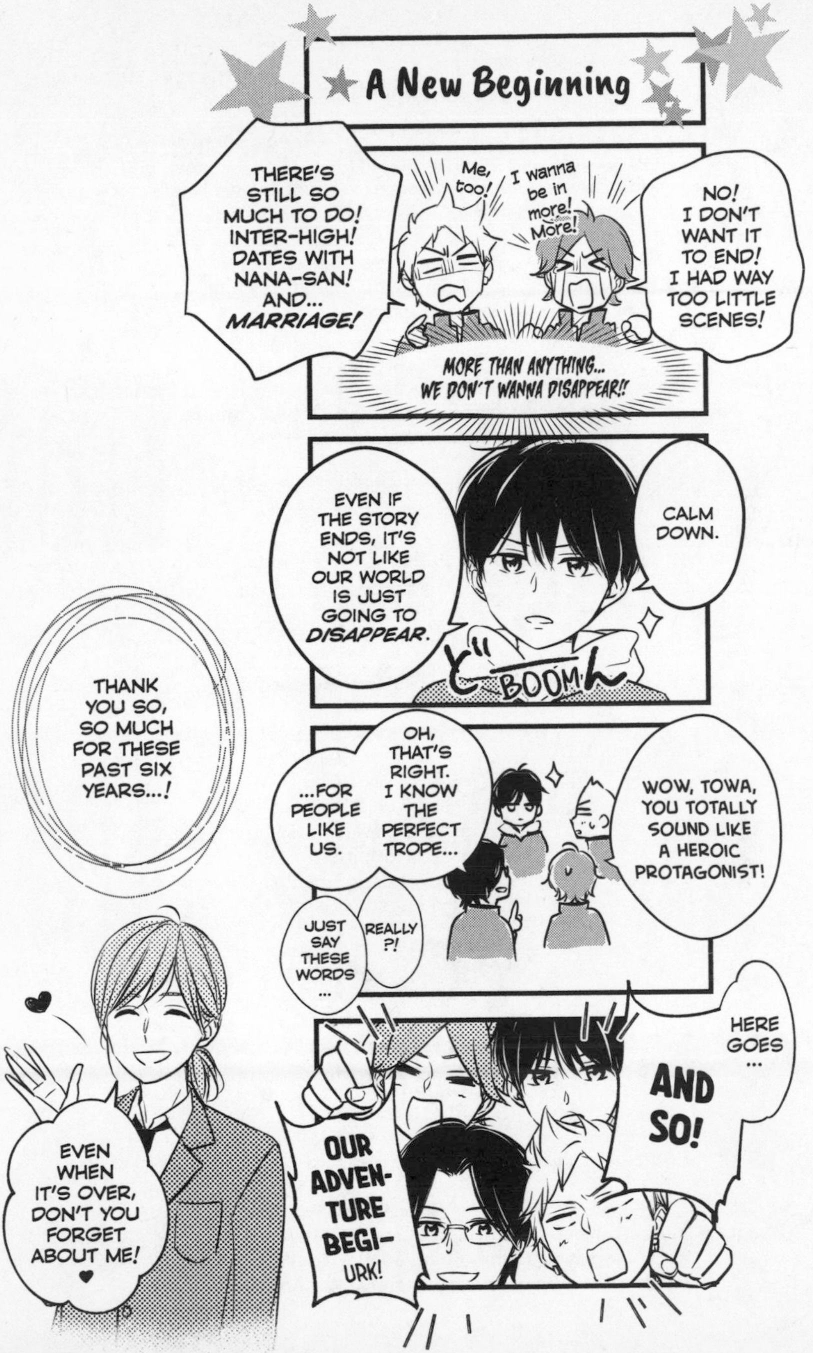
A New Beginning
NO! I DON'T WANT IT TO END! I HAD WAY TOO LITTLE SCENES!
I wanna be in more! More!
Me, too!
THERE'S STILL SO MUCH TO DO! INTER-HIGH! DATES WITH NANA-SAN! AND... MARRIAGE!
MORE THAN ANYTHING... WE DON'T WANNA DISAPPEAR!!
CALM DOWN.
EVEN IF THE STORY ENDS, IT'S NOT LIKE OUR WORLD IS JUST GOING TO DISAPPEAR.
BOOM
WOW, TOWA, YOU TOTALLY SOUND LIKE A HEROIC PROTAGONIST!
OH, THAT'S RIGHT. I KNOW THE PERFECT TROPE...
...FOR PEOPLE LIKE US.
REALLY?!
JUST SAY THESE WORDS...
HERE GOES...
AND SO!
OUR ADVEN-TURE BEGI- URK!
THANK YOU SO, SO MUCH FOR THESE PAST SIX YEARS...!
EVEN WHEN IT'S OVER, DON'T YOU FORGET ABOUT ME! ♥

A Kodansha Comics Trade Paperback Original
*Waiting for Spring* 14 copyright © 2020 Anashin
English translation copyright © 2021 Anashin

All rights reserved.

Published in the United States by Kodansha Comics, an imprint of Kodansha USA Publishing, LLC, New York.

Publication rights for this English edition arranged through Kodansha Ltd, Tokyo.

First published in Japan in 2020 by Kodansha Ltd, Tokyo.

ISBN 978-1-64651-148-8

Printed in the United States of America.

www.kodanshacomics.com

9 8 7 6 5 4 3 2 1
Translation: Alethea Nibley and Athena Nibley
Lettering: Sara Linsley
Editing: Haruko Hashimoto
Kodansha Comics edition cover design by Phil Balsman

Publisher: Kiichiro Sugawara

Director of publishing services: Ben Applegate
Associate director of operations: Stephen Pakula
Publishing services managing editor: Noelle Webster
Assistant production manager: Emi Lotto, Angela Zurlo

**EVER AFTER**

Mitsuki and Towa have BALTIMORE COUNTY PUBLIC LIBRARY about his own future romance! However, in the background, Kyōsuke has been having his own girl problems—will his first love return his affection? Meanwhile, Nanase and Ryūji bump into their own relationship issues, and Aya must cope with his heartbreak once more.

**FINAL VOLUME!**

"Soothing and sweet. It'll make the heart of every shojo fan beat faster."
—Awkward Dangos

"[A] light romance that gives us a heroine and heroes we can root for...simultaneously fluffy, and grounded, and all fun."
—Anime News Network

396-BAC-998

Novel

**KODANSHA COMICS**

T AGES 13+

USA $10.99
CAN $14.99

www.kodanshacomics.com
ISBN 978-1-64651-148-8
EAN
51099
9 781646 511488